The

WESTMINSTER
CONFESSION
OF FAITH

FOR STUDY CLASSES

Jim Stelling
5/12/19

The

WESTMINSTER
CONFESSION
OF FAITH

FOR STUDY CLASSES

Second Edition

G. I. WILLIAMSON

P&R

PUBLISHING

P.O. BOX 817 • PHILLIPSBURG • NEW JERSEY 08865-0817

Page design and typesetting by Lakeside Design Plus

Printed in the United States of America

ISBN-10: 0-87552-593-8
ISBN-13: 978-0-87552-593-8

Contents

To Grace

Preface to the Second Edition

It is now some forty years since the late Mr. Charles H. Craig read and approved my manuscript for this book. I think he was more confident than I was that it would prove to be of use to Reformed and Presbyterian churches. That it is sill useful enough to warrant a second edition, however, may well have surprised him as it has the author. My gratitude to Mr. Craig is only surpassed by my gratitude to God for allowing me to be a teacher, through this book, of so many of God's people throughout the English-speaking world.

It may surprise some that so few changes have been made. But there is good reason. I remember reading a series some years ago in the *Christian Century* magazine. Various noted clergymen of modernistic denominations told how much their thinking (and theology) had changed over the years. With me it is quite different. I believe today, more than ever before, that the doctrines set forth in the Westminster Confession of Faith are true and therefore do not need to be changed. They are not, of course, infallibly stated. Only the Bible is infallible. But even today—after some 350 years—the amazing thing is that the Westminster Assembly got it so right that little needs to be changed.

It is therefore my hope that this study will continue to serve the church in these early years of the twenty-first century.

Sheldon, Iowa
August, 2003

Preface to the First Edition

Though office-bearers of most Presbyterian churches are still required to affirm adherence to the Westminster Confession of Faith "as containing the system of doctrine taught in the Holy Scriptures," it can hardly be denied "that the Confession no longer holds the same place in the mind of the church as it did in the past."[1] When the author was a student in seminary, he became aware of the fact that a brief statement of faith (The Confessional Statement of 1925) had virtually replaced the Westminster Confession of Faith as the creedal standard of the United Presbyterian Church of North America. Careful study of the two documents led to the author's conviction that it was the Westminster Standard, rather than the present-day convictions of the church, which was in accord with Scripture. The conclusion was reached that the chief cause of this lamentable situation was simply ignorance of the contents of this great Confession. This in turn led to the humble effort which produced this study manual.

This manual was written in a home mission charge for the purpose of recovering with certainty and fullness the rich heritage of the Reformation faith. Whatever may be the weaknesses of this study manual on the Westminster Confession of Faith, the author can testify that a study of this Confession, as a body of doctrines provable from Scripture, has been of inestimable benefit to the faithful congregation that patiently studied—and thus helped to write—the lessons of this book. Should this manual assist others also to see that system of doctrine set forth in Scripture, all of the labors of its author will be abundantly rewarded.

1. George S. Hendry, *The Westminster Confession for Today* (Richmond, Va.: John Knox Press, 1960), 11.

A special word of acknowledgment is due to Dr. William Young, who originally suggested that this study material be published, and to Dr. Robert L. Reymond and Dr. David Freeman for valuable suggestions regarding format and style.

Auckland, New Zealand
July, 1964

1

I. Of the Holy Scriptures

1. *Although the light of nature, and the works of creation and providence, do so far manifest the goodness, wisdom, and power of God, as to leave men inexcusable; yet they are not sufficient to give that knowledge of God, and of his will, which is necessary unto salvation: therefore it pleased the Lord, at sundry times, and in divers manners, to reveal himself, and to declare that his will unto his Church; and afterwards, for the better preserving and propagating of the truth, and for the more sure establishment and comfort of the Church against the corruption of the flesh, and the malice of Satan and of the world, to commit the same wholly unto writing; which maketh the holy Scripture to be most necessary; those former ways of God's revealing his will unto his people being now ceased.*

This section of the Confession teaches us (1) that God reveals himself in two distinct ways to man: in nature and in Scripture, (2) that no man can evade constant confrontation by that which reveals the living and true God (even without Scripture), (3) that all men are without excuse for their ignorant and sinful condition, and (4) that Scripture is necessary for true and saving knowledge of God because therein alone is revealed God's redemptive provision.

It has long been the habit among Christians (even of Reformed persuasion) to speak of the insufficiency of natural revelation, as if there were something defective in the revelation it makes of God. This may be seen in the traditional use of the theistic proofs.

(1) From the world as a great effect we may argue the possibility of a great cause.

(2) From the apparent order and design in the world we may argue the possibility of a designing intelligence.

(3) From the apparent rule of the world by moral law we may argue the possibility of a moral law-giver.

After these, and similar arguments, were developed and brought together, it was hoped that unbelievers might be convinced that (a) "a god" probably exists; and that (b) if he does exist, he might possibly be the God of the Bible. Only when the possibility of the existence of "God" was thus "proved" was it expected that the unbeliever would admit further evidence that might confirm that God really does exist. Observe that in this scheme the creature fixes the terms under which God must present his credentials. Facts are not allowed to say, "The true God is," but only, "A god may possibly exist."

What is wrong with such an approach? Simply this: every fact (and the sum total of all facts) *proves* the existence of the God of the Bible. And there is good reason. This God is. He always was. He existed before anything was made. And the whole universe exists only because he planned it. Every detail of the related aspects of existence has the precise character and purpose that God intended. It therefore has meaning that is God-given. "The heavens declare the glory of God; and the firmament shows His handiwork. . . . There is no speech nor language where their voice is not heard" (Ps. 19:1, 3). Everything in heaven and earth says that the true God is, that he is glorious, that he is Creator and ruler of all, and that we are his creatures.

Man was once God's true image. He alone among the creatures could think thoughts of his Creator. Before sinless man the whole creation (including man's own being) was an unclouded mirror in which God could be seen with clear vision. In the mind of man God's revelation came to self-conscious reinterpretation. It was the task of man to become conscious of all the meaning deposited by God in the universe. Man began this task (Gen. 2:19–20). He used God-given powers of investigation to discover the true (that is, God-imprinted) meaning of nature. When Adam named something in the world of nature, he was simply reading the name (meaning) put there by God.

We must observe, however, that even before the fall of man God revealed himself in word as well as in nature. Nature revealed all that Adam needed for a right knowledge of the nature of God and the world. But how could Adam know the will or purpose of God? And how could he know what his own will and purpose ought to be? The answer is: only by special (word) revelation.

In order for man to be the image and likeness of God two things were essential. His being must be like God's, and his will or purpose must also be like God's. The being of God is not a matter of choice. Neither is the being of man a matter of choice. He is God's image. To be other than this would be to be other than human. As long as men are men they exist in God's image. It therefore follows that human existence is such as to compel the sense of deity within man. All men know God, the true God, the only God. They do not merely have the capacity for knowing him; they actually do know him, and cannot possibly evade knowing him.

However, the purpose of man is a matter of choice. As God is free to do as he will, so man (being created in the divine image) is free to do as he will. But even in his freedom of will man cannot escape the absolute control of God because the being of man (he is only an image) is wholly dependent upon God. In setting his will against the will of God revealed by the Word of God, man can only violate, but can never destroy, his dependent relationship to God. He is metaphysically God's image, although he is ethically God's likeness no longer. Man's determination to be independent of God is doomed to frustration, and he is clearly and constantly reminded of this through natural revelation. Natural revelation never ceases to declare to sinful man the fact that the true God is, and that man's very existence is wholly dependent upon God. In order to continue in rebellion against God, therefore, a man must lie to himself about the situation. He must suppress the truth in unrighteousness (Rom. 1:18). This suppression of the truth (whereby sinful men refuse to know either themselves or the true God aright) is wholly due to sin, and not in any way due to an insufficiency or defect in natural revelation.

However, the revelation of God before the fall differed from that which God has given since the fall, and this is true of both natural and special (or word) revelation. The two forms of revelation are always coordinate. Natural and special revelation before the fall were related to, and designed to operate through, Adam's obedience. The fall rendered this revelation inoperative. Revelation now speaks in relation to man's fallen condition. Natural revelation not only declares the attributes of God (as it did from the beginning), but also reveals the wrath of God against all unrighteousness and ungodliness of men (about which it did not previously need to testify, for the simple reason that there was then no unrighteousness or ungodliness of men). That natural revelation so testifies now is taught in the Bible (Rom. 1:18; 2:14–15). Certain changes were introduced in the natural order (Gen. 3:17–19) so that nature would testify to man's folly and ruin. As the regularity and peacefulness of man's original environment had testified in every way to God's goodness, so now the turmoil and violence of the environment testify that God is angry with sinners every day. This is why it is no easier for sinners to accept God's revelation in nature than for them to accept his revelation in Scripture. Natural revelation is hard for the sinner to read, not because it does not say enough, nor because it does not speak clearly enough, but because it says too much only too clearly.

Just as the test of man's obedience came by way of word revelation, so the remedy for man's present need comes by way of word revelation. Only the gospel can supplement natural revelation in such a way as to (a) disclose the means of removing God's enmity (Rom. 1:17; 2 Cor. 5:18–21) and (b) make man once more a willing subject of the will of God (Rom. 12:1–2). Therefore, it has pleased God to make such a revelation by a gradual process which is now completed, with the result that his saving Word is now deposited in the Bible. As Scripture says, (a) "God . . . at various times and in various ways spoke in time past to the fathers by the prophets" and then, (b) "in these last days [has] spoken to us by His Son" (Heb. 1:1–2). The culmination came when (1) the final revelation of God "began to be spoken by the Lord," and then (2) "was confirmed to us by those who heard Him" (that is, the apostles and other eyewitnesses; Heb. 2:3). God gave this confirmation by granting the apostles power (a) to perform great signs and wonders and (b) to distribute special charismatic gifts according to his will.

It will be noted that the Confession sharply contradicts the view popularized today by the neo-Pentecostal movement. In essence this view would have us believe that we can have the same charismatic gifts today—such as prophecy, speaking in tongues, and healing—that we read occurred in the age of the apostles. This is a very serious error. In essence it is a result of a failure to grasp the biblical teaching concerning the history of salvation. The Bible itself makes it clear that there are many things in the history of redemption that cannot, and will not, be repeated. There will never again be a universal flood, or a crossing of the Red Sea, or a virgin birth. Never again will there be an outpouring of the Holy Spirit such as took place on the day of Pentecost. The sending of the Holy Spirit is just as much an unrepeatable event as the birth of Christ was. It is for this reason that the miracles—the signs and wonders—that we read of in the Bible were not constantly occurring but, rather, centered on the major events in the process of revelation. Note, for instance, how few the miracles are in the Bible until we come to the time of Moses (the author of the first part of the Bible). Note also how the signs and wonders that we read of in the book of Acts are always associated with the presence of the apostles. For these, and similar facts, there is a reason. The reason is that these signs and wonders were given by God to attest and confirm that these men were his spokesmen. And since this process came to completion in the finished work of Christ, and the testimony of these men is now deposited in the Scriptures, the Bible alone is God's present revelation. Of this we shall see more in the sections that follow.

QUESTIONS

1. How many kinds of revelation are there? Name them.
2. It has been imagined by some that natural revelation spoke clearly to Adam (some even imagine that he needed no word revelation before the fall), but that it does not speak clearly to us. Disprove.
3. Is there proof for the existence of God? Where?
4. What is wrong with the traditional proofs for the existence of God?
5. What are the two aspects of man's nature as the image of God?
6. Which of these could man lose?
7. Which of these was produced wholly by God?
8. Which of these was partly produced by man?
9. Was natural revelation alone sufficient before the fall? Why?
10. What does natural revelation declare *now* that it did not declare *before* the fall of man?

11. Does man still exist in the image of God?
12. What prevents men from having consciousness of the true and living God who hates sin?
13. Why must the remedy for man's condition come by special (word) revelation?
14. What is the fundamental error of the "charismatics"?
15. What was the purpose of the signs and wonders that we read of in the Bible?
16. Do we limit God when we say that these do not occur today?

I, 2–5

2. *Under the name of holy Scripture, or the Word of God written, are now contained all the books of the Old and New Testaments, which are these:*

Of the Old Testament

Genesis	I Kings	Ecclesiastes	Obadiah
Exodus	II Kings	The Song of Songs	Jonah
Leviticus	I Chronicles	Isaiah	Micah
Numbers	II Chronicles	Jeremiah	Nahum
Deuteronomy	Ezra	Lamentations	Habakkuk
Joshua	Nehemiah	Ezekiel	Zephaniah
Judges	Esther	Daniel	Haggai
Ruth	Job	Hosea	Zechariah
I Samuel	Psalms	Joel	Malachi
II Samuel	Proverbs	Amos	

Of the New Testament

The Gospels according to	Corinthians I	Titus	The First, Second, and Third
Matthew	Corinthians II	Philemon	Epistles of John
Mark	Galatians	The Epistle to the Hebrews	The Epistle of Jude
Luke	Ephesians		The Revelation
John	Philippians	The Epistle of James	
The Acts of the Apostles	Colossians	The First and Second Epistles of Peter	
Paul's Epistles to the Romans	Thessalonians I		
	Thessalonians II		
	Timothy I		
	Timothy II		

All which are given by inspiration of God to be the rule of faith and life.

3. *The books commonly called Apocrypha, not being of divine inspiration, are no part of the canon of the Scripture, and therefore are of no authority in the Church of God, nor to be any otherwise approved, or made use of, than other human writings.*

4. *The authority of the holy Scripture, for which it ought to be believed, and obeyed, dependeth not upon the testimony of any man, or church; but wholly upon God (who is truth itself) the author thereof: and therefore it is to be received, because it is the Word of God.*

5. *We may be moved and induced by the testimony of the Church to an high and reverent esteem of the holy Scripture. And the heavenliness of the matter, the efficacy of the doctrine, the majesty of the style, the consent of all the parts, the scope of the whole (which is, to give all glory to God), the full discovery it makes of the only way of man's salvation, the many other incomparable excellencies, and the entire perfection thereof, are arguments whereby it doth abundantly evidence itself to be the Word of God: yet notwithstanding, our full persuasion and assurance of the infallible truth and divine authority thereof, is from the inward work of the Holy Spirit bearing witness by and with the Word in our hearts.*

These sections of the Confession teach us (1) that because of man's lost condition, God has revealed himself and his will through a historical process, (2) that he has for good reasons permanently inscripturated that revelation, (3) that it is now complete, (4) that it is contained in the sixty-six canonical books, and (5) that this is evident from the fact that they are inspired as no other writings are.

God's special revelation after the fall could help man only if it came with power (a) to restore him to his place as God's image-likeness (Eph. 4:23–24; Rom. 12:2; Col. 3:10); and then (b) to control and sustain him as God's image-likeness in perpetuity (2 Cor. 3:18; Rom. 8:29). God's revelation, to be effectual, had to disclose redemptive information *plus* moral directives. The Scripture contains both. Redemption came in a series of acts accompanied by God's interpretation of those acts. The Old Testament records a series of God's acts preparatory to the actual accomplishment of redemption, along with such explanations as would advance human understanding of God's plan. The New Testament records the culminating act (the redemption accomplished by Jesus Christ) and the final interpretation of it in the apostolic doctrine. When redemption was finished in *deed,* it was also completed in *word* (Heb. 1:1–2). The reason is that the completion of redemption leaves nothing more to be explained.

But why has God chosen *this means* to preserve that revelation? The answer is that this means is better than other means commonly relied upon among men. It is better than tradition, for example. And it is not only better for *preserving* the truth, but also for *propagating* it. But of this we shall see more under section 8.

A more important question at this point is this: How do we know that this book is the Word of God, and how can we be sure that only this book is the Word of God? We can be sure that this book is the Word of God because of the evidence which proves it to be. And that evidence is both internal and external to the Word of God.

A. The internal evidence is complex. We shall simply indicate in part what that evidence is.

(1) The Old Testament claims to be the very Word of God. For example, David said: "The Spirit of the Lord spoke by me, and His word was on my tongue" (2 Sam. 23:2).

(2) The New Testament writers readily accepted the Old Testament as the Word of God. For example: "they raised their voice to God with one accord, and said: 'Lord, You are God, who made heaven and earth and the sea, and all that is in them, who by the mouth of Your servant David have said . . .' " (Acts 4:24–25). Or as Luke said: "Blessed is the Lord God of Israel, for He has visited and redeemed His people . . . as He spoke by the mouth of His holy prophets, who have been since the world began" (Luke 1:68–70). Christ and the apostles constantly quote the Old Testament as the Word of God (Matt. 5:18; John 10:35).

(3) Christ promised to give his apostles the Holy Spirit so that they could also write the New Testament Scriptures (John 14:26). "But the Helper, the Holy Spirit, whom the Father will send in My name, He will teach you all things, and bring to your remembrance all things that I said to you" (John 14:26). "But when the Helper comes, whom I shall send to you from the Father, the Spirit of truth who proceeds from the Father,

He will testify of Me. And you also will bear witness, because you have been with Me from the beginning" (John 15:26–27).

(4) The apostles later received the fulfillment of this promise (Acts 2:1–4) so that the apostles could say, "Therefore he who rejects this does not reject man, but God, who has also given us His Holy Spirit" (1 Thess. 4:8). "These things we also speak, not in words which man's wisdom teaches but which the Holy Spirit teaches," the apostle said (1 Cor. 2:13).

(5) The apostles treated each other's writings as the Word of God, putting them on a level with the Old Testament (2 Peter 3:15–16).

(6) The Bible contains information which, in the nature of the case, could have come only from God, namely, creation and the new heaven and new earth of the future (Gen. 1–2; Rev. 21–22).

(7) The Bible contains many predictions concerning events which were later fulfilled. We shall give a few. Concerning Christ the Messiah, the most important subject of prophecy, we find predictions: (a) of the nation, tribe, and family from which he was to come (Gen. 12:3; 18:18; 21:12; 22:18; 26:4; 28:14; 49:8–10; Pss. 18:50; 89:4, 29, 35–37); (b) of the place of his birth (Micah 5:2) (see Luke 2:1–7); (c) that he was to be born of the virgin (Isa. 7:14); (d) that he would be a prophet (Deut. 18:15, that is, the *final* prophet), priest (1 Sam. 2:35; Ps. 110:4, that is, the *final* priest), and king (2 Sam. 7:12–16, that is, the *everlasting* king); (e) that he would be hated and persecuted (Pss. 22:6; 35:7, 12; 109:2; Isa. 53:3–9); (f) that he would ride into Jerusalem upon a lowly ass (Ps. 118:26; Zech. 9:9; cf. Matt. 21:1–11); (g) that he would be sold for thirty pieces of silver (Zech. 11:12); (h) that he would be betrayed by one of his familiar friends (Pss. 41:9; 55:12–14); (i) that he would be forsaken even by his disciples (Zech. 13:7); (j) that he would be accused by false witnesses (Pss. 27:12; 35:11; 109:2); (k) that he would not plead at his trial (Ps. 38:13; Isa. 53:7); (l) that he would be mocked, spit upon, insulted (Ps. 35:15, 21), scourged (Isa. 50:6), and crucified (Ps. 22:14, 17); (m) that his persecutors would offer him gall and vinegar (Pss. 22:15; 69:21), part his garments and cast lots for his vesture (Ps. 22:18), mock him (Pss. 22:6–8; 109:25) and pierce him (Zech. 12:10; 13:7; Ps. 22:16); not a bone would be broken (Ps. 34:20); he would die with malefactors (Isa. 53:9–12), and be buried with the rich (Isa. 53:9); (n) that there would be an earthquake at his death (Zech. 14:4); (o) that he would rise again from the dead (Ps. 16:10; Hos. 6:2–3); (p) that he would ascend into heaven (Pss. 16:11; 24:7; 68:18;

110:1); (q) that Judas would die suddenly and miserably (Pss. 55:15; 109:17); and many others could be added.

(8) The Bible, though written by many different prophets and apostles, who lived in different times and places, and under very different circumstances, customs, and the like, has never been shown to contradict itself. (Many people *say* that the Bible contradicts itself, but no one has yet proved that it does in even a single instance.)

(9) The Bible teaches a plan of salvation and a system of ethics which human wisdom could not devise. Indeed, human wisdom cannot even receive such without supernatural grace.

B. The external evidence is subordinate, but important.

(1) The Church in all ages has acknowledged the Scriptures to be the Word of God. This cannot be a primary proof since the Church can and often does err. Yet it is no small thing that the Church even in its darkest days has acknowledged that the Bible is the Word of God.

(2) The Bible has been subject to God's special care, so that it has been preserved as no other writing on earth. (For proof of this, see John H. Skilton, "Transmission of the Scriptures," in *The Infallible Word,* ed. N. B. Stonehouse and P. Woolley [Philadelphia: Presbyterian Guardian, 1946], pp. 137–87.) Of this we shall see more under section 8.

But if Scripture *is* the Word of God, then obviously it must possess divine authority within itself. And if it does possess within itself divine authority, then it cannot and need not depend on anything else (other than God). Authority can depend only on that which is higher than itself. The authority of man can depend on the authority of man, but only if the authority depended upon is higher. Thus the authority of an ambassador to another nation depends upon that of the secretary of state, and the secretary of state is under authority of the president (Luke 7:7–8). But God is the highest authority. The word of an ambassador may have to be backed up by that of the secretary of state. But who can back up the authority of the Word of God but God himself?

The Roman Catholic Church nowhere reveals its supreme audacity more clearly than it does here. Rome says that the Bible is the Word of God. But it also says that the certainty of this is dependent upon the testimony of the Church. Thus the Baltimore Catechism (Q. 1327) states that "it is only from Tradition (preserved in the Catholic Church) that we can know which of the writings of ancient times are inspired and which are not inspired." Concerning the testimony of the Bible, God's Word, that the Bible is in fact God's Word, a testimony found in many texts, a Roman Catholic textbook says this: "Even though these texts from Scripture are exceedingly clear, they cannot possibly be our main proof that the Bible is the inspired Word of God (F. J. Ripley, *This Is the Faith* [Westminster, Md.: Newman, 1952], p. 41). Much more important than what God says about his Word, according to Rome, is what the Church says. "The Scripture needed a guarantee of authenticity. The Church alone could give that guarantee; without the Church it cannot exist" (Ripley, p. 45). Note that Rome does not hesitate to say that God *cannot* guarantee his own Word: only man, collective man (the Church), can. What is this but to put the creature above the Creator?

Sometimes Protestants have unwittingly done this too. It has often happened in the dealing of Christians with unbelievers. The unbeliever claims that he sees nothing in the Bible to demand belief that it is the Word of God. And the believer has all too often, in effect, granted that the unbeliever has had some justification for his position. The believer may even imagine that he can find a "neutral" starting point at which he and the unbeliever are in agreement. Then, it is thought, a series of arguments can be erected on that neutral starting point which in the end might possibly prove that the Bible is the Word of God (or perhaps that it is not). Thus human reason or archaeology or history may be made the starting point, and unconsciously this starting point becomes the "higher authority" and judgment bar before which God must pass muster. This in effect makes some authority higher than the authority of God. And this cannot be done (cf. Heb. 6:16–18).

The fact of the matter is that the Bible cannot possibly be proved to be God's Word by anything external to God himself. This does not mean that the testimony of the Church is useless. A guide who points out various masterpieces in an art gallery is of use. He does not *make* doubtful paintings into masterpieces. He does not even *prove* masterpieces to be such. But he may be the instrument by which we are brought to see the *intrinsic qualities* which make them to be masterpieces. So the Church may point out that the Bible is the Word of God. But this is possible only because it is *God's* Word—because it already displays everywhere within itself the excellencies which belong to word-divinity. It must *be* there in order to be *seen to be* there. As John Murray puts it: "The authority of

Scripture is an objective and permanent fact residing in the quality of inspiration." He also maintains that "faith in Scripture as God's Word . . . rests upon the perfections inherent in Scripture and is elicited by the perception of these perfections" ("The Attestation of Scripture," in *Infallible Word,* ed. Stonehouse and Woolley, p. 45).

However, as Murray himself asks: "If Scripture thus manifests itself to be divine, why is not faith the result in the case of every one confronted with it? The answer is that not all men have the requisite perceptive faculty. Evidence is one thing, the ability to perceive and understand is another." As 1 Corinthians 2:14 reminds us, "the effect of sin is not only that it blinds the mind of man and makes it impervious to the evidence but also that it renders the heart of man utterly hostile to the evidence" (Murray, p. 46). It is only when God gives "the spirit of wisdom" that the eyes of our understanding are enlightened (Eph. 1:17–18). But there are some who remain "in the futility of their mind, having their understanding darkened, being alienated from the life of God, because of the ignorance that is in them, because of the blindness of their heart; who, being past feeling, have given themselves over to lewdness" (Eph. 4:17–19). Such, of course, are utterly incapable of handling evidence, no matter how obviously divine it may be. Their devotion to "ungodliness" is such that they feel constrained to "suppress the truth in unrighteousness" (Rom. 1:18).

"The two pillars of true faith in Scripture as God's Word are the objective witness, and the internal testimony" (Murray, p. 51). The internal testimony of the Holy Spirit does not convey to us new truth content. God's whole truth to man is contained in Scripture. The Holy Spirit so works in the hearts of the elect that in the end they react properly to the truth which is actually confronting them in the Bible.

The Barthian or neo-orthodox view, which is so popular today, maintains that the Bible "contains" the Word of God, or that it "becomes" the Word of God to the reader. But the cause of this, in the Barthian view, is not objective perfection in the Bible, but wholly a subjective activity of God in the reader. Because this view rejects the *permanent* and *inherent* perfection of the written Word of God, it really has no "Word of God" at all. To call one's inward reaction to the Word of God the Word of God is to reject the Word of God and to enthrone the word of man. Neo-orthodoxy is really neo-modernism, and more dangerous because it is more deceiving. The Bible must have a subjective effect on me to be of help to me, but it can be of help to me only if it is forever and inherently the infallible Word of God. All I need is to see what it already is. This is the orthodox view.

QUESTIONS

1. What is the "proof" that the Bible is inspired?
2. How does the Bible express the claim that it is inspired?
3. Why can't the authority of the Bible depend on the testimony of any man or church?
4. What is Rome's audacious claim?
5. How do Protestants sometimes subordinate the authority of Scripture to men?
6. Where must the evidence of Scripture's divinity be sought?
7. If the evidence is there, why does not faith always result when men are confronted with that evidence?
8. When the Confession speaks of the Holy Spirit "bearing witness," does it mean that new truth content is conveyed to the mind?

I, 6

6. *The whole counsel of God concerning all things necessary for his own glory, man's salvation, faith and life, is either expressly set down in Scripture, or by good and necessary consequence may be deduced from Scripture: unto which nothing at any time is to be added, whether by new revelations of the Spirit, or traditions of men. Nevertheless, we acknowledge the inward illumination of the Spirit of God to be necessary for the saving understanding of such things as are revealed in the Word: and that there are some circumstances concerning the worship of God, and government of the Church, common to human actions and societies, which are to be ordered by the light of nature, and Christian prudence, according to the general rules of the Word, which are always to be observed.*

This section teaches (1) that God's finished revelation (now inscripturated) is entirely sufficient for all of man's spiritual needs, (2) that it is sufficient for all time (it cannot be added to), and (3) yet it is sufficient in terms of principles rather than details (leaving it to men to apply general principles according to their image function in particular instances).

The following is given in support of the Confession's teaching that the Bible is a finished product and entirely sufficient for all our needs.

Christ said that he was "the truth" (John 14:6), and we believe he embodied the whole truth (Col. 2:9). Is this not the point of comparison in the opening statement of the Epistle to the Hebrews? "God . . . at various times and in various ways spoke in time past to the fathers by the prophets," but now he "has in these last days spoken to us by His Son" who is the "express image of His person." Is this not a contrast between that which was provisional and that which is final, between that which was incomplete (and therefore constantly being added to) and that which is complete (and therefore incapable of being added to)? But the truth which Christ contained within himself, he in turn, according to his own testimony, disclosed to others. "All things that I heard from My Father I have made known to you" (John 15:15). If Christ, at the time of his incarnation, could say "I have made known . . . all," then how can anyone maintain that there might be more needed before Christ returns?

Christ made a disclosure of all truth to the apostles. We see, then, that Paul could rightly claim that he had declared "the *whole* counsel of God" (Acts 20:27). "I kept back nothing that was helpful," says Paul (v. 20). Every apostle could make the same claim. How, then, could there remain anything yet to be disclosed which would be of any profit? And even if the apostles had failed to disclose to us (by means of a written record) what Christ disclosed to them, would it not be impossible for anyone but an apostle to supply the deficiency? But Paul's testimony in 2 Timothy 3:15–17 plainly indicates that there is no such deficiency, since the Scriptures are able to furnish the believer unto perfection. And if the holy Scriptures were not sufficient and finished, what would a comparison between Hebrews 10:10 (or 10:12; 7:27) and Jude 3 lead to? Can Christ's "once for all" sacrifice be added to? If it cannot, then how can "the faith . . . once for all delivered to the saints" be added to? And how could Paul in Ephesians 6:11 encourage us to "put on the *whole* armor of God" in order to "be able to stand against the wiles of the devil"? One part of this panoply is "the sword of the Spirit, which is the word of God" (v.17). But if God's Word is not yet complete, how could that armor be whole?

Would it not then be defective? And if it were defective, how could we be able to stand?

Revelation 22:18–19 also teaches the impossibility of addition to the Bible. Some argue that John was merely forbidding any addition to the particular book he was then writing, namely, the book of Revelation. But everyone knows that John was the last surviving apostle, writing the final book. He was conscious of this fact. And then note the peculiar expression he uses in 22:18. The word translated "to" is not ordinarily translated "to." It is the Greek word *epi,* which means "on, upon, or above." It thus would indicate addition to that which was under it, or to what had gone before. If John wrote the last book, what better way to deny that anything else could be added to the whole Bible, than to deny that anything could be added on top of this book? And then, too, we might just as well argue that John forbade only this one book to be tampered with by way of subtraction. Who can imagine that John would allow us to "take away" from the words in other books of the Bible only to raise a protest if we took away from his book?

Man needs no knowledge of God's will which is not either "expressly set down in Scripture" or deducible from Scripture "by good and necessary consequence." The Mosaic law, for example, is not expressed by way of abstract principles. Moses declared the law in terms of concrete instances. But, as John Murray says, "these concrete instances are not to be isolated from the kind of relationship which they exemplify" (*Principles of Conduct,* [Grand Rapids: Eerdmans, 1957], p. 255). Even though the Ten Commandments in some cases are stated in terms of a concrete example (such as adultery as a concrete instance of sexual sin), yet they exemplify far-reaching principles. Because these principles are so all-encompassing we ought to do all ("whether you eat or drink, or whatever you do") to the glory of God. And because each person must, as an image of God personally responsible to God, apply these principles to his own particular circumstances, it is of the utmost importance to insist upon Christian liberty (see chapter XX).

We may cite as examples of "circumstances concerning the worship of God, and government of the Church . . . which are to be ordered by the light of nature, and Christian prudence, according to the general rules of the Word" such things as the place and time (on Sunday) of congregational assembly. In Acts 2:46 we read that the early Christians met "in the temple" and also "from house to house." That the "fair-minded" Jews in Berea who "received the word with all readiness" had a synagogue (Acts 17:10–11) is not condemned. But possession of a church building is certainly not considered as essential to the existence of a Christian church (cf. Acts 18:7). Nor is the Bible seen to prescribe a certain hour for the assembly of the congregation. Paul and Silas worshiped God at midnight (Acts 16:25). This seems to have happened also at Troas (Acts 20:7). But this was just as often not the case (Acts 16:13). The principle remained always in effect (Ex. 20:8), but the principle was carried out under varied circumstances concerning which God had not given every possible direction.

We are not at liberty to modify the principle in any degree. But we are at liberty to work out the principle according to changes in circumstances. (We may move the place of assembly from one building to another or from one hour to another, but not from one day to another.) A fire might deprive a congregation of its accustomed place of meeting. Another place would have to be selected, at least temporarily. So circumstances of divine worship would be changed by common agreement. But nothing other than the circumstances could be changed legitimately. It would still be required that the congregation meet on the Lord's Day, and the elements of divine worship prescribed by the Bible would still compose the entire content of the exercises of that day. We see this distinction in matters of worship and government. The day of worship is ordained of God, the circumstances of time (on the Lord's Day) and place are left to men. The content of divine worship is prescribed by God, the circumstances of the particular order are left to men. The organization of the Church with presbyteries and general assembly is of divine appointment, but the details of church order are left to circumstances. There is liberty, but only within the strict limits of the law of God laid down by way of principles revealed in the Scripture.

QUESTIONS

1. Cite Scripture proof that God's Word is now complete.
2. Cite Scripture proof that God's Word discloses all of his will for man.
3. Why is guidance given in terms of general principles rather than particular directions? (Two reasons may be given.)

4. How can the Bible suffice for all men in all times and places?
5. Give examples of things which are circumstances and things which are principles of worship and government.
6. Give an example to show that the general principles of the Word of God must control circumstances, and that the circumstances must not control (or be allowed to cause violation of) principles of the Word of God.

I, 7

7. *All things in Scripture are not alike plain in themselves, nor alike clear unto all: yet those things which are necessary to be known, believed, and observed for salvation, are so clearly propounded, and opened in some place of Scripture or other, that not only the learned, but the unlearned, in a due use of the ordinary means, may attain unto a sufficient understanding of them.*

This section teaches (1) the doctrine called the perspicuity of Scripture (which literally means the "see-through-ableness" of Scripture), and (2) that the unscholarly as well as the scholarly may therefore, by proper use of means, attain to a correct and saving understanding of Scripture.

It is the original lie of Satan that God, speaking in his Word, needs an interpreter to give man infallible guidance (Gen. 2:17; 3:4). This ancient error now is supreme in the Roman Catholic Church. Thus the Baltimore Catechism (Q. 1328) asks: "How can we know the true meaning of the doctrines contained in the Bible?" Answer: "We can know the true meaning . . . from the Catholic Church which has been authorized by Jesus Christ to explain His doctrines, and which is preserved from error in its teachings by the special assistance of the Holy Ghost." Thus, while affirming that God has spoken to men in the Bible, the Roman Catholic Church teaches that God has not made clear what he means, and so above the Word of God must stand the authoritative interpretation of the Church (which, we are to presume, has an expert opinion about what God's Word means). This also means that Rome would have us trust in the clear word of man rather than the obscure Word of God.

The Reformed faith views the matter precisely in reverse, holding that Scripture alone expresses divine truth with perfect clarity, and so regarding the Scriptures alone as finally authoritative. The interpretation of the Church (as in its creeds) must always, therefore, be regarded as less than a perfectly clear expression of divine truth, and as necessarily subordinate to Scripture. The authority of creeds is *determined by* Scripture, not *determinative of* Scripture. They have authority only if, and to the extent that, they truly are faithful to Scripture.

To say that God has spoken clearly is not, however, the same as to say that there is nothing "deep" or "profound" in Scripture. Peter reminds us that there are in Scripture "some things hard to understand" (2 Peter 3:16). It is not the Scriptures but some *things* in Scripture which are declared difficult to understand, and even if these things are drawn out of Scripture and correctly interpreted (or taught) by the Church, they would still be (by definition) "hard things" to understand. There is no question but that "untaught and unstable people" may, and often do, twist the hard things of Scripture "to their own destruction." But those who will study diligently and with stability (not just with spasmodic spurts of effort) will know the truth of the deep things of God. The fact that God has spoken clearly about hard things does not make them easy. The clearest possible expression of Einstein's theory of relativity does not make it simple. But if God *has not* spoken clearly, how can we be sure that others understand what we cannot?

The final proof for this, as for all other doctrines, must be found in Scripture. The following Scripture data are given by A. A. Hodge in his commentary:

(a) All Christians without distinction are commanded to search the Scriptures (2 Tim. 3:15–17; Acts 17:11; John 5:39).

(b) Scriptures are addressed either to all men or to the whole body of believers (Deut. 6:4–9; Luke 1:3; Rom. 1:7; 1 Cor. 1:2; 2 Cor. 1:1, and note the opening salutation of the Epistles).

(c) The Scriptures are affirmed to be perspicuous (Ps. 119:105, 130; 2 Cor. 3:14; 2 Peter 1:18–19; 2 Tim. 3:15–17).

(d) The Scriptures present themselves as a direct divine law to be personally obeyed by men (Eph. 5:22, 25; 6:1, 5, 9; Col. 4:1; Rom. 16:2).

QUESTIONS

1. What does "perspicuity" of Scripture mean?
2. What is the Roman Catholic doctrine on this same point?
3. Contrast Roman Catholic and Reformed views of the creeds.
4. Does the doctrine of the perspicuity of Scripture teach that there is nothing difficult to understand in Scripture?
5. What must the humblest as well as the most learned Christian do to understand the Scriptures? Do you think that those who complain of Scripture being too hard to understand have ever really done this?
6. How does Scripture itself indicate that God regards his Word as clear enough for all to understand?
7. What do you think are "the ordinary means" which must be duly used? (Section 9 of this chapter gives a partial answer.)

I, 8

8. *The Old Testament in Hebrew (which was the native language of the people of God of old), and the New Testament in Greek (which, at the time of the writing of it, was most generally known to the nations), being immediately inspired by God, and, by his singular care and providence, kept pure in all ages, are therefore authentical; so as in all controversies of religion, the Church is finally to appeal unto them. But, because these original tongues are not known to all the people of God, who have right unto, and interest in the Scriptures, and are commanded, in the fear of God, to read and search them, therefore they are to be translated into the vulgar language of every nation unto which they come, that, the Word of God dwelling plentifully in all, they may worship him in an acceptable manner; and, through patience and comfort of the Scriptures, may have hope.*

This section teaches (1) what languages the original Bible was written in: namely, the Hebrew and Greek, (2) that the original manuscripts were divinely inspired, (3) that final authority resides in these original texts alone, (4) that God has preserved this text in a state of essential purity, and (5) that this text should be translated into the vernacular for the profit of all believers.

Strictly speaking, there is only *one* Bible. We commonly, but incorrectly speak as though there were many. We speak of "the Protestant Bible" and "the Roman Catholic Bible." We speak of "the King James Bible" and "the New Bible." The truth is that there are many versions (or translations) of the Bible. But there is only one Bible. It is that body of words which were written down in ink upon parchments or vellum by those persons whom the Holy Spirit employed as instruments through which to impart his revealed truth. The only Bible which is properly in view when we speak of "The Bible" is this *original* text deposited in the autographs of the inspired writers. This divine text was originally contained in the written form in those documents (pieces of material with Hebrew and Greek letters, words, and sentences inscribed on them). This text was, in its entirety and in every least part thereof, absolutely infallible and perfect in every way. It is to this original text that Paul refers when he says that it was "given" to us. It is to the perfection of this original text that he refers when he says that it was "given by inspiration of God," and is therefore "profitable," etc. (2 Tim. 3:16).

Now it must be remembered that we do not today possess the leaves of parchment or vellum upon which this divine text was first written. We do not now possess the document so inspired of God as to be perfect in every way. Making use of this fact, modernists (who disbelieve the perfection of the original text of Scripture) have long argued that Reformed Christians have no infallible Bible to which they may appeal. "What use," they ask, "is an infallible Bible when no one possesses it?"

This brings us to the matter of God's "singular care and providence" by which he has "kept pure in all ages" this original text, so that we now actually possess it in "authentical" form. And let us begin by giving an illustration from modern life to show that an original document may be destroyed, without the text of that document being lost. Suppose you were to write a will. Then suppose you were to have a photographic copy of that will made. If the original were then destroyed, the photographic copy would still preserve the text of that will *exactly the same as the original itself.* The text of the copy would differ in no way whatever from the original, and so it would possess exactly the same "truth" and meaning as the original.

Now of course photography was not invented until long after the original copy (or rather, manuscript, since the original was not a "copy") of the Bible had been worn out or lost. How then could the original text of the Word of God be preserved? The answer is that God preserved it by his own remarkable care and providence. Let us illustrate this in figure 1, which shows the working of God's providential control of the preservation of the true text of the Bible through history.

Fig. 1

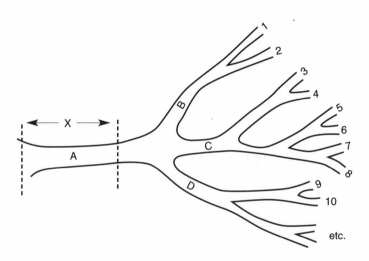

In this simplified diagram the original manuscript of the Bible is represented by letter A. X represents the duration of its existence, during which time several copies (B, C, D, etc.) were made. These in turn became the basis for later copies (1, 2, 3, etc.).

Now it must be granted that while A was entirely perfect (without any error whatsoever) because of God's immediate inspiration, yet copies B, C, D, and copies 1, 2, 3, etc., being made by uninspired persons who made mistakes common to men, were not entirely perfect. We must assume that copy B, for example, would contain very slight imperfections as compared with A (such as misspelled words, possibly a word or two left out, etc.). This same process would again be true of later copies, with this additional fact being evident: while those who made copies 1, 2, 3, etc., would make further errors of their own, they would also unavoidably transmit the mistakes already present in the copies from which their copies were made. That is, in addition to mistakes of their own, they would reproduce all previous errors located in B, C, etc.

At first sight it would seem that with the disappearance of A (probably worn out with use) the text would be doomed to progressive corruption thereafter. But such is not the case. The reason is that God has exercised control over all the elements and agencies concerned with the preservation of the sacred text. We see that God determined that early copies of the original would be made. True, each erred in a slight degree, but they did not all err in the same points. Being human, the copier of manuscript B would make a mistake here and there. Likewise would the copiers of C and D. But they would each err in a different, individual way. So that where B erred, C and D would not err. In effect, C and D would thus bear witness against the error of B. And so, while the true (or perfect) original text would not be entirely reproduced in any single copy, yet it would not be lost or inaccessible because by the majority testimony of the several copies, error would always be witnessed against. The true text would be perfectly preserved within the body of witnesses.

The diagram shown above is, of course, simplified. Actually, there are thousands of handwritten manuscript copies of the biblical text. And it is not always easy to organize them according to their proper genealogy. But in spite of the complexity of the matter, there can be no doubt that the process outlined above has actually been operative. By a diligent study of the many textual witnesses remaining from the ancient world, by just such a process as we have sketched here, the text of the Greek New Testament stands before our eyes today with assured integrity.

The manual effort to produce copies of the text of the Bible was not operative in a vacuum, however. We must briefly note other factors controlled by divine providence which played a part in the preservation of the true text of Scripture. (1) The first churches founded outside Palestine were in the ancient world of Greek language and culture. Greek was the native language of Ephesus, Corinth, and Thessalonica. Thus the language in which Paul and the other apostles wrote was the everyday spoken language of the Christians of that era. They heard the marvelous word of God in their own tongue. This tended to produce in the company of believers a "memorized" Bible. Naturally, therefore, any errors made by copiers of the Bible would usually be noticed by the people. (Just consider how quickly you notice the differences in a new translation, when they concern some familiar part of Scripture such as the Lord's Prayer, or the Twenty-third Psalm!) Remember, too, that in a day when there were no printing presses and only a few precious copies of the Bible, the people had to memorize much more than we do today. Thus it was that especially in the Greek-speaking Church, from the very beginning, the Greek New Testament had living witnesses who helped reduce the errors of copiers to an exceedingly small amount. (2) Then, when the Reformation came, God in his providence had enabled mankind to discover mechanical means of printing. Because of this, the text of Scripture could be reproduced in thousands of copies without progressive deterioration in accuracy.

Thus, as declared by the Confession of Faith, the infallible text of the Word of God has "by . . . singular care and providence [been] kept pure in all ages," so that we do now actually possess before our very eyes the "authentical" text of the Word of the living God. We may say concerning the actual words that we see on the pages of the Greek New Testament, "Behold, these are the very words which have come forth from the mouth of God. Amen." (We may point out in closing our discussion of this section that God has similarly preserved the text of the Old Testament—through manuscript witnesses, and through the careful oversight of Hebrew-speaking Jews, who by their familiarity with the text of the Old Testament in their own language quickly detected accidental errors in copy-work.)

QUESTIONS

1. How many "Bibles" are there (in the ultimate sense)?
2. Give the correct definition of "the Bible."
3. Do we actually possess the original manuscripts upon which the Word of God was originally written?
4. What does the modernist say about the "original, infallible Word of God"?
5. Could a copy of the infallible Word of God be as infallible as the Word of which it is a copy? Explain.
6. Were the early copies perfect?
7. What two chief factors worked to preserve the perfect text even through imperfect copiers?
8. Which of these do you believe more important?

9. Why is it no longer necessary that preservation of the true text depend on the Greek-speaking Church?
10. What is the glorious result of God's singular care and providence so far as the Scripture is concerned?

I, 9

9. *The infallible rule of interpretation of Scripture is the Scripture itself: and therefore, when there is a question about the true and full sense of any Scripture (which is not manifold, but one), it must be searched and known by other places that speak more clearly.*

In this section we learn (1) that Scripture interprets itself, (2) that difficult places are clarified by the parallel passages which speak more clearly, and (3) that the sense of Scripture is one (not many).

We have already seen that Roman Catholicism and other false religions join in the denial that the Bible is God's complete revelation. They have in common the denial of the sufficiency of Scripture (against which remember 2 Tim. 3:15–17). These religions also share another characteristic, namely, the denial that the Bible is capable of being understood without reference to any outside interpreter. For example, Pope Leo XIII in 1893 declared that "God has entrusted the Scriptures to the Church," by which of course he meant the Roman Catholic Church. For this reason, he said, the Church is "the perfectly trustworthy guide and teacher," so that the true sense of the Scriptures is to be considered "that sense which has been and is held by our Holy Mother the Church, whose is the judgment of the true sense and interpretation of the Holy Scriptures, so that nobody is allowed to explain Holy Scripture contrary to that sense or to the unanimous opinion of the Fathers." Obviously, under this system, it becomes quite unnecessary to read the Bible. Christ said, "Search the Scriptures!" Paul said, "Be diligent to present yourself approved to God, a worker who does not need to be ashamed, rightly dividing the word of truth" (2 Tim. 2:15). But Rome says, "God cannot speak clearly, so you must listen to me. I will make clear to you what he is trying to say!"

This same tendency may be seen in the Jehovah's Witnesses' teaching. It is well known that this religion disseminates *The Watchtower* and other literature in an endless stream. A constant part of this stream is the *Scripture Studies*. Here is what *The Watchtower* (July 1, 1957) had to say about the comparative value of the Bible itself and the *Scripture Studies* put out by this religion:

> Furthermore, not only do we find that people cannot see the divine plan in studying the Bible by itself, but we see, also, that if anyone lays the Scripture Studies aside, even after he has used them, after he has become familiar with them, after he has read them for ten years—if he lays them then aside and ignores them and goes to the Bible alone, though he has understood his Bible for ten years, our experience shows that within two years he goes into darkness. On the other hand, if he had merely read the Scripture Studies with their references, and not read a page of the Bible, as such, he would be in the light at the end of the two years, because he would have the light of the Scriptures.

Rome and the Jehovah's Witnesses sect agree in their basic attitude toward the Word of God. The psalmist said, "Your word is a lamp . . . and a light" (Ps. 119:105). But Rome and the other false religions call that light "darkness."

Against this stands the Reformed faith. As Cornelius Van Til reminds us, "No human interpreter need come between the Scripture and those to whom it comes." This view is opposed to clericalism. But "this does not mean that men who place themselves with us under the Scriptures, and who are ordained of God for the preaching of the Word cannot be of service to us in the better understanding of Scripture." Again, this Reformed stand does not mean that every portion is equally easy to understand. What it means is "that with ordinary intelligence any person can obtain" from the Word of God itself "the main point of the things he needs to know" (Van Til, *Introduction to Systematic Theology,* [Nutley, N.J.: Presbyterian and Reformed, 1974], p. 140).

This doctrine can, of course, be abused. It is abused by those who cry "No creed but Christ!" and then ignore the great creeds of the Church. In an odd way this itself is a denial of the clarity of Scripture, for it proceeds upon the assumption that in all history no one before us has been able to see the truth contained in God's Word. It is precisely because we believe that the Bible is plain that we value the creeds. Hence, the creeds are evidence that the Bible is clear. The creeds represent the consensus of many, who therein testified that they plainly saw the same great truth revealed in the Bible. This does not mean that the creeds are ever on a par with the Bible. They must always be kept subordinate to the word of Scripture. They cannot be regarded as infallible. That attribute belongs to God's Word alone. But because men have seen the plain truth revealed in Scripture and have expressed that truth in creedal form, the truths contained in the creeds possess a measure of authority. Precisely to the degree that they are "agreeable to and founded on the Word of God" are they useful and authoritative. But we do not go to the creeds to see if the Bible is true; we go to the Bible to see if the creeds are true. And we could not do this if the Bible was not clear and self-interpreting. In fact, creeds could not have been formulated in the first place if Scripture was not self-interpreting.

QUESTIONS

1. False religions deny that the Bible is God's complete revelation. What other aspect of revelation do they deny?
2. In such a religion is the Bible important or necessary to the individual believer (according to the view of that religion)?
3. Reconcile any apparent conflict between the Reformed insistence that the Bible is self-interpreting and the Reformed teaching that there are to be ministers of the Word ordained with authority to teach the Word in the churches.
4. Are all portions of the Scripture equally simple to understand? If not, does this change the fact that they are self-interpreting? Explain.
5. Why is creedless Christianity a perversion of this doctrine?
6. Why do creeds (which are agreeable with Scripture) have authority?

I, 10

10. *The supreme judge by which all controversies of religion are to be determined, and all decrees of councils, opinions of ancient writers, doctrines of men, and private spirits, are to be examined, and in whose sentence we are to rest, can be no other but the Holy Spirit speaking in the Scripture.*

Here we are taught that there is but one supreme judge in religious controversies, namely, the Scriptures.

This section of the Confession has to do with the application of the infallible rule of faith and practice to particular situations or questions. As we have already noted, the Roman Catholic Church maintains that it has power to interpret infallibly the infallible Word of God (the Bible) so that the faithful adherents of the Church will know in a particular situation what to believe. When the pope speaks officially, the Catholic doctrinal controversies are then settled. When the pope proclaimed the doctrine of the assumption of Mary, all Roman Catholics were then conscience-bound to believe it.

Reformed Christianity refuses to allow the conscience to be bound by anything except the infallible Word of God itself, as it interprets itself to the individual conscience of the believer. This does not mean that the truly Reformed church will remain silent on controversial matters. It means only that a truly Reformed church will make no attempt to require the conscience to bow to anything other than the Word of God. It is the task of the Church to express, set forth, or declare what the Word of God says so that the individual believer will be able himself to prove what the will of God is (Rom. 12:2). A true church simply declares the Word of God. It is not a legislative body. It does not make laws which bind the consciences of the subjects of Jesus Christ the king. It merely states the king's laws so clearly that they who fail to heed will be without excuse. (But the Roman Church claims precisely this legislative power to *make* laws for the subjects of Christ.)

This section of the Confession should be compared with chapter XXXI on Synods and Councils, especially sections 3–5. We have account of such a synod or council in Acts 15. Therein we learn how the Church ought to settle controversies ministerially on the basis of the Bible ministerially declared, rather than on the basis of new laws added to the content of the Bible. In Acts 15 we learn (1) that a controversy had arisen in the Antioch church (v. 1); (2) that a synod or council was sought in order to settle the controversy (vv. 2–3); (3) that such a synod was called (v. 4); (4) that the nature of the controversy was stated to this synod (vv. 4–5); and (5) the synod then proceeded to settle the matter (vv. 6–30). Most important is to notice how it was settled. It was settled by appeal to the Bible (or special apostolic revelations which became part of the Bible)

(vv. 14–18 etc.). When the synod came to certainty regarding the teaching of the Word of God, it was able to declare that teaching (vv. 28–29). They had not presumed to judge the matter in and of themselves, but had in every way acknowledged the Scripture as supreme judge. It is true that the synod expected the churches to receive the declaration with reverence and submission (vv. 28–29), but this was expected because said declaration was consonant with the Word of God. It was the Word of God declared which had the authority, and not the synod apart from that Word.

When a synod makes a declaration "apart from the Word of God" it is without divine authority. An example is provided by the 1934 General Assembly of the Presbyterian Church in the USA. This decision declared that it was the solemn obligation of every member of that denomination to contribute money to the support of the mission boards of the church even though there were, at that very time, modernists (who denied the very faith of the church) serving under the boards. The Assembly said that the obligation to support the mission boards was as definite as the obligation to observe the Lord's Supper. J. Gresham Machen and others refused to obey this mandate on the grounds that a synod cannot require as a duty what is contrary to the Bible. In rejecting the error of the highest court of the church Machen and others appealed to the supreme authority, which is the holy Scriptures.

Synods and councils (or general assemblies) may err. Many have erred. They are therefore never to be made the rule of faith and practice, but only to be used as a help to a proper observance of the rule of faith and practice which is the Bible. In a truly Reformed church there will be, and ought to be, frequent synodical declarations. But any member (or lower court) of the church will be, and ought to be, free to dissent from the declarations of the synod, provided he does so on the ground of appeal to the higher authority of the Word of God. (Of this we shall have more to say in our discussion of chapter XXXI.)

QUESTIONS

1. What is the difference between the Roman Catholic and Reformed churches with regard to the supreme judge in matters of religious controversy?

2. Can the Church speak infallibly? If not, then how can it speak with authority or value?
3. In the Synod of Jerusalem did Peter act as pope? Who made the decision? Upon what was this decision based?
4. Can you cite Scripture (a) to prove that it is the duty of believers to partake of the Lord's Supper? and (b) to prove that it is the duty of believers not to support "missionary" work performed by modernist unbelievers?

2

II. Of God, and of the Holy Trinity

1. *There is but one only living and true God, who is infinite in being and perfection, a most pure spirit, invisible, without body, parts, or passions, immutable, immense, eternal, incomprehensible, almighty, most wise, most holy, most free, most absolute, working all things according to the counsel of his own immutable and most righteous will, for his own glory; most loving, gracious, merciful, long-suffering, abundant in goodness and truth, forgiving iniquity, transgression, and sin; the rewarder of them that diligently seek him; and withal most just and terrible in his judgments; hating all sin, and who will by no means clear the guilty.*

2. *God hath all life, glory, goodness, blessedness, in and of himself; and is alone in and unto himself all-sufficient, not standing in need of any creatures which he hath made, nor deriving any glory from them, but only manifesting his own glory in, by, unto, and upon them: he is the alone foundation of all being, of whom, through whom, and to whom are all things; and hath most sovereign dominion over them, to do by them, for them, or upon them, whatsoever himself pleaseth. In his sight all things are open and manifest; his knowledge is infinite, infallible, and independent upon the creature, so as nothing is to him*

> *contingent or uncertain. He is most holy in all his counsels, in all his*
> *works, and in all his commands. To him is due from angels and*
> *men, and every other creature, whatsoever worship, service, or*
> *obedience, he is pleased to require of them.*

These sections teach (1) that there is but one living and true God, (2) that he is spirit, (3) that he possesses certain perfect incommunicable attributes, (4) that he possesses certain perfect communicable attributes, and (5) that he is not dependent upon any created thing, but rather absolutely independent of and sovereign over all.

Scripture says: "He who comes to God must believe that He is, and that He is a rewarder of those who diligently seek Him" (Heb. 11:6). It is also declared, in this same epistle, that "faith is . . . the evidence of things not seen" (Heb. 11:1). The doctrine of God begins, therefore, with the assertion that God is. And to the truth of this assertion (as Scripture informs us) *everything* testifies. What else do the heavens declare? What else does the firmament show (Ps. 19)? Some would seek to "prove" the existence of God, as if the evidence is hard to find. It would be more correct to say that the evidence is impossible to find when one is dead in trespasses and sins. But the evidence is impossible to escape anywhere when one is regenerated by God's Holy Spirit. In our discussion of chapter VI we will show why sinful men have such difficulty in seeing the evidence for the existence of God. And in our discussion of chapter X we will discover how it is that Christians have no such difficulty. For these reasons we do not believe that we should try to "prove" that God exists. As our text reminds us (Heb. 11:6), we cannot come to God until after we have been able to believe that he is.

When we speak of God as being pure spirit, we mean that he does not have a body like men. "God is Spirit," said Jesus (John 4:24). "When the Scriptures, in condescension to our weakness, express the fact that God hears by saying that he has an ear, or that he exerts power by attributing to him a hand, they evidently speak metaphorically, because in the case of men spiritual faculties are exercised through bodily organs. And when they speak of his repenting, of his being grieved, or jealous, they use metaphorical language also, teaching us that he acts toward us as a man would when agitated by such passions" (A. A. Hodge).

Because God is pure spirit, he is not subject to limitations of any kind. There is no place from which God is absent. "Where can I go from Your Spirit? Or where can I flee from Your presence? If I ascend into heaven, You are there; if I make my bed in hell, behold, You are there" (Ps. 139:7–8). Moreover, it is to be emphasized that at whatever specific place a man might be, at that place not merely a part of God but God himself in all his glory and majesty is present. When we say that God is omnipresent, we mean that the whole or complete and infinite God is to be found everywhere at the same time.

God is also infinite in that he is omnipotent; that is, he has unlimited ability to do whatsoever it is his good pleasure to do. "All the inhabitants of the earth are reputed as nothing; He does according to His will in the army of heaven and among the inhabitants of the earth. No one can restrain His hand or say to Him, 'What have You done?' " (Dan. 4:35). God has been able to predestinate all things because he not only can, but does actually work "all things after the counsel of His [own] will" (Eph. 1:11).

God is, again, infinite in knowledge, or omniscient. "His understanding is infinite" (Ps. 147:5). There never was a time when God did not know everything. He knows (and always has known) the future as he knows the past. "Even from the beginning I have declared it to you; before it came to pass I proclaimed it to you" (Isa. 48:5). We know things mediately; God knows them immediately (not through, or by means of, the senses). We know things successively (one thing after another) but God knows by one all-comprehending insight. We know only in part, but God's knowledge is exhaustively complete. We know as lowly creatures; he knows as exalted Creator. His knowledge is on a totally different level from ours. "Such knowledge is too wonderful for me; it is high, I cannot attain it" (Ps. 139:6). As Paul said, "For who has known the mind of the Lord?" (Rom. 11:34). Who can possess within the limits of a creaturely mind the orbit of God's thought? Who can even understand a single aspect of truth *as God understands it?* Even when we come to know the truth we must confess—at every point—that there is in that which we know a depth (an element of mystery) which is beyond us. All right understanding of God's revelation (truth) requires that we bow in wonder, and adore God who alone can fully understand.

And finally, God is eternal. He is "the same yesterday, today, and forever" (Heb. 13:8). There is never the least shadow of turning in him. He is in every respect exactly what he always has been, and always will be.

In saying that these qualities belong to God, we are "attributing" such to him. We therefore call these his "attributes." And the above-mentioned attributes are sometimes called *incommunicable* because they belong to God alone and cannot be communicated by God to his creatures. It is the possession of these attributes (eternity, infinity, and immutability) which distinguishes God from all other beings. There are, however, *communicable* attributes also. This means that God not only has qualities which he shares with none, but also has qualities which he does—*in a measure*—bestow upon such creatures as he pleases. Thus God has being (Ex. 3:14), wisdom (Ps. 147:5), power (Rev. 4:11), holiness (Rev. 15:4), justice, goodness, and truth (Ex. 34:6–7). But so do certain creatures, in a certain measure, namely, men and angels. God has all these qualities in an unlimited degree. The creatures who possess such qualities possess them only in a limited way.

This may be understood by means of an illustration. Hold a mirror before you. You will see an image of yourself. Now observe the many qualities which you and your image have in common! In one sense they are the same and yet, in another sense, they are not. For you are living being and the image is not. You exist on an entirely different level than does your image. The qualities belonging to your image in the mirror are but a reflection of your qualities. There is a dimension belonging to your attributes which does not belong to those of your image. So it is with God and man, his image. All of God's attributes possess that higher level of glorious and perfect existence which our creaturely attributes do not. The wisdom belonging to God (and the power, holiness, justice, etc.) is infinite, eternal, and unchangeable wisdom, but our wisdom is finite, temporal, and changeable, at best, a mere reflection of God's. We must therefore be careful to remember that in speaking of the communicable attributes of God, we do not mean that man is on the same level with God in anything.

God is the great original. Everything else is, in one way or another, a mere reflection of him. How simple this great truth. Yet how seldom do we see it consistently maintained in the thinking of men. "As though He needed anything, since He gives to all life, breath, and all things" (Acts

17:25). As if anyone could do anything that would benefit him (Job 22:2). Is it not perfectly evident that the creature could never do anything more excellent than reflect God as his image? How can a reflection add anything to that which it reflects? The unavoidable truth is that God alone is in and of himself really "something." And man (as also any other creature) is, in and of himself, nothing. For he is utterly dependent upon God. Since God alone has independent existence, is it not also evident that he has dominion over his creatures to do by them, for them, or with them, whatever he pleases? As if anyone—whose very being is from God— could do anything that God had not determined to have done. Even evil has come into existence because it was God's good pleasure to permit it, in order that by means of it his good purpose might be accomplished (Isa. 45:7). But this enters the realm of the decrees of God, to which we shall return in the next chapter.

Questions

1. Where is proof to be found of the true God's existence?
2. What do we mean when we call God a "spirit"?
3. Why does Scripture speak of God as having hands, feet, etc.?
4. What is meant by the term "incommunicable"?
5. What is meant by the term "attributes"?
6. What are the incommunicable attributes of God?
7. What is meant by the term "communicable"?
8. What are some communicable attributes of God?
9. Does our knowledge of a particular fact or truth (for example) have the same qualities as does God's knowledge of that fact or truth?
10. What does God receive?
11. What simple truth of the doctrine of God is seldom consistently maintained in the thinking of (even Christian) men?

II, 3

3. *In the unity of the Godhead there be three persons, of one substance, power and eternity: God the Father, God the Son, and God the Holy Ghost. The Father is of none, neither begotten nor proceeding;*

> *the Son is eternally begotten of the Father; the Holy Ghost eternally*
> *proceeding from the Father and the Son.*

The two sections of the Confession preceding this one have given us a definition of the essence of God. This section describes the manner in which God exists. Thus we learn (1) that this one God (as defined) exists in three distinct persons, (2) that each of these three persons is fully God (not parts of God), and (3) that these three equal persons have personal distinctions one from the other.

The doctrine of the Trinity is the great stumbling block to the Jew and Muslim. They accuse Christians of worshiping new and different gods from that of Old Testament monotheistic teaching. The question therefore naturally arises, "Is the doctrine of the Trinity revealed in the Old Testament, or is it revealed merely in the New Testament?" Strange as it may seem, it is not exactly correct to say that it is revealed in either. As B. B. Warfield once said, "We cannot speak of the doctrine of the Trinity . . . if we study exactness of speech, as revealed in the New Testament, any more than we can speak of it as revealed in the Old Testament. The Old Testament was written before its revelation; the New Testament after it. The revelation itself was made not in word but in deed. It was made in the incarnation of God the Son, and the outpouring of God the Holy Spirit. The relation of the two Testaments to this revelation is in the one case that of preparation for it, and in the other that of product of it."

God revealed himself by supernatural deeds, along with which he gradually gave more and more verbal interpretation. Only as God's plan of redemption was fully worked out, was God himself fully made known. God could have announced at the very beginning that there were within the unity of his being three distinct persons. But who could have understood? But when, in the fullness of time, each of the three persons actually wrought before the eyes of men those mighty deeds of redemption which each person of the Godhead was to do in the plan of salvation, who could not understand? Thus in Scripture we have the record of that which God has done, and what he said by way of interpretation. And the proof of the doctrine of the Trinity is supplied in the recorded fact that the Father manifestly is God, that Jesus just as clearly is God, and so also the Holy Spirit.

This is not to say, however, that the God revealed in the Old Testament is other than the Triune God. The God revealed in the Old Testament is fully God (and triune), though not fully revealed in the Old Testament. This being the case, it is inevitable that many things in the Old Testament can be understood only in the light of the (now fully revealed) doctrine of the Trinity. For example, in Genesis 1:1–3 we discern distinct references to God, God the Spirit, and God the Word. In Genesis 1:26 God takes counsel with himself, and speaks with himself of fashioning man "in Our image." How could this be if God be not three as well as one? In Genesis 11:5, 7 we read that the Lord came down to see the city and tower of Babel, and yet speaking of this says, "Let *Us* go down."

Again, we discover that a certain "Angel of Jehovah" frequently appeared to the people of God in the Old Testament. He had the appearance of a man (Gen. 32:24) and yet is recognized as being God (v. 30). This Angel, recognized as being God, is, however, also described as being sent by God (Ex. 23:20–24, 25). The true believer was therefore to acknowledge that this Angel sent by God was God. He had power to "pardon . . . transgressions," for God said, "My name is in him" (Ex. 23:21). Yet, while (1) the Old Testament believer was to know that the true God was one, (2) that yet the Angel of God (sent by God) was God also, (3) there was also a clearly recognized presence of God the Holy Spirit (Ps. 51:11; cf. 1 Sam. 16:13–14) distinct from either "God" or "the Angel."

Thus while the Old Testament believer did not yet see so full a manifestation of the three persons as we have seen (in Christ's becoming incarnate, and the Holy Spirit's being poured out at Pentecost), yet undeniably the God who was being revealed in Old Testament history (little by little) is this God and no other. Because we now know him to be such, these Old Testament accounts make perfectly good sense, which otherwise they would not. There are also, in prophecy, statements which, though perhaps not fully understood at the time (1 Peter 1:10–11), are such as to require the doctrine of the Trinity for their fulfillment. Thus Isaiah tells Israel that the Lord God will give a virgin-born son who will be Immanuel (which means "God with us") (Isa. 7:14). He is also called "the mighty God" (9:6). How could God send God, if there is not a plurality of persons in the divine essence? These are but examples of the fact that while the doctrine of the Trinity is not (fully) revealed in the Old

Testament, yet the God who is revealed there (in a partial and prepara-tory way) is none other than the Triune God.

The New Testament was written after the trinitarian nature of God had been completely manifested. The apostles became very conscious of the fact that while God remained invisible in the heavens, yet at the same time he stood incarnate before them in the flesh. They saw God (in the flesh) pray to God in heaven. Then when they saw him ascend into heaven, they witnessed the coming of the Holy Spirit. In such passages as Luke 3:22 we even see all three persons simultaneously manifested to the apostles' very senses. Who can speak from heaven but God? Who can command the wind and the waves, change water to wine, and raise the dead, but God? And who can come as a rushing mighty wind to enable weak and sinful men to speak the wondrous things of God?

So it was that the apostles quite simply had no choice but to recognize that the one living and true God exists in three persons. They were simul-taneously confronted with three who were God, and yet with over-whelming conviction they acknowledged these three to be one God. Thus Matthew 28:19, speaking of this one God, says that we are to be baptized "in the name [not names] of the Father and of the Son and of the Holy Spirit." Matthew would be guilty of faulty expression if either of two things were true: (1) if the Father, Son, and Holy Ghost did not possess an identical being (for otherwise he would have said "names"), and (2) if that one being named is not existent in three persons (for oth-erwise he would not have implied that "the name" is shared by each of the three). If there are not three persons who are God, and if there is more than one God, Matthew speaks incorrectly. But this is impossible to one inspired as he was. As the ancient text reminds us (1 John 5:7), "There are three . . . the Father, the Word, and the Holy Spirit; and these three are one." The formulation of our Confession (and similar ortho-dox creeds) is simply a key which fits all the facts as no other doctrine does or can.

QUESTIONS

1. Is the doctrine of the Trinity revealed in the Old Testament? In the New Testament?
2. Is the God revealed in the Old Testament the Triune God? How can this be proved?

3. Cite an Old Testament text to prove that God is not a single person.
4. Cite a text which indicates that the Angel of Jehovah is Jehovah (God).
5. Cite a prophetic text which shows that God promised to send God incarnate.
6. Why did the apostles accept the "doctrine" of the Trinity?
7. What two essential elements of the doctrine of the Trinity are taught in the baptismal form of Matthew?
8. The Larger Catechism states that each of the three persons of the Godhead is seen to be God because Scripture attributes to each of them such names, attributes, works, and worship as are proper to God only. Can you cite Scripture references showing that the names, attributes, works, and worship proper to God are associated with each of the three persons (the Father, the Son, and the Holy Ghost)?

3

III. Of God's Eternal Decree

1. *God from all eternity did, by the most wise and holy counsel of his own will, freely and unchangeably ordain whatsoever comes to pass; yet so as thereby neither is God the author of sin, nor is violence offered to the will of the creatures, nor is the liberty or contingency of second causes taken away, but rather established.*

2. *Although God knows whatsoever may or can come to pass upon all supposed conditions, yet hath he not decreed any thing because he foresaw it as future, or as that which would come to pass upon such conditions.*

This section of the Confession teaches us (1) that God has predetermined all things that happen, (2) that this predetermination (plan) is eternal, (3) that there is nothing too large or small to be excluded from this predetermination, (4) that this does not make God the author of sin, (5) that God does not force men to do what they do not want to do (in the way of sin), (6) that this does not destroy "freedom" or cause-and-effect relationships (rather, it is the very basis upon which these exist), and finally, (7) that this sovereign plan of God is not "conditioned upon" anything foreseen by him (which would make God dependent upon something outside himself).

What distinguishes a person from a thing (or being without personality) is that a person acts according to purpose. God is an infinite, eternal, and unchangeable person. Therefore his plan or purpose must ever have been a part of his infinite, eternal, and unchangeable existence. So Scripture testifies: "Known to God from eternity are all His works" (Acts 15:18). Scripture speaks of this as "the eternal purpose which He accomplished" (Eph. 3:11). It is an unchangeable purpose (Heb. 6:17). The infinity of it is seen in the fact that we are predestined "according to the purpose of Him who works *all* things according to the counsel of His will" (Eph. 1:11).

Little wonder that Christ could say confidently that not even a sparrow "falls to the ground apart from your Father's will" (Matt. 10:29), and that even "the very hairs of your head are all numbered" (v. 30). As the Bible declares that the whole system of things is controlled by God (Eph. 1:11), it declares with equal insistency that every single thing, however small and insignificant it may seem to us to be, is ordered by God ahead of time in his perfect plan. Even what seems to us to be a chance event can therefore be prophesied ahead of time by the true prophets of God (see 1 Kings 22:1–40, especially vv. 28, 34, 37).

The free actions of men are also predestined by God. Please note: these acts are both *free* and *predestined*. That is, those who commit these acts do so because they want to. And yet the acts which they do are predetermined by God so that Scripture says they *must* happen. Christ said, "Offenses *must* come, but woe to that man by whom the offense comes!" (Matt. 18:7). This statement recognizes two things: (1) the certainty of the occurrence of a future event, and (2) that those who will perform the act will do so freely and therefore with guilt. So in Acts 2:23 we read of Christ "being delivered by the determined counsel and foreknowledge of God," and yet also as "taken by lawless hands . . . [and] crucified, and put to death." "For truly against . . . Jesus . . . both Herod and Pontius Pilate, with the Gentiles and the people of Israel, were gathered together, to do whatever [God's] hand and purpose determined before to be done" (Acts 4:27–28).

As God predetermines evil actions which are freely performed, so he predetermines good actions which are also freely performed. Christians repent, believe, and seek to do the will of God because they want to. But in this case "it is God who works in [them] both to will and to do for His good pleasure" (Phil. 2:13). There is, in this case, an internal operation of God's Spirit, which is wholly absent from the wicked. But this still does not mean that the good (converted) any more than the wicked (unconverted) are not acting freely in doing what God has predestined that they shall do.

Freedom may be defined as "the absence of external coercion." If a man is not forced by any power outside himself to do that which is contrary to what he wants to do, then we may properly say that he is "free." The wonder of God's predestination is that God does leave men free in this sense, even though he predestines everything that every man will ever do. Some people use the word "freedom" in another sense, however, which is false in the extreme. They mean, by the "freedom" of man, that man has *power* or ability to do good or evil at any moment of time. To say that a man is able to do good or evil is very different from saying that a man is at *liberty* to do what he desires. We believe that the natural man has liberty but not ability to do what is right. For the truth is that man, while free from coercion from the outside, *is not free from the control of his own nature.* He who is evil by nature must of necessity do evil (just as a corrupt tree must of necessity produce corrupt fruit, Matt. 7:17–19). Just as we may say that God is good and therefore cannot do evil, so we may say that man (by nature) is evil and cannot (of himself) do good.

In the case of the unconverted who are not elect, the very fact that they are never regenerated by God makes it inevitable that they will do evil for the simple reason that this is the one thing that they want to do (Gen. 6:5; Pss. 14, 53). In the case of the elect, God regenerates, effectually calls, and sustains in grace, and then—because these are made new creatures (with new desires, new natures)—they will do the good that God has predestined for the simple reason that they want to. In either case there is entire absence of external coercion, and yet the will of God is surely done. Even where internal power is exerted (in the case of the converted), it does not force man to do what he does not want to do, but rather creates a new will which is in accord with the will of God.

Some have thought that God makes predestination depend on what he foresees. Thus many have held that God predestines to everlasting life those he foresees will by their own power turn unto him. This contradicts Scripture, which teaches clearly (1) that no man has the power to do this by nature, (2) that such power is a gift of God, and (3) that the gift is given to those chosen of God *for* the gift. It is not, then, a question of predestination *or* foreknowledge. It is, and can be, only a question of predestination *and* foreknowledge.

This we may indicate by asking two simple questions: (a) Does God know for certain what will happen before it happens? All Christians would no doubt say yes. (b) But if God knows that a thing is certain to happen before it happens, we may then ask, what makes it certain? There can be but one answer: God makes it certain. We are unable to escape the conclusion that God foresees with certainty only because he guarantees the certainty he foresees. Things are "predestined according to the purpose of Him who works all things according to the counsel of His will" (Eph. 1:11). God foresees that the elect will be "holy and without blame before Him" (Eph. 1:4), and that they will experience "sanctification by the Spirit and belief in the truth" (2 Thess. 2:13). But this is foreseeable only because he "chose us in Him before the foundation of the world" (Eph. 1:4). His predestination is the cause of the holiness which he foresees. He does not choose us because he foresees that we will believe, but he foresees that we will believe because he has chosen us. Only thus are works wholly excluded (Eph. 2:8–10).

QUESTIONS

1. What distinguishes a "person" from all other beings or things?
2. What kind of "plan" or "purpose" must of necessity belong to an "infinite, eternal and unchangeable" personal being?
3. Cite a Scripture text proving that all existence is controlled by God.
4. Cite a Scripture text proving that the most minute details of existence are controlled by God.
5. Cite a text proving that seemingly accidental events are controlled by God.
6. Cite a text proving that evil acts are predetermined by God.
7. Cite a text proving that evil acts are nevertheless "free."
8. Cite a text proving that "good" acts done by regenerate persons are predetermined by God, and yet also "free."
9. What do we mean when we say that a man is "free," or acts "freely"?
10. Why are the unregenerate, though free, certain to do only evil?

11. Why are the regenerate, though free, certain to please God?
12. Can God foresee (or foreknow) before he predetermines? Vice versa? Why?

III, 3–5

3. *By the decree of God, for the manifestation of his glory, some men and angels are predestinated unto everlasting life; and others foreordained to everlasting death.*

4. *These angels and men, thus predestinated, and foreordained, are particularly and unchangeably designed, and their number is so certain and definite that it cannot be either increased or diminished.*

5. *Those of mankind that are predestined unto life, God, before the foundation of the world was laid, according to his eternal and immutable purpose, and the secret counsel and good pleasure of his will, hath chosen in Christ, unto everlasting glory, out of his mere free grace and love, without any foresight of faith or good works, or perseverance in either of them, or any other thing in the creature, as conditions, or causes moving him thereunto; and all to the praise of his glorious grace.*

The preceding sections have shown that God predetermines all events of every kind that come to pass. These sections further expound one aspect of that totality of predetermined things, namely, the eternal destiny of men and angels. These sections teach (1) that God decrees who shall be saved and who shall be left in their lost estate, (2) that this determination is unchangeable, (3) that God's decision is not based on any condition which he foresees will be fulfilled by them, and (4) that the ultimate purpose which God has in this is the manifestation of his own glory.

That God is the one who determines who will, and who will not be saved, is one of the clearest teachings of Scripture. The reason that it is so seldom acknowledged is due to human perversity rather than any obscurity in Scripture teaching. And the chief cause of man's constant misreading of Scripture regarding this matter is his perennial desire to have a better opinion of himself than is warranted. If we can but remember that no man deserves anything but wrath and damnation, if we can but face this solemn and awful reality, if we can but keep this truth ever before us, we will then be in a position to accept what Scripture so clearly says. And Scripture simply says this: that God gives to some men what they most assuredly and richly deserve (namely, damnation) while to others he gives the wholly unmerited gift of salvation (which they in no way deserve).

The classic Scripture example is that of Jacob and Esau. They were twins. By nature they had everything in common. Their heredity was the same, as was their environment. Yet before they were born, or had done anything good or bad, "that the purpose of God according to election might stand" (Rom. 9:11), Jacob was chosen to eternal life, and Esau was passed by and left to the punishment he deserved. And concerning this obvious discrimination the apostle simply says, "He has mercy on whom He wills, and whom He wills He hardens" (Rom. 9:18). And lest we should try to subvert the plain import of these words, he goes on to insist that God, as a potter, has "power over the clay, from the same lump to make one vessel for honor, and another for dishonor" (Rom. 9:21). God has a *right* to give damnation to Esau, who deserves damnation, and eternal life to Jacob, who also deserves damnation.

But what is of cardinal importance is to recognize that God's sovereign determination of the destinies of the souls of men is not conditional. There was no difference between Jacob and Esau for the sake of which God chose the one and rejected the other. We do not say that there is no difference between the elect and nonelect. But we say that the difference is the *result* of God's sovereign discrimination rather than the *cause* of it. As God said to Pharaoh and the Egyptians, "I will make a difference between My people and your people" (Ex. 8:23).

We may see this more clearly, perhaps, with the following facts in view: (1) Scripture says that salvation is wholly of grace and that works are in no way the cause of it lest man should have something to boast of in the matter (Eph. 2:8–9; Rom. 11:6). And if salvation is "by grace, then it is no longer of works; otherwise grace is no longer grace" (Rom. 11:6). One can as well mix fire and water as grace and works. They are absolutely exclusive the one of the other. If salvation is by God's grace (pure, unmerited favor)—and Scripture says it is—then there is no room at all for works (that is, activity of man as an originating cause). When it is said that God gives grace to certain persons because he foresees that they will do (work) this or that, then we have salvation by works (in this case, "foreseen works"), and grace is overthrown. (2) Scripture tells us that repentance and faith are themselves a part of the gift which God gives. And what is a part of a gift cannot be the cause of the gift itself. (3) Scripture plainly states that men are by nature "dead in trespasses and sins" (Eph. 2:1, 5). Faith and repentance are activities, not of the dead, but of new creatures "quickened from the dead." Obviously then, it would be impossible for God to give the gift of life to those who already have life. (4) Scripture informs us that divine election is *not* conditioned upon something in the creature, *but rather* upon something in God. It is the good pleasure, the delight of God, which is the basis of election. (See Luke 10:21.) As the potter is controlled in his selections by his own good pleasure, so God is determined only by that good pleasure which is within himself.

And why has God elected some? Why has he also left some to perish in their sins? (Observe: we are not now asking why he chose the ones he did while passing by the rest, but why he chose any while passing by others.) The answer is: for his own glory. God will bring glory to himself, or rather will manifest his glory. He will display the perfection of his holiness by wrath against sin in the destruction of the wicked, and he will display the perfection of his mercy and love in saving the elect. Is there anyone disposed to argue that God has no right to do these things? (Read Rom. 9:20–21.)

QUESTIONS

1. Why is the doctrine of predestination so seldom acknowledged even though it is so clearly taught in Scripture?
2. What does sinful man deserve?
3. What classic example in Scripture proves this doctrine?
4. How much did they have "in common" to begin with? At the "end"?
5. How does this case prove that it was God (alone) who made them to differ?
6. What Scripture asserts that God has "the right" to do this?
7. What is meant by saying that God's predestination is not "conditional"?

8. If man could fulfill some condition upon which basis God would then elect him, what teachings of Scripture would be denied?
9. Why has God chosen the ones he has chosen?
10. Why has God chosen some and passed others by?

III, 6

6. *As God hath appointed the elect unto glory, so hath he, by the eternal and most free purpose of his will, foreordained all the means thereunto. Wherefore they who are elected, being fallen in Adam, are redeemed by Christ; are effectually called unto faith in Christ by his Spirit working in due season; are justified, adopted, sanctified, and kept by his power through faith unto salvation. Neither are any other redeemed by Christ, effectually called, justified, adopted, sanctified, and saved, but the elect only.*

This section of the Confession teaches (1) that God "in determining *the ends* he intends to accomplish . . . at the same time determines *the means* by which he intends to accomplish them," (2) that God has determined that the elect shall be saved (ordinarily) by "effectual calling, justification, adoption, sanctification and perseverance in grace," and (3) that those for whom the divinely appointed means of grace are lacking are not among the elect (with such exceptions as are noted in chapter X, section 3).

God gives us our daily bread. But he employs complex means and agencies to do so. There must be sunshine and rain, harvest and distribution. Without these things there would be no such result. So it is in the effecting of our redemption. We are, as Peter says, "elect according to the foreknowledge of God the Father," but it is only "in sanctification of the Spirit, for obedience and sprinkling of the blood of Jesus Christ" (1 Peter 1:2). Or as he again tells us, we must "be even more diligent" (2 Peter 1:10) not because there is no such thing as election, but because there is. We are called—by means of this diligence—to make our "call and election sure" (2 Peter 1:10). Our diligence will prove to be the means by which that divinely ordained end is realized. For this reason Paul links divine predestination (the end) with calling, justification, and glorification (the means to this end) (Rom. 8:30). He recognizes an inseparable link between the end decreed by God, and the steps leading to the end.

It is the Reformed teaching that all the works of God, and of the three persons of the Godhead, are in perfect harmony. The plan of God is never contradicted by the works of God by which the plan is executed. Thus, as God the Father elected some to everlasting life, so he decreed all the means necessary to the accomplishment of that end. Christ was given to make atonement for the sins of the elect, and the Holy Spirit was given to apply to the elect the redemption accomplished by Christ. The Father planned to save some, Christ died to save them, and the Holy Spirit sees to it that they do actually come to possess salvation.

But some have departed from the truth in this matter. Their view may be summarized as follows: "Out of infinite pity and universal benevolence, God determined to give his Son to die so that all mankind, ruined by the fall, might be redeemed from the curse of the law; but, foreseeing that if left to themselves all men would certainly reject Christ and be lost, God, in order to carry out and apply his plan of human redemption, and moved by a special love to certain persons, elected them out of the mass of mankind to be recipients of the special effectual grace of the Holy Ghost, and thus to salvation." Such teaching may be made to sound quite pious, and attractive to sinful men. It is always comforting to believe that somehow God's saving grace is for all alike. But comforting though it may be, it cannot be maintained together with a consistent view of God (unless one simply denies damnation altogether). One can consistently hold that God bestows *saving* grace on all men and that all men will be saved. One can also consistently maintain that God bestows saving grace upon some men only and that only they will be saved. But one cannot consistently maintain that God has universal saving grace which does not universally save. And the attempt invariably results in a deficient doctrine of God. However, so great is the desire of sinful man to make God's saving grace universal, that there has been repeated lapse from purity of conception regarding this truth.

A notable example is provided by a creedal revision which took place in the United Presbyterian Church of North America. From 1858 until 1925 the United Presbyterian Church held this doctrine (consistent with the Word of God):

> We declare, that our Lord Jesus Christ did, by the appointment of the Father, and by his own gracious and voluntary act, place himself in the room of a definite number who were chosen in him before the foundation of the world, so that he was their true and proper legal surety; and as such, did, in their behalf, satisfy the justice of God, and answer all the demands which the law had against them, and thereby infallibly obtain for them eternal redemption.

But in 1925 the United Presbyterian Church changed its testimony to a position inconsistent with the Word of God:

> We believe that our Lord Jesus Christ, by the appointment of the Father, and by his own gracious and voluntary act, gave himself a ransom for all, that as a substitute for sinful man his death was a propitiatory sacrifice of infinite value, satisfying Divine justice and holiness, and giving free access to God for pardon and restoration; and that this atonement, though made for the sin of the world, becomes efficacious to those only who are led by the Holy Spirit to believe in Christ as their Savior.

The differences are evident. (1) One statement says Christ was a substitute for some men; the other, that he was a substitute for all men. (2) One statement says he suffered the penalty of some men, the other, that he suffered the penalty of all. (3) One statement says he (by his finished work) obtained eternal redemption for those he represented; the other, that he merely gave free access to God for the obtaining of redemption, and this for all. Now if we were to ask, "Why is it that some men only, and not all, are actually saved in the end?" the answer would be clear and consistent in the one case, and hopelessly contradictory in the other.

The 1858 doctrine would teach us that some men are saved because God (the Father, the Son, and the Holy Ghost) acted to save them. But if we consider the 1925 doctrine we note that a specific statement is added showing that only some are actually saved because the Holy Spirit's work is not in harmony with that of God the Son! For even "though" Christ's sacrifice was "made for the sin of the world" as "a ransom for all," yet it becomes efficacious "to those only who are led by the Holy Spirit to believe in Christ." This is sad beyond words, because it would sacrifice the scriptural doctrine of God in order to give some saving grace (which, however, does not save) to everyone. We say "sacrifice the scriptural doctrine of God" because a God in which there are persons in sharp disagreement is not the true and living God of Scripture. (God the Son died to save everyone, but the Holy Spirit leads only some to repentance and faith.) It is no exaggeration whatever to say that such a God as this does not even exist. How amazing the perversity and darkness of man—to sacrifice the true doctrine of God for universal saving grace which (by their own account) does not work anyway!

QUESTIONS

1. Read Acts 27:14–44. What divine end was promised by God (v. 24)? What means did the inspired apostle require for attaining this end (v. 31)? Was the end reached? Were the means used as required? Which then was ordained (decreed, or predetermined) by God, the end or the means?
2. What is wrong with this popular statement: "If I'm elect, then I'll be saved no matter what I do"?
3. By what is the plan of God never contradicted?
4. Why may we not say that Christ's death was intended for the salvation of all?
5. What words in the 1925 doctrine of the United Presbyterian Church are wrong?
6. State precisely what the death of Christ is supposed to actually secure under the respective views of 1858 and of 1925.
7. How does the 1925 doctrine in effect abolish God?

III, 7–8

7. *The rest of mankind, God was pleased, according to the unsearchable counsel of his own will, whereby he extendeth or withholdeth mercy as he pleaseth, for the glory of his sovereign power over his creatures, to pass by, and to ordain them to dishonour and wrath for their sin, to the praise of his glorious justice.*

8. *The doctrine of this high mystery of predestination is to be handled with special prudence and care, that men attending the will of God revealed in his Word, and yielding obedience thereunto, may, from the certainty of their effectual vocation, be assured of their eternal election. So shall this doctrine afford matter of praise, reverence, and admiration of God, and of humility, diligence, and abundant consolation, to all that sincerely obey the gospel.*

These sections of the Confession teach us (1) that God has sovereignly determined to withhold his saving grace from some men, (2) that this "withholding" or "passing by" is wholly an effect of his own unsearchable counsel, (3) that it is for his own glory, (4) that while his decree is sovereign as respects the particular persons, it is just, because of their sin, (5) that this doctrine is to be taught, and with great care, in order that it may bring good to believers and glory to God, and (6) that this doctrine (despite the enmity it arouses in unbelievers) is full of God's blessing to those who receive it aright.

We must observe that God's decree, as respects the "reprobate" (non-elect, or unbelieving), consists of two distinct aspects. First, God has determined to pass *them* by. When it is asked, "Why has God determined to withhold his saving grace from (or to pass by) this particular individual (as in the case of Esau) rather than his brother (Jacob)?" we can only answer: "Because it was his good pleasure to do so." He has mercy on whom he will have mercy, and hardens whom he will harden (Rom. 9:18). The reason that God determines to pass by a particular individual is not the existence of sin in that particular individual. If that were the reason, then all men would be reprobate. For it cannot be too often insisted that the elect and reprobate are, considered in and of themselves, without difference in this respect. Both are sinful. That which moves God to take the one and pass by the other is therefore wholly within himself. We cannot go beyond this—God elects or passes by as, and because, it pleases him. Such reasons as God may have for this discrimination are wholly within himself and hidden from our view. But of one thing we may be sure: there is *nothing whatever in us* that provides God with a reason for electing one and passing by another.

Secondly, God has determined to treat those whom he does pass by in strict justice. Thus we must say that, while sin is in no way the reason for passing by the reprobate, it is the whole (or only) reason for the damnation which they receive. As Paul said: "Let no man deceive you with empty words, for because of these things [i.e., the sins mentioned by Paul] the wrath of God comes upon the sons of disobedience" (Eph. 5:6). The sins mentioned are not the reason why some are left in their sin, but the sin in which they are left brings the wrath of God upon them.

Again we must observe the perversity of human nature. This is seen in the fact that this doctrine is so often either abused or refused. It is abused by those who say that if (a) God has withheld saving grace from some men, passing them by (which is true), then (b) it is God's fault, and not theirs, that they receive such horrible punishment (which is not true). This is diabolical for the simple reason that God's withholding of grace does not make the sinner guilty and liable to punishment; it merely leaves him in that condition. "The wrath of God *abides* [or, *remains*] on him" (John 3:36). The reason for the horrible punishment of the reprobate person is not God's act of passing him by, but his own wickedness and sin. This doctrine is refused by those who say that such a God as would do this is unfair, arbitrary, and unjust. No doubt this doctrine is "a stone of stumbling and a rock of offense," but this is only because "they stumble, being disobedient to the word, to which they also were appointed" (1 Peter 2:7–8). In other words, this merely proves the point. God is sovereign. He is *not* unjust. No descendant of Adam and Eve deserves anything but God's wrath and curse.

Therefore, when God sovereignly decides that some shall receive what they do not deserve, the sinner may rail against him as arbitrary and unjust. But the real problem here is in the sinner, not in God. For, as the apostle said: "O man, who are you to reply against God?" (Rom. 9:20).

There is no question but that this doctrine arouses man's enmity. It could not be otherwise, inasmuch as this doctrine resolutely denies the supreme claim of sinful man—to be "as god," that is, the supreme arbiter of his own destiny. For this reason some have suggested that it would be better not to mention the doctrine of predestination at all. But this is nothing but a sinful catering to the desires of sinful men and an insult to God. We believe that this doctrine ought by all means to be taught. It ought to be taught because it is revealed in the Word of God. And it ought to be taught with special prudence and care—that is, with special pains and fullness of explanation to expound its meaning completely and to track down and obliterate every vain objection raised by sinful men. And even if this does not have the desired result with respect to those who (because they are reprobate) hate this doctrine, it will still be to the glory of God that it has been expounded, and it will also be to the good and comfort of true believers who are by means of this doctrine brought to see that their salvation is wholly of God, and that they owe him all praise and honor for having dealt so mercifully with them out of his mere good pleasure.

We are well aware, of course, that the doctrine of predestination is often considered better unmentioned for another reason also—namely, because it is thought that it will encourage indolence and presumption in those who are not offended by it. But this is *not* the case with true believers. No doubt there are those who misuse this doctrine, as there are those who hate this doctrine. Yet the fact remains that the apostles taught this doctrine in order that believers might "be even more diligent to make [their] call and election sure" (2 Peter 1:10). The truth is that, when this doctrine is *not* taught with care and prudence, the danger of false presumption is increased. When the doctrine is taught fully, clearly, and honestly—without reservation—the desired diligence and humility will be the God-given result. There is little doubt that in our day, when this doctrine is so little mentioned and almost never handled with special prudence and care, the result has been lamentable. The evidence certainly does not show that neglect of this doctrine has produced that humility, diligence, and abundant consolation that marked the Church in better days when this doctrine was so handled.

QUESTIONS

1. Precisely what has God determined to do with respect to the reprobate?
2. Why has God passed by these particular persons?
3. Why do they receive damnation?
4. How has this doctrine been abused?
5. Why has this doctrine been refused?
6. Is God "arbitrary" in his actions?
7. Is it wrong for God to be "arbitrary" in his actions?
8. What text of Scripture shows that reprobation (God's withholding of grace, and passing by) does not make a sinner guilty and liable to punishment?
9. Should this doctrine be taught? Why? How?

4

IV. Of Creation

1. *It pleased God the Father, Son, and Holy Ghost, for the manifestation of the glory of his eternal power, wisdom, and goodness, in the beginning, to create, or make of nothing, the world, and all things therein, whether visible or invisible, in the space of six days, and all very good.*

This section of the Confession teaches us (1) that the world is not self-existent or eternal, (2) that it derives existence from the true God, (3) that he made all things of nothing, (4) that he then formed the universe through process until it was "very good" in his sight, and (5) that he did all this for his own glory.

Scripture begins with an assertion: "In the beginning God created the heavens and the earth" (Gen. 1:1). The world is created, not self-existent, and it is God, the true God, who caused it to be. Modern "scientific" dogma, on the other hand, teaches (1) that the universe is self-existent or eternal, (2) that it does not have a derived subsistence (i.e., that it was not created out of nothing), (3) that the present form of the world is the result of a process of selection controlled, not by God, but by the "principle" of "the survival of the fittest," and (4) that there is no "ultimate" reason for it all.

What must be stressed, however, is that the above-mentioned process—called evolution—is strictly speaking merely a "theory" and a dogma. Although it has been "believed" and "accepted" for more than a century now, there is still *not one iota of "proof" that it is true.* It is thus needlessly assumed that there *may be,* or that there actually is, conflict between genuine science and the Bible. If "genuine science" be taken to mean "truth" drawn from natural revelation, such is impossible, for the simple reason that God is the author of both the "book of nature" and the "book of life" (the Bible). Truth is simply that which really is. There is only one truth, because there is only one reality. Therefore, if the Scriptures are true, they merely tell us what really is (or was, or will yet be). When by investigation men also discover what really is in the world of nature, they simply grasp another aspect of the same total truth. So there cannot be any conflict between them. The *only reason* for conflict is that men have erred either (a) in their investigation of the facts, or (b) in their theories about the facts, or (c) in both. It is a fact that Christ rose from the dead (1 Cor. 15). So when a biologist, examining thousands of "other facts," theorizes about life while starting with the assumption that no one ever did—or could—die and then rise again from the dead, he errs in both ways. "Science" has noted that various orders of life "formed" through process. But when it theorizes from this that life started by itself, and directed itself from stage to stage, it is neither scientific nor true. Evolutionists have made many worthwhile observations, but they have not proved and cannot prove that things caused themselves to be, for this is not true.

Perhaps the chief point at which it is commonly thought that science "contradicts" Scripture is where the Bible says that the process of forming the original stuff of creation into its finished state took place in six days. Such undeniable facts as fossils are said to be "proof" that this is not "possible." But in such an assertion there are hidden assumptions:

First, there is the assumption that the production of fossils is very slow and time-consuming. But there is much to be said for the opposite view. There are beautifully preserved fossils of fern leaves, with even the most minute parts perfectly preserved. We find it difficult to believe that a thing so fragile could have been preserved except by some very quick process, because it is so highly "perishable." Perhaps, after all, the *belief* that fossils were caused by a cataclysm such as the flood is less incredible

than the *belief* that they were slowly produced over vast stretches of pri-
mordial time.

Second, there is the assumption that the vast stretches of time which
produced fossils cannot have come after the events recorded in the six
days of biblical creation. Or in other words, that the events described in
the biblical creation narrative are precisely those events which require
great eons of time. We might reply to this that the Bible is as indefinite
about the length of time which followed creation as it seems to be definite about the length of time required by creation. We ought not so easily to assume, therefore, that the fossils have not all been deposited since
the six days of creation.

Third, there is the assumption that the six days of creation (as recorded
in the Bible) present us with a creation which occurred in six twenty-
four-hour days. In reply we may observe that long before "modern science" challenged Bible believers, there were Bible believers who held
on biblical grounds that creation did not occur in six twenty-four-hour
periods. They recognized that the Hebrew term (*yom*) is not restricted to
this sense. (See John 8:56; Isa. 49:8; Hosea 2:15; Ps. 110:3; Job 15:23.)
Augustine, for example, recognized that one of the "days" of creation
effected the conditions necessary for solar time. Other Bible believers
have suggested that the six days of creation were six days during which
God revealed to Moses the story of creation. No one saw it happen but
God. Moses could "see it" only by way of visions. And these visions may
have taken six days to unfold.

Finally, there is the assumption that such a process as is recorded in
the creation account (and as is theorized of in modern science) could
not have occurred in six twenty-four-hour days. Another way of putting it is this: it is assumed that God could not (or would not) have quickly
produced the world which so evidently bears the appearance of great
age. But if we merely *suppose* that God created man, we are immediately
confronted with such a necessary "appearance of age." If God created
Adam as an adult person, he would have appeared as an adult appears to
us now, and yet would really have had no long period of prior development. The Christian position is that God did so create Adam. And so
in this instance it is compelled to assume the very difficulty supposed by
scientific dogma. Why should we then care to avoid this difficulty
respecting the rest of creation? For our part we can see no good reason

to doubt that God did create the world in six brief days, with the appearance of age (that is, with maturity) in the things created, and that the fossils were caused by a great catastrophe, probably the flood, which occurred after creation. (Though the Bible does not use modern scientific terms such as "twenty-four-hour days," we believe the Genesis record intends us to think of days much like our own with respect to duration.) See *The Genesis Flood* by J. C. Whitcomb and H. M. Morris (Philadelphia: Presbyterian and Reformed, 1961).

QUESTIONS

1. Who created the world?
2. What are the basic points of dogma held by "modern science"?
3. Is there any proof for the theory of evolution? Why?
4. What is truth?
5. Where is truth found?
6. What are some common false assumptions of those who accept modern scientific dogma?
7. State concisely your reply to each of these false assumptions.
8. What is your view of the "days" of Genesis 1?
9. Is the Hebrew term for "day" always used to denote a twenty-four-hour period?
10. Is there any good reason not to believe that God created the world in six twenty-four-hour days? If so, state same.

IV, 2

2. *After God had made all other creatures, he created man, male and female, with reasonable and immortal souls, endued with knowledge, righteousness, and true holiness after his own image, having the law of God written in their hearts, and power to fulfill it, and yet under a possibility of transgressing, being left to the liberty of their own will, which was subject to change. Beside this law written in their hearts, they received a command not to eat of the tree of the knowledge of good and evil; which while they kept, they were happy in their communion with God, and had dominion over the creatures.*

This section of the Confession teaches (1) that man was God's crowning work of creation, (2) that the whole human race descended from one human pair, (3) that man was made in the image of God, (4) that God furnished Adam with a sufficient knowledge of his will (the law written in his heart, plus a special directive to test his obedience), and (5) that Adam was capable of due obedience but also of falling.

The Bible and evolutionists superficially agree in regarding man as the highest creature on earth. Both acknowledge that there was an advance from lower to higher forms. But whereas evolutionists attribute this to blind mechanical forces, the Bible attributes it immediately to God. The Christian need not doubt that God employed in the creation of man many of the basic structural designs which he first used on lower forms of life. But there can be no yielding at one point: man did not "gradually emerge" from the slime, but was created by an immediate divine act in which matter and spirit were fused together and given existence as a living soul. There may have been creatures other than apes with physical characteristics similar to those of man. But there never was any species of "man" before God breathed from himself the breath of life into that dust which he had formed as the receptacle for it. And apart from the fall, there has been no change in that species.

We cannot allow that the human species derives from any prior lower species. That man had no prehuman ancestry is clear from the fact that it was only when God breathed into him that man *became* a living soul, whereas the animals already were that, according to the Genesis account (cf. Gen. 1:30 and 2:7). Scripture does not, of course, inform us *how* God formed the body of man, nor does it indicate how much time this may have taken. What it does tell us is that at the moment God breathed into that form (of dust) the breath of life, a man came into being. Before that, man was not. Since that time man has remained essentially the same, except for sin. "So God created man in his own image" (Gen. 1:27). "And the Lord God formed man of the dust of the ground, and breathed into his nostrils the breath of life; and man became a living being" (2:7).

What must be remembered, in sharp contrast to evolutionary dogma, is that there was at the very beginning of man's existence a highly developed intelligence. Human life was very far from that of the presumed "caveman" at the beginning. It was not on a mere animal level. To the contrary, man originally had a much more perfect knowledge and a higher moral character than he has ever had since the fall. "God made man upright" (Eccles. 7:29). He began with the law written in man's heart (Rom. 2:15). This does not deny progress in human knowledge, nor does it deny that Einstein knew much more than Adam did. But it does affirm that Adam's knowledge was perfect as far as it went (and this even Einstein could not claim), and that it was much more penetrating than is commonly supposed. A man who could look for many years out of a dirty window might learn more than another man who looked out of an open door for a day. But there is no doubt as to who would see more clearly. Adam's knowledge might be more "primitive" in that it was less technical and composite. But it was certainly not primitive in the sense that evolutionary dogma would have us to think.

Again, modern science and the Bible superficially agree that the whole human race has descended from one original pair. It would be too much for the scientist to believe that the same incredible accident could have happened more than once on the same planet at approximately the same time! Thus it has become a "sin" against science to teach that one race is "superior" to another. But the Christian believes that God "has made from one blood every nation of men to dwell on all the face of the earth" (Acts 17:26). And the Christian resists all racist pride, not on the basis of the evolutionary dogma of man's greatness, but the biblical doctrines of creation and the fall. There is no man who is not to be highly valued, because every man retains the imprint of God's image. But no man is to be too highly exalted, because every man also bears the dreadful taint of sin.

But what is meant by "the image of God"? Some have argued that the image of God is found exclusively in man's soul, and not his body, since God is a pure spirit. Of these, some have said that the soul itself bears the image of God, while others have said that it contains that image. However, it is mere assumption to say that the body cannot be (in part) the image of God. Perhaps this notion is a holdover from the ancient pagan notion that the spirit is good and the (material) body evil. At any rate, it would seem to be more scriptural simply to affirm that man (in the totality of his physical-spiritual being) *is* (rather than merely contains) the image of God. In Scripture the soul (or mind) is shown to be a union of body and spirit, and not just a spirit contained within the body. In any case, man's capacity to exercise lordship over the earth as God's image-bearer was as physical as it was spiritual.

We also believe that man was originally an image of the Triune God in that he was made to function as prophet, priest, and king. As there are in God three persons in one essence, so in Adam's personality there was the endowed capacity for knowledge, holiness, and righteousness. As a prophet man was endowed with the physical senses and mental ability to learn the truth. As a priest he possessed the sensibility and desire to worship God in true holiness. And as a king he possessed the physical and mental power and ability to subject in righteousness all things to the purpose and will of God. In the Godhead it is characteristically the Father to whom knowledge and purpose are attributed, the Son who dedicates all to the worship and delight of the Father, and the Holy Spirit who carries into execution the determinations of the divine Being. In the complexity of human personality we believe there *is* (and even more, in sinless man there *was*) a reflection of this.

Questions

1. In what do evolutionists and Christians superficially agree?
2. Why do we say this agreement is superficial?
3. Is it anti-Christian to believe that God employed many basic structural designs in lower forms of life and then later in creating man?
4. At what precise point must the Christian never yield respecting man's creation?
5. Is it possible that man may have developed from lower forms of "semi-human" beings? Why?
6. What does evolutionary dogma say about "early" human existence?
7. What does the Bible say about "early" human existence?
8. In what sense was Adam's knowledge primitive?
9. Why do scientists believe in the unity of the human race?
10. Why do Christians believe in the unity of the human race?
11. Which is correct: the soul is the image of God, the soul contains the image of God, man has the image of God, or man is the image of God?
12. Why may it be that the body has traditionally been excluded from the image?
13. If God is triune, and man is God's image, then what must we see in the unity of human personality?
14. Do you find Scripture evidence for this diversity?

5

V. Of Providence

1. *God, the great Creator of all things, doth uphold, direct, dispose, and govern all creatures, actions, and things, from the greatest even to the least, by his most wise and holy providence, according to his infallible foreknowledge, and the free and immutable counsel of his own will, to the praise of the glory of his wisdom, power, justice, goodness, and mercy.*

This section of the Confession teaches (1) that God, who created all things, also sustains them in being, (2) that he exercises over them complete control, (3) that this control regards all creatures and their actions as well as events in the natural world, (4) that this absolute control effects the execution of God's fixed plan, and (5) that all this has as its end the manifestation of the glory of God.

Two errors are excluded by the formulation of this section of the Confession. The first is that error which teaches that things happen by *chance.* The second error is that which teaches that things happen by a blind mechanical necessity or *fate.*

The belief that events just "happen" without any certain and necessary relationship to God or to other things in his control is essentially pagan. And yet, no doubt without realizing this, there are many Protestants who believe that the most momentous things happen by chance. Arminianism teaches that the will of man acts without any predetermined certainty. There is no necessary reason why a particular individual should refuse or accept the gospel. The will of man according to this view is, so to speak, balanced on a razor's edge between two equal possibilities. God makes no determination but leaves it up to the individual himself to decide whether or not he will be saved. And so without any predetermined and necessary reason, in some cases it just "happens" that Christ is chosen, while in other cases it also just "happens" that he is rejected.

The Reformed Confession teaches, on the contrary, that nothing just happens, not even in the case of the exercise of man's own will. If "the king's heart is in the hand of the Lord" so that "he turns it wherever He wishes" (Prov. 21:1), then there can be no such thing as chance. "There are many plans in a man's heart, nevertheless the Lord's counsel—that will stand" (Prov. 19:21). We cannot of course explain *how* God exercises this absolute control of genuinely free agents. We know only that he does.

However, even apart from this mystery, we may observe that even in God the will is not free to operate in a random or chance way. The will of God is determined by the character of God. God cannot lie (Heb. 6:18). There is no "chance" that he ever will. Similarly, the will of man is determined by the character of man. And so long as the character of a man is sinful and corrupt (as received by ordinary generation from Adam), there is no "chance" that he will do that which is pleasing to God. "Can the Ethiopian change his skin or the leopard its spots? Then may you also do good who are accustomed to do evil" (Jer. 13:23). But when God regenerates a man so that he receives a new and different character, there is no "chance" that he will *not* begin to do good. "For it is God who works in you both to will and to do for His good pleasure" (Phil. 2:13).

The error which teaches that things happen by a mechanical fate has something in common with the true doctrine, namely, that things are absolutely predetermined. But the similarity is only formal. There is all the difference in the world between the certainty of mechanical fate and the certainty of divine decree. Mechanical fate is at the very heart meaningless, merciless, and hopeless. But the certainty of divinely ordered providence is meaningful, merciful, and hopeful.

But *how* can God control everything? The ways of God are mysterious to us, and far above us, no doubt. Yet we are much aided if we keep such Scripture teachings as these firmly in mind: (1) God made everything. How then can it be a marvel if he is able to exercise absolute control over that which he has made? (2) God has perfect foreknowledge (Acts 15:18; 1 Peter 1:2). It is not difficult to see that this contributes immeasurably to an effective control of things! (3) God is omnipotent. He is able to do what he will at any place and at any time. He is free to "inject" into the world supernatural power drastically "changing" existing conditions. (Thus his miracles!) (4) God is free. He is not prevented from doing all his holy will.

Such considerations as these do not give us the knowledge of *how* God controls all things, but they do evidence the fact *that* he is able to do so. Above all, the infallible Scripture asserts that God actually does exercise such absolute control of all things. "He does according to His will in the army of heaven and among the inhabitants of the earth. No one can restrain His hand or say to Him, 'What have You done?' " (Dan. 4:35). "Whatever the Lord pleases He does, in heaven and in earth, in the seas and in all deep places" (Ps. 135:6). Unable as we are to fathom it, yet God works all things after the counsel of his will (Eph. 1:11).

To summarize the matter: because God *controls* the universe, *chance* is ruled out, and because it is *God* who controls the universe, *fate* is ruled out also.

QUESTIONS

1. There are two errors ruled out by this section of the Confession: the first teaches that things happen by _____. The second teaches that things happen by _____.
2. With which of these errors are the Arminians in (perhaps unconscious) agreement?
3. Cite a Scripture text which proves that the will of man is not unpredictable.
4. What scriptural teaching about God helps us to understand why there are some things that man cannot do?
5. Why is there no chance that an unconverted man will do the will of God, or that a converted man will not begin to do the will of God?

6. What is the difference between fate and divine sovereignty?
7. What teachings of Scripture aid us in believing that God controls everything?
8. Cite a Scripture text to prove that God controls everything.

V, 2–7

2. *Although in relation to the foreknowledge and decree of God, the first cause, all things come to pass immutably and infallibly, yet, by the same providence, he ordereth them to fall out according to the nature of second causes, either necessarily, freely, or contingently.*

3. *God in his ordinary providence maketh use of means, yet is free to work without, above, and against them, at his pleasure.*

4. *The almighty power, unsearchable wisdom, and infinite goodness of God so far manifest themselves in his providence that it extendeth itself even to the first fall, and all other sins of angels and men, and that not by a bare permission, but such as hath joined with it a most wise and powerful bounding, and otherwise ordering and governing of them, in a manifold dispensation, to his own holy ends; yet so as the sinfulness thereof proceedeth only from the creature, and not from God; who, being most holy and righteous, neither is nor can be the author or approver of sin.*

5. *The most wise, righteous, and gracious God doth oftentimes leave for a season his own children to manifold temptations and the corruption of their own hearts, to chastise them for their former sins, or to discover unto them the hidden strength of corruption, and deceitfulness of their hearts, that they may be humbled; and to raise them to a more close and constant dependence for their support upon himself, and to make them more watchful against all future occasions of sin, and for sundry other just and holy ends.*

6. *As for those wicked and ungodly men whom God as a righteous judge, for former sins, doth blind and harden, from them he not only*

*withholdeth his grace, whereby they might have been enlightened in
their understandings and wrought upon in their hearts, but sometimes
also withdraweth the gifts which they had, and exposeth them to such
objects as their corruption makes occasion of sin; and withal, gives
them over to their own lusts, the temptations of the world, and the
power of Satan: whereby it comes to pass, that they harden
themselves, even under those means which God useth for the
softening of others.*

7. *As the providence of God doth, in general, reach to all creatures; so,
after a most special manner, it taketh care of his Church, and
disposeth all things to the good thereof.*

These sections of the Confession are directed against certain erroneous
inferences which men have drawn from the doctrine stated in section 1
of this chapter. Here we are taught (1) that God's absolute sovereignty
does not destroy the integrity of man's liberty, (2) that it does not deny
the operation of second causes, (3) that God is, however, free to overrule these "laws" (and causes) when he pleases, (4) that God ordered even
the fall of man without himself doing any evil, and (5) that God's sovereignty extends even to the inward operations of men's hearts (in both the
saved and the lost) without participation in sin.

Whenever the biblical doctrine of divine sovereignty is taught, certain
objections seem to arise quite spontaneously from the sinful human heart.
We list several, seeking to show how the Scripture replies to each.

(1) "If God controls everything, then I am not responsible for what
I do."

This objection is really based upon the assumption that when God
controls human actions he forces us to do his will whether we want to
or not. If God forced me to sin against my will, then God would be
responsible for my sin and not I. But Scripture is at pains to teach us that
we are responsible precisely because we do our own will when we sin.
Because God is the infinite, eternal, and immutable one, he is able to
allow us to do as we please (within the limitations of opportunity and
ability) and yet render certain that we will do what he has predetermined
that we will do. This is the lesson of the relationship between Joseph and
his brethren (Gen. 37–50). "As for you," said Joseph to his brothers, "you
meant evil against me; but God meant it for good, in order to bring it

about as it is this day, to save many people alive" (Gen. 50:20). They did evil. They did it freely. Yet they also did the will (decree) of God.

(2) "If God controls everything, then things will turn out the same no matter what I do."

This objection is false because it contains a real contradiction. On the one hand, there is the supposition that God controls everything. But then, on the other hand, there is the foreign and contradictory supposition that certain personal actions may happen in a random and uncertain way. It says, in effect, that if all things are fixed by divine decree, then it makes no difference whether events a, b, and c happen: we will still arrive at event d. But the obvious fact is that a, b, and c are events just as d is, and the starting supposition is that God controls them all. Therefore, if God controls all things, it is obvious that they will work out only if each event leading to event d also works out according to plan. Divine foreordination does not make our actions unimportant, but rather makes them exceedingly important. Thus Peter says, "Brethren, be even more diligent to make your call and election sure, for if you do these things you will never stumble" (2 Peter 1:10). If God has elected us, then far be it from us to say that we will be saved no matter what we do. We must know that we can be saved only as we do that which God says the elect will do, namely, "be even more diligent. . . ."

(3) "If God controls everything, then he must be the author of sin."

Was it the will (or plan) of God that Adam should fall? Do the wicked hands of men do only what God has before determined to be done (Acts 4:28)? Surely the Scripture avoids even the appearance of evading such an admission. "I form the light, and create darkness: I make peace, and create evil: I the Lord do all these things" (Isa. 45:7 KJV). Certainly there is no inclination in Scripture to deny God's absolute sovereignty, even in this extremity, merely because of offensive consequences which may seem to flow from it. However, Scripture is equally insistent that God is not the author of sin. "God cannot be tempted by evil, nor does He Himself tempt anyone" (James 1:13). The apparent contradiction has been expressed this way: (a) God is the author of all that is. (b) Sin is. (c) Yet God is not the author of sin. But the contradiction is only apparent. For God is *not* the author of all that is, although he has decreed all. Satan and his host (of men and angels) are the "authors" of sin, although God has created them and decreed even their sin without being himself the author of it.

(4) "If God controls everything, then how can we account for (a) the sins of the righteous, and (b) the prosperity of the wicked?"

It may seem to human wisdom that it would be best for God to control men in such a way that the elect (after regeneration) were immediately perfect in righteousness. Likewise it might seem wise to permit the reprobate to proceed to unrelieved wickedness. But such is not the case. God's ways are not our ways (Isa. 55:8). How then are we to account for the sins of the saints and the "goodness" of the reprobate?

Scripture says that "whoever has been born of God does not sin" (1 John 3:9). And yet Scripture also says that "if we say that we have no sin" or that "we have not sinned, we make Him a liar, and His word is not in us" (1 John 1:8, 10). There is a contradiction, then, but the contradiction is in the regenerate man, not the Scriptures. The regenerate man sins, but he cannot give himself to the willful and continual practice of sin. "For His [God's] seed remains in him; and he cannot sin, because he has been born of God" (1 John 3:9).

Paul said: "It is no longer I who do it, but sin that dwells in me. . . . For I delight in the law of God according to the inward man. But I see another law in my members, warring against the law of my mind, and bringing me into captivity to the law of sin which is in my members" (Rom. 7:20–23). This does not mean that Paul is not the guilty one. If that were so, he would not call himself a "wretched man" (7:24). He does not mean that there are "two Pauls" either, as some have maintained: "the old man" and "the new." For while it is "the new man" alone which is the "real" Paul, the remnants of the "old" are present, and able to lash out furiously against the "new." The "new man" cannot lose the conflict. But neither can the "new man" prevail without much bitter conflict. Above all, we must realize that there would be no conflict in the first place had not God created a new man (Eph. 2:15). This "new creature" may seem frightfully weak (Heb. 5:12–14) at first, yet where he truly exists, he will surely prevail. But in no sense whatever do the "new man" and his activities originate from the powers belonging to a man "by nature." Sometimes we forget this. We forget that all that we are in and of ourselves is sin. So God sometimes leaves us for a season to manifold temptations and the corruptions of our own hearts (1 Peter 1:6).

Whenever God so chastises us, the remnants of our old nature express their natural character, and we learn anew that we can do nothing of ourselves. We are thus brought to seek salvation wholly in, and by the work of, God.

The reason why the wicked (or reprobate) on the other hand so often do that which is (outwardly) "good" is that they too have the remnants of their old nature. But in their case "the old nature" traces back to the sinless nature that belonged to Adam before the fall. The conscience still retains some recollection of the law of God which was written there in the beginning (Rom. 2:14–15). But the "new man" is sinful, corrupt, and fallen. The conscience (or alter ego) objects to what the ego wishes to do. The two constantly fight. But, as we all know, the conscience does not rule over so much as testify against. However, sometimes God causes the conscience to overrule and restrain even the reprobate. Through the operation of the Holy Spirit and through such agencies as law, civil government, social custom, desire for approval, and fear of punishment, the reprobate may actually do that which is "good." We may diagram the two cases in figure 2.

By means of the instruments of common grace God is able to restrain (b) and give considerable influence to (a) in the reprobate. By means of the instruments of special grace God is able to increase (d) and decrease (c) in the elect. (This process is not finished until the end of life.) God

FIG. 2

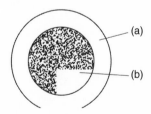

A. The Reprobate Mind
(a) the "outer" remnants of man's paradise nature
(b) the new center (ego) of man's fallen sinful nature

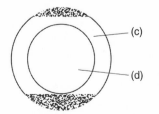

B. The Regenerate Mind
(c) the remaining "outer" remnants of man's fallen sinful nature
(d) the new center (ego) of man's nature in Christ

never "nurtures" (b) or (c), but he may so withdraw special grace that (c) "erupts" in a frightful way (as in David) in order that his people will recognize that (d) is wholly from him.

The final section stresses that the providence of God is concerned in a special way with his redemptive program. We need to know not only the fact that all things work together, or that they do so because God is in control, but also that this is all for the good of those who love God, being called according to his gracious purpose (Rom. 8:28). And that purpose is to sum up all things in the glorious person and work of his son Jesus (Eph. 3:11).

QUESTIONS

1. Name the common objections to the doctrine of absolute sovereignty.
2. Refute same.
3. Why do the elect sometimes sin so grievously?
4. Why do the reprobate sometimes act better than we might expect them to?
5. Is it correct to speak of a Christian as both an old and new man?
6. Is a Christian "responsible" for the sin he does under the influence of "the remnants of his old nature"?
7. Does Figure 2 imply that some acts which we do are entirely sinless and that others are entirely sinful (i.e., without alleviation)?
8. Explain and harmonize Paul's statements in Romans 7:20 and 7:24.
9. Why is the final section of this chapter of the Confession important?

6

VI. Of the Fall of Man, of Sin, and of the Punishment Thereof

1. *Our first parents being seduced by the subtilty and temptation of Satan, sinned in eating the forbidden fruit. This their sin God was pleased, according to his wise and holy counsel, to permit, having purposed to order it to his own glory.*

2. *By this sin they fell from their original righteousness and communion with God, and so became dead in sin, and wholly defiled in all the faculties and parts of soul and body.*

These sections teach (1) that the human race stems from two (and only two) real people, (2) that the record of Genesis 3 is historical (not symbolical or mythical in character), (3) that the first sin was foreordained, and (4) that by this sin our first parents (a) lost communion with God, (b) fell under his wrath and curse, and (c) became totally depraved.

"The fall of man needs as much emphasis as his creation" (C. Van Til). This is especially true today because of widespread dominance of neo-orthodox theology. Neo-orthodoxy (which is supposed to mean "new orthodoxy") arose in early-twentieth-century Europe from the spiritual ruins of an older "rationalism." The "rationalists" enthroned human reason and made the Bible subservient to it. When Karl Barth (the originator of neo-orthodoxy, which is therefore also called "Barthianism") first appeared on the scene speaking with great power against the emptiness of the old rationalism, many were impressed. He even revived the terminology of the historic Christian faith, speaking of "creation," "the fall," and "election." Many hailed him as a prophet who would lead the Church back to the orthodox faith.

But the sad truth was that Barth (and others who soon followed) did not replace the authority of man's reason with the authority of the Bible. They were merely exchanging the old form of reliance upon the supremacy of man's reason with a new form of the same evil. Thus neo-orthodoxy claimed that it affirmed the doctrine of the fall, but then denied that there was an actual historical person who at a particular time and at a specific location on earth ate a real piece of forbidden fruit. It affirmed that the doctrine of the fall is "true," but it meant thereby only that there is nonhistorical (or symbolic, or mythical) meaning in it. It meant that the Bible is "true" much as Aesop's fables are "true." "The creation and the fall," says Barth, "lie behind the historical."

Why did neo-orthodoxy take such a contradictory position? Why did it attempt to affirm (that the Bible teaches truth) and deny (that what the Bible says is actually true) at the same time? The answer is that these modernists (for that is what neo-orthodoxy really is: modernism) wanted to have their cake and eat it too. They wanted to be accepted as Christians *and* respected by this world. Because the earlier "rationalists" created a climate of opinion which regarded as completely outdated the idea of putting God's Word above human wisdom and science, the neo-orthodox theologians could not dare hope to find acceptance if they did such an old-fashioned thing. Respectable people had long since agreed that the Bible could not be considered scientifically accurate or historically dependable. But the neo-orthodox theologians realized that without the things spoken of in the Bible there was no "Christianity" left. Not wanting this, they were determined to believe those things anyway—but not in such a way as to offend the "modern world."

This led to a complete dilemma. There were but two choices: (1) either accept the authority of God's Word and lose standing with this world, or (2) retain the approval of the world, and reject the authority of the Bible. It was the latter which was chosen, but the ingenuity of the neo-orthodox theologians was seen in their ability to camouflage the loss of biblical authority. They did it by removing doctrine from history. And so long as they did not say that these doctrines are really true (that is, that they actually happened in history), they were free to say that they are symbolically true (that is, that they are above and beyond our world). In this way they were free to preach about such things as "the fall" without losing their self-respect and standing with the world.

All this is only a working out in Adam's children of the principle evident in his first sin. Adam's first sin was an attempt to have truth apart from subjection to the word of God. The tree in the garden was "the tree of the *knowledge* of good and evil." By accepting, without question, what God said about that tree, Adam could gain true understanding of its meaning and purpose. God's interpretation of things was original and determinative. Adam's interpretation could be right only if it was non-original and determined. But as soon as Adam sought to know (make interpretation) apart from subjection to God's word (Gen. 3:6), he was lost, and wholly in error. And as soon as the authority of God's word was rejected (3:4) and the authority of man's own reason enthroned (3:5–6), it became necessary for Adam to deny that the "fall" had happened as God said. Thus we note (3:12) that Adam begins to act as if the original defect was not *his* act, performed in actual history, but rather something inherent in creation itself, and thus—in a sense—prior to, or "behind" history. Adam seeks to "explain" the fall, not in terms of what actually happened (what he actually did) at a particular time and place, but in terms of what lay behind all history. And what lies behind history? Only the creative work of God. Thus Adam of old (and the neo-orthodox and their successors today) would ultimately place the blame for man's plight upon God himself!

This diabolical condition of man's heart we call "total depravity." We say that as a consequence of what Adam (an actual man, the first man) did (at a real place and an actual time), all men are, by nature, "wholly defiled in all the faculties and parts of soul and body." By this we do not mean (a) that fallen man is "stupid" or of a "low I.Q." whereas Adam before the fall was "brilliant," nor (b) that Adam had a nature like our own with added powers (beyond the power of reason, emotion, and the will), nor (c) that by the fall the faculties of human nature were meta-physically destroyed, or blotted out of existence. What we mean is that the whole of human nature was ethically perverted so as to become wholly contrary to God. Thus every part of that which constitutes man's created nature was polluted and corrupted. Therefore, (d) when we speak of "total depravity," we do not mean that man's nature is so sinful in degree that nothing "human" remains, and that he has become a "pure" devil rather than a man. The "total" in "total depravity" refers to the *extent* of the damage rather than the *degree.*

Let us illustrate. Take a glass of water. Stir in a teaspoon of deadly poison. The whole glass of water is ruined. But it could be "ruined even more" by adding another teaspoon of poison, and then another and another. However, one teaspoon spreads the poison throughout. So it is with the effects of Adam's first sin: it has poisoned the whole of our human nature. But this does not mean that this or that particular man is already as evil as he can ever become. By and by the lost will become totally evil *in degree,* as they are now totally depraved *in extent.* But there are, for the present, certain instrumentalities of God which retard and restrain man's depravity in order that life in this world might be tolerable. (Of this we shall say more later.)

A totally depraved man may have high intelligence. He may devise intricate systems of thought and deeply probe the mysteries of nature. His intellect is not annihilated by sin, nor is it made inoperative. But it invariably works error. Every man (who is not redeemed) worships and serves the creature rather than the Creator (Rom. 1:25). He deifies something other than God. He makes himself, or something in the created world, his ultimate reference point. Because every thought proceeds from a starting point other than that of humble subjection to the Word of God, it necessarily follows that "every intent of the thoughts of his heart [is] only evil continually" (Gen. 6:5).

Again, a totally depraved man may have a very strong will! When Christ said, "No man can come to Me unless the Father . . . draws him" (John 6:44), he did not mean that sinful men lack will power. What he meant was that because it is the disposition of sinful men to do their own will rather than the will of God, they are incapable of submitting their own will to his. The one thing that an independent will cannot do is to willingly submit, thereby ceasing to be independent.

Finally, the same may be said of human affections. They may be, and often are, quite strong in a sinner. But they are also invariably sinful. "There is none who seeks after God" (Rom. 3:11). The affections are set upon the things of this world, rather than the Creator.

And so it is that because man is corrupt and polluted in every part, he sins continually. "Every intent of the thoughts of his heart" [is] "only evil continually" (Gen. 6:5). He cannot do anything that is not sin from God's point of view. Neither can he do anything to escape, because there is no escape for such an "ego," but to die. This the gospel demands (Matt. 16:24). But this no man can agree to do (John 6:44). But thanks be to God, this *is* freely given to them whom the Father has chosen in Jesus Christ (see chapter X).

QUESTIONS

1. Why does the fall of man need much emphasis today?
2. What does neo-orthodoxy (the term itself) mean?
3. From what did it arise?
4. Why did it sound promising at first?
5. What is its tragic defect (basic to all other defects in it)?
6. When neo-orthodoxy says that a thing is "true" doctrine, what does it mean?
7. Why does neo-orthodoxy take such a position?
8. What choice were neo-orthodox theologians forced to make?
9. How were the neo-orthodox theologians more ingenious (and therefore more dangerous) than the older rationalists and modernists?
10. How does the neo-orthodox attitude resemble that of Adam?
11. By "total depravity," which do we mean:
    (a) that Adam had a nature like ours with added powers,
    (b) that nothing human remains in sinful men,
    (c) that every faculty of man's nature is corrupt and polluted,
    (d) that fallen man is stupid whereas Adam was brilliant,
    (e) the faculties of human nature were annihilated by the fall?
12. By "total depravity," do we mean that the extent of the damage or the degree of the damage is complete in fallen human nature?

13. Does man (being totally depraved) do anything that is not sinful? Why?

VI, 3–4

3. *They being the root of all mankind, the guilt of this sin was imputed, and the same death in sin and corrupted nature conveyed to all their posterity, descending from them by ordinary generation.*

4. *From this original corruption, whereby we are utterly indisposed, disabled, and made opposite to all good, and wholly inclined to all evil, do proceed all actual transgressions.*

These sections of the Confession teach us (1) why we are totally depraved, and (2) how actual transgressions are the effect of this condition.

The facts concerning our lost condition are few and simple to state: (1) Adam sinned and fell, becoming totally depraved. (2) In Adam, we sinned and fell, becoming totally depraved. (3) Thus we are born in sin (Ps. 51:5) and are evil from our youth up (Gen. 8:21). And therefore, (4) death reigns over us all (Rom. 5:12). In other words, if we ask why death reigns over all men, we hear the reply, "Because all have sinned, even tiny infants that die as soon as they are born." If we then ask *how* all did sin, the answer must be, "By one man." Adam's sin is our sin. And because it is, we therefore share the penalty with him.

These are the facts, and they are simple enough to state. But they are far from being simple to explain or to understand. For the age-old question is: "How can a just God condemn me for what another has done?" Or to put it another way, "How can it be that I sinned in Adam when I did not even exist yet?" The answer is, first of all, that God has declared it to be so, even though we may not understand how. And we know that it is just for God to do so, because he always does what is right.

We believe that part of the difficulty that is experienced with this teaching is due to the failure to recognize the corporate aspect of human existence. The Bible does not regard the human race as so many iso-lated individuals, each separately created by God (as were the angels), but as an organic unit created in one man—and then, one pair—having the power to produce offspring in their own likeness and image. Adam and Eve were the "root of all mankind." Therefore, we are members one of another. God has made "from one blood every nation" (Acts 17:26).

Some limit this "organic" union of human beings to the body only. They are called "creationists." They believe that by a mysterious process not understood by man, parents generate a new body from themselves, and that God then (some say at the moment of conception, others say at a later time) creates a new soul and places it within the body. This view we believe to be in error. It is the soul as much as the body that bears the imprint of original sin. How could the soul be created sinful by God? We believe that there is as much evidence that children resemble their parents in mind or soul as there is that they resemble their parents in body. And again, how can we say that Adam begat in his own image and likeness if he did not beget a soul as well as a body in his children?

"Traducianists" believe that parents beget both the body and soul of their children by a mysterious process not understood by man. They do not (as is often thought) believe that this requires a dividing up of the substance of the soul (as it does not require the dividing up of the substance of the body). The Scripture itself speaks a language which seems to us to require such a view (Heb. 7:10; Gen. 46:26 KJV).

Yet it is to be recognized (on either view) that while Adam's descendants derive their nature from Adam, they do not actually become existing persons until the time decreed by God. I, therefore, cannot say that I was *personally* present or that I *personally* acted when Adam sinned. How then can his act be mine? The answer is that God has ordered human life by the principle of representation. By this principle, which is operative in many spheres of life, one person may act for another in such a way that the act of the one is regarded as the act of the other. For example, the father is the head of the house, according to divine appointment. If he moves to another country and there establishes legal citizenship for himself, he also establishes the same for his children that are born there. Again, the civil ruler (whether he be king or president) represents the whole nation. If this ruler embarks upon an act of war, then the nation (and every citizen thereof) is at war. And another nation would regard itself as at war, not with the ruler of that nation alone, but with the whole nation as well. Likewise, the act of Adam was the act of all men because he represented them. Therefore, the guilt of his sin was imputed (regarded as theirs) as it was also conveyed to them.

Only the first sin of Adam was performed for all. This act was a probationary test, in which Adam acted as a representative person. But after that act was performed, Adam no longer acted as a representative person. His other sins were therefore not laid to the charge of other men. As a president ends his term of office, and then no longer acts for others, so Adam terminated his representative actions with that one sin. By that one act he (and we) became corrupt and guilty. But after that, all of the acts of Adam were to his own account, as all of our acts are to our own account. However, the damage was done. He, and we, became totally depraved. And because our condition was that of being "wholly defiled in all the faculties and parts of soul and body," it followed that continual transgressions proceeded out of this condition. By "actual transgressions" the Confession means every sin which has followed the original sin of Adam. And it teaches that all other sins are the natural consequence of that first sin. "For out of the heart proceed evil thoughts, murders, adulteries, fornications, thefts, false witness, blasphemies" (Matt. 15:19).

QUESTIONS

1. State the basic facts concerning our lost condition.
2. Are these facts simple to understand or to explain?
3. How do we know that it is right for God to condemn us for Adam's sin?
4. What teaching of the Bible is often overlooked in this matter?
5. What does the "creationist" teach as to the derivation of the soul?
6. What does the "traducianist" teach as to the derivation of the soul?
7. Which do you favor, and why?
8. In either case, what other principle helps explain our guilt in Adam's sin?
9. Why was only the first sin of Adam our responsibility?
10. How are all other sins related to this one?

VI, 5–6

5. *This corruption of nature, during this life, doth remain in those that are regenerated: and although it be through Christ pardoned and mortified, yet both itself, and all the motions thereof, are truly and properly sin.*

6. *Every sin, both original and actual, being a transgression of the righteous law of God, and contrary thereunto, doth, in its own nature, bring guilt upon the sinner, whereby he is bound over to the wrath of God, and curse of the law, and so made subject to death, with all miseries spiritual, temporal, and eternal.*

These sections of the Confession teach us (1) that depravity remains in believers in this life, (2) that it is pardoned through Christ, (3) that it is progressively destroyed in them, (4) that it and the products of it are truly sin even in the believer, and (5) that this corruption as well as what it produces are so truly sin as to rightly bring us under God's wrath and curse (unless and until the sovereign grace of God secures our release).

We have already suggested (by our diagram in V, 2–7) the relationship between the old nature and the new in a Christian believer. And we stress, again, that it is not to be supposed that the believer is two persons, the old man and the new. This will not comport with the plain declarations of Scripture. "Therefore, if anyone is in Christ, he is a new creation; old things have passed away; behold, all things have become new" (2 Cor. 5:17). "Or do you not know that as many of us as were baptized into Christ Jesus were baptized into His death? Therefore we were buried with Him through baptism into death, that just as Christ was raised from the dead by the glory of the Father, even so we also should walk in newness of life . . . knowing this, that our old man was crucified with Him, that the body of sin might be done away with, that we should no longer be slaves of sin" (Rom. 6:3–4, 6). As it is perhaps most succinctly expressed: "you have put off the old man with his deeds, and have put on the new man who is renewed . . . according to the image of Him who created him" (Col. 3:9–10). It is for this reason that Paul can say, without hesitation, "I delight in the law of God according to the inward man"

(Rom. 7:22). And the psalmist can say, "Oh, how I love Your law! It is my meditation all the day" (Ps. 119:97).

Yet we must note that a misunderstanding of this glorious truth has led to two exceedingly serious errors: (1) The first is the error of *perfectionism*. Perfectionism teaches that the believer *is* (or at least, *may* in this life *become*) not merely a new creature in Christ, but a new creature from which all sin (or, as some say, all "known" sin) is absent. This is contradicted by the uniform and continual warnings of Scripture. "If we say that we have no sin, we deceive ourselves, and the truth is not in us," says the apostle John (1 John 1:8). "If we say that we have not sinned, we make Him a liar, and His word is not in us" (1:10). James says, "We all stumble in many things" (James 3:2). And the wisdom of God says that "there is not a just man on earth who does good, and does not sin" (Eccl. 7:20). This testimony is confirmed by the confession of God's people. Even the most eminent acknowledged that their sin was ever with them (Rom. 7:14–25; Ps. 51).

There can be no doubt, therefore, that the Confession is correct when it states that "corruption of nature, during this life, doth remain in those that are regenerated," even though "it be through Christ pardoned and mortified." The evidence that one is a regenerate person is not the vain delusion that one is free from all corruption and sin, but rather the existence of a proper sense of Christ's pardon and of the working of the Spirit within us, enabling us to strive earnestly to die unto sin and to live unto righteousness. The faithful believers that we come to know in Scripture never claimed perfection in this life, but they did claim the pardon of their sins through Christ's atonement, and they also manifested an unremitting fight against sin.

(2) The other error is that of *antinomianism*. The essence of this deadly error is the notion that no matter how much my old nature may influence me to sin, it makes no difference because "it is not I that do it, but the old man or nature that is with me." The antinomian does not claim perfection. He may even admit the most scandalous wickedness. But he disclaims all responsibility. He blames all the sinning on the "old" nature and insists that he is responsible only for the acts of the "new" nature.

Certain expressions of the apostle Paul may be quoted in what can be made to seem a support of this view. He says, for example, "it is no longer I who do it, but sin that dwells in me" (Rom. 7:17). And, again, "I see another law in my members, warring against the law of my mind, and bringing me into captivity to the law of sin which is in my members" (7:23). But putting this construction on these statements of Paul is false because it overlooks completely the way in which Paul "takes the blame" for this situation. "I am carnal," he says (7:14). "For I know that in me (that is, in my flesh) nothing good dwells" (7:18). Paul does not pretend that he can blame his sins on "the old man" as though they were not his. He does indeed inform us that his sins arise from the motions of his old nature as they survive in him. Yet he clearly indicates that he must fight against them and continue doing so until they are wholly destroyed. So the antinomian ends up saying the same thing the perfectionist says: "I have no sin." In this he deceives himself and shows that the truth is not in him. For both the remaining corruption, and all the motions thereof, are truly and properly sin.

The true state of the case is this: in an unregenerate person corruption rules, but in a regenerate person the Spirit of God and the law of God have the dominion (Rom. 8:7–14). In the unregenerate man, sin reigns. In the regenerate man, sin does not reign although it does survive.

We might illustrate with reference to the Second World War. Before the Allied forces landed at Normandy, the Axis powers had control of Europe. The "hit and run" commando raids gave the Axis powers some trouble but did not challenge their control. The work of conscience in the unregenerate is like this "trouble." It can offer some resistance but cannot challenge the reign of sin. But when the Allies landed in force they took control, and the Axis powers were "on the run." The Axis forces were still able to cause a great deal of trouble, but they could not win.

So it is with the believer. When he is regenerated, the Spirit of God dwells in him, and he is from that moment on under the sovereign control of Christ, and not of sin. Paul says, "Sin shall not have dominion over you" (Rom. 6:14). But the dislocated forces of the enemy are far from being destroyed merely because they have been routed. They can, and will, carry on a prolonged holding action, causing as much trouble as possible. So it is with surviving sin in the believer. But here the illustration fails, for the paradox is that the believer must sorrowfully recognize that the "alien" force is somehow a part of himself. So that, even though he is a new creature in Christ Jesus, yet (because of this contradiction) he is also a wretched man who serves the law of sin with distressing frequency (Rom. 7:24–25).

Perhaps the most wicked thought of all is that which suggests that sin is somehow less heinous if it is committed by the Christian. We might rather say that sin is much more heinous if it is committed by the Christian, for there are many things which aggravate the situation. The Christian has strength that the non-Christian does not have; he has knowledge that the unbeliever lacks; most of all, he has a realization of the terrible consequences of sin because he has seen what it cost the Savior to blot them out. It is well to remember, therefore, not only that "whoever commits sin also commits lawlessness, and sin is lawlessness" (1 John 3:4), but also that "if we sin willfully after we have received the knowledge of the truth, there no longer remains a sacrifice for sins, but a certain fearful expectation of judgment" (Heb. 10:26–27). "Every sin . . . being a transgression of the righteous law of God . . . doth . . . bring guilt upon the sinner," but he who sins with impunity shall find no escape from the consequences of his sin. "What shall we say then? Shall we continue in sin that grace may abound? Certainly not! How shall we who died to sin live any longer in it?" (Rom. 6:1–2). Yes, sin continues to "live" (that is, to survive) in the believer, but it is a horrible perversion of the truth to think that the believer may live in sin.

QUESTIONS

1. Is the believer both "the old man" and "the new man"?
2. Prove this to be correct from Scripture.
3. What does "perfectionism" teach?
4. What does "antinomianism" teach?
5. Give a Scripture reference to refute "perfectionism."
6. Give a Scripture reference to refute "antinomianism."
7. What is the difference between the status of indwelling sin in the unregenerate man and the regenerate man?
8. What pernicious error is suggested (and condemned) in Rom. 6:1–2?
9. Why is sin more heinous in a believer than it is in an unbeliever?
10. What is "willful sin"?

CHAPTER

7

VII. Of God's Covenant with Man

1. *The distance between God and the creature is so great that although reasonable creatures do owe obedience unto him as their Creator, yet they could never have any fruition of him as their blessedness and reward, but by some voluntary condescension on God's part, which he hath been pleased to express by way of covenant.*

This section of the Confession teaches us (1) the basic distinction between the Creator and the creature, (2) that the creature (because he *is* the creature) owes obedience to the Creator, (3) that the Creator owes nothing to the creature, and (4) that therefore all blessing and/or reward from God can come only by way of "condescension" on God's part (that is, by grace) and so by way of sovereignly disposed covenant.

It is not enough that the sinner denies his sin, denies, that is, the truth about his fallen estate. But much worse, being evil, the sinner now in effect denies even his creaturehood. The essential or basic impiety of man is that he considers himself to be independent of God. God says to man, "Without Me you can do nothing" (John 15:5). To which, man replies (like Nebuchadnezzar of old), "I have done it 'by my mighty power and for the honor of my majesty' " (cf. Dan. 4:30). The perennially popular doctrine of "man's free will," which teaches that man rather than God determines destiny, is but an instance of this basic impiety.

The Reformed churches have guarded against this impiety to a greater degree than most, and yet even among them it has not always come to full and proper expression that "the distance between God and the creature is so great that . . . they could never have any fruition of him as their blessedness and reward, but by some voluntary condescension on God's part, which he hath been pleased to express by way of covenant." It has sometimes been the custom, even in Reformed churches, to describe a covenant as "an agreement between two or more persons." There is, in such language, at least the danger of suggesting that God and man are equal parties in the disposition of the covenant—as if each agreed to terms sovereignly imposed by the other! The truth is, however, that "the distance between God and the creature is so great" that we cannot properly entertain such thoughts. And this is quite as true as respects the covenant of works as in the case of the covenant of grace. In fact, the covenant of works too was essentially a matter of grace. Adam did not have any sovereign claim to God's blessing and rewards. It is often unconsciously assumed that Adam, being righteous, had some inherent right to demand of God. But Scripture says, "If you are righteous, what do you give Him? Or what does He receive from your hand?" (Job 35:7). Even if a man could say that he had done all the will of God, he would still be an unprofitable servant, having done only what it was his duty to do (see Luke 17:10)!

But this common failing is not countenanced by our Confession. Rather it insists upon the immeasurable chasm that separates the creature and the Creator. And it acknowledges that all of God's covenant dealings with men are both sovereign and gracious. They are imposed by the will of God, and not at all by the will of man (Isa. 40:13–17). Furthermore, they benefit the creature only, and not the Creator (Acts 17:25). The only "conditions" or "obligations" to which God "agrees" in such covenants are self-imposed by his own gracious promises. He is bound by nothing but his own holy Word. Had Adam obeyed, God would surely have given him a great reward, but not because Adam demanded it. He would have given it only because it is his good pleasure to confer upon the creature gifts which none can ever earn, not even by sinless obedience (which is after all but the debt we already owe).

QUESTIONS

1. What does the depraved sinner deny besides the fact that he is depraved?
2. Have Reformed Christians failed to consistently acknowledge "the distance between God and the creature"?
3. How have they done so?
4. What would God have owed a sinlessly perfect, or perfectly obedient, man?
5. By what is God "bound" in his covenant(s)?
6. By whom is a covenant instituted?

VII, 2–3

2. *The first covenant made with man was a covenant of works, wherein life was promised to Adam, and in him to his posterity, upon condition of perfect and personal obedience.*

3. *Man by his fall having made himself incapable of life by that covenant, the Lord was pleased to make a second, commonly called the covenant of grace: wherein he freely offered unto sinners life and salvation by Jesus Christ, requiring of them faith in him, that they may be saved, and promising to give unto all those that are ordained unto life his Holy Spirit, to make them willing and able to believe.*

We here consider the two covenants revealed in Scripture. Note again that both are covenants of grace in the sense that both express the mercy of God upon those who have no inherent claim upon him.

The first covenant was a covenant of works. The grace of God was seen in this covenant when life was promised Adam (and his posterity) upon condition of perfect and perpetual obedience (which Adam owed God even apart from any such gracious blessing). The fall, however, rendered man totally unable to meet the conditions of that covenant, so God mercifully instituted a new covenant called the covenant of grace. Both covenants were gracious, but the second rightly deserves to be called by that name because God himself provides the work required to meet the conditions of the covenant whereby his people are saved.

The elements which constituted the "covenant of works" are not formally stated in Scripture. They are nevertheless clearly implied. The tree of life was in the midst of the garden. So was the tree of the knowledge of good and evil from which Adam was forbidden to eat upon pain of death. Clearly held before him was the alternative of obedience and life, or disobedience and death. It can be legitimately inferred from Genesis 2:17 that the Lord required "perfect and personal obedience" since the least infraction of his will was threatened with death. Because the elements of a covenant are thus present, the apostle Paul raises the hypothetical situation that, if a man were to keep all God's commandments, he would receive the reward of life (Gal. 3:12).

Some object to speaking of "a covenant of works" on the grounds (a) that such a covenant is not formally stated in Scripture, nor is the phrase (covenant of works) even found in Scripture, and (b) that such a designation falsely suggests that the works of man could have merited God's blessings. These objections are not convincing. The doctrine of the Trinity is not formally stated in Scripture either, but it is "there" by implication. The same may be said for the phrase "covenant of works." The second objection is more formidable. And yet, no such charge can be laid against our Confession, for even in calling it "a covenant of works," the Confession carefully guards against the very danger that is being warned about. Moreover, the designation "covenant of works" has the merit of focusing upon the precise element which distinguishes the one covenant from the other, namely, the fact that the obedient works of man were the condition laid down by the Lord in that covenant for the granting of his gracious gift of life. It also pinpoints the precise matter in which the difference from the covenant of grace is to be seen. For, as Paul says, if we are saved by grace, "then it is no longer of works; otherwise grace is no longer grace. But if it is of works, it is no longer grace; otherwise work is no longer work" (Rom. 11:6).

The covenant of grace, quite as much as the covenant of works, was sovereignly imposed by God. God did not consult man to see if he would like such a covenant and then (partly on man's terms) institute it. God did not consult man. He consulted only himself. The covenant of grace was an agreement not between God and man but between the persons of the Godhead. God the Father agreed to give his Son (John 3:16; Matt. 25:34; Rev. 13:8). Christ agreed to give his life a ransom for many (John 10:17–18). And the Holy Spirit agreed to make actual application of this redemption to those whom the Father had chosen (Rom. 8:9, 14, 16).

The Arminian view is that Christ died for all men. By this, they say, he has procured their removal from the covenant of works and introduced them into the provisions of the covenant of grace. Therein he offers to all men individually eternal life on a new and easier basis than that of the covenant of works. God required complete and perpetual obedience to the whole law in Adam's case. But now he requires only that men fulfill the (much easier) conditions of faith and repentance and evangelical obedience. God then confers his reward in the same way for the fulfillment of these conditions of the covenant of grace as he formerly did for the fulfillment of the conditions of the covenant of works. It is easy to see that mere terminology cannot hide the fact that "evangelical works" are still works, and that a covenant which has conditions that man fulfills by his "works" is not really a covenant of grace in the proper sense at all.

The Reformed view is that all conditions of the covenant of grace are really fulfilled by the work of God. Part of this work is done *for* us by Christ. Part of it is done *in* us by his Holy Spirit. It is true that one condition of the covenant of grace is faith in Jesus Christ. But this condition is fulfilled because the Lord himself gives faith to his people (Eph. 2:8; 1:17). The life and salvation offered in the Arminian version of the gospel is merely a potential or possible salvation, because it depends upon certain actions and attitudes that do not yet exist, and will not exist unless men originate them. But the life and salvation offered sinners in the Reformed version of the gospel is actual, because it depends upon God alone not only for the end to be attained, but also for the creation of those attitudes and actions in us that are necessary for the receiving of that end.

We do not, of course, receive possession of salvation until certain conditions are realized in us. We must repent, and exercise faith in Christ in order to possess the salvation he has secured for us. But this cannot be called "conditional" in the Arminian sense (which is really of the same essential character as the covenant of works). It is "conditional" only in the sense that it depends upon certain effects of the work of the Holy Spirit in the hearts of God's elect. (Of this we shall see more in chapters X, XIII, and XIV.)

QUESTIONS

1. Why is it proper to speak of the "covenant of works" as a biblical teaching though it is not technically designated as such in Scripture?
2. What reasons are given by those who object to speaking of a covenant of works?
3. What answers may be given to these arguments?
4. What merit has this designation (covenant of works)?
5. What is meant by saying that the covenant was sovereignly imposed?
6. State the Arminian conception of the condition of the covenant of grace.
7. State the Reformed conception of the condition of the covenant of grace.

VII, 4–6

4. *This covenant of grace is frequently set forth in the Scripture by the name of a testament, in reference to the death of Jesus Christ the testator, and to the everlasting inheritance, with all things belonging to it, therein bequeathed.*

5. *This covenant was differently administered in the time of the law, and in the time of the gospel; under the law it was administered by promises, prophecies, sacrifices, circumcision, the paschal lamb, and other types and ordinances delivered to the people of the Jews, all fore-signifying Christ to come, which were for that time sufficient and efficacious, through the operation of the Spirit, to instruct and build up the elect in faith in the promised Messiah, by whom they had full remission of sins, and eternal salvation; and is called the Old Testament.*

6. *Under the gospel, when Christ the substance was exhibited, the ordinances in which this covenant is dispensed are the preaching of the Word, and the administration of the sacraments of Baptism and the Lord's Supper, which, though fewer in number, and administered with more simplicity and less outward glory, yet in them it is held forth in more fullness, evidence, and spiritual efficacy, to all nations,*

both Jews and Gentiles, and is called the New Testament. There are not therefore two covenants of grace differing in substance, but one and the same under various dispensations.

These sections of the Confession teach us (1) that the word "testament" is a biblical term for the covenant of grace, (2) that the covenant of grace has in all ages been the same in substance, (3) that it has been differently administered (without any alteration in its essence), and (4) that there are only two covenants disclosed in Scripture, the covenant of works and the covenant of grace.

A striking example of the type of error against which this section of the Confession testifies is found in modern dispensationalism. Dispensationalism is found today in many denominations, even that officially profess adherence to the Westminster standards. It is often difficult to deal with dispensational error because dispensationalists generally adhere to such fundamentals of the faith as the infallibility of the Bible, the doctrine of the virgin birth of Christ, and the bodily resurrection. Most dispensationalists are, in this sense, adherents of the historic Christian faith. It must be said, however, that dispensationalism is clearly in opposition to the Confession of Faith, in that it teaches that God has employed, in different periods of history, entirely distinct (or even contrary) principles of redemptive dealing with mankind.

For example, it is the common teaching of dispensationalists that God has a different purpose for, and method by which he administers salvation to, Jews and Gentiles. Dispensationalists, therefore, speak of several covenants. The Scofield Reference Bible speaks of the Edenic, Adamic, Noahic, Abrahamic, Mosaic, Palestinian, Davidic, and New Covenants. This divides history into various dispensations—Innocency, Conscience, Human Government, Promise, Law, Grace, and Kingdom—in each of which the method by which God dispenses saving benefits is quite different. And these differences are such as would suggest that God's way of saving in one dispensation is not even essentially the same as is the case in another. Against this and all similar errors, our Confession teaches the essential unity of the one (and only) covenant of grace by which, since the fall, God has alone dealt with sinners, although it is acknowledged that there have been changes in the manner of administration of that covenant as God's revelation was being unfolded.

What might be called "the element of truth" in the dispensational view is the fact that there have been changes in the administration of the covenant. But the changes have been changes of growth and development rather than radical discontinuity. It is not even wrong to speak of various "dispensations" provided we do not deny the unity of the covenant in all periods. For example, (1) God, immediately after the fall, gave the human race a rudimentary knowledge of the plan of salvation by a redeemer (Gen. 3:15). At this time he also revealed the elementary fact that man's sinful nakedness could be covered only by sacrificing the life of a substitute (Gen. 3:21; also 4:1–8). (2) Later on God revealed more fully to Noah the scope and grandeur of his redemptive purpose (Gen. 9:8–17, 26–27). But there was no change in the applicableness of what had previously been revealed (Gen. 8:20–22). (3) At the time of Abraham (Gen. 17:7–8; 22:18) much more was given. The promise of a redeemer was more specific. The grandeur of the purpose of God was more distinctly made known. The Church was organized as a distinct visible organization, separated from the world by the sign of circumcision. (4) And then through Moses the content of the covenant of grace was revealed in still greater detail and fullness. The simple theme of blood sacrifice (which was at the heart of divine revelation from the beginning) was elaborately explained in this ritual of the tabernacle and temple services. And the ethical provisions of the covenant were expounded in the moral law. But through all these "dispensations" God was always leading his people to find their salvation in Christ alone. And it never was imagined that there was any other way of salvation than that of forgiveness through the atoning blood. Rather we might say that the more revelation given, the more clearly it was understood that there was, is, and ever shall be only one way of salvation, namely, that which is provided by God in Christ the Redeemer.

All of this leads to certain important conclusions. (1) Upon the basis of this one covenant, there is one true Church extending through all ages (Acts 7:38; Eph. 2:11–20; Rom. 11). The fact that the Scriptures speak of the Church as an organism continuing through all history is a corollary of the unity of the covenant. (2) The Old Testament ordinances were in anticipation of redemption through Christ and are therefore superseded by the New Testament ordinances which have the same essential meaning (retrospectively, in part). It is because of the unity of the covenant in all dispensations that the apostle can interchange the terminology of the ordinances of the Old and New Testament periods (1 Cor. 5:7; Col. 2:11–12). Because circumcision and baptism and again the Passover and the Lord's Supper are signs and seals of the same covenant, the apostle can call the one by the name of the other. This would not be true if there were any change in the essence of the covenant. But it would be true if the change were only in administration. The only "difference" then is that which comes with growth unto completion. The covenant of grace has not changed, but because it is now fully revealed and wholly accomplished, it may be seen with greater simplicity, clarity, fullness, and efficacy than was the case in any previous era.

QUESTIONS

1. What is the basic error of dispensationalism?
2. What does the dispensationalist mean by various dispensations?
3. Is it improper to speak of various dispensations?
4. What does the Reformed Christian mean by this term?
5. What change does the Reformed Christian recognize in the various dispensations?
6. What are important corollaries of the doctrine of the covenant (i.e., that there is but one covenant of grace in all dispensations)?

8

VIII. Of Christ the Mediator

1. *It pleased God, in his eternal purpose, to choose and ordain the Lord Jesus, his only begotten Son, to be the Mediator between God and man; the Prophet, Priest and King; the Head and Saviour of his Church, the Heir of all things; and Judge of the world; unto whom he did from all eternity give a people to be his seed, and to be by him in time redeemed, called, justified, sanctified, and glorified.*

This section of the Confession teaches us (1) that God has, from eternity, chosen a definite number of Adam's posterity to be saved through the redemptive work of Christ, (2) that he also, from eternity, promised to give these elect persons to Christ as the reward for his suffering, (3) that Christ engaged to perform and suffer all that was necessary to that end, (4) that this messianic work required Christ to be the prophet, priest, and king of his elect people as head and Savior of the Church, and (5) that he must also be heir and judge of the world.

Christ is called the second Adam, or to be more precise, "the last Adam" (1 Cor. 15:45). This is by virtue of the fact that Adam was the first and Christ the last person in human history to be a covenant head, or representative person. He came to undo for many what Adam did, and to do for them what Adam failed to do.

When Adam was sinless, he was possessed of a clear mind, a pure heart, and a right will. In this sense it is proper to speak of him as a prophet, priest, and king. (1) As a prophet, Adam was able to "think God's thoughts after him." He could interpret the works of God, and speak the truth of God for the whole creation. (2) As a priest, he was able to dedicate himself to God as a "living sacrifice." He himself, and all that he surveyed, he was to devote to the worship of God. (3) As a king, he was qualified to subdue and rule all in accordance with right knowledge and holy devotion. His activities were to be in conformity with, and expressive of, the will of God. Of course we do not say that there was in Adam a consciousness of these three offices as such, nor do we mean that he was called a prophet, priest, and king in the official sense. What we mean is that the work or activity of a prophet, priest, and king was implicit in Adam's headship. Had he not sinned, it would have become more patent. But the fall of Adam ended all this.

God then began to prepare to send "the last Adam." And it is highly significant that much of the Old Testament revelation in preparation for his coming centered in the three "anointed" (that is, messianic) offices of prophet, priest, and king. We believe it was because of the sinful depravity of man that God instituted three distinct and separate offices, borne by separate lines of individuals, from that which had originally been part and parcel to sinless manhood. By thus instituting each office, distinct from the others, God could reveal the dismal imperfection of man's nature, and also show something of the perfection which was to be required of his Son. We shall briefly summarize the unfolding revelation of each of these offices.

Prophet

The term "prophet" is first used of Abraham (Gen. 20:7). But from the earliest beginning of history, certain persons served as spokesmen of the truth of God; Enoch (Jude 14; Gen. 5:18), Noah (2 Peter 2:5; 1:20–21), Isaac (Gen. 27:28–29, 40), and Jacob (Gen. 49, especially verses 8–11) did so. Moses was the first to be designated a prophet with that prominence that we usually associate with the term. And in Deuteronomy 18:15–20 God promised that there would follow him a succession of prophets, until at last there would arise a supreme prophet (like unto Moses) whose words would have final authority. Such a succession of prophets did indeed follow throughout the remainder of Old Testament history. But it is a noteworthy fact that none has arisen since the coming of Jesus Christ and the completion of the Bible.

Priest

The word "priest" is first mentioned with reference to the mysterious Melchizedek (Gen. 14:18). This is important because there is no record of his beginning or end. And the prediction of Psalm 110:4 was that Jesus would be "a priest forever after the order of Melchizedek." This indicated that he would have an eternal and unchangeable priesthood (Heb. 7:24). But even before Melchizedek, the offering of blood sacrifices was a "priestly" activity (Gen. 4:1–5; 8:20; 12:8). Thus Abraham was a priest (Gen. 13:4; 22:13), as were Isaac (26:25) and Jacob (33:20; 35:7). Again, however, it was not until the Mosaic era that a special (or distinctly designated) office was instituted. Aaron was the first to hold this office, which—unlike the prophetic office—was hereditary (Ex. 29:29; Num. 25:12–13). Inauguration to this office was by "anointing." And he who held the office had to be consecrated (Ex. 29:29–31), free of bodily defects (Lev. 21:16–23), and clothed with garments symbolic of holiness (Ex. 29:29). Finally, it was revealed concerning this office too, that there would be a succession of priests but only until a supreme priest would arise whose work would abide forever (see 1 Sam. 2:35–36).

King

The first king in Israel's history was Saul. Moreover, the original desire of the people to have a human visible king was condemned (1 Sam. 10:19). Yet from the beginning of history the special task of ruling in obedience to God's will was a subject of divine revelation. Adam was to rule (Gen. 1:26), as was Noah after the fall (9:2). Abraham was a king in the sense that he was regarded as the equal of other kings (Gen. 14:1–2, 13, 17–24). His wife was called a princess (17:15) and of her a succession of kings was promised (17:16). Jacob prophesied that the scepter, the symbol of kingly rule, would not depart from the tribe of Judah until the supreme ruler had come (Gen. 49:10). Thus in spite of the divine disapproval of the reason for which the Israelites desired a king, the institution of the monarchy was clearly part of the eternal plan and will of God (1 Sam. 8:20 compared with 8:22). But then the Lord promised a line of descendants from David terminating in the supreme king who would rule forever (2 Sam.

7:12–16; Pss. 2, 45, 72, 110). This office too required the act of "anointing" (from which comes the word "Messiah") of those inaugurated.

When Christ came, he fulfilled the requirements which God had laid down for each of these three offices. During the Old Testament period these offices had been held by true and false prophets, good and evil priests, righteous and wicked kings. From the good and true something was learned concerning the glory of the future Messiah. From the evil and false something was learned of man's inability and need for divine intervention. In Christ the promise was fulfilled and the failure overcome. (1) As our prophet he revealed to us the will of God for our salvation. He not only did so when he was in the days of his flesh (that is, while on earth) but also does so today. Christ executes the office of a prophet in revealing to us, by his Word and Spirit, the will of God for our salvation. (2) As our priest he offered himself as a sacrifice to satisfy divine justice and to reconcile us to God. And he continues to intercede for us, applying to us the benefits of his one perfect oblation. (3) As our king he subdues us to himself, rules and defends us, and continues daily to do so as he causes the kingdom of darkness to recede and the kingdom of grace to advance on earth.

It is Christ, in the plenitude of his three offices, who is the head and Savior of his Church. And it is in terms of this plenitude that he is to be worshiped and honored. Where he is not so acknowledged, neither is he head and Savior, and such cannot be his Church. (1) For example, modernists stress the kingship of Christ but neglect his other offices. They no doubt sincerely desire to see men and nations ruled by Christian principles. But Christ cannot be king where he is not first acknowledged as prophet and priest. Those who do not accept the Bible as the infallible revelation of his will do not recognize him as prophet. And those who avoid the substitutionary atonement do not recognize him as priest. Therefore their efforts to build the kingdom are in vain. (2) On the other hand, many fundamentalists acknowledge Christ as prophet and priest. They accept the Bible as his infallible Word and trust in his atonement for forgiveness of sin. But they do not believe that he is ruling right *now* *as* a king; they believe that he will do so only in the future. They therefore take a generally pessimistic view of the world and consider it more or less fruitless to seek to apply the principles of Christ's word to society.

Happily many fundamentalists are inconsistent and so do not fully deny in practice what they deny in theory. Yet it must be said that where the theory is put into practice, Christ's honor is denied, and the character of the true Church lacking.

We have already considered God's eternal election (III, 3–4) and covenant (VII). We shall consider the design of Christ's atonement under section 5 below. But we must here briefly consider Christ's universal lordship over creation. He who is prophet, priest, and king, the head and Savior of the Church, is also heir of all things and judge of the world. The head of the Church is also the Lord of creation. And he rules both the Church and the creation pursuant to his redemptive purpose (Eph. 1:22; 4:15; Col. 1:18; 2:19). This is a truth quite commonly ignored today. It is ignored in a multitude of public and interfaith religious observances. Thus to God, but not Christ, is ascribed the praise for the rule of nature and the operations of providence. It is thought that when we speak of the headship over creation, Christ may be bypassed and that only the Father need be mentioned. But the truth is that God the Father has given all things into the hands of the God-man Jesus Christ. And no one comes unto the Father except through him (Phil. 2:6–11; Eph. 1:22–23; Matt. 28:18; Acts 2:36).

QUESTIONS

  1. Why is Christ called "the last Adam"?
  2. What are the three offices implicit in Adam's work and explicit in Christ's?
  3. Why were these offices separated by the Old Testament institution of God?
  4. Concerning the office of prophet:
   (a) Who is first named a prophet in Scripture?
   (b) With whom does the office itself properly begin?
   (c) What fact is specially noteworthy as respects this office?
  5. Concerning the office of priest:
   (a) Who is first named a priest in Scripture?
   (b) Why is this important?
   (c) With whom did the succession of priests begin?
  6. Concerning the office of king:
   (a) Who was the first king in Israel?

(b) When were kings first mentioned by the Lord to his people?

(c) Was it the will of God for Israel to have a king?

7. Briefly define each of Christ's three offices. (See Shorter Catechism, 24–26.)

8. Which offices of Christ do modernists deny or at least neglect?

9. Which office of Christ do fundamentalists sometimes neglect?

10. How do those who acknowledge Christ in his three offices sometimes dishonor him?

VIII, 2

2. *The Son of God, the second person in the Trinity, being very and eternal God, of one substance and equal with the Father, did, when the fullness of time was come, take upon him man's nature, with all the essential properties and common infirmities thereof, yet without sin; being conceived by the power of the Holy Ghost, in the womb of the Virgin Mary, of her substance. So that two whole, perfect, and distinct natures, the Godhead and the manhood, were inseparably joined together in one person, without conversion, composition, or confusion. Which person is very God and very man, yet one Christ, the only mediator between God and man.*

This section of the Confession teaches us (1) that Christ is God, (2) that he is also man, having supernaturally entered into human nature without sin, and (3) that he is yet one person, Christ the only mediator between God and man.

John the apostle said, "By this you know the Spirit of God: Every spirit that confesses that Jesus Christ has come in the flesh is of God, and every spirit that does not confess that Jesus Christ has come in the flesh is not of God. And this is the spirit of the Antichrist, which you have heard was coming, and is now already in the world" (1 John 4:2–4). The seriousness of heresy with respect to the doctrine of Christ is plain: "Whoever transgresses and does not abide in the doctrine of Christ does not have God. He who abides in the doctrine of Christ has both the Father and the Son. If anyone comes to you and does not bring this doctrine, do not receive him" (2 John 9–10). With such warnings as this it is not surpris-

ing that the history of the Church is not one of sweet peace. Christ came
not to send peace on earth but a sword. That sword is his Word, and it
divides men wherever it goes (Rev. 1:16; Heb. 4:12; Matt. 10:34–36).
The Church is in the world to do battle with the kingdom of error, and
from the beginning Satan has opposed the Church's only weapon of
offense—the Word of God—with subtle error.

During the first two centuries after Christ was on earth the battle
between truth and error was doctrinally generalized. The early Christians
were called upon to defend the Christian faith as a whole against all-out
pagan opposition. Gnosticism was Satan's great counterfeit in those days.
It was a false, but not wholly unattractive caricature of the whole Christian system. Many were led away from the historic Christian faith (that
is, faith based upon real events which took place in history) by this
suprahistorical faith (that is, faith based upon vain speculations of things
supposedly lying behind history).

During the third and fourth centuries the attack became less generalized and was concentrated primarily on the doctrine of the Trinity. During this period the Church faced monarchianism (a heresy which made
Christ and the Holy Spirit subordinate to the Father, not only in their
redemptive work, but in their very essence), modalistic monarchianism
(which taught that God is one person who assumes three identities—
Father, Son, and Holy Spirit—but only one at a time), and Arianism
(which taught that Christ and the Holy Spirit were merely creatures).
Against these and similar errors the Councils of Nicea (A.D. 325) and
Constantinople (A.D. 381) began to hammer out the statement of the
Church's faith in the great creedal documents. The biblical faith was thus
expressed in conscious opposition to the subtle and innocent-sounding,
but actually deadly, errors of Satan.

But no sooner had the Church survived Satan's attack on the doctrine
of the Trinity than there began an attack upon the doctrine of Christ.
Roughly between the fifth and seventh centuries there arose (1) Apolli-
narianism (which taught that Christ was God, but that he did not possess
a true—or complete—human nature; Apollinaris taught that Christ had
a body and a soul, but that in place of a human spirit Christ had the divine
Logos, or Word); (2) Nestorianism (which taught that the Christ consists of two separate persons, the one divine and the other human, rather
than being one person having two natures); (3) Eutychianism (also called

monophysitism, which taught that in the person of Christ incarnate there was but a single, and that a divine, nature). There were others, but these were prominent and they show the persistency with which error respecting the person of Christ abounded in that era.

Against these the Church formulated the true doctrine of Christ's person at the Council of Chalcedon in A.D. 451. And it is the substance of this creed which is embodied in, and even more succinctly stated by, this section of the Westminster Confession of Faith. Centuries of deadly conflict between Satan and the Church are crystallized in these words: "that two whole, perfect, and distinct natures, the Godhead and the manhood, were inseparably joined together in one person, without conversion, composition, or confusion." If it be true that "he who forgets the past is condemned to live it over again," then it is a tragedy of the greatest magnitude that this history and the fruits of it have been forgotten. The mushrooming growth of many modern cults which do little more than repeat the ancient errors would seem to confirm the truth of this proverb. The testimony of this section of the Confession is confirmed as follows:

Christ's divine nature
- Eternal (John 17:5, 24)
- Omnipotent (Matt. 8:27)
- Omniscient (Luke 6:8)
- His supernatural paternity was respected in his human conception (Luke 1:35).

His human nature
- Began in time (Gal. 4:4)
- Was by human generation from Mary's substance (Luke 1:35)
- Was subject to the limitations, etc., incident to human existence (i.e., growth, hunger, sorrow, pain, limitations of knowledge, etc.) (Heb. 2:17; 4:15)

His uni-personality
While it is clear from Scripture that Christ's human nature was genuine and complete, as was his divine nature, and that they ever remained distinct within his person (there was no mixture, dissolution, or confusion between the two natures), yet the Scripture is equally insistent that Christ was but *one person*. Neither God nor men ever addressed him or

dealt with him as one or the other, nor did he ever act at any time as if he were one or the other. The modern practice of making pictures of Christ as if his human nature could properly be portrayed by itself is not only a serious error in doctrine; it is *impossible* in fact. For this reason the Westminster Larger Catechism consistently declares "the making of any representation of God, of all or of any of the three persons, either inwardly in our mind, or outwardly in any kind of image or likeness of any creature whatsoever" a violation of the Second Commandment (Q. 109). For just as God is one God, and yet three eternally distinct persons, so Christ is one person, and yet has two entire natures which are distinct from one another in the unity of his person. The scriptural proof for this is to be found in such texts as Acts 20:28. There we read that "God . . . purchased with His own blood" the Church. But Scripture says that God is a spirit (John 4:24). And Jesus said that "a spirit does not have flesh" (Luke 24:39) and can therefore have no blood. The statement found in Acts 20:28 is therefore possible only because the person who purchased the Church is both God and man. Because he is one person with two natures, we may speak of him as God and also as shedding human blood.

QUESTIONS

1. Why is it not surprising that the history of the Church has been one of conflict?
2. In this battle what is the Church's only offensive weapon?
3. In this battle what is Satan's weapon?
4. In what sphere of doctrine did the Church first do battle?
5. What sphere next engaged the Church in conflict?
6. At what two early councils, and in what years, did the Church formulate the doctrine of the Trinity against the errors that had arisen?
7. At what council and in what year did the Church defend the true doctrine of the person of Christ?
8. How many natures has Christ?
9. How many persons is Christ?
10. Why is it wrong to make pictures to represent Christ?
11. How does such a text as Acts 20:28 confirm the doctrine set forth in the Confession?

VIII, 3

3. *The Lord Jesus, in his human nature thus united to the divine, was sanctified and anointed with the Holy Spirit above measure; having in him all the treasures of wisdom and knowledge; in whom it pleased the Father that all fullness should dwell: to the end that being holy, harmless, undefiled, and full of grace and truth, he might be thoroughly furnished to execute the office of a mediator and surety. Which office he took not unto himself, but was thereunto called by his Father, who put all power and judgment into his hand, and gave him commandment to execute the same.*

In this section of the Confession we learn (1) how the human nature of Christ was equipped for his mediatorial work, (2) why it was necessary that he also be God to perform this work, (3) how he was divinely called to this office, (4) that he was invested with requisite authority and ability, and (5) that he was ordained to execute this work.

Remembering that the human nature of Christ did not cease in any way to be human (limited, finite, etc.) when taken into unity with his divine nature, we may understand how it was necessary that he be furnished by God with what he needed to fulfill his office. He was, apart from sin, as we are. And even without sin, he was not qualified or authorized to perform the messianic task (Heb. 2:11) until he received a special call from God (Heb. 5:4). It was necessary, in other words, that he receive divine orders to fulfill the task (Heb. 5:1; Luke 4:18).

The Old Testament persons anointed of God to hold messianic offices by way of anticipation were supernaturally endowed for their work by a special operation of the Holy Spirit distinct from such operations as he may have performed for (or in) them personally (see 1 Sam. 10:1, 6 compared with 1 Sam. 28:16; Judg. 14:6; 16:20). This special operation of the Spirit was outwardly symbolized by anointing with oil. Christ was not anointed with oil, but he was anointed with the Holy Spirit without measure, that is, not in the limited way in which the Old Testament persons were who typified him (John 3:34; Luke 4:18). Obviously the Savior did not have need of the Holy Spirit for personal salvation, since he was without sin. But he *did* need the Holy Spirit to enable him, human as he was, to accomplish the work of redemption. It can be unhesitatingly said that Christ at all times performed his preaching, worked his miracles, and yielded perfect obedience, in entire dependence upon the supernatural power of the Holy Spirit (Acts 10:38). Thus he said, "I do nothing of Myself" (John 8:28). His constant praying evidences his entire dependence upon God. In the end, his human nature sank under the total infliction of the curse of God; and the inability of his human nature to bear this awful damnation, for which he died (albeit, by his own willing submission), shows us that there was no power inherent in his human nature apart from the Spirit of God.

It is equally true and important that he was possessed of a divine nature. Thus he was, in and of himself, able to lay down his life and take it up again (John 10:17). Endowment by the Holy Spirit as to his human nature could not have given him this divine authority and power. He that would be sovereign over death, as well as subject to death, must be God and not just man. A man may in a sense be said to lay down his life, perhaps, but he must be more than a mere man to take it up again. Furthermore, if he was not God and thus infinite in his capacity for suffering, how could he have suffered the limitless wrath of God in three days? Because he was infinite in his divine nature he was able to offer that which is greater in value than is required by the sins of the whole world.

Finally, we may ask such questions as these: How could he have access to God on our behalf with guaranteed efficacy? How could he certainly defeat all of his and our enemies? How could he send us his Holy Spirit? How could he do these things if he were not God as well as man? Again, if he had not been God and man in one person, these diverse requirements would not have been met in that one work of redemption. Because he united in himself the requisite conditions and possessed the necessary qualifications, he was able to accomplish our redemption as the one mediator between God and man.

QUESTIONS

1. Why was it necessary for Christ to be furnished with the power of the Holy Spirit?
2. Did the presence of the Holy Spirit in Old Testament prophets (or priests or kings) necessarily indicate that they were regenerate persons? Why?
3. How does the Savior's reception of the Holy Spirit confirm this?

4. What are some of the things Christ did, for which it was necessary that he be human?

5. What are some of the things Christ did, for which it was necessary that he be divine?

6. Why was it also necessary that he unite two natures in one person?

VIII, 4

4. *This office the Lord Jesus did most willingly undertake, which, that he might discharge, he was made under the law, and did perfectly fulfill it; endured most grievous torments immediately in his soul, and most painful sufferings in his body; was crucified, and died; was buried, and remained under the power of death, yet saw no corruption. On the third day he arose from the dead, with the same body in which he suffered; with which also he ascended into heaven, and there sitteth at the right hand of his Father, making intercession; and shall return to judge men and angels at the end of the world.*

This section of the Confession teaches us (1) that Christ voluntarily took upon himself the mediatorial office (2) with the estate of humiliation which was necessary for the accomplishment of our redemption, as well as the estate of exaltation wherein he now continues to apply the benefits of his mediatorial work.

The voluntary character of the entrance of God the Son into human nature, and the messianic offices, is everywhere affirmed in Scripture. In Hebrews 2:12–17, for example, we read of him, "I will declare Your name to My brethren; in the midst of the assembly I will sing praise to You." This, a quotation from Psalm 22:22, is the Spirit of Christ speaking through David (Acts 4:25) concerning his entrance into human flesh. It is voluntary. "Inasmuch . . . as the children have partaken of flesh and blood, He Himself likewise shared in the same" (Heb. 2:14). But there was a difference. He chose to become man. "For indeed He does not give aid to [or take hold of] angels, but He does give aid to the seed of Abraham" (Heb. 2:16). He exercised free choice. He imposed this condition upon himself. And the same is true of his death. Of his own life he said, "No one takes it from Me" (John 10:18). He "gave Himself for [us]" (Gal. 2:20).

Christ's voluntary assumption of the messianic offices entailed the state of humiliation requisite to the accomplishment of the task. This was made quite clear prior to his coming. He was to be subject to humiliation in that he (1) would experience human birth (Isa. 7:14; 9:6; Gen. 3:15; 17:7; Ps. 72; Heb. 2:12–17), (2) would be born in a low condition (Ps. 22:9–12; Micah 5:2; Job 25:6; Ps. 22:6), (3) be made under the law (Ps. 40:6–8; Heb. 10:4–10; Pss. 45:6–7; 72:1), (4) render perfect obedience to the law (Ps. 45:7; Ex. 28; Ps. 40:8–10), (5) undergo the miseries of this life, the wrath of God, and the accursed death of the cross (Ps. 22; Isa. 53), and (6) die, be buried, and continue under the power of death for a time (Pss. 118:22; 16:9–11; Isa. 53, especially v. 8).

It was also necessary that he subsequently experience a glorious estate of exaltation. For the Scripture required him (1) to rise again from the dead on the third day (Pss. 16:10; 49:15; 68:18; Eph. 4:8–10), (2) to ascend into heaven (Pss. 47:5; 24:7–10), (3) to sit at the right hand of God the Father, there to intercede for us, reign over us, and rule all things (Pss. 16:11; 90:1; Dan. 7:13–14; Zech. 6:12–13), and (4) to come again—at the last day—to judge the living and the dead (Ps. 98:9; this will be discussed under chapter XXXIII).

It is not necessary to labor here to show that these predictions (except for the last) have been fulfilled by our Lord according to the witness of the New Testament. While the voluntary character of his work is clearly affirmed, it is also testified that each of these steps was divinely prescribed and necessary to the successful completion of the redemption of the Lord's people (see Luke 2:49; 4:43; Matt. 16:21; Luke 22:37; 24:44; compare also Larger Catechism, 46–56).

QUESTIONS

1. Cite Scripture proof that Christ's humiliation was voluntary.
2. How can Christ's mediatorial work be described as voluntary and yet a necessity?
3. What particular conditions pertaining to the humiliation of Christ were required by the Old Testament revelation?
4. What particular conditions pertaining to the exaltation of Christ were required by the Old Testament revelation?

5. Is there evidence of the absolute fulfillment of these conditions by Christ in the New Testament?

6. What is the one required work of Christ in his estate of exaltation that yet remains wholly future?

VIII, 5

5. *The Lord Jesus, by his perfect obedience and sacrifice of himself, which he through the eternal Spirit once offered up unto God, hath fully satisfied the justice of his Father; and purchased not only reconciliation, but an everlasting inheritance in the kingdom of heaven, for all those whom the Father hath given unto him.*

This section of the Confession teaches us (1) that Christ made satisfaction to God for those whom he represented, (2) that this satisfaction was by active and passive obedience, and (3) that by this satisfaction Christ secured complete redemption for those whom he represented.

Here we consider the doctrine of "particular" or "definite atonement." It has sometimes been called the doctrine of the "limited atonement," because the Reformed Confessions acknowledge that Christ was a substitute for some men rather than all men. It is most unfortunate, however, that this phrase has given rise to the misconception that it is the Reformed churches that "limit" the atonement, whereas the Arminian groups do not. The truth is really the exact opposite. It is the Arminian system that "limits" the atonement while the Reformed system does not.

In order to show this we need only to ponder the following fact: the Arminian (and likewise, the Lutheran and Roman Catholic) is compelled (by the plain teaching of Scripture) to admit that only some men actually will be saved. Only those who subscribe to the totally unscriptural idea of a universal salvation deny this. All who maintain the historic Christian faith in even the broadest sense agree that only some shall be saved. Therefore, there is no disagreement as to whether or not the work of Christ ultimately terminates in the salvation of only a limited portion of the human race. If all who accept the scriptural dictum thus "limit" the ultimate number that shall be saved to merely a part of the human race, it is quite unjust when Reformed Christians alone are held in disrepute for "limiting" the atonement.

The precise difference between the Reformed Confessions and those of the Arminians and others is not the ultimate *effect* of the atonement, but rather the original *design* of it. The real question is this: When Christ died, was it his plan or design (and that of the Father who gave him) to save all men or some men only? The Reformed churches have always answered that the works of God are never inconsistent, and that those who are actually saved are those whom it was ever God's design to save. But the Arminian (and Lutheran and Roman Catholic) churches have ever endeavored to find some way to make the work of Christ distributively the same for all men. They say that the design of the atonement was to provide "equal" benefits for all men. This, however, necessitates a profound lowering of the conception of what Christ's atonement is. Because they wish to say that Christ did as much for any particular man as he did for any other, namely, make salvation possible, they cannot quite say that Christ did enough to actually secure the salvation of anyone. If they were to do so, then they would logically be compelled to say that all will be saved. If the work of Christ is the same for all men, then it cannot actually do for any what it does not do for all. Since the work of Christ does not secure salvation for all, it must not secure salvation for any. It secures, then, only the possibility, or chance, or opportunity for salvation, and this, supposedly, for all.

In 1925 the United Presbyterian Church of North America sought to accommodate the Reformed faith to just such a view. Setting aside the Westminster Confession of Faith at this vital point, Article XIV of the new creed stated that Christ "gave himself a ransom for all." No doubt the authors of this new creed abhorred Arminianism. Yet they could not avoid the inexorable logic of their own Arminian assumption. In order to say that Christ died equally for all, they could not avoid saying that his atonement secured only "free access to God for pardon and restoration." In other words, it secured something less than complete salvation; it secured only the access to it.

This is truly "limited" atonement in the reprehensible sense. For this is a false limitation placed upon it by men. And it wounds the gospel at its very heart. For it is the witness of the Bible (and our Reformed Confession) that the work of Christ did much more for sinners than to merely gain them "access to God *for* pardon and restoration." What it gained for sinners was precisely pardon and restoration. Christ actually took upon himself the sin and punishment of his people (Isa. 53; Rom. 5:19; Heb. 10:14; 9:25–26). They in turn receive the imputed righteousness of Christ (2 Cor. 5:21. And that *is* pardon and restoration. They are pardoned because their sin is punished in Christ. And they are restored because his righteousness becomes theirs.

Thus it becomes painfully clear that the only way to extend the design of the atonement so as to include everyone equally within its provision is to denature it and to eliminate its substitutionary character. If Christ did not actually take upon him my sin, guilt, and punishment, then what shall I do? If he merely opens the way of access to God so that I can go there with my sin and guilt, woe is me, for I am surely undone. Yet that is the most that we can attribute to Christ's death if we try to hold that it was designed for the equal benefit of all men (that is, to open heaven to all, in order that they might each come to ask for pardon and restoration). But if we hold, with Scripture, that in this, as in all other redemptive works of God, he had in view a special people, then we may magnify its power and rest our faith securely therein.

So the crucial question is this: what does the Scripture teach? And the answer is that the Messiah was named Jesus because he would *save his people* from their sins (Matt. 1:21). He gave his life a ransom for *many* (Matt. 20:28). He promised that he would actually save *all that the Father had given him* (John 6:37, 39). In Romans 8:29 the apostle states that only those who are predestined of God to subsequently receive salvation do actually receive the same. Each particular benefit of salvation is therefore unfolded to them (Rom. 8:30). But the basis of it all, he says, is that God "spared not His own Son, but delivered Him up for us all" (8:32). And he specifically says that by "us all" he means none other than "God's elect" (8:33). It is because they are elect that they are the recipients of the atonement of Christ, and it is no wonder that, God having given his Son unto death for them, he will also with him freely give them all things (8:32).

And if this is not sufficient, we have the words of Jesus himself, by which he plainly declares what the design or purpose of his atonement was to be. "For I have come down from heaven, not to do My own will, but the will of Him who sent Me. [And] this is the will of the Father who sent Me, that of all He has given Me I should lose nothing, but should raise it up at the last day" (John 6:38–39). "I do not pray for the world," he said, "but for those whom You have given Me, for they are Yours. And all Mine are Yours, and Yours are Mine" (John 17:9–10). "I lay down My life for the sheep" (John 10:15). These words were not spoken by one who intended that his death would benefit all men in the same way. And certainly they do not indicate a mere intention of making salvation *possible.* They are the words of one who intended to actually (and completely) save his people from their sins.

It is true, of course, that certain texts of Scripture can be quoted in such a way as to seem to suggest a universal design of the atonement (such as Heb. 2:9; 2 Cor. 5:14–15; 1 John 2:2; 1 Tim. 4:10). Concerning such texts the following may be said: (1) The context is often ignored. For example, in Hebrews 2 the writer is speaking of "the many sons" whom Christ will bring to glory, and not of all men. Therefore, when the writer speaks in this context of Christ tasting death for everyone, there is no legitimate reason to extend the scope of his remark beyond the limits of those under discussion. Why should we not acknowledge the author's right to speak of Christ's tasting death for every one of those concerning whom he is speaking?

(2) A second reason for misinterpretation is the failure to discern the proper meaning of Scripture terms by a comparison of Scripture with Scripture. It just so happens that Scripture employs universal expressions to describe phenomena which are merely general and not absolute. For example, Matthew 3:5–6 says that when John the Baptist was preaching, "Jerusalem, all Judea, and all the region around the Jordan went out to him and were baptized by him in the Jordan, confessing their sins." But this *all* was clearly meant in a general sense—not in an absolute sense— since Scripture also informs us that the Pharisees and lawyers did not accept the baptism of John (Luke 7:30). In 1 John 5:19 John says, "The whole world lies under the sway of the wicked one," and yet he also says that "we are of God." In other words the phrase "the whole world" is not intended to include absolutely everyone, including John himself. Why then cannot Christ be the Savior of all men in a general sense (that is, some from every tongue and tribe and nation) while yet not in the absolute sense?

(3) Finally, it is to be remembered that there are certain gracious benefits which accrue to the whole human race from the atonement of Christ

other than that of eternal salvation. There is a sense in which Christ *is* "the Savior of all men," as there is another sense in which he is "especially [the Savior] of those who believe" (1 Tim. 4:10). The death of Christ has secured temporal benefits for the whole human race *and* a delay in the execution of the sentence of damnation. (See Gen. 8:20–9:17 for the provisions of the covenant of grace applicable to all men.)

QUESTIONS

1. In Reformed teaching what does "limited atonement" mean?
2. What terms are more appropriate?
3. In what does Reformed, Arminian, Lutheran, and Roman Catholic doctrine agree (i.e., as respects the number of the saved)?
4. The precise difference between Reformed Christians and others concerns not the ultimate effect of the atonement, but what?
5. How does the opposing view "limit" the atonement?
6. When the United Presbyterian Church tried to universalize the design of the atonement, what was the unavoidable consequence?
7. What must the atonement of Christ secure for you to be of any benefit that can be called "saving"?
8. Cite a text in which Christ clearly states the design of his death.
9. Cite a text which seems applicable, on first sight, to the opposing view.
10. Give the proper interpretation of 1 Timothy 4:10.
11. State the principles that are often overlooked in interpreting such texts.

VIII, 6–8

6. *Although the work of redemption was not actually wrought by Christ till after his incarnation, yet the virtue, efficacy, and benefits thereof were communicated unto the elect in all ages successively from the beginning of the world, in and by those promises, types, and sacrifices wherein he was revealed and signified to be the seed of the woman which should bruise the serpent's head, and the lamb slain from the beginning of the world, being yesterday and today the same, and forever.*

7. *Christ, in the work of mediation, acteth according to both natures; by each nature doing that which is proper to itself: Yet, by reason of the unity of the person, that which is proper to one nature is sometimes in Scripture attributed to the person denominated by the other nature.*

8. *To all those for whom Christ hath purchased redemption, he doth certainly and effectually apply and communicate the same; making intercession for them, and revealing unto them, in and by the Word, the mysteries of salvation; effectually persuading them by his Spirit to believe and obey; and governing their hearts by his Word and Spirit, overcoming all their enemies by his almighty power and wisdom, in such manner and ways as are most consonant to his wonderful and unsearchable dispensation.*

These sections teach us (1) that the benefits of Christ's atonement have been applied to the elect in all ages even though they were not actually accomplished until the incarnation, (2) that these benefits were applied prior to the incarnation by types and ordinances different from those of the present, (3) that Christ's mediatorial work involves both natures concurrently, (4) that Christ effectually applies redemption to those for whom he purchased it, and (5) the manner in which he does this.

We have previously discussed the unity of the covenant (VII, 4–6). In that discussion we endeavored to show that in all "dispensations" salvation was by faith in Christ's atonement, and that the changes evident there were merely those required by progress in divine revelation. But the salvation of God's people in all ages was through the cross of Christ alone. David recognized that God did not regard the Old Testament sacrifices as efficacious in themselves (Ps. 51:16). The very design of the sacrificial system of the Old Testament was partly to show that it could not "make him who performed the service perfect" (Heb. 9:9) in order that believers might look forward to that one offering by which Christ "has perfected forever those who are being sanctified" (Heb. 10:14). The law was a mere shadow (Heb. 10:1), but it was a shadow "of the good things to come" and therefore a means by which believers received the benefits of Christ before the work had actually been done.

We have also seen (VIII, 1–3) that Christ's mediatorial work concurrently involves both natures. We shall confine our remarks here, therefore, to the subject of the present application of redemption to the elect. The plan of salvation is self-consistent. Those chosen of the Father were purchased by Christ. And those purchased by Christ are effectually called into his kingdom. "All that the Father gives Me will come to Me" (John 6:37). "Them also I must bring, and they will hear My voice" (John 10:16). The manner in which Christ accomplishes this is briefly described in section 8 of this chapter of the Confession. But it is unfolded in detail in the chapter entitled *Of Effectual Calling* (X). Here it is important to stress that Christ does effectually apply redemption to all those for whom he died.

In grasping this fact we will find it helpful to remember the following truths: (1) Christ freely and sincerely offers salvation to all who hear the gospel, whether they are elect or not. "For," as Jesus himself said, "many are called, but few are chosen" (Matt. 20:16). "Come to Me, all you who labor and are heavy laden, and I will give you rest," he cried (Matt. 11:28). "How often I wanted to gather your children together," said Christ regarding Jerusalem, "but you were not willing" (Matt. 23:37). (2) Christ promises that no one who accepts his offer will be cast out. "The one who comes to Me I will by no means cast out" (John 6:37). To say that Christ effectually applies redemption to his elect must not be twisted or perverted to mean that he restrains others from accepting his grace. (3) The difficulty with those who are not effectually called is wholly within themselves. They are dead in trespasses and sins (Eph. 2:1–5). They will not come to Christ (Matt. 23:37). They consider his gospel a foolish thing (1 Cor. 1:23; 2:14). It is not because of what Christ does, but because of what they are and what they do, that they cannot come to Christ (John 6:44). (4) That the elect do come is only because Christ enables them to do so. He creates a new heart (Ps. 51:10) within them so that they will want to accept the salvation that he freely gives to all who will receive it. "No one knows . . . who the Father is except the Son, and the one to whom the Son wills to reveal Him" (Luke 10:22). "But God has revealed them to us through His Spirit." Therefore we can truly say: "Now we have received, not the spirit of the world, but the Spirit who is from God, that we might know the things that have been freely given to us by God" (1 Cor. 2:10, 12).

QUESTIONS

1. Did Old Testament believers regard their sacrifices as inherently efficacious? Prove from Scripture.

2. Who effectually applies salvation to the elect?
3. Cite Scripture proof that Christ applies redemption to those for whom he died.
4. To whom does Christ offer salvation? Prove this.
5. How many of those who accept this offer will be saved? Prove this.
6. Why do all except the elect refuse this offer?
7. Why do all the elect without exception accept this offer?

9

IX. Of Free Will

1. *God hath endued the will of man with that natural liberty, that it is neither forced, nor by any absolute necessity of nature determined, to good or evil.*

2. *Man, in his state of innocency, had freedom and power to will and to do that which is good and well-pleasing to God; but yet mutably, so that he might fall from it.*

3. *Man, by his fall into a state of sin, hath wholly lost all ability of will to any spiritual good accompanying salvation; so as a natural man, being altogether averse from that good, and dead in sin, is not able, by his own strength, to convert himself, or to prepare himself thereunto.*

4. *When God converts a sinner, and translates him into the state of grace, he freeth him from his natural bondage under sin, and by his grace alone enables him freely to will and to do that which is spiritually good; yet so as that, by reason of his remaining corruption, he doth not perfectly nor only will that which is good, but doth also will that which is evil.*

5. *The will of man is made perfectly and immutably free to do good alone in the state of glory only.*

These sections teach us (1) that man, by nature, possesses a free will, (2) that this freedom or liberty means that man is not forced to will that which is contrary to his nature or desire, and (3) that man in four estates enjoys the same liberty but different degrees of ability to do good or evil.

It is all too common to bring the railing accusation against the Reformed faith that it denies free will. Many reject the Reformed faith (or Calvinism) out of hand because they assume that divine sovereignty (of which predestination is but one aspect) cancels all true human liberty and responsibility. Yet, ironically, no other system of teaching safeguards true human liberty and responsibility as does the Reformed faith.

But in order to grasp this fact we must carefully note what freedom of the will is and what it is not. By free will we mean that man's will is not coerced. We mean that man is not forced by some external force greater than himself to do something he does not want to do. We mean that man is free to do what he wants to do within the limits of his ability. What else can freedom or liberty be than to do as we please?

However, we must carefully note that liberty is not identical with ability. Confusion of these distinct things accounts for much false thinking on the subject of free will. Many people really mean *ability* when they say *liberty*. They speak of man being free to do good or evil when they really mean to say that men are able to do good or evil. In this they seriously err. For the Bible clearly and consistently teaches (1) that man is *free* to do good or evil, that he is at liberty to do either, but (2) that he is *able* to do only evil because of his fallen condition (Deut. 30:19; John 6:44).

The source of this common confusion is revealed for us in Christ's teaching in Matthew 12:33 where he says, "Either make the tree good and its fruit good, or else make the tree bad and its fruit bad; for a tree is known by its fruit." The will is a faculty of man's soul or personality. The will is therefore determined by the soul (self, ego, or personality) of the man. It cannot escape the moral character out of which it comes. If the soul is entirely corrupt so that its knowledge and desire are defective and rotten, it follows that it can *will* to do only that which is evil. Thus complete liberty exists even though there is total inability to do good.

Man originally had a sinless personality. He desired only that which was good and well-pleasing to God. He was free to do that which was according to his own desire. And because his nature was wholly uncorrupted his desires were only good. He had complete liberty and also ability to do good. He had no more liberty to do good than has fallen man, but he had complete ability, which is totally absent in fallen man.

With sin's entrance man lost *ability* to do good, not liberty. This was due to the fact that one sin, as God had warned, was sufficient to destroy the pure nature from which alone the good fruit of right action could issue. Before the fall man was at liberty to do either good or evil, and he was able to do either. After the fall he remained free to do either good or evil, but he was able to do only evil. Now "every intent of the thoughts of his heart was only evil continually" (Gen. 6:5; compare 8:21; 1 Cor. 2:14; Pss. 14, 53). The prophet put it like this: "Can the Ethiopian change his skin or the leopard its spots? Then may you also do good who are accustomed to do evil" (Jer. 13:23). Sinful man cannot even do that one good thing necessary to bring his deliverance. No man is able to come to Christ (John 6:44). But this is due to his own nature; he is not kept from any good by external force or coercion. He is kept from it by the very "laws" of his own depraved character.

Just as a corpse has arms and legs which lie unused because the one who exercised them is dead, but which are used again when God resurrects the body, so it is with the will of man. He is spiritually dead. He is able to do good only as he is regenerated in order that he may again possess the good heart to will and to do God's good pleasure (Eph. 2:1–7; John 3:3; Phil. 2:13). The regenerate man possesses the same liberty that Adam had before the fall and that sinners had after the fall. The difference between an unregenerate man and a regenerate man is one of ability, not liberty. Both are free to do good, but only the regenerate man is *able* to do good. And he is able because God the Holy Spirit has given him a new heart (Eph. 2:10; 1 John 5:18; Ezek. 36:26). He is made a new creature (Gal. 6:15). Therefore, he has ability to will and to do what is good.

Yet the regenerate man's ability is not identical with that which Adam originally had. Adam was once able to do God's will perfectly. The regenerate man is not yet able to do God's will perfectly. This does not mean that he is not a new creature indeed. He is. He does truly delight in the will of God. He does persist in the way of righteousness (1 John 3:9). Sin cannot prevail in him as it formerly did (1 John 3:3; Eph. 5:9; Rom. 6:14). But sin is present with him (Rom. 7:21). The reason for this is that those who are new creatures in Christ are in the process of being made holy. They are not finished products even though they are wholly changed in essence. They are only what they ought to be "in principle." Some day they will be what they ought to be "in detail." But now God's work is being wrought in them. He now works in them to will and to do, more and more, of his good pleasure.

By and by God's work in the regenerate will be done (with glorification). But even then, man will possess essentially the same liberty that he now has. The difference, again, will be in the measure of his ability, not liberty, to do good. He will then be able to do only that which is right. This will be because his nature will then be confirmed in holiness and wholly contrary to all evil. He will no longer be susceptible to sin's attraction. He will not even possess the slightest desire to do anything evil anymore. May the Lord grant that both author and reader may see that day.

QUESTIONS

1. What false accusation is frequently made against the Reformed faith?
2. What do we mean by "free will"?
3. What do we not mean by "free will"?
4. What two distinct things do people often confuse in discussions of this matter?
5. State the two facts taught in the Bible concerning our liberty and ability.
6. What is it that determines the will?
7. In what estates is man at liberty (to do good or evil)?
8. In what estates is man able to do good?
9. In what estates is man able to do evil?
10. Prove from Scripture that fallen (unregenerate) men cannot will anything spiritually good.
11. Why is the regenerate man not able to do good perfectly in this life?

10

X. Of Effectual Calling

1. *All those whom God hath predestinated unto life, and those only, he is pleased, in his appointed and accepted time, effectually to call, by his Word and Spirit, out of that state of sin and death in which they are by nature, to grace and salvation by Jesus Christ; enlightening their minds spiritually and savingly to understand the things of God; taking away their heart of stone, and giving unto them an heart of flesh; renewing their wills, and by his almighty power determining them to that which is good; and effectually drawing them to Jesus Christ; yet so as they come most freely, being made willing by his grace.*

2. *This effectual call is of God's free and special grace alone, not from any thing at all foreseen in man; who is altogether passive therein, until, being quickened and renewed by the Holy Spirit, he is thereby enabled to answer this call, and to embrace the grace offered and conveyed in it.*

These sections of the Confession teach us (1) who they are who are effectually called, (2) when, (3) by what means, (4) from what moral and spiritual condition, (5) to what moral and spiritual condition, (6) in what manner they are effectually called, and (7) that this effectual call is wholly of God.

We here begin a survey of the *ordo salutis*—the order of the application of redemption to the elect. In this order we distinguish the following: (1) the free offer of salvation in the gospel (God's general *call*), (2) *regeneration* (the creative act of God making the elect new beings in heart), (3) *conversion* (the exercise of that new heart in responding to the gospel in repentance and faith), (4) *justification* (the judicial act of God upon repentance and faith by which he declares and constitutes his elect "just" or righteous), (5) *adoption* (the act by which God admits them into the rights and privileges of sons of God), (6) *sanctification* (the work of God's Spirit by which the elect are enabled to persevere in faith unto ever greater conformity to the will of God), and (7) *glorification* (by which, at the resurrection of the body, the believer is at last constituted perfect in Christ in both body and soul, forever).

The first phase of the application of redemption is ordinarily effectual calling. We say "ordinarily" because there are certain exceptions. Section 3 of this chapter speaks of those who "are incapable of being outwardly called by the ministry of the Word," such as infants dying in infancy and persons who suffer from severe mental disorder. Such, of course, could not receive saving grace in quite the same way as others. In their case regeneration would take place apart from the ministry of the Word. And it is worth pausing to note that it is only supposedly harsh Calvinism which is able to offer a reasonable hope for such cases on the basis of its principles. Those who restrict the scope of divine sovereignty in order to suspend the operations of grace upon the powers of man must logically pay a heavy price at this very point. They can offer no hope— *on their principles*—to those who they must admit have no ability or power! Yet the absolute sovereignty of God in the salvation of men does not conflict with the fact that in all ordinary cases God employs the means which he himself has ordained. In all cases, except those specified, effectual calling is accomplished through the instrumentality of the preaching of the gospel. "It pleased God through the foolishness of the message preached to save those who believe" (1 Cor. 1:21).

God has commanded his Church to go into all the world to preach the gospel to everyone (Matt. 24:14; 28:19; Acts 1:8). The reason is that "faith comes by hearing, and hearing by the word of God" (Rom. 10:17). This does not mean that every human being in history will hear the gospel. Many will not (Eph. 2:11–12). God has appointed some to dwell in darkness until the set time for deliverance to come (Acts 17:26–27). And as there were nations appointed to darkness before Christ came, so God appointed the Jews (except for a remnant) to walk in darkness in this present era, until the fullness of the Gentiles is brought in (Rom. 11:25). Yet in the Old Testament era some Gentiles were effectually called, as in the New Testament era some Jews are also.

One of the fascinating facts of redemptive history is the way in which God has controlled all things in such a way that all who are elect (except such cases as previously mentioned) do actually hear the gospel in order that they might be saved. He saw to it that Rahab and Ruth heard the gospel. He sees to it that elect Jews (as well as others) hear it today. And so in the general task of expanding the witness of the Church to all the world, there is a divine control exercised so that the elect will hear the call of God.

Consider the case of Paul's second missionary journey. The whole world lay before him. Where then should he go? One choice would seem as good as the other. But when Paul thought to go into Bithynia, the Spirit of God intervened (Acts 16:7). He was directed, instead, to go to Macedonia. And so it came to pass that Lydia—whose heart the Lord opened—heard the Word of God, and that she heeded the things which were spoken by Paul (16:14). So it was, too, that the Philippian jailer was saved (16:30–34), and the Thessalonian church established. In this way, too, a few were brought to salvation in Athens, and a great many in Corinth. At Corinth God revealed his sovereign control over the distribution of his gospel unto men. God told Paul why he brought him to that place, instructing him to boldly preach the gospel, saying, "I am with you, and no one will attack you to hurt you; for I have many people in this city" (18:10). God sees to it that the elect hear his voice. "And other sheep I have which are not of this fold," said Jesus; "them also I must bring, and they will hear My voice" (John 10:16).

The gospel, then, comes to the elect. But it also comes to others with whom they are intermingled. It comes with good offers of grace and salvation to all. It makes no discrimination, and neither must those who preach it. Yet it is only some who are willing to receive it. And the question is: why do some accept and others reject this offer of eternal salvation? The answer is that it is contrary to the will and the desire of men to accept it, until—in the case of some—their basic nature is changed.

This change is the result of the instantaneous creation of a new heart in them by the almighty power of the Spirit of God. "I will give you a new heart and put a new spirit within you" (Ezek. 36:26). This is the "new birth" (John 3:3–6), the "new creation" (Eph. 2:10), which is likened in Scripture itself to being "raised from the dead." A careful study of John 3:1–8 will show that this sovereign work of the Holy Spirit is (1) *prevenient* (that is, it precedes all spiritual activity of man which pertains to salvation), (2) *monergistic* (that is, it is accomplished solely by the power of the Holy Spirit), (3) *mysterious* (it cannot be observed or described), (4) *sovereign* (it takes place when and where the Spirit wills), and (5) *effectual* (it invariably produces the desired result: the person consequently has spiritual abilities previously lacking—he can see and enter the kingdom).

Regeneration is something that man has no part in, so far as doing anything is concerned. He is wholly passive therein. He is not performing or operating in regeneration. Rather, he is operated on, and the result of that operation is that he has another heart or mind. This regeneration is closely associated with the preaching of the gospel (in ordinary cases), but it is not the gospel which regenerates. It is the Holy Spirit. We may think of the Word of God as the instrument employed by God to effect this regeneration, but the regenerating is done, not by the gospel itself, but only by the Holy Spirit who is pleased to operate by means of it.

This regeneration effects an essential change in the whole personality—the reason, the emotions, and the will. Such a one who is regenerated begins, immediately upon regeneration, to think differently, to feel differently, and to will differently than before. And because this is so, he will thankfully accept the free offer of the gospel. So God's call becomes effectual. It is effectual in every such case. Every elect person is enabled to repent and believe. And he does so because he begins to act out of a new nature created or implanted by regeneration. "So then it is not of him who wills, nor of him who runs, but of God who shows mercy" (Rom. 9:16). "Therefore He has mercy on whom He wills, and whom He wills He hardens" (9:18).

Arminianism evades the plan of Scripture by trying to make the work of God depend upon a work of man. It says that God foresees who will accept the gospel. Then because God foresees that a particular person will accept the gospel, he regenerates him when that time comes. But this makes regeneration a reward conferred rather than a gift which enables.

Under this view Paul would have said, "So then it *is* of him who wills, and of him who runs . . . and *not* of God who shows mercy." And under this view God would "have mercy on whom He must have mercy (because they are more worthy), and He would harden no one."

QUESTIONS

1. List the seven steps of the *ordo salutis* and define each.
2. How many of these steps does "effectual calling" embrace?
3. To whom ought the gospel to be preached?
4. To whom shall the gospel certainly be preached?
5. Why was Paul directed to Macedonia rather than Bithynia?
6. To what two classes of men does the gospel come?
7. Why do they react differently to the free offer of salvation?
8. According to John 3:1–8, describe the Holy Spirit's work of regeneration.
9. With what does Scripture compare regeneration?
10. What part does man perform in regeneration?
11. What is essentially changed in regeneration?
12. What do regenerated persons invariably do with the gospel offer?
13. How has Arminianism denied the truth regarding the Holy Spirit's work of regeneration?

X, 3

3. *Elect infants, dying in infancy, are regenerated and saved by Christ through the Spirit, who worketh when, and where, and how he pleaseth. So also are all other elect persons, who are incapable of being outwardly called by the ministry of the Word.*

This section of the Confession teaches (1) that there are some human beings "who are incapable of being outwardly called by the ministry of the Word," (2) that such may be elected, and (3) that in such cases the Spirit works when, where, and how he pleases.

Except in such cases as these, regeneration takes place in connection with the use of the means of grace which God himself has appointed. But there are some who are incapable of understanding the Spirit's word, not merely for reasons of spiritual inability but also from natural incapacity. That is, because of dying in infancy or being mentally deficient, they would not be able to understand the gospel *even though regenerated.*

It must be admitted, of course, that the Scripture does not say very much concerning the salvation of such persons, certainly not directly. Christ said that little children and even tiny infants are, as such, members of the kingdom (Luke 18:15–16 and parallel passages). And David expresses himself in such a way as to imply that infants dying in infancy may be saved (2 Sam. 12:23). But beyond these few statements, and such good and necessary inferences as may be drawn from such Scriptures, we are strictly limited in what we may legitimately say in this matter. It is important to note, therefore, that the original formulation of the Westminster Confession does carefully observe this limitation. It says only "elect infants, dying in infancy," without attempting to speculate about how many or few the number of such persons may be. And the same is true of "all other elect persons, who are incapable of being outwardly called by the ministry of the Word." Conceivably these could be very few in number, or very many. The important thing is that since the Scripture does not give us much information, we must not act as if it does. For this reason we believe that the so-called declarative statement appended to the Confession of Faith by the Presbyterian Church in the U.S.A. and retained today by the United Presbyterian Church is unwarranted, to say the least.

But here we have a strange thing. Calvinism is often looked upon as stern and forbidding. Many are horrified at the teaching of predestination and total human inability. Salvation that is possible for all, and that becomes actual by something that each is able to supply, seems more attractive than a salvation that is certain only for some because none can do anything. But the truth is that Calvinism is merciful and the opposing view is harsh, because the latter denies salvation to the weak and helpless, granting it only to the strong and able (supposedly). How can infants dying in infancy "decide" for Christ? How can the mentally deficient, of their own will, choose him, when they cannot even understand the meaning of simple words? Arminianism sounds very appealing when men imagine that they have ability to do in their own strength what must be done for salvation. But it offers no comfort at all for those who are helpless (such as infants dying in infancy).

Only if Calvinism is true is there reason to hope for the salvation of such as these.

We rejoice in this and gladly assert that it is only on the basis of pure Reformed doctrine that there is a basis of hope for infants dying in infancy and others of like incapacity. But we regard it as perverse when this hope is made a sweeping claim (as in the Declaratory Statement mentioned above). It is to be suspected that the basis of this statement is not so much the text of the Bible as it is the humanistic notion that God could not justly condemn such helpless individuals. With this sentiment our Confession and the Bible have nothing to do. All men sinned in Adam and fell with him in his first transgression (Rom. 5:12). It is wholly within the just administration of God therefore to condemn all to everlasting punishment. If infants dying in infancy are human, they are also such as sinned in Adam, and they are therefore guilty and liable to damnation. If they are to be saved, it can never be "because it would be unjust for God to condemn them," but only because he has elected them to eternal life which they do not deserve.

We can assert that there are elect infants who die in infancy. We can also assert that believers have special warrant to hope that their infants who die in infancy are such (Luke 18:15–16; 2 Sam. 12:23; Acts 2:38–39; Ezek. 16:20–21). Beyond this we may not go. We may legitimately hope, but we may not demand.

QUESTIONS

1. Name the exceptions to the teaching that salvation is by effectual calling.
2. Does the Reformed faith (or Calvinism) provide hope for more or fewer souls than does Arminianism?
3. Why?
4. What text of Scripture affirms that infants may be regenerated as infants?
5. What careful limitation of Scripture does the Confession observe?
6. What unwarranted declaration is maintained by the United Presbyterian Church?
7. What important teaching of Scripture does this undermine?
8. Are all infants of believers necessarily elected?

X, 4

4. *Others, not elected, although they may be called by the ministry of the Word, and may have some common operations of the Spirit, yet they never truly come unto Christ, and therefore cannot be saved: much less can men not professing the Christian religion be saved in any other way whatsoever, be they ever so diligent to frame their lives according to the light of nature and the law of that religion they do profess; and to assert and maintain that they may is very pernicious, and to be detested.*

This section of the Confession teaches us (1) that those who are not elected will not be saved (2) because they will not come to Christ (3) even though they may hear the Word and be powerfully affected by supernatural forces, and (4) that the light of nature affords those untouched by the gospel with no basis for saving faith, for which reason they are without God and without hope.

Out of the totality of men only some hear the gospel. Of this number only some are savingly affected by it. Only the elect respond to it, and this they do only after—and because—God gives them a new heart by the creative power of his Holy Spirit in regeneration. This inward ability is bestowed upon the elect only, and this is why they come to Christ to be saved. The credit therefore belongs to God alone.

But what of the others who hear? First, let it be remembered that they also are called by the ministry of the Word. And this call is "genuine." It is "sincere." God entreats them to come to Christ. He takes no delight in the fact that they refuse to listen (God *never* takes delight in sin! Ezek. 18:32; 2 Peter 3:9).

Second, we must appreciate the extent to which even such persons may experience the power of the gospel. Christ's parable of the sower and the soils reminds us that it is possible to give every appearance of being in possession of faith and obedient for a time, and even to evidence great zeal for the things of Christ, and then to lose all interest or even to lapse into hostility to the kingdom. The Scripture speaks of those "who were once enlightened . . . and have tasted the good word of God and the powers of the age to come" (Heb. 6:4–5). Peter uses strong words to describe the miserable case of those who have experienced these things only to fall back into their old ways (2 Peter 2:20–22). "The Scripture itself, therefore, leads us to the conclusion that it is possible to have very uplifting, ennobling, reforming, and exhilarating experience of the power and truth of the gospel, to come into such close contact with the supernatural forces which are operative in God's kingdom of grace that these forces produce effects in us which to human observation are hardly distinguishable from those produced by God's regenerating and sanctifying grace, and yet be not partakers of Christ and heirs of eternal life" (John Murray, *Redemption Accomplished and Applied* [Grand Rapids: Eerdmans, 1955]).

Third, we must observe that the one fatal defect is that "they never truly come to Christ." They seem to do so. But they do not really do so. They have no genuine repentance and faith. And *for this reason* they cannot be saved. The entire fault lies in them (just as, in the case of the elect, the entire credit belongs to God). Of all who hear the gospel and perish the words of Jesus are true: "you are not willing to come to Me that you may have life" (John 5:40). It is true, of course, that they *are not willing* because they are totally depraved by nature. It is also true that God alone can replace that totally depraved heart with a new heart which will want to come to Christ. But God owes this gift to none. And those who do not receive it still have no one to blame but themselves for rejecting the offer of God's grace.

If those who hear the gospel and fail to accept it cannot be saved, what about those who are not touched by it at all? If they are "diligent to frame their lives according to the light of nature" or "the law of that religion they do profess," will they not be accepted of God? It would not be an exaggeration to say that there has been a revolution in the attitude of Protestants concerning this question. Prior to the modernist-fundamentalist controversy in the early decades of the twentieth century, most Protestant denominations in the United States maintained foreign mission work because it was believed that men would eternally perish without the knowledge of Christ. Then came the startling thesis expressed by the "Layman's Inquiry" into the basis of foreign missions (entitled *Rethinking Missions*) which suggested that the foreign mission program should be one of learning as well as teaching, and that the foreign missionary should seek a synthesis with other religions rather than only conversions from them.

Sixty years and more have passed. And now the leaders of the ecumenical movement (as disclosed by the statements of the missions section of the World Council of Churches) openly assert that the adherents of "pagan" religions may be "saved" without hearing the gospel of Christ at all. And in more and more instances the older Protestant denominations have placed primary emphasis upon works of relief, medicine, education, and the like rather than upon the preaching of the gospel in their foreign mission fields.

But the truth is that this is a useless enterprise in the long run. There is a relationship between these social and economic blessings and the gospel. We enjoy these blessings because, to an extent, the gospel has leavened our society. And to the extent that the true gospel is forgotten or rejected, the benefits that we have enjoyed will disappear. It is even more evident that the transformation of the so-called underprivileged or underdeveloped nations will never be possible without that inward change of heart that only the gospel can bring.

What will millions of dollars, or even billions, do for a country where the cow is worshiped and human life devalued? But above all, we must face the fact that apart from any temporary alleviation of man's misery by outside help through social and economic aid, the souls of men are doomed without the gospel of Christ. It is this conviction which always has and always will provide the sense of urgency and perspective that the missionary task requires. "Nor is there salvation in any other, for there is no other name under heaven given among men by which we must be saved" (Acts 4:12). "He who has the Son has life; and he who does not have the Son of God does not have life" (1 John 5:12).

QUESTIONS

1. Divide the human race into three classes (in relation to the gospel).
2. Is God's call "sincere"? Prove this.
3. To what extent may a person be affected by the gospel without true conversion?
4. Why do such persons fail to come to Christ?
5. Is this the fault of God? Explain.
6. Who receives the blame for the end that overtakes unbelievers?
7. Who receives sole credit for the end enjoyed by true believers?
8. Can those who do not hear the gospel be saved through their own religion?

9. Why is it ultimately fruitless to attempt to "help them" through social and economic aid alone?

10. What is the present-day attitude among modernists toward "pagan" religions?

11. Cite Scripture proof for the original Protestant position expressed in our Confession of Faith.

11

XIV. Of Saving Faith
and
XV. Of Repentance unto Life

XIV, 1–3

1. *The grace of faith, whereby the elect are enabled to believe to the saving of their souls, is the work of the Spirit of Christ in their hearts, and is ordinarily wrought by the ministry of the Word: by which also, and by the administration of the sacraments, and prayer, it is increased and strengthened.*

2. *By this faith, a Christian believeth to be true whatsoever is revealed in the Word, for the authority of God himself speaking therein; and acteth differently upon that which each particular passage thereof containeth; yielding obedience to the commands, trembling at the threatenings, and embracing the promises of God for this life and that which is to come. But the principal acts of saving faith are, accepting, receiving, and resting upon Christ alone for justification, sanctification, and eternal life, by virtue of the covenant of grace.*

3. *This faith is different in degrees, weak or strong; may be often and many ways assailed and weakened, but gets the victory; growing up*

in many to the attainment of a full assurance through Christ, who is both the author and finisher of our faith.

XV, 1–5

1. *Repentance unto life is an evangelical grace, the doctrine whereof is to be preached by every minister of the gospel, as well as that of faith in Christ.*

2. *By it a sinner, out of the sight and sense, not only of the danger, but also of the filthiness and odiousness of his sins, as contrary to the holy nature and righteous law of God, and upon the apprehension of his mercy in Christ to such as are penitent, so grieves for and hates his sins as to turn from them all unto God, purposing and endeavoring to walk with him in all the ways of his commandments.*

3. *Although repentance be not to be rested in as any satisfaction for sin, or any cause of the pardon thereof, which is the act of God's free grace in Christ; yet is it of such necessity to all sinners that none may expect pardon without it.*

4. *As there is no sin so small but it deserves damnation; so there is no sin so great that it can bring damnation upon those who truly repent.*

5. *Men ought not to content themselves with a general repentance, but it is every man's duty to endeavor to repent of his particular sins particularly.*

At this point we depart from the order of the Confession of Faith so that we may discuss conversion in its logical relationship to effectual calling. Calling becomes effectual when conversion ensues. Only as conversion takes place are there effected justification, adoption, sanctification, and perseverance. This is not to find fault with the order in which the Confession of Faith deals with these doctrines. Evidently the reason for the order of the Confession is the desire to consider first the acts of God, and then the response of man (in repentance and faith). This is perfectly acceptable. But it is also helpful to view the *ordo salutis* in sequence. And to do so we need to place conversion (repentance and faith) after effectual calling.

To begin with, we must observe that regeneration is inseparable from its effects. And one of the effects is faith. Another is repentance. Regeneration is the renewing of the heart or mind, and the renewed personality must and will act according to its nature. In faith and repentance we simply see the new nature beginning to assert itself. Likewise it must be stressed that repentance and faith are the activity of the sinner alone, as regeneration is the act of God alone. It is God who regenerates, and it is the sinner who repents and believes. Finally, we must realize that repentance and faith are inseparable. There cannot be one without, or apart from, the other. For this reason we will in this instance consider these chapters together. Conversion follows regeneration, but repentance and faith accompany rather than follow one another.

True conversion is a complex matter. It involves a full-orbed transformation of the heart, mind, or personality of a man. As the lowly caterpillar is metamorphosed into a beautiful butterfly, so the sinner becomes a saint by the renewing of his mind (Rom. 12:2). Because man was made in the image of God, there is diversity within the unity of his personality. He has the faculties of reason, affection, and will. He can think or reason. He can feel deep desires. And he can choose between various alternatives. And full-orbed conversion involves all of these in their unity and diversity. Without any one of them, without all of them, the total personality does not experience true conversion.

Repentance and faith are two aspects of this full-orbed transformation of the soul. Repentance denotes that aspect of change whereby the soul turns from sin and experiences true abhorrence of it. Faith denotes that aspect of change whereby the soul turns to Christ and experiences supreme attachment to him. Both phases of this complete turning involve the total personality—reason, affections, and will. We may diagram this in figure 3.

It is important to emphasize that anything less than full-orbed conversion will not do. We shall cite certain examples. (1) Many "revival meeting" conversions fail to stand the test of time. This is well known, but the reason is often overlooked. In such cases it is obvious that the feelings, affections, or emotions are deeply involved. Then in response to the evangelist's pleading the will is exercised as the sinner "comes forward." What then is lacking? It is knowledge that is lacking. And without a scriptural knowledge of one's own depravity (on the one hand) and Jesus Christ's work of redemption (on the other hand) there can be no

FIG. 3

Conversion circle

1. Man must know his lost condition (Rom. 3:20; Ps. 51:3–4; Ezek. 36:31).
2. Man must have a broken and contrite heart (Jer. 31:19; Ps. 51:17; 2 Cor. 7:10f.).
3. Man must turn from the ways of sin (Acts 26:18; Ezek. 14:6; 2 Cor. 7:11).

Conversion

knowledge

Repentance   feeling   Faith

will

(The dotted line indicates that there is no hard and fast break between repentance and faith.)

1. Man must know the divine remedy for sin (Rom. 10:13–17; Ps. 9:10; Phil. 3:8).
2. Man must feel drawn to Christ with heart assent (John 4:42; 1 Thess. 2:13).
3. Man must turn to Christ to rely upon him alone for salvation (Acts 15:11; 16:31; Phil. 3:9).

true conversion. Because one important aspect of the person has been neglected, there is a defective conversion in spite of all appearances to the contrary.

(2) One of the dangers in an orthodox church is that knowledge and activity may pass for true conversion. Those who regularly hear sound preaching of doctrine, and who have certain group activities that are Christian, must ever be reminded that there is no true conversion without contrition and conviction of heart. In this sense there is such a thing as "dead orthodoxy." It is religion without feeling. It is also without hope.

(3) Another common condition is that in which sinners possess an adequate knowledge of the law and gospel of God, together with deep feelings of contrition and conviction, and yet never actually turn from death in sin to life in Christ. We might call this "spectator" religion. Christianity is, to them, like a great stage drama—they know it by heart—and it moves them deeply every time they see it—but they never become "part of the drama." This is not conversion. And it leads only to sorrow and death.

The Confession speaks of repentance and faith as "graces." That is, they are divine gifts (Acts 11:18; Eph. 2:8). When God regenerates a person, he implants the seed (or beginning) of repentance and faith. It is improper therefore to think of either repentance or faith as mere momentary acts. They are, rather, permanent states or conditions expressive of the soul. We may speak of the initial act of repentance and faith. But with this initial act begins an activity that never ceases thereafter (Luke 22:32). Because faith and repentance are given by God they cannot fail.

QUESTIONS

1. Why does the Confession probably follow the order it does rather than that of the *ordo salutis?*
2. Where does "conversion" come in the *ordo salutis?*
3. What is the relationship between regeneration and conversion?
4. Can faith and repentance separately exist? Why?
5. Why must we call conversion a complex matter?
6. What are the three faculties of man's soul?
7. What are the two phases or parts of conversion?
8. Describe three types of defective conversions.
9. Why are repentance and faith called graces?
10. Are these momentary acts or constant conditions of the soul?

XIV, 1–3; XV, 1–5 (continued)

In this section we shall briefly consider certain classic errors in the realm of repentance and faith.

One such error is the Roman Catholic dogma of penance. According to A. A. Hodge, "Romanists distinguish penance (1) as a virtue, which is internal, including sorrow for sin and a turning from sin unto God, (2) as a *sacrament,* which is the external expression of the internal state. This sacrament consists of (a) *contrition* (i.e., sorrow and detestation of past sins, with a purpose of sinning no more), (b) *confession* (or self-accusation to a priest having jurisdiction and the power of the keys), (c) *satisfaction* (or some painful work, imposed by the priest and performed by the penitent, to satisfy divine justice for sins committed), and (d) *absolution* (pronounced by the priest judicially and not merely declaratively)" (*The Confession of Faith* [London: Banner of Truth, 1958], p. 214). And as Hodge points out, in this view this painful work "makes a real satisfaction for sin" and is "absolutely essential: the only means whereby the pardon of sins committed after baptism can be secured." There is, then, in the Roman Catholic view of repentance, as at least a prominent element, the notion that the sinner can and must pay for his own sins and thus win the favor of God.

It is no exaggeration to say that the biblical view of repentance is precisely the opposite of this. True repentance is a recognition of the fact, conviction of the fact, and assent to the fact that there is no possible way in which the sinner could satisfy divine justice other than to experience eternal damnation. Indeed, it is precisely this recognition, conviction, and assent which also require him to trust in the suffering satisfaction of Christ alone for salvation. We could not more radically misconceive repentance than to regard it as a work performed. Rather is it the abject realization that the favor of God can never thus be won at all.

The Arminian doctrine of "evangelical repentance" is also seriously in error. The doctrine teaches that repentance precedes regeneration. It is based upon the assumption that the unregenerate man is not really nor utterly dead in sin nor destitute of all powers unto spiritual good, but that he can yet hunger and thirst after righteousness and offer the sacrifice of a contrite and broken spirit which is pleasing to God (Canons of Dordt, III–IV, "Rejection of Errors," par. 4). This state of mind or heart is held to be a self-generated act of obedience, in return for which God bestows the gift of eternal life.

It is not as obvious that Arminianism treats repentance as a work, as does the Roman Catholic view, but there is no essential difference. For again, we must insist that repentance, far from being a meritorious act of obedience well pleasing unto God and bringing in return his blessing and reward, is rather a consciousness of one's total inability to please God or to do anything deserving of his blessing and reward. This is precisely the psychological as well as theological reason why there can be no true repentance without faith in Christ. When one is conscious of complete inability to do anything that would turn away God's wrath and curse and win his favor, he is ready to trust in Jesus Christ who has borne that wrath and curse and won his favor as the substitute for his people.

In the realm of faith, as in that of repentance, some have intruded the doctrine of human ability and merit. But as John Murray has said, "Faith is not something that merits the favor of God. All the efficacy unto salvation resides in the Savior. As one has aptly and truly stated the case, it is not faith that saves but faith in Jesus Christ; strictly speaking, it is not even faith in Christ that saves but Christ that saves through faith" (*Redemption Accomplished and Applied* [Grand Rapids: Eerdmans, 1955], p. 139). "The specific character of faith is that it looks away from itself and finds its whole interest and object in Christ. He is the absorbing preoccupation of faith." Anything other than utter trust in and dependence upon Christ is not faith in the scriptural sense.

QUESTIONS

1. What elements of the Roman Catholic teaching concerning penance (when considered apart from the errors) are proper to a view of repentance?
2. What is the element which is precisely opposed to biblical repentance?
3. What does the biblical conception stress against this?
4. What assumption underlies the Arminian conception of repentance?
5. In what way is it essentially the same as the Roman Catholic doctrine?
6. What must be stressed in opposition to the Arminian view?
7. What must be rigidly excluded, at all cost, from the true view of repentance and faith?

XV, 6

6. *As every man is bound to make private confession of his sins to God, praying for the pardon thereof, upon which, and the forsaking of them, he shall find mercy; so he that scandalizeth his brother, or the Church of Christ, ought to be willing, by a private or public confession and sorrow for his sin, to declare his repentance to those that are offended, who are thereupon to be reconciled to him, and in love to receive him.*

This section of the Confession teaches us the Protestant doctrine of confession, which is (1) that all sins are to be confessed to God, and (2) that certain sins should also be confessed to those against whom they have been committed.

It is commonly thought that only Roman Catholics are under obligation to confess their sins. The truth is that the scope of this duty is nowhere recognized as it is in the churches that are faithful to the Reformation. The Reformed faith recognizes, as Roman Catholicism cannot, the true magnitude of this duty. Its view is correspondingly deeper and more searching. (1) This is true, in the first place, because of the recognition that all sin must be confessed to God rather than merely to man. "If we confess our sins, He is faithful and just to forgive us our sins, and to cleanse us from all unrighteousness" (1 John 1:9). It is much more awesome to face God than to face man. It is also efficacious, whereas no mere man has the power to forgive sins. "For this cause everyone who is godly shall pray to You in a time when You may be found," says David (Ps. 32:6). (2) The Reformed view is true, secondly, because of the recognition that the sinfulness of the heart is more to be confessed than even the sins which proceed from it (Pss. 51; 38:3–10). It is easier to recite a list of sins than it is to mourn the defilement of the heart. (3) Thirdly, confession is a duty which requires much greater constancy than is true on the Roman Catholic view. "Evening and morning and at noon I will pray, and cry aloud, and He shall hear my voice" (Ps. 55:17).

But how can a defiled sinner stand before that holy God who is a consuming fire? Does he not *need* a priest who can stand between? He does indeed need one who can (1) remove God's wrath, and (2) absolve his own guilt and remove defilement. But no priest of Rome can do so for the simple reason that he also is defiled. And it is the glory of the gospel of Christ and the Reformed Confession that they inform us of the only Savior and priest who is able to do what the situation requires. He was "made like His brethren, that He might be a merciful and faithful High Priest in things pertaining to God, to make propitiation for the sins of the people" (Heb. 2:17). By the sacrifice of himself he removed God's wrath *and* our defilement. He then ascended up on high in order to make intercession for us. For this reason we are commanded in the Word of God to acknowledge none other to be our priest. We are not to imagine that he "cannot sympathize with" our infirmities, but we are to come boldly to him for mercy and relief (Heb. 4:15–16). Therefore no sin can be removed until it is confessed unto God through him.

Our primary duty is to regard all sin as an offense against God. And we are to confess all our sins to him (Ps. 51:4). However, Scripture also requires that we confess our sins *against* one another *to* each other. "Confess your trespasses to one another," says the apostle (James 5:16). This duty is implied in the Lord's Prayer (Matt. 6:12). As we are to seek forgiveness by confessing our trespasses to those against whom we have sinned, so we are to be ready to forgive any who trespass against us (Luke 17:3–4). Only one against whom the sin was committed can forgive. Apart from those offenses against individuals which ought to be confessed to them individually, and against corporate bodies which ought to be confessed publicly, all confession and forgiveness are between the sinner and his Lord.

QUESTIONS

1. Does Roman Catholicism require confession of sin more than does the Reformed faith?
2. In what ways does the Reformed faith recognize the magnitude of this duty as Roman Catholicism does not?
3. Do we need a priest in confession of sin? Why?
4. Why can a Roman priest not satisfy our need in confession of sin?
5. Why may we have confidence that Christ is not "too high" to supply this need?
6. Why may we have confidence that Christ is able to supply this need?
7. What sins are to be confessed to men as well as to God?
8. What sins are not to be confessed to men but only to God?

12

XI. Of Justification

1. *Those whom God effectually calleth he also freely justifieth; not by infusing righteousness into them, but by pardoning their sins, and by accounting and accepting their persons as righteous: not for anything wrought in them, or done by them, but for Christ's sake alone; not by imputing faith itself, the act of believing, or any other evangelical obedience, to them as their righteousness; but by imputing the obedience and satisfaction of Christ unto them, they receiving and resting on him and his righteousness by faith: which faith they have not of themselves, it is the gift of God.*

2. *Faith, thus receiving and resting on Christ and his righteousness, is the alone instrument of justification; yet is it not alone in the person justified, but is ever accompanied with all other saving graces, and is no dead faith, but worketh by love.*

These sections teach us (1) that those who are effectually called (regenerated and converted) are also justified, (2) that justification is judicial, (3) that it is effected by imputation, (4) that it is conditioned by, and instrumentally applied through, faith (which is a gift from God), and (5) that while justification is by faith alone, it is invariably productive of good works.

Only those who are effectually called of God are also justified by him. Paul expresses this succinctly when he affirms that "whom He predestined, these He also called; whom He called, these He also justified; and whom He justified, these He also glorified" (Rom. 8:30). Justification is never found by itself. It is one link in the golden chain of the redemptive work of God. Justification is by faith. But there can be no faith except in one who is regenerated by the Spirit of God. And regeneration is accomplished in those whom the Lord has chosen from the foundation of the world (Eph. 1:4–5, 11; 2:4–10).

But what is justification? It is "an act of God's free grace, wherein he pardoneth all our sins, and accepteth us as righteous in his sight, only for the righteousness of Christ imputed to us, and received by faith alone" (Shorter Catechism, Q. 33). It is God's answer to our most perplexing need: how can sinful man be just with God? The lamentable fact is that we are all wrong with God. We have sinned and come short of his glory (Rom. 3:23). "Far too frequently we fail to entertain the gravity of this fact. Hence the reality of our sin and the reality of the wrath of God upon us for our sin do not come into our reckoning. This is the reason why the grand article of justification does not ring the bells in the innermost depths of our spirit" (John Murray, *Redemption Accomplished and Applied* [Grand Rapids: Eerdmans, 1955]). Only when we realize, by God-given grace and conviction, what utter sinfulness and pollution dwell in the very depths of our nature can we learn what it means to be justified.

Central to a right grasp of this great article of our faith is the fact that "it is God who justifies" (Rom. 8:33). Justification is that which we do not and cannot effect for ourselves. It is "not any religious exercise in which we engage however noble and good that religious exercise may be" (Murray, *Redemption*). This fact is underscored by another. Justification does not mean that one is to *be*, or be made, or *become* inherently good, holy, or upright. To the contrary, it is the *sinner* who is justified, and at the very instant that he is declared just by God, he remains inherently sinful and unworthy.

This does not mean that internal holiness is left unprovided for in the plan of salvation. Not at all. True believers are sanctified, as surely as they are justified. They are required to engage in the task of "perfecting holiness in the fear of God" (2 Cor. 7:1), "without which no one shall see the Lord" (Heb. 12:14). This personal, internal, inherent holiness must and shall be realized by a process which takes time. But justification does not take time. Neither does it await completion of sanctification. It is *not* a process, but an instantaneous act of God, applied without delay to the (as yet) unsanctified sinner as soon as he believes. He is then and there, and from that time forth, regarded by God as if he were perfectly righteous.

Justification is not a term meaning to make a person holy. It is rather a legal declaration. It is in this sense that we find it in Scripture. "If there is a dispute between men, and they come to court, that the judges may judge them," it is their duty to "justify the righteous and condemn the wicked" (Deut. 25:1). This text speaks of human judges, and it stresses the obligation to declare the righteous to be righteous, and the wicked to be guilty. Imagine what a travesty of justice it would be if they did otherwise! But if the word "justify" meant "to actually make righteous," it would be hard to see that the Lord would condemn such. What is more pleasing to him than for the wicked to forsake wickedness and be righteous? So then, if the human judge cannot justify the wicked, then neither can the term "justify" mean to make the wicked man just. It means to declare, rather than to constitute, him what he is. When the publicans justified God (Luke 7:29), they did not make him just; they only declared him to be just. And conversely, when the judge condemns the wicked (Deut. 25:1), he does not make him wicked; he only declares that he is wicked. Justification, like condemnation, is a judicial declaration. And thus justification is said to be judicial. It concerns that judgment which is declared. We must therefore carefully distinguish between such an act as regeneration (which institutes a change of nature) and justification (which declares a change of status). "The distinction is like that of the distinction between the act of a surgeon and the act of a judge. The surgeon, when he removes an inward cancer, does something in us. That is not what a judge does—he gives a verdict regarding our judicial status" (Murray, *Redemption*).

But here is the marvel of justification. God does what a human judge cannot and must not do. He declares righteous those who are really ungodly (Rom. 4:5; 3:19–24). If men were to do so it would be abomination (Prov. 17:15). But God does so and yet is not unrighteous in doing it. The question is: how? The answer is: God provides a just and legal basis upon which to declare the unrighteous to be just. And he does this by *imputation*. By imputation he is able to cause the sinner to legally possess a righteousness and to be freed from unrighteousness even while a sinner. And having thus *constituted* sinners righteous, he is able to *declare* them to be such.

Imputation means to "reckon, think, or regard." When an innocent man is reckoned or thought to be guilty, he will complain that men are falsely *imputing* guilt to him. They consider him to be what he actually is not. So it is with us. God (without doing wrong) regards us to be righteous. The reason that God can do this is that Christ kept the law perfectly and thus worked out a perfect righteousness which he then freely offered to the Father on our behalf for this purpose. God is able to reckon us free from guilt. The reason is that Christ placed himself in our room and stead so that God could consider our guilt to belong to him. He was condemned just as we are justified. We speak of "double imputation" because of Christ's active (perfectly obeying God's law) and passive (fully suffering the penalty of the law against sin) obedience. God regards his righteousness to be ours, and our guilt to be his. Without imputation of both (our guilt to him and his righteousness to us) there would be no basis for justification. But upon this basis God is able to declare us righteous in his sight. And this declarative act is justification.

From this it clearly emerges that the *sole ground* of our justification is the obedience of Christ. It cannot be, in any sense, our own righteousness. This thought is beautifully expressed by Paul: "I also count all things loss for the excellence of the knowledge of Christ Jesus my Lord, for whom I have suffered the loss of all things, and count them as rubbish, that I may gain Christ and be found in Him, not having my own righteousness, which is from the law, but that which is through faith in Christ, the righteousness which is from God by faith" (Phil. 3:8–9). Since we have no righteousness of our own, and since we must have *perfect* righteousness before God in order that he might declare that we are righteous, there can be no mixture of our own righteousness with that of Christ imputed to us. Saving faith is simply "receiving and resting on Christ and his righteousness," and is for this reason "the alone instrument of justification." God requires of us nothing except utter reliance upon the righteousness and satisfaction of Christ.

This means that at the instant we begin to trust in Christ we are then and there declared to be legally without sin, guilt, or future punishment. This declaration cannot depend upon anything done by the sinner.

Faith—which is not "doing" something ourselves, but only our depending upon what Christ has done—instantaneously results in complete and eternal justification, provided it be true faith. If it is true faith, it will also produce good works, which are the one sure evidence of it. Of this we shall have more to say in our discussion of chapter XVI.

QUESTIONS

1. With what is justification always linked?
2. What is man's most perplexing question?
3. What do we need to realize to properly respond to the doctrine of justification?
4. Who justifies?
5. What does justification *not* mean?
6. Does this mean that sinners will be saved without personal holiness?
7. How long does justification take?
8. What does "justify" mean? Prove from Scripture.
9. Why do we call justification a "judicial" act?
10. Is it wrong for men to justify the ungodly? Why?
11. Is it wrong for God to justify the ungodly? Why?
12. What basis has God provided in order that he might justly justify?
13. What does "imputation" mean?
14. What does "double imputation" mean?
15. Why must the obedience of Christ be the *sole ground* of our justification?
16. Are we saved by "faith alone"?
17. Are we saved by faith that is alone?

XI, 3–6

3. *Christ, by his obedience and death, did fully discharge the debt of all those that are thus justified, and did make a proper, real, and full satisfaction to his Father's justice in their behalf. Yet, in as much as he was given by the Father for them, and his obedience and satisfaction accepted in their stead, and both freely, not for any thing in them, their justification is only of free grace; that both the exact*

justice and rich grace of God might be glorified in the justification of sinners.

4. *God did, from all eternity, decree to justify all the elect; and Christ did, in the fullness of time, die for their sins, and rise again for their justification: nevertheless they are not justified until the Holy Spirit doth in due time actually apply Christ unto them.*

5. *God doth continue to forgive the sins of those that are justified; and although they can never fall from the state of justification, yet they may by their sins fall under God's fatherly displeasure, and not have the light of his countenance restored unto them, until they humble themselves, confess their sin, beg pardon, and renew their faith and repentance.*

6. *The justification of believers under the Old Testament was, in all these respects, one and the same with the justification of believers under the New Testament.*

These sections teach us (1) that Christ has provided the basis for our justification, (2) that this is of free grace (since Christ's placing himself in our stead was voluntary, as was God's accepting him as our substitute), (3) that the justification of the elect was eternally decreed, historically accomplished by Christ, and yet is applied only in time by the Holy Spirit, (4) that God justifies sinners even with respect to sins committed after they believe, (5) that this does not mean that they cannot and do not fall under his displeasure and chastisement, and (6) that justification is essentially the same for all believers in all ages.

We have already shown that Christ provided the basis for our justification by his active and passive obedience (VIII, 5; XI, 1–2). We have also proved that this was wholly voluntary on his part, as was God's accepting him as our substitute (John 10:17–18; 1 Tim. 2:6; Eph. 5:2). The following facts indicate that "justification is only of free grace." (1) It was an act of free grace that God permitted another to be our substitute. (2) It was an act of free grace that God gave his only begotten Son to be our substitute. (3) It was an act of free grace that God chose many out of a lost race to be represented by him. (4) It was an act of free grace that God bestowed the rewards which are the inheritance of the redeemed because of Christ's finished work (see A. A. Hodge, *The Confession of Faith* [London: Banner of Truth, 1958], p. 186).

There are some who have held that the elect are justified from eternity. And the Bible does speak of these as "written in the Book of Life of the Lamb slain from the foundation of the world" (Rev. 13:8). The error in this view is the failure to make distinction between the decree (or plan) of God, and the execution of that decree. It is true that God foreordained the justification of the elect. Thus Paul could speak of "the Scripture foreseeing that God would justify the Gentiles by faith" (Gal. 3:8). But he does not say that God already had justified them. As Peter said, the sacrifice of Christ (which is the basis for justification) "indeed was foreordained before the foundation of the world, but was manifest in these last times for you" (1 Peter 1:20). One could as well say that the elect are already glorified, even risen from the grave, as to say that they were justified from eternity. Justification is an event that takes place in time just as much as is glorification (Rom. 8:30). Thus we must reject the notion that the elect have been justified from eternity.

But others have said that we are justified from the time that Jesus finished his mediatorial work. The advocates of this view point out that Christ *"was* delivered up because of our offenses, and *was* raised because of our justification" (Rom. 4:25). God already "made Him . . . to be sin for us" (2 Cor. 5:21) and "by one offering He has perfected forever those who are being sanctified" (Heb. 10:14). This view may be made to sound quite plausible, more so than the "justification from eternity" view. But we must reject it as firmly as we must reject the other. The error in this view is the failure to distinguish between the work of Christ, which is the basis for justification, and the work of the Holy Spirit, by which, on that basis, sinners are actually put in possession of righteousness before God. As Paul says in Colossians 1:21, we "who once were alienated and enemies in [our] mind by wicked works, yet *now* He has reconciled" us to God. For a time, even though the work of Christ was finished, we remained the enemies of God. Then we were effectually called and enabled to repent and to believe. *Now* we are reconciled to God and justified in his sight. For this reason Scripture says, "We have believed in Christ Jesus, that we might be justified" (Gal. 2:16).

Faith is antecedent to justification. Justification follows faith in due order. Imputation, which provides the conditions requisite for God's declaration, is itself contingent upon faith. "It shall be imputed," says Paul, "to us who believe in Him" (Rom. 4:24). Therefore, we must say that while God provided the basis for justification in the finished work of Christ, yet the actual application of such to men is distinct from it. This may be seen from the fact that men were justified before the work of Christ was finished (Ps. 32:1–2). And it is even more clearly seen in the fact that men living since the work of Christ has been completed are justified only when they believe. "And by Him everyone who believes is justified from all things" (Acts 13:39).

One of the basic errors of Roman Catholicism is confusion of justification and sanctification, that is, between legal and inherent righteousness. Rome teaches that at certain times (such as immediately after baptism, or reception of one of the other sacraments) a person is "just." What is meant, however, is that the person is actually made internally holy and not just legally righteous before God. This holiness, according to Rome, can then be partially or even totally destroyed by sin, venial or mortal. A person may cease to be just. He must again be justified through sacramental grace. And on it goes in a constant cycle. Sin nullifies sacramental grace, and then sacramental grace nullifies sin. This is a doctrine that gives no peace (see Rom. 5:1). One can never be certain of his standing with God. But more than this, it does not make sense. For if sacramental grace actually produced inward holiness, then why would that person ever sin again? If justification meant perfect inward holiness, then there could be no further sin, because a "perfect tree will bring forth perfect fruit" (see Luke 6:43–45).

This difficulty is removed when we distinguish between justification and sanctification. In justification the sinner is once and for all *declared* holy, legally absolved from all guilt and punishment of sin, whether original or actual, past or future. In sanctification the sinner is gradually and progressively *purged* of all pollution and practice of sin, so that sin is progressively weakened (in the long run), and inherent holiness becomes progressively stronger, until finally the person becomes (at death) actually as righteous as he has long been legally.

"If we say that we have no sin, we deceive ourselves, and the truth is not in us" (1 John 1:8). Rome does say this; it says that sacramental grace can render the sinner (at least momentarily) sinless in this life. The Reformed faith, with a proper distinction between justification and sanctification, never says, "We have no sin." But it does say, with respect to true believers, "We have no guilt" (Heb. 10:14). There can be "no condemnation to those who are in Christ Jesus" (Rom. 8:1). Being justified, they can never be anything but legally righteous in his sight.

Does this mean that God will view lightly the actual sins of his justified people? "Shall we continue in sin that grace may abound?" (Rom. 6:1). Some, recognizing the provision made by justification (i.e., that believers can never fall from that state), have foolishly suggested this. But there are two reasons for rejecting this evil suggestion. (1) The first reason for rejecting this evil suggestion is the fact that it envisions a condition which the Scripture declares to be a delusion. It is a delusion to imagine that a justified person can also continue to live in sin. The great truth which is the antidote to this evil thought is that a person who is *really* justified will also possess all other saving graces including the determination to strive after holiness of heart and life. If a person is really justified, it is because he has true faith. But if a person has true faith, it will be productive of good works. "Faith . . . if it does not have works, is dead" (James 2:17). It would be no more foolish to pretend to have justification without faith than it would to pretend to have justification without abhorrence of sin.

(2) But a second reason for rejecting this evil suggestion is that Scripture teaches so clearly God's displeasure against the sins of his people. When true believers (such as David, Moses, or Peter) did become presumptuous or careless, they soon discovered his fatherly displeasure, and they learned what it was to be deprived of the light of his countenance (Pss. 32, 51). The chastisements of God are as "painful" (Heb. 12:11) as they are beneficial for the children of God. And there is not one child of God, who sins against him, who does not in a measure learn what his chastisement means (Heb. 12:8). Even if a believer should fall into this sad error (of believing that because he is justified he may continue in sin), he would soon regret his mistake. For the hand of the Lord will teach that one his displeasure against such, even if that one neglects his Word.

One thing remains to be mentioned. It is the doctrine of justification as it relates to the covenant. Dispensationalism, which we have previously discussed, is particularly dangerous here in that it tends to deny, or at least to obscure, the fact that "the justification of believers under the Old Testament was [essentially] one and the same with the justification of believers under the New Testament." For example, it is sometimes said that in the Mosaic dispensation men were supposed to be justified by keeping the law. The truth is that the law was given to Moses in order to make men the more conscious of their need of the tabernacle, and thus of Christ (Gal. 3:21–24). There was as much "grace" as there was "law" in the Mosaic era. The revelation of God in the tables of stone was accompanied by the pattern of the tabernacle shown to Moses in the mount.

QUESTIONS

1. How may it be shown that "justification is only of free grace"?
2. What is meant by "justification from eternity"?
3. What distinction must be made to avoid this error?
4. What is meant by "justification from Calvary"?
5. What distinction do advocates of this view fail to make?
6. When does justification actually take place? Prove this.
7. What confusion is made in the Roman Catholic view of justification?
8. If justification were what Rome says it is, why would the results of justification be different from what Rome says they are?
9. What distinction safeguards the Reformed doctrine of justification?
10. Does justification from the guilt of all sin encourage sinning? Why?
11. What is the error of dispensationalism as respects this doctrine?

CHAPTER

13

XII. Of Adoption

1. *All those that are justified God vouchsafeth, in and for his only Son Jesus Christ, to make partakers of the grace of adoption; by which they are taken into the number, and enjoy the liberties and privileges of the children of God; have his name put upon them; receive the Spirit of adoption; have access to the throne of grace with boldness; are enabled to cry, Abba, Father; are pitied, protected, provided for, and chastened by him as by a father; yet never cast off, but sealed to the day of redemption, and inherit the promises, as heirs of everlasting salvation.*

This chapter of the Confession teaches us (1) that those who are effectually called (regenerated in order that they might respond to the gospel) and justified (declared just by God) also have conferred upon them the grace of adoption, (2) that adoption is closely related to regeneration and justification, but distinct from them, and (3) that the elect are thereby made children of the living God.

Adoption, like the other aspects of the application of redemption, is inseparably connected with (1) the eternal decree of God, and (2) the mediatorial work of Christ. We are "predestined . . . to adoption as sons" (Eph. 1:5). Because "He chose us in Him before the foundation of the world, that we should be holy and without blame before Him" (v. 4), he ordered not only the end from the beginning, but also every step necessary to the attainment of that end. One step that is necessary to the attainment of this end is adoption. God chose his elect not only to be regenerated, justified, sanctified, and glorified, but also to be adopted. Therefore, we note that the Lord Jesus Christ did his work in order that we might be adopted, as well as called, justified, sanctified, and glorified. "God sent forth His Son, born of a woman, born under the law, to redeem those who were under the law, *that we might receive the adoption of sons*" (Gal. 4:4–5). To receive the Holy Spirit is to receive "the Spirit of adoption" (Rom. 8:15). One cannot receive the Spirit nor can one trust in Christ apart from adoption. "But as many as received Him, to them He gave the right to become children of God, even to those who believe in His name" (John 1:12).

But what is adoption? "Adoption, as the term clearly implies, is an act of transfer from an alien family into the family of God himself" (John Murray, *Redemption Accomplished and Applied* [Grand Rapids: Eerdmans, 1955]). It means that those who were by nature children of wrath, children of darkness, even children of Satan (Eph. 2:3; Col. 3:6; John 8:44), are constituted the children of light and of God.

Contrary to the widely accepted doctrine of modernism, God is *not* the Father of all men. There is, of course, a sense in which God sustains a relationship to all men that has fatherly aspects. He is the Creator of all. He does good to all. In him we live and move and have our being. And there is divine mercy and compassion extended toward all men that cannot be denied (1 Tim. 4:10; Ezek. 18:23). If the concept of "fatherhood" meant no more than this, there would be little objection to speaking of "the fatherhood of God" or "the brotherhood of men." But the biblical concept of the relationship existing between God and man, and between men, requires us to reject this way of speaking. Because of the fall of man, the relationship between God and man can no longer be *called* that of father and son. Rather, this father-son relationship exists between Satan and man. We are properly "children of the devil" (1 John 3:10) rather than the children of God by nature. We must admit this because "whoever does not practice righteousness is not of God, nor is he who does not love his brother" (v. 10). Since men do not honor and obey God, they can hardly be called his sons, and they can hardly be called brothers when they do not love one another. The terms "father," "son," and "brother" belong within the sphere of intimate and loyal family relationship, and therefore they simply do not apply to those who are out-side of Christ's family.

But it is precisely such a relationship that is the possession of all who are in saving union with Christ by effectual calling, conversion, and jus-tification. When one becomes a believer in Christ, then may he say with wonder and thanksgiving: "Behold, what manner of love the Father has bestowed on us, that we should be called children of God! Therefore the world does not know us, because it did not know Him. Beloved, now we are children of God" (1 John 3:1–2).

It is equally important to distinguish the sonship belonging to believ-ers from the unique sonship which belongs only to Christ. Christ is the Son of God and he is the brother of believers. He is not the only son, in other words, but he *is* the only son who is not adopted (John 1:14; 3:16). When modernism speaks of our sonship as if it were the same as Christ's, it does grave injustice to his deity. Christ is begotten, not adopted. His sonship is eternal. It had no beginning. He is equal with the Father in power and glory. Our sonship is of another order. We are made to be God's sons in God's appointed time. Our sonship is due to a change in our status. Christ's sonship is due to the eternal generation of the Father. Yet this does not alter the fact that "the God and Father of our Lord Jesus Christ" is also our God and our Father (1 Peter 1:3, 17). "My Father [is] your Father," said Jesus, "and My God . . . your God" (John 20:17). The difference is not that we have a different father and God. The difference is that the God-man is, as to his divine nature, of one substance with the Father, whereas we are mere men and sons of the Father only by adoption.

But we must not let the difference between our sonship and that of Christ in any way minimize the wonder of our status as adopted. For the wonder is that, despite this infinite difference, we are—by adoption—taken into the number of and enjoy all the liberties and privileges of the children of God. We are joint heirs with Christ. If Christ is "heir of the world," that is no great wonder when viewed from the standpoint of his being very and eternal God (Rom. 4:13). But "the Spirit Himself bears witness with our spirit that we are children of God, and if children, then heirs—heirs of God and joint heirs with Christ" (Rom. 8:16–17). And that is all the more astounding precisely because we are mere men, and unworthy sinners besides.

One of the chief privileges belonging to those who receive the grace of adoption is prayer. Only those who are adopted can pray in a manner acceptable unto God. Thus the Spirit given in effectual calling is the Spirit of adoption, whereby believers are enabled to pray (Rom. 8:15). The Spirit enables us to realize that we are sons and to exercise the privilege of prayer as sons. "The Spirit also helps in our weaknesses. For we do not know what we should pray for as we ought, but the Spirit Himself makes intercession for us with groanings which cannot be uttered" (8:26).

Finally, we note that God treats such persons as children. They receive his pity and protection (Ps. 103:13; Prov. 14:26). They are under his watchful providence (Matt. 6:30–32; 1 Peter 5:7). He also subjects them to appropriate discipline because they are his sons (Heb. 12:6–11). But above all, he keeps them in safety even to the end (Rom. 8:23, 28, 38–39). Of these things we shall have more to consider in chapters XIII, XVII, and XVIII.

QUESTIONS

1. With what is adoption inseparably connected?
2. Give proof that God's predestination is unto adoption if it is to eternal life.
3. What is adoption?
4. Is God the father of all men? Explain.
5. Are all men "brothers"? Explain.
6. In Scripture the terms "father," "son," and "brother" belong to what sort of relationship?
7. What is the difference between our sonship and the sonship of Christ?
8. Does this difference decrease or increase the wonder of our sonship? Why?
9. Can those who are not adopted sons of God acceptably pray? Why?

14

XIII. Of Sanctification

1. *They who are effectually called and regenerated, having a new heart and a new spirit created in them, are further sanctified, really and personally, through the virtue of Christ's death and resurrection, by his Word and Spirit dwelling in them; the dominion of the whole body of sin is destroyed, and the several lusts thereof are more and more weakened and mortified, and they more and more quickened and strengthened, in all saving graces, to the practice of true holiness, without which no man shall see the Lord.*

2. *This sanctification is throughout in the whole man, yet imperfect in this life; there abideth still some remnants of corruption in every part, whence ariseth a continual and irreconcilable war, the flesh lusting against the spirit, and the spirit against the flesh.*

3. *In which war, although the remaining corruption for a time may much prevail, yet, through the continual supply of strength from the sanctifying Spirit of Christ, the regenerate part doth overcome; and so the saints grow in grace, perfecting holiness in the fear of God.*

These sections of the Confession teach us (1) that the regenerate nature in believers is, by God's Word and Spirit, enabled to develop, (2) that in this development the believer dies more and more unto sin and lives more and more unto righteousness, (3) that this work of sanctification pervades the whole man, (4) that it is never perfect in this life (i.e., complete victory over sin is not attained in this life), but (5) that genuine progress is made in that all true believers do strive to perfect holiness in the fear of God.

Sanctification is closely associated with effectual calling and regeneration. Like these it is a work of God in us. Sanctification is the continuation of that which is begun in effectual calling and regeneration. Regeneration is the renewal of our whole nature. Calling becomes effectual when that new nature consciously responds to the gospel in repentance and faith. Sanctification simply continues the nurture and development of that new nature which is brought into being by regeneration and into operation by effectual calling.

But why is it that the believer invariably dies more and more to sin and lives more and more unto righteousness? The answer is: because "whoever has been born of God does not sin, for His seed remains in him; and he cannot sin, because he has been born of God. In this the children of God and the children of the devil are manifest" (1 John 3:9–10). If a person is united to Christ and adopted into his family, then he is dead to sin in the sense that it no longer has the dominion over him. The governing disposition of such a person is the law of God which is written in the heart (Rom. 7:22). It is not that he is sinless, but rather that he cannot go on any longer yielding himself as the servant of sin. He is, in fact, utterly at war with sin even though it may at times manifest its power within him (Rom. 7:14–25). Above all, he can never abandon himself to sin again (1 John 4:4; 3:9). Appearances to the contrary prove, not that regenerate persons may abandon themselves to sin, but only that men may appear to be regenerate without really being so (1 John 2:19).

Perfectionism teaches three major errors against the true doctrine of sanctification. (1) It teaches that only some (possibly but a very few) believers attain freedom from the dominion of sin. This is contradicted by the teaching of Scripture which says that "as many as are led by the Spirit of God, these are sons of God" (Rom. 8:14). Therefore to say that one "is born of God" is to say that "he cannot sin" (1 John 3:9). To say that one is justified by grace is to say that sin will not have dominion over him (Rom. 6:14). (2) Perfectionism also teaches that one may be justified without also—at the same time—having victory over the dominion of sin. We have already answered this error. And finally, (3) it teaches that the victory that is attainable in this life is a freedom from sinning, or at least from consciously sinning. This is contradicted by the warnings of both Paul and John (Rom. 7:14–25; 1 John 1:8, 10). Even if a person were not "conscious of sinning," he ought to be conscious that it is a sin to say that he has no sin.

The doctrine of sanctification does not teach that sin is obliterated in every, or even in any, true believer in this life. It teaches us that there is rather a radical breach with the power and love of sin. It teaches us that established within us are a new power and love which necessitate an incessant conflict with sin. The dominion of sin is broken, though the presence of sin is not entirely eliminated. Just as penicillin may break a fever, thus destroying the dominion of a disease, and yet some time elapses before every trace of the disease is eliminated, so it is with sin. Just as the Allied armies invaded Europe and destroyed the threat of Hitler's hope of world dominion, and yet required much more time to eradicate every vestige of it, so it is with sin. Sin no longer commands the heart. The main lines of communication have been destroyed. The control center is now in the hands of God. But the alien force still carries on harassment of all kind with all the skill, cunning, and desperation of a defeated foe. As Murray has aptly said: "There is a total difference between surviving sin and reigning sin." It is impossible that a true believer will rest content with his sin, indulging it freely, turning the grace of God into lasciviousness. Only if we "by the Spirit . . . put to death the deeds of the body" shall we "live" (Rom. 8:13). And it is a noteworthy fact that the greater the progress that one makes in sanctification, the greater will be the distress over the sin that yet remains in the life of the believer (Rom. 7:24).

It is very necessary to make clear that it is the Holy Spirit that sanctifies us. It may be asked how this can be the case when so difficult and relentless a task (conflict with sin) is ours. How can a struggle that engages every ounce of my strength and will be the work of the Holy Spirit? The answer is that "it is God who works in us" in order that we might "will and do" (Phil. 2:13). It is God who creates that new nature which must engage in conflict with sin. And it is the same God who strengthens, encourages, warns, and enables us to do what we must do. All work which is performed by us in sanctification is the effect of that which God has done and is doing in us by his Holy Spirit. His work does not make our work unnecessary but rather makes it certain. When we find ourselves willing and able to fight against sin, we may know that God works in us by his might and power. Of ourselves we can do nothing. We can do all things through Jesus Christ who strengthens us. And this brings us to mention the means of grace. It has pleased God to strengthen us in this warfare by means of the Word, sacraments, prayer, and discipline. The Holy Spirit makes these effectual to the sanctification of believers.

QUESTIONS

1. Of what is sanctification a continuation?
2. Why do true believers invariably experience sanctification?
3. What is the status of sin in a believer?
4. What errors does perfectionism teach respecting sanctification?
5. What is the scriptural answer for each?
6. Who sanctifies true believers?
7. Does this make effort on the part of the believer unnecessary? Why?
8. What is the relationship between man's work and God's work in sanctification?
9. What means has God provided for our sanctification?

15

XVI. Of Good Works

1. *Good works are only such as God hath commanded in his holy Word, and not such as, without the warrant thereof, are devised by men out of blind zeal, or upon any pretense of good intention.*

2. *These good works, done in obedience to God's commandments, are the fruits and evidences of a true and lively faith; and by them believers manifest their thankfulness, strengthen their assurance, edify their brethren, adorn the profession of the gospel, stop the mouths of the adversaries, and glorify God, whose workmanship they are, created in Christ Jesus thereunto; that, having their fruit unto holiness, they may have the end, eternal life.*

These sections of the Confession teach (1) the nature and (2) the source of good works, (3) that truly good works are such by warrant of divine commandment only, (4) that truly good works can spring only from the inward root of true repentance and faith, (5) that the effects and uses of good works are (a) the expression of the believer's gratitude, (b) the confirmation of faith, (c) the edification of others, (d) the manifestation of faith to others, (e) the refutation of the adversaries of God, and (f) the glorifying of God, and (6) that good works are necessary.

What are "good works"? How about a donation to the Red Cross or perhaps part-time work with the Boy Scouts? It is commonly thought that anything done out of charity or kindness qualifies as a "good work." But according to the Scripture it is not so. Two requirements are set forth in Scripture in order that a work may be truly "good." (1) It must be in conformity with the revealed will of God. It must be that which God himself has commanded in his holy Word. "Then it will be righteousness for us, if we are careful to observe all these commandments before the Lord our God, as He has commanded us" (Deut. 6:25). (2) It must also spring from a "good conscience." It must be done with sincerity of heart as an act of service to God. "For we are confident that we have a good conscience, in all things desiring to live honorably" (Heb. 13:18).

The impossibility of an unbeliever doing good works is due to the fact that his heart (or conscience) and the law of God are not in agreement the one with the other. For example, there are those who sincerely think that they are performing "good works" when they abstain from marriage out of regard for a tradition or ecclesiastical commandment. But Scripture says this is due to the fact that "their own conscience [has been] seared with a hot iron" (1 Tim. 4:2). In spite of any sincerity they may have, their "good work" is actually sin because it is contrary to God's will. Again, there are those who are quite sincere in thinking that total abstinence from the use of certain material things is a "good work," whereas it is really sin because they are "subject . . . to regulations—'Do not touch, do not taste, do not handle' . . . according to the commandments and doctrines of men" rather than God (Col. 2:20–22).

It is even possible for men to commit the most terrible crimes under the conviction that they are doing service to God (John 16:2). And the reason is that obedience to conscience is obedience to evil in the case of an unregenerate man. "Even their mind and conscience are defiled" (Titus 1:15). We might compare their case with that of a man who has defective weights and measures. No matter how "sincere" he might be about the weight and measurement of the things he sells, he will be in error because his standards are not in conformity with the instruments in the Bureau of Standards in Washington, D.C. Only if he discovers what is wrong with his instruments can he stop being in error. And so it is with those who are regenerated by the Spirit. They begin to bring the conscience into line with the law of God. And the more they succeed in doing so, the more they may do "good works."

But let us suppose for a moment that an unregenerate man sees the works of a believer and decides to imitate him. Is it not possible that he could do many of the same things? Indeed it is. "Works done by unregenerate men may be things which God commands, and of good use both to themselves and others." An unbeliever may place a ten dollar bill in the offering plate for the support of the preaching of the true gospel of Christ. Yet we must still deny that he has done a "good work." And we *must* do so, not because he lacks outward conformity with the law of God in this instance. No, but it is still not truly a good work because "whatever is not from faith is sin" (Rom. 14:23). A man must not merely do what God commands, but he must do it because he recognizes that it is God's will and wants to obey him. "Without faith it is impossible to please Him" (Heb. 11:6).

Because of this double principle the unbeliever is *never* able to do truly good works. Moreover, even the true believer is sometimes unable to do truly good works, because there is imperfect conformity of conscience to the Word of God. This is not often enough appreciated. The truth is requisite to sanctification and good works (John 17:17). The extent to which our consciences are illuminated by the truth of God, and not *merely* the earnestness with which we heed the voice of conscience, determines whether we are able to do good works.

Neglect of this truth has sometimes led to a serious perversion of the Word of God. This is the case when the weaker brother is looked upon as the more pious, and the stronger brother as less so. Paul said, "Receive one who is weak in the faith, but not to disputes over doubtful things" (Rom. 14:1). And what was the weakness of this brother? It was that he felt obliged—out of conscience—to abstain from all use of meat. (We could substitute some other substances in our modern age.) At this point it is clear that this brother was weak not because he did not have a *strong* conscience, but rather because his conscience misdirected him. He was weak because his conscience was not in full agreement with the Word of God (1 Tim. 4:4). And in the area of his weakness we cannot deny that this brother erred—*either* by eating meat against his own conscience, *or* in the conviction that it was sin to do something that is not really sinful per se.

In a situation like this one a weaker brother cannot avoid error unless, and until, his weakness is overcome. Now to be sure, this weakness is not to be overcome by lack of charity. The stronger brother ought not to seek to induce the weaker brother to violate his own conscience. He should avoid every occasion of presenting a temptation to sin, for every violation of conscience is sin. But we cannot but protest against the modern notion that the weakness of such a brother should therefore be made the rule of practice for those who are strong. This would be sin twice compounded. It is sin to allow ourselves to be conscience-bound not to do something *even though* it is known to be acceptable unto God. The answer is not capitulation to the demands of the weaker brother, then, but rather it is to seek to educate the conscience of the weaker brother. This is very different from tempting him to act against conscience. And meanwhile, the strong person has every right to say with the apostle, "Why is my liberty judged by another man's conscience?"

We are not suggesting that any Christian is immediately or perfectly delivered from this difficulty. We all have need of sanctification through the truth. But the true believer is to some extent, and more and more as the truth of God is formed in his soul, delivered from ignorance in order that he might serve God with a clear and enlightened conscience. There is in every such man a measure of genuine agreement between his conscience and the will of God. "For we are His workmanship, created in Christ Jesus for good works, which God prepared beforehand that we should walk in them" (Eph. 2:10).

QUESTIONS

1. What is the commonly accepted notion of "good works"?
2. What are the two essentials of truly good works?
3. Why can an unbeliever never do truly good works?
4. Can an unbeliever do "the same thing" a believer does? If so, why is it not a good work when he does it?
5. Why will even "sincere" acts done out of "conviction of conscience" be evil in the case of unbelievers?
6. Why is the believer sometimes unable to do truly good works?
7. What is meant by a "weaker brother"?
8. Should we seek to induce him to do what we think is right?
9. What should we do to overcome his weakness?
10. Why is it wrong to let a weaker brother determine our actions?
11. Is any Christian free from this difficulty?

12. Why is growth in knowledge of truth essential to strong Christian character?
13. What is invariably found in true believers?

XVI, 3–6

3. *Their ability to do good works is not at all of themselves, but wholly from the Spirit of Christ. And that they may be enabled thereunto, besides the graces they have already received, there is required an actual influence of the same Holy Spirit to work in them to will and to do of his good pleasure; yet are they not hereupon to grow negligent, as if they were not bound to perform any duty unless upon a special motion of the Spirit; but they ought to be diligent in stirring up the grace of God that is in them.*

4. *They who in their obedience attain to the greatest height which is possible in this life, are so far from being able to supererogate, and to do more than God requires, as that they fall short of much which in duty they are bound to do.*

5. *We cannot, by our best works, merit pardon of sin, or eternal life, at the hand of God, by reason of the great disproportion that is between them and the glory to come, and the infinite distance that is between us and God, whom by them we can neither profit nor satisfy for the debt of our former sins; but when we have done all we can, we have done but our duty and are unprofitable servants; and because, as they are good, they proceed from the Spirit; and as they are wrought by us, they are defiled and mixed with so much weakness and imperfection that they cannot endure the severity of God's judgment.*

6. *Yet notwithstanding, the persons of believers being accepted through Christ, their good works also are accepted in him, not as though they were in this life wholly unblamable and unreprovable in God's sight; but that he, looking upon them in his Son, is pleased to accept and reward that which is sincere, although accompanied with many weaknesses and imperfection.*

These sections of the Confession teach us (1) that the Christian's ability to do good works is not of himself but only of the Holy Spirit, who dwells in him, (2) that the Holy Spirit exerts a constant influence in the believer, (3) that this does not provide occasion for indolence nor does it in any way deny duty to exercise diligence, (4) that works of supererogation are impossible, (5) that no believer ever performs his duty perfectly in this life, (6) that our best works are without merit or perfection, and (7) that the good works of believers are accepted and rewarded only for Christ's sake.

It is basic to all right thinking about the good works of Christians to recognize that all is of God (Rom. 11:36). "Without Me you can do nothing" (John 15:5), said Jesus to his own disciples. God does not regenerate the believer and then leave him to accomplish what he can by his own power. Rather it is God's sovereign power that is operative so as to complete and perfect that work which is begun in regeneration. "As the branch cannot bear fruit of itself, unless it abides in the vine, neither can you, unless you abide in Me. I am the vine, you are the branches. He who abides in Me, and I in him, bears much fruit; for without Me you can do nothing" (John 15:4–5).

Good works are the product and evidence of the work of God in us. Just *how* the Spirit accomplishes this work is a mystery. His ways are past our finding out. But we do know that it is through, or by means of, the truth (John 17:17). As we gain true knowledge, we are brought under the inward control of the principles of the Word of God. As a result we are able to know what the good and acceptable and perfect will of God is (Rom. 12:1–2). We do not pretend to know how the Spirit does this work; we know only that God's Word requires us to acknowledge that he does do it, so that we will praise the Spirit for everything good that we are able to do.

But to say that the generative source of all our good works is God is in no way to suggest that negligence, slothfulness, or carelessness is excusable, as if we were not bound to perform any duty unless we felt a special motion of the Holy Spirit directing us to do it. There are those who excuse themselves from duties on this ground. They know (1) that God commands them to do good and (2) that they have no ability to do good works unless it is given by the Spirit, and so (3) they excuse their failure to do good works on the grounds that they are unable to do them because the Spirit has failed to move them. But this is mere pretense. They pretend that they would be delighted to do good works if only they "could," whereas, in reality, they could do them if they but "would," that is, if they had a right attitude of mind and heart. But the lack of "a right attitude of mind and heart" is not evidence that the indwelling Spirit has failed to give some special motion needed at the moment. It is, rather, evidence that the heart is unconverted, and that the Spirit does not dwell within. Such individuals are really without excuse (Rom. 1:20; 2:1). They are without excuse because such a condition of heart is entirely their own doing.

The cause of man's depravity and inability is sin. And there is no excuse for sin. A true believer will not make excuse for sin, nor will he wait for some special motion of the Spirit before he strives to do his duty. He will strive to do his duty because, having a converted heart in which the Spirit dwells, he will desire to do what is right. Moreover, the believer learns in Scripture that the Spirit does not work in spurts. (Rom. 8:14, "For as many as are *ever-being-led* by the Spirit of God, these are sons of God," is the sense of the original.) Neither can the "motions" of the Spirit be observed or felt. The effects of his work may be felt, but the activity itself is spiritual (John 3). Indeed, if we may speak properly of "feeling" in this matter, it is the "feeling" that the believer has respecting Scripture as a result of the Spirit's work in him. The believer feels the power and authority of the warnings and exhortations of Scripture which require him to do his duty. "Be even more diligent," says Peter (2 Peter 1:10). "Do not become sluggish," warns the Epistle to the Hebrews (6:12). "Stir up the gift of God," says Paul (2 Tim. 1:6). And Jude even demands to keep "building yourselves up" and "keep yourselves in the love of God" (Jude 20–21).

"If anyone thinks himself to be a prophet, or spiritual, let him acknowledge that the things which I write to you are the commandments of the Lord," says Paul (1 Cor. 14:37). The evidence that one possesses the Spirit of God, therefore, is that one will feel or acknowledge the authority of that Word which lays duty upon him. He will be led by the Spirit through the Word. Those who wait upon a special motion of the Spirit demonstrate that they are possibly unregenerate and certainly mistaken about the way in which the Spirit works obedience in the hearts of his own. Those who do their duty because they humbly reverence the will of God revealed in Scripture, and they only, have warrant to believe that they are the children of God indeed (1 John 2:4–5).

Section 4 of this chapter of the Confession is addressed to the Roman Catholic doctrine of works. This teaching is that at least a few sinful people, having received divine grace, have been capable of doing, not merely all their duty, but more besides. The Baltimore Catechism (Art. 1125) speaks of the "superabundant satisfaction of the Blessed Virgin Mary and of the saints." This "superabundant satisfaction" is defined as "that which they gained during their lifetime but did not need, and which the Church applies to their fellow-members of the communion of saints." This superabundance of works of merit fills the "treasury of merits," from which the less fortunate may draw.

We have already shown that perfection in this life is never attained by *any* believer (chapter XIII), not to mention the truly ungodly thought that one could be "better than perfect." Indeed it would be difficult to think of a doctrine more openly hostile to the teaching of Scripture. For it seems that God, in the Scripture, went out of his way to show us that even the most eminent prophets and apostles were sinful men even to the end (Rom. 7:14–25). Isaiah did not hesitate to say, including himself, that "our righteousnesses are like filthy rags!" (64:6). No wonder the psalmist asks, "If You, Lord, should mark iniquities, O Lord, who could stand?" (130:3). And if this be so, how much more impossible the incredible presumption so clearly evident in Rome's false doctrine of superabundant works done by Mary and the saints (see Luke 17:10; Job 22:2–3; 35:7)!

The marvel is not that the good works of believers are so "great," but rather that they are accepted and rewarded at all. If even "our righteousnesses are like filthy rags," if even our best works are "defiled and mixed with . . . much weakness and imperfection," how is it that they are even called good works at all? The answer is that believers have union with Christ. And just as the *person* of believers is accepted by God because of their union with him, though they are sinners and imperfect, so it is with their *works*. We must "do all in the name of the Lord Jesus," that is, in his mediation.

As A. A. Hodge has put it: "It is all of grace—a grace called a reward added to a grace called a work." That is, both are of God. "God promises to reward the Christian just as a father promises to reward his child for doing what is its duty, and what is for its own benefit alone. Because a certain gracious proportion has been established between the grace given in the reward and the grace given in the holy exercises of the heart and life:—

the more grace of obedience, the more grace of reward—the more grace on earth, the more glory in heaven—because God so wills it, and because the grace given and exercised in obedience prepares the soul for the reception of the further grace given in the reward" (*Commentary on the Confession of Faith* [London: Banner of Truth, 1958], p. 228). "For whoever has, to him more will be given, and he will have abundance; but whoever does not have, even what he has will be taken away from him" (Matt. 13:12). They who excel others in works will therefore have the greater reason to humbly acknowledge that they owe the greater debt of gratitude to God.

Questions

1. What is basic to all right thinking about "good works"?
2. Does a regenerate person have the power or ability to do good works? Explain.
3. How does the Holy Spirit enable believers to do good works?
4. What excuse do some give for not doing their duty?
5. What is the real source of their inability?
6. When does the Spirit move believers to do their duty?
7. What "feeling" may properly be attributed to, and called an evidence of, the work of the Spirit in true believers?
8. What may be wrong with those who wait upon a special motion of the Spirit?
9. What is the one sure way to know that the Spirit dwells in us?
10. What does the Roman Church mean by "works of supererogation"?
11. What doctrine, already proved, refutes this error? Cite Scripture.
12. If even our best works are imperfect, why does God accept and reward them?
13. Who has the greater reason to be humble before God—the great or the lowly in gifts and attainments, accomplishments, and rewards? Why?

XVI, 7

7. *Works done by unregenerate men, although, for the matter of them, they may be things which God commands, and of good use both to themselves and others; yet, because they proceed not from a heart*

> *purified by faith, nor are done in a right manner, according to the*
> *Word, nor to a right end, the glory of God; they are therefore sinful,*
> *and cannot please God, or make a man meet to receive grace from*
> *God. And yet their neglect of them is more sinful, and displeasing*
> *unto God.*

This section of the Confession teaches us (1) that unregenerate men may do (what we shall call) *formally* good works, (2) that these are nevertheless inherently wicked works (as God sees them), and (3) that notwithstanding, the neglect of such formally good works is more wicked still.

By "formally good works" we mean actions which—considered in themselves—are the same as the good works that true believers may perform. We have already seen *why* the wicked cannot perform any good works whatsoever (XVI, 1–2). But it is of no little importance to insist that the wicked can and do perform those works which are "formally good." If it were not so, it is hard to see how there could be a human society in which believers and unbelievers could exist together. And it is a matter of common observation that there is much "good" in unconverted men. The sole reason for this "goodness," however, is the influence of the restraining hand of God (V, 2–7). The conscience of man is not permitted to wholly extinguish the recollection of the commandments of the law (Rom. 2:14–15). Culture, tradition, and civil authority as well as the convicting power of the gospel upon unbelievers, may stimulate the conscience to exercise to a high degree restraint upon the wicked heart.

Yet even so, when viewed in relationship to God, the very "good works" of evil men (for which the Christian gives thanks to God) may be exceedingly heinous sins. For example, a very wealthy man has made his money through devious means. His conscience warns him of the judgment to come. He therefore decides to do some great humanitarian work which will "make up for his sins" and "appease the wrath of God." He therefore builds a great hospital for the alleviation of human suffering. And so it comes to pass that many humble believers receive the blessing of proper medical care. Surely such Christians would give thanks to God that this rich man had been moved to such a "good work." And rightly so. But it is no exaggeration to say that in God's view of it, this "good work" might well be the crowning blasphemy, the supreme wickedness, in the life of that sinner, for what could be more wicked than to seek by one's own works to "make up for sin," and to "appease the wrath of God," instead of trusting in the work of Jesus Christ? Augustine was not exaggerating when he called such "good works" *splendid sins*. That is just what they are: splendid in one way, but in another way nothing more than sins. And all that is "splendid" in them comes from "outside the sinner," while all that is "sinful" is his own.

It would be a grave mistake, however, to think that such a sinner would be better off without the "splendid" sins. If our rich man had done nothing, he would have been worse still. For in that case he would have added this sin to all the rest: that he resisted even the conviction and warning of God completely, as it came through his conscience. Outright blasphemy against the Holy Spirit is unpardonable. Again, perhaps we can illustrate: John Dillinger was a vicious criminal. His whole life was criminal because he lived outside of and against the law. Yet it is known that he showed certain kindness and loyalty to his associates in crime and even to "good people" who were not immediately connected with his crimes. There was then, in a sense, "good" in John Dillinger. And he would have been still worse if he had treated everyone violently, even to the point of killing them all. This does not mean that he was law-abiding in part of his life. To the contrary, he was in rebellion against the law all the time. But it simply recognizes that the absence of his "better activities" in his life of crime would have rendered him worse still.

QUESTIONS

1. What do we mean by "formally good works"?
2. Is it important to acknowledge such? Why?
3. Why do evil men do such "good works"?
4. Why must these good works yet be called sins?
5. Should believers give thanks to God for these "splendid sins"? Why?
6. If these "splendid" acts are only "sins," why would the perpetrator of them be worse off for not having done them?

16

XVII. Of the Perseverance of the Saints

1. They whom God hath accepted in his Beloved, effectually called and sanctified by his Spirit, can neither totally nor finally fall away from the state of grace; but shall certainly persevere therein to the end, and be eternally saved.

2. This perseverance of the saints depends, not upon their own free will, but upon the immutability of the decree of election, flowing from the free and unchangeable love of God the Father; upon the efficacy of the merit and intercession of Jesus Christ; the abiding of the Spirit, and of the seed of God within them; and the nature of the covenant of grace: from all which ariseth also the certainty and infallibility thereof.

3. Nevertheless they may, through the temptation of Satan and of the world, the prevalency of corruption remaining in them, and the neglect of the means of their preservation, fall into grievous sins; and for a time continue therein: thereby they incur God's displeasure, and grieve his Holy Spirit; come to be deprived of some measure of their graces and comforts; have their hearts hardened, and their consciences wounded; hurt and scandalize others, and bring temporal judgments upon themselves.

These sections of the Confession teach us (1) that true believers cannot fall from grace (that is, totally or finally), (2) that they will certainly persevere, (3) that this certainty is not because of anything originating in them but in God only (the decree of election, the merits and intercession of Christ, the indwelling Holy Spirit who enables them to persevere, and the provisions of the eternal covenant), and (4) that this certainty in no way denies that true believers may fall into grievous sins for a time, the occasions of such lapses being (a) the temptations of the world, (b) the seductions of Satan, (c) the remaining corruption of their own nature, and (d) the neglect of the means of grace; and the effects of such lapses being (a) to displease and to grieve God, (b) to deprive themselves of a measure of God's grace and comfort, (c) hardening their own hearts, (d) wounding their own consciences, (e) incurring temporal judgments, and (f) causing others to stumble.

When a person has been regenerated by the Holy Spirit and truly converted unto Christ (by repentance and faith), is it possible to again become a child of wrath and of eternal destruction? The answer of the Scripture is clear and emphatic: no, it is not possible. "He who believes in the Son *has* everlasting life" (John 3:36). "He who hears My word and believes in Him who sent Me has everlasting life, and *shall not come into judgment, but has passed from death into life*" (John 5:24). Here we have God's Word for it that when a man has once exercised faith in Jesus Christ, he cannot come into judgment any more. He has passed from that judgment never to return again. The Christian then ought to be "confident of this very thing, that He who has begun a good work in you will complete it until the day of Jesus Christ" (Phil. 1:6). It is not for nothing that God promised, "I will put My fear in their hearts so that they will not depart from Me" (Jer. 32:40).

It must be admitted that experience often *seems* to contradict this teaching. Who cannot think of someone who became a member of the Church, giving evidence of great interest in divine things and zealously using the means of grace for considerable time, who yet, later on, fell away from the fellowship of Christ into complete neglect and even antagonism? Such a person indeed seems to have "fallen from grace." We say "seems," because the apostle John tells us what really happens in such cases. "They went out from us," he says, "but they were not of us; for if they had been of us, they would have continued with us; but they went out that they might be made manifest, that none of them were of us" (1 John 2:19). Such cases prove, not that believers can fall from grace, but only that we can be misled by false appearances and professions. The apostle John felt the difficulty presented by such cases, but he insisted that true believers cannot fall from grace—"for if they had been of us," he says, "they would have continued." He said this because he knew from the Word of God what he could not know from appearances only, namely, that believers cannot fall from grace.

But if this is true, we may now ask, why is it that true believers cannot fall from grace? Is it because of something in the power of the believers themselves? Or is it the power of God that prevents this? The answer again is unmistakable. True believers "are kept by the power of God through faith for salvation," says Peter (1 Peter 1:5). Here we see the vast difference between the Reformed faith on the one hand, and Roman Catholicism and Arminianism on the other hand. For these latter systems agree in teaching that it is the power of man as well as that of God, yes, even more than the power of God, which keeps the saved from being lost. And this is true not only at the beginning of the process but all the way to the end.

At the beginning, salvation is said to be possible or available for all. But the sinner himself must, by his own power, do the one thing necessary to make that "possibility" become a "reality." In this view God is like a gas station owner. He has a great storehouse of power just waiting to be tapped. But it is up to the sinner to drive in and say, "Fill 'er up." All that power is "powerless" until the sinner "makes his move." This view is very appealing to the sinner naturally, because it leaves him in command even of the power of God.

But what sounds attractive at the beginning loses its appeal when we consider the end. For as soon as we have started, the Roman Catholic and Arminian begin to break the sad news. We liked it when we were told that we could start the trip by our own free will and power. But now we learn the bitter fact that we can also "run out of gas" and "fail to make our destination" by the same free will and power. The power of God that is powerless until the sinner makes his move at the beginning can become just as powerless at any later time if the sinner wills it to be so. If at any time he falters and chooses unbelief rather than faith, sin rather than godliness, falling away rather than perseverance, he at that moment loses all power of a saving sort. He is right back where he started. And there is nothing the power of God can do about it. The Roman Catholic and the Arminian are consistent! At least they are honest enough to admit that grace which is not sovereign at the beginning is not sovereign to the end. Salvation which depends upon man is no more dependable than man himself.

In contrast to this the Reformed faith begins with the frank recognition that if God were to merely make salvation "possible" for men— leaving it up to them whether or not to turn this possibility into reality— none would be saved, because man is totally unable to do so. He loves evil too much to turn by himself to good. But in resting all hope for the sinner upon the election of the Father, the atonement of the Son, and the regeneration of the Holy Spirit, the Reformed faith not only speaks to the need of the helpless sinner *at the beginning,* but does so also *to the end.* It prefers to offend angry sinners in order to give them a salvation that cannot fail. And fail it cannot. For if it is God alone who saves, then we have a salvation which cannot fail. A salvation which depends upon God entirely is entirely dependable. And that is what this doctrine teaches. The Lord who says "I give them eternal life," is also able to guarantee that "they shall never perish, neither shall any one snatch them out of My hand" (John 10:28).

Having said all this, however, we must still defend the emphasis given by the Confession of Faith in calling this chapter "Of the Perseverance of the Saints." Having advertised the fact that it is the power of God alone which renders the saints secure, we must stress with even greater urgency the necessity of perseverance on the part of believers. When we say that the ultimate basis of perseverance is the Holy Spirit's operation in believers, we do not mean that it is the Holy Spirit who perseveres. "The true doctrine is not that salvation is certain if we have once believed, but that perseverance in holiness is certain if we have truly believed." The doctrine is "not that persistent effort on our part is not necessary in order" to be saved, "but that in this effort we are certain of success; for it is God that worketh in us both to will and to do of his good pleasure" (A. A. Hodge, *Commentary on the Confession of Faith* [London: Banner of Truth, 1958]).

The infallible certainty of salvation as respects true believers does not, however, render their perseverance any easier, as though the Christian were playing a game instead of fighting a stiff battle. We believe that those who claim that it is simple to overcome life's tribulations and trials because they have "taken Christ" deceive themselves as well as others. The true description of the battle of perseverance is rather to be found in the agonized cries of the psalmist, "My sighing is not hidden from You. My heart pants, my strength fails me. . . . Those also who seek my life lay snares for me; those who seek my hurt speak of destruction, and plan deception all the day long. . . . For I said, 'Hear me, lest they rejoice over me, lest, when my foot slips, they exalt themselves against me.' For I am ready to fall, and my sorrow is continually before me" (Ps. 38:9–10, 12, 16–17). It is, in other words, a struggle all the way. And it is a struggle that engages all that is in us. But it is a struggle from which a true believer, as distinguished from a mere pretender, will never turn away until the battle is won and the goal is reached. As our Lord said to his disciples, "He who endures to the end shall be saved" (Matt. 24:13).

It is evident from Scripture that while true believers never fall totally or finally from grace, they can and do fall or lapse therein. This is the biblical doctrine of backsliding, and it is illustrated in the lives of even such great men as Noah, Moses, David, and Peter. They all fell into lamentable sin for a time, after they had become true believers. It may be wondered how sin can rise up like this in those in whom the Spirit dwells. There are various reasons, one or more of which will be seen in every case. There is the attraction of the world (1 John 2:15). There is the temptation of Satan (Mark 1:13; Matt. 26:70, 72, 74). There is the corruption remaining in a believer's heart (James 1:13–14). And there is the neglect of the means of grace (Heb. 10:24–25).

Yet we must not from these tragic lapses form a wrong estimate of these holy men of God. The Scripture records their lapses, not to encourage us to sin, but to warn us against such. And, as we read of their lapses, so we read of God's displeasure (2 Sam. 11:27), their own loss of comfort and assurance (Ps. 51:8, 10, 12), the harm that was done to their own hearts and consciences (Ps. 32:3–4), and the dishonor brought upon the cause of God and truth (2 Sam. 12:14). Such tragic falls we should never make light of. We should contemplate them only with fear and trembling. Such things should remind us of Peter's warning: "If the righteous one is scarcely saved, where will the ungodly and the sinner appear?" (1 Peter 4:18). It is not as if the true believer need have no concern about falling, or that he can fall without any serious harm. No, the truth is that even the believer is saved with nothing to spare. But the point is that he *is* saved. And he is saved because, even if he does fall (as these great men of God did), he will soon again rise up to do battle with sin, and will (except for such tragic lapses) continue in that conflict to the end. If Christians would study the way in which these men rose up from such lapses to strive for God once more, they would never be tempted to a false and easy view of security, but would hold the true doctrine of perseverance.

QUESTIONS

1. Can a true believer fall from grace? Cite Scripture proof.
2. What common experience seems to contradict this teaching of Scripture?
3. What does the apostle John say that such cases really prove?
4. Why cannot true believers fall entirely from grace?
5. How do Roman Catholicism and Arminianism seek to make the gospel attractive to sinners at the beginning?
6. What is the price that they pay for this later on?
7. What great benefit has the Reformed believer when he accepts the offensive biblical teaching that salvation is wholly by the power of God?
8. Does this doctrine teach that salvation is certain if we have once believed whether or not we continue to strive? (Answer in a sentence.)
9. Does the security of believers make perseverance easier? Cite proof.
10. Can true believers fall? Cite proof.
11. Give an example of that which may occasion such a fall.
12. Give an example of a consequence of such a fall.
13. The record of the lapse of such saints is not to teach us how to fall, but rather what?

17

XVIII. Of Assurance of Grace and Salvation

1. *Although hypocrites, and other unregenerate men, may vainly deceive themselves with false hopes and carnal presumptions of being in the favor of God and estate of salvation, which hope of theirs shall perish; yet such as truly believe in the Lord Jesus, and love him in sincerity, endeavoring to walk in all good conscience before him, may in this life be certainly assured that they are in the state of grace, and may rejoice in the hope of the glory of God, which hope shall never make them ashamed.*

2. *This certainty is not a bare conjectural and probable persuasion, grounded upon a fallible hope; but an infallible assurance of faith, founded upon the divine truth of the promises of salvation, the inward evidence of those graces unto which these promises are made, the testimony of the Spirit of adoption witnessing with our spirits that we are the children of God: which Spirit is the earnest of our inheritance, whereby we are sealed to the day of redemption.*

These sections of the Confession teach us (1) that there is a false assurance in which unregenerate men sometimes indulge, in which they are deceived, and in which they will finally be discovered, (2) that there is a true assurance, in which true believers are not deceived but, rather, infallibly confirmed, and in which they will not be confounded, and (3) that this infallible assurance rests upon (a) God's infallible Word, (b) the graces in the believer's heart of which the Word speaks, and (c) the testimony of the Spirit which enables the believer to confirm the one by the other.

The Scripture says that men are prone to deceive themselves as well as others. "The heart is deceitful above all things, and desperately wicked" (Jer. 17:9). "For if anyone thinks himself to be something, when he is nothing, he deceives himself" (Gal. 6:3). Such was the Pharisee described by our Lord (Luke 18:10–14). He was confident that all was well with his soul. But he only deceived himself. It is sometimes the case that a man "blesses himself in his heart, saying, 'I shall have peace,'" and yet is such that "the Lord would not spare him" (Deut. 29:19–20). No matter how confident he may be, "the hope of the hypocrite shall perish" (Job 8:13). Indeed the strength of such confidence may be the measure of his iniquity, as was true in the days of Jeremiah. Those who confidently said, "The temple of the Lord, the temple of the Lord, the temple of the Lord are these," were relying on "lying words that cannot profit" (Jer. 7:4, 8). The joy of such may be great but it will not last (Job 20:5).

And yet there is such a thing as true assurance of good estate with God. "The Spirit Himself bears witness with our spirit that we are children of God," says the apostle (Rom. 8:16). "We know that we know Him," says John (1 John 2:3). "We know that we have passed from death to life" (1 John 3:14). And Scripture is not content merely to say that there *is* such a thing as right assurance, but exhorts believers to "show the same diligence to the full assurance of hope until the end" (Heb. 6:11), "be even more diligent to make your call and election sure" with the promise that "if you do these things you will never stumble" (2 Peter 1:10). If a man may confidently believe that he is saved while in reality he is not saved, it is also true that a man may confidently believe that he is saved and actually be saved. And he not only may be confident of this fact, but he may also know that he is not deceived.

What then is the difference between true and false assurance? (1) There is a difference, first of all, in the qualities manifested therein. As A. A. Hodge succinctly tells us, (a) true assurance begets unfeigned humility; false assurance begets spiritual pride (1 Cor. 15:10; Gal. 6:14), (b) true assurance leads to increased diligence in the practice of holiness; the false leads to sloth and self-indulgence (Ps. 51:12–13, 19), (c) true assurance leads to candid self-examination and to a desire to be searched and corrected by God; the false leads to a disposition to be satisfied with appearance and to avoid accurate investigation (Ps. 139:23–24), and (d) the true leads to constant aspirations after more intimate fellowship with God, which is not true of false assurance (1 John 3:2–3). It is not the *strength* of one's conviction which proves the validity of his assurance, but the *character* of one's conviction. A man may be fanatically sure that he is saved, but this may mean only that he is "sincerely wrong."

(2) The second difference between true and false assurance is the basis of it. True assurance rests upon three things, all of which are absent in the case of those who possess false assurance. (a) True assurance rests upon the infallible certainty of what God says about us in the Bible. False assurance rests upon what man says about himself (Heb. 6:17–18; Ps. 118:8; Prov. 28:26). (b) True assurance rests upon the evidence presented by the actual possession of those graces unto which God's promises are made. False assurance rests upon the mere semblance of such (2 Cor. 1:12; 1 John 2:3; 3:14; 1 Peter 2:10; Luke 18:10–14). (c) True assurance rests upon the testimony of the Holy Spirit within our hearts (as he applies the Word of God), so that we know that we are the children of God. False assurance rests upon the testimony of the spirit of error as it suppresses the Word of God (Rom. 8:15–16; 2 Thess. 2:9–12). This means, above all, that true, infallible assurance comes by the Spirit and Word of God.

God has said certain infallible things in his Word. He has said that whoever believes in Christ already possesses life everlasting (John 3:36). He also infallibly declares that "he who keeps His commandments abides in Him . . . and by this we know that He abides in us, by the Spirit whom He has given us" (1 John 3:24). The same God who declares these things also produces them in the elect. He enables us to believe in Christ and keep his commandments. Therefore, when we *do* believe in Christ and keep his commandments, the Holy Spirit enables us to know that we do. And because we know that we believe in him and that we keep his commandments, we can then possess true assurance.

We believe that God's Word is infallible in all that it says, and therefore also *when it speaks of us*. It is of paramount importance to insist that this infallible assurance is never ours by some private revelation by the Spirit. To claim assurance on the basis of a witness of the Spirit apart from, or additional to, the Bible is to claim a false assurance. God's Word is sufficient. By Scripture alone "the man of God may be complete, thoroughly equipped" (2 Tim. 3:16–17). In effecting infallible assurance in the hearts of believers, the Holy Spirit does not impart new revelation (because there is no need for new revelation). He applies that which is already revealed, namely, the scriptural truth that believers shall be saved. By bringing the sure Word of God (with the infallible promises it contains) *and* the actually existing graces of the heart (with respect to which these promises are made) together, the Spirit enables the believer to say with assurance, "I am a child of God, and will be forever."

Some have maintained that the Holy Spirit communicates assurance to the believer immediately, that is, apart from the Scripture. And Romans 8:16 is claimed in support of this view: "The Spirit Himself bears witness with our spirit that we are children of God." It is true that the Spirit himself bears witness. But he bears witness *with* our spirit jointly, and not *to* it directly. In other words God exerts an immediate influence upon the spirit of man, but not by speaking to man's spirit apart from the Scripture. Rather, the immediate influence is such that man and God speak together—man by saying, "I am saved because I am a true believer," and God by saying, "He who believes in the Son has everlasting life" (John 3:36). When our spirit is brought into conformity with God's Spirit and Word, what we say will be consonant with what the Spirit says in Scripture. Thus the assurance that "we are children of God" comes, not from a witness by the Holy Spirit alone, but from a joint witness effected by the Holy Spirit as our word becomes in agreement with his Word. The special or personal aspect of this consists, not in what God says alone, but rather in the fact that we are by his grace enabled to say of ourselves what he says of true believers in Scripture. "The whole counsel of God concerning all things necessary for . . . man's salvation, faith and life, is either expressly set down in Scripture, or by good and necessary consequence may be deduced from Scripture: unto which nothing at any time is to be added, whether by new revelations of the Spirit, or traditions of men" (I, 6).

Questions

1. Is man easily deceived in religious matters? Cite Scripture proof.
2. Why did the Pharisee think that he was "right with God"?
3. Does the Scripture affirm that there is valid assurance?

4. Is it the duty of believers to endeavor to possess this assurance? Prove.
5. In what two important ways do true and false assurance differ?
6. State at least two qualities belonging to true assurance.
7. State at least two qualities belonging to false assurance.
8. What is the basis of true assurance?
9. What is the basis of false assurance?
10. Which is more important in true assurance—God's Spirit or his Word?
11. What false interpretation is given to Romans 8:16 by those who believe in an immediate testimony of the Spirit (apart from Scripture)?
12. State the true relationship of the Spirit and Word of God in this "witness" which belongs to the believer.
13. Why does it dishonor the Spirit when we seek "new revelations"?

XVIII, 3–4

3. *This infallible assurance doth not so belong to the essence of faith, but that a true believer may wait long, and conflict with many difficulties, before he be partaker of it: yet, being enabled by the Spirit to know the things which are freely given him of God, he may, without extraordinary revelation, in the right use of ordinary means, attain thereunto. And therefore it is the duty of every one to give all diligence to make his calling and election sure, that thereby his heart may be enlarged in peace and joy in the Holy Ghost, in love and thankfulness to God, and in strength and cheerfulness in the duties of obedience, the proper fruits of this assurance; so far is it from inclining men to looseness.*

4. *True believers may have the assurance of their salvation divers ways shaken, diminished, and intermitted; as, by negligence in preserving of it; by falling into some special sin, which woundeth the conscience, and grieveth the Spirit; by some sudden or vehement temptation; by God's withdrawing the light of his countenance, and suffering even such as fear him to walk in darkness, and to have no light: yet are they never utterly destitute of that seed of God, and life of faith, that love of Christ and the brethren, that sincerity of heart and conscience*

of duty, out of which, by the operation of the Spirit, this assurance
may, in due time, be revived, and by the which, in the mean time,
they are supported from utter despair.

These sections of the Confession teach us (1) that a man may be a true
believer though he lacks infallible assurance that he is, (2) that he ought,
nevertheless, to attain this assurance, (3) that the possession of it inclines
men, not to looseness, but to diligence, (4) that those who have such
assurance may have it shaken, diminished, and intermitted (because of
negligence, sin, temptation, or trial), and (5) that whether or not the
believer has assurance, yet he does have security because of God's seed
and operation in him, out of which he may gain, or regain, assurance in
due time.

There is a great difference between believing in Jesus Christ (without
which we cannot be saved) and believing that we truly believe in him
(without which, important as it is, salvation is possible). The man who
cried, "Lord, I believe; help my unbelief" (Mark 9:24), surely had faith
in Christ, but he was not sure of his own faith. Just as a man may be sure
that he is saved and yet not be saved, so a man may be saved (by faith in
Christ) and yet not be sure that he is saved. Infallible assurance is not of
the essence of saving faith. This may be proved from the following considerations: (1) The Bible does not say that we *must* have infallible assurance to be saved, but only that we must have faith in Jesus Christ (Mark
5:36; John 11:26). We *ought* to have such assurance. We absolutely *must*
have faith. (2) The Scripture shows that true believers have lacked such
infallible assurance (Matt. 26:22; Pss. 31:22; 51:12). David asks for a
restoration, not of salvation, but of the joy of salvation, and probably such
assurance was central to that joy. (3) There are many exhortations in the
Bible urging believers to strive for, and attain unto, this assurance (Heb.
10:22; 6:11; 2 Peter 1:10). But if all true believers were required to have
full assurance as the essence of saving faith, there would be no need to
exhort them because, being believers, they would on this view already
have it.

But such exhortations also teach us that believers may and *ought* to
attain unto full assurance even though it is not of the essence of faith.
"And we desire that *each one of you* show the same diligence to the full
assurance of hope" (Heb. 6:11). Indeed, for this very reason "have been

given to us exceedingly great and precious promises" (2 Peter 1:4). Contrary to popular opinion, full assurance is not meant only for a few who are spiritually "elite"; it is something that all Christians ought to possess. And it is something that even the lowliest may come to possess by a proper and diligent use of the means of grace. Whoever will be diligent in seeking it will also make his calling and election sure (2 Peter 1:10). And by a neglect of the means of grace even the most gifted may lack what the lowly possess.

It is sometimes charged that such assurance will lead to carelessness and neglect. This would be true, perhaps, if God gave assurance by a direct revelation *to* the believer apart from the Scripture. But since God communicates the assurance that we are the children of God only by bringing our spirits into concurrence with his Spirit and Word, we see how false this is. For the precise way in which our spirits are enabled to bear witness with God's Spirit is *by giving diligence*. As we (by God's strength and grace) diligently use the appointed means of grace, striving after holiness in conformity with the commandments of God, we attain unto and sustain assurance. Since this assurance is the fruit of diligence it cannot lead to carelessness. The tree determines the nature of the fruit, and not vice versa. Assurance is a fruit of grace. The tree from which it comes is that working of the Spirit of God which makes a believer diligent from the heart to keep God's commands. The root is grace, the tree is diligence, and the fruit is assurance.

Since assurance is the fruit and not the root, it follows that it may at times be shaken, diminished, and intermitted. Such was the case with Job (Job 6:4; 23:3–7; 29:2–5). Such was probably the case with Peter (Matt. 26:69–75; Luke 22:32). The causes of the lack of assurance in those who have previously possessed it are varied. Peter neglected to pray (Luke 22:46). David was confronted with sudden temptation. Job was subjected to many grievous afflictions. There may be other causes. There may be a combination of causes. But the important fact is that even true believers, who have known full assurance, may lose it for a time or in a measure. And they may cry out with the psalmist, "Lord, why do You cast off my soul? why do You hide Your face from me?" (Ps. 88:14; read the whole Psalm). However, even in the slough of despond, the downcast *believer* looks to God. Even in doubt and trouble he cries, "O Lord, God of my salvation, I have cried out day and night before You. Let my prayer come before You; incline Your ear to my cry" (Ps. 88:1–2). And this makes all the difference. For "whoever has been born of God . . . His seed remains in him" (1 John 3:9). Even in great distress and doubt he cries to his heavenly Father, and continues to do so until the light of the Father's countenance is known by him once more.

"I cried out to God with my voice—to God with my voice; and He gave ear to me" (Ps. 77:1). "For this cause everyone who is godly shall pray to You in a time when You may be found: surely in a flood of great waters they shall not come near him" (Ps. 32:6). The true believer may not be sure of himself. Yet even in his sore distress he cries unto God because he is a true believer. Thus it cannot be that the root of assurance has been destroyed. So by "the operation of the Spirit, this assurance may, in due time, be revived." And in any event, believers "are supported from utter despair." " 'For this is like the waters of Noah to Me; for as I have sworn that the waters of Noah would no longer cover the earth, so have I sworn that I would not be angry with you, nor rebuke you. For the mountains shall depart and the hills be removed, but My kindness shall not depart from you, nor shall My covenant of peace be removed,' says the Lord, who has mercy on you" (Isa. 54:9–10).

Questions

1. Give proof to support the statement that assurance is not necessary to salvation.
2. In "faith" a Christian has confidence in _____.
3. In "assurance" a Christian has confidence in _____.
4. Who ought to have full assurance? Cite proof.
5. Who may have full assurance?
6. Why cannot full assurance *produce* neglect and carelessness?
7. Why may true assurance be shaken, diminished, or intermitted?
8. Cite a biblical instance of this.
9. What does every believer still do in spite of lack of assurance?
10. Why does he do this?
11. Why is it never "impossible" to "revive" lost assurance?

18

XIX. Of the Law of God

1. *God gave to Adam a law, as a covenant of works, by which he bound him, and all his posterity, to personal, entire, exact, and perpetual obedience; promised life upon the fulfilling, and threatened death upon the breach of it; and endued him with power and ability to keep it.*

2. *This law, after his fall, continued to be a perfect rule of righteousness; and, as such, was delivered by God upon Mount Sinai in ten commandments, and written in two tables: the first four commandments containing our duty towards God, and the other six our duty to man.*

These sections of the Confession teach us (1) that the law of God exhibits the standard of perfect obedience which God imposed upon Adam at creation, (2) that its demands were absolute, and (3) that this law, the demands of which have never ceased to stand for all men everywhere, was revealed in summary (by way of general principles) at Sinai on two tables of stone.

The law of God is central to the message of the Bible. Only Jesus Christ eclipses the law in importance. And he came not "to destroy . . . but to fulfill" the law (Matt. 5:17). It would be difficult to make a more radical error than to think of the law of God as something merely transient or mutable. For the law (that is, the moral law) simply states what God requires of man. So long as God is the immutable God and man is man, there can be no revocation of the law. "The entirety of Your word is truth, and every one of Your righteous judgments endures forever" (Ps. 119:160). "You have founded them forever" (v. 152). Because he is the everlasting and holy God, and we are his creatures, this law has incessant relevance.

This does not mean that God gave Adam the law in an externally revealed and codified form. "For the law was given by Moses" (John 1:17). Paul teaches us that the law was first transcribed in the human conscience (Rom. 2:14–15). It was "written in the hearts" of men. This, however, does not mean that Adam was conscious of the Ten Commandments in the same way that we are. To us the law is a negative power which incites our enmity. In him it was a positive sense (perhaps like an intuition) which incited love of God and of good. But the difference was in Adam's relation to the law, not the law itself. What was right for Adam and wrong for Adam is precisely the same as that which is commanded of and forbidden us by the Ten Commandments. Adam broke the law. But he and his children ceased not to be men. The only change was in their relationship to the law. The law had been the way of life to them. Now it was the way of death. They had ceased to live by it and had come to live against it. Both consciously and unconsciously sinful men now seek to "suppress the truth in unrighteousness" (Rom. 1:18).

And yet in at least two important ways, men testify that they are obligated to keep the law of God: (1) All men exercise moral judgment. However sinful they may be, they still exercise moral judgment against the sins of others. "Therefore you are inexcusable, O man, whoever you are who judge, for in whatever you judge another you condemn yourself; for you who judge practice the same things" (Rom. 2:1). Even though men are liars, they condemn lies. (2) All men are likewise possessed of conscience. They "show the work of the law written in their hearts, their conscience also bearing witness, and between themselves their thoughts accusing or else excusing them" (Rom. 2:15). Man's inherent sense of right and wrong is due to the fact that he cannot escape the claims of the law of God.

Of those who deny the permanent relevance of the law, none are to be so sharply condemned as Christians. There are professing Christians who say that Christ has delivered them from the obligation to keep the law. "We are not under law but under grace," they cry (misusing Rom. 6:14). Of this we shall have more to say under sections 6–7. Suffice it to say that the truth lies in the opposite direction: the Christian above all is obligated to keep the law. "Whoever therefore breaks one of the least of these commandments, and teaches men so, shall be called least in the kingdom of heaven; but whoever does and teaches them, he shall be called great in the kingdom of heaven" (Matt. 5:19). To deny that Christians are obligated to keep the law of God is to deny that Christians are to love God and their neighbor. For on these two hangs all the law of God (Matt. 22:37–40).

From the summary that Christ makes—that we are to love God with all our heart, soul, mind, and strength, and our neighbor as ourselves—we may rightly infer the two divisions of the law of God. We need not think that the two divisions required the use of the two stones which God gave to Moses. It is more likely that the entire law was written on each of the two stones, as was customary in the ratification of a covenant in ancient times. In any case we believe that the division is consonant with our Lord's statement, and that the interpretation of the Westminster Larger and Shorter Catechisms is correct. We therefore conclude this section with a brief resumé of the Ten Commandments.

The Love of God—Man's Duty to God Vertically

(1) The First Commandment teaches us *whom* we are to worship. We are to worship the true God only. And in no instance may we properly give the worship that is due him to any other, nor may we in any sense acknowledge any other god to be a legitimate object of worship. (This commandment is frequently violated when Christians act as if Jews or Unitarians practice legitimate worship, or even worse, when they join with them in worshiping a god who has no son (2 John 9; 1 John 5:12).

(2) The Second Commandment teaches us *how* we are to worship. We are to worship God only as he has commanded us to worship him. Any thing that man devises, invents, or imagines corrupts the true reverence and worship of God. (This commandment is frequently violated when Christians have "pictures" of Jesus. When it is said that they are legitimate because they are not used in worship, we reply that they are not legitimate because one cannot have a proper thought or feeling with

respect to Christ other than that of reverence and worship. Study the Westminster Larger Catechism, Q/A 109 carefully.)

(3) The Third Commandment teaches us *who* they are that worship God acceptably. They are those who profess his name (take his name) with true sincerity of heart. It is as useless to worship the true God (even in the right manner) with insincerity as it is to worship a false god or to worship the true God in an unacceptable way. (This commandment is frequently violated, at least to a degree, even by Christians. This happens, for example, when they do not concentrate intently upon the Word of God when they gather together for worship. See Luke 8:18; Prov. 8:34.)

(4) The Fourth Commandment teaches us *when* we are to worship and serve God. We are to spend one whole day each week in worship and six days in serving God. The one day that belongs to God is a day of rest, that is, of cessation from the labor and recreations that are proper on the other days (except for works of necessity, piety, and mercy). (This commandment is frequently violated. It is violated in two ways. It is violated when the Lord's Day is desecrated. It is also violated when one of the other six days is designated as a holy day by mere human authority, as in the case of Christmas or Good Friday. See Gal. 4:9–11; Col. 2:16–17.)

The Love of Man—Man's Duty to God Horizontally

(5) The Fifth Commandment teaches us the duty to respect and to obey all God-given authority. All authority is of God. The authority that belongs to parents, employers, church officers, and civil rulers, is from God (Ex. 20:12; Eph. 6:5; Acts 20:18–21; Rom. 13). This commandment also teaches those who administer such authority in subordination to God that they must be obedient to God's law themselves as well as require all due obedience from their subjects. (This commandment is commonly violated today by parents who fail to require obedience from their children. This is a desecration of divine authority. And it is certain to have evil consequences for the children. See Prov. 29:15.)

(6) The Sixth Commandment teaches us reverence for human life because man was created in the image of God. It is important to note that this commandment forbids murder but not every form of killing. It is legitimate to kill animals for food (Gen. 9:3). It is even a divine *require-ment* that murderers be executed by civil authority (Gen. 9:6). And God also sanctions self-defense even though it results in human death, whether

such defense be personal or national (Num. 35:31; Ex. 22:2; Rom. 13:1–4). (This commandment is often violated by intemperance. God does not forbid the temperate use of material things. But intemperance is wrong because it is a violation of the Sixth Commandment. Consult the Larger Catechism, Q/A 136.)

(7) The Seventh Commandment teaches us to guard the sanctity of sex and marriage. This commandment forbids everything which destroys, undermines, or tends to undermine, the unity of husband and wife according to the original divine institution. It therefore forbids not only adultery, fornication, and divorce, but even the least inclination of lust out of which such wicked sins come. (This commandment is frequently violated by the deliberate perusal of literature, motion pictures, and television programs which excite lustful thoughts and desires. Consult the Larger Catechism, Q/A 139.)

(8) The Eighth Commandment teaches us the divine sanction of personal property. This commandment stands in opposition to every form of private or public endeavor to claim possession of property except by inheritance or in return for money or labor. The Scripture does not countenance the doctrine which teaches that wealth is necessarily wrong in and of itself. Many utopian schemes of which Marxism is an example hold that private property is the root of all evil, so that human ills can be alleviated if personal property is eliminated, either by force or violence or by confiscatory taxation. Under the canopy of this error civil authorities are sometimes guilty themselves of stealing.

(9) The Ninth Commandment teaches us the sanctity of truth. Satan's kingdom is a kingdom of falsehood, lies, and deceit. The kingdom of Christ is a kingdom of truth, candor, and integrity. When we speak, we ought to be sure of two things: (a) that we really mean what we say, and say what we mean, and (b) that what we say is in accordance, not merely with our intention, but also with the facts. (Gossip is a form of lying, even if we sincerely believe what we are relating. To repeat hearsay as if it is reliable is to evidence no love of the truth. It is just as truly a violation of this command when we "sincerely" relate that which is not true, as when we "insincerely" relate something that happens to be true. Consult the Larger Catechism, Q/A 145.)

(10) The Tenth Commandment teaches us that "the heart is deceitful above all things, and desperately wicked" (Jer. 17:9). The requirement is

that we learn to be content with what the Lord our God has given us. All discontent, envy, and covetousness are in essence a complaint against God's dealings with us. They are idolatry because they challenge his divine authority. This is the root of all kinds of other sins (Larger Catechism, Q/A 147, 148).

The more one meditates on the perfect law of God, as summarized in these ten principles, the more marvelous will it appear. There is no duty taught in any portion of Scripture which is not implicit here. There is no duty that can be legitimately imposed upon a believer which is not already imposed here. "God alone is Lord of the conscience, and hath left it free from the doctrines and commandments of men which are in anything contrary to his Word, or beside it," and the reason is that the whole duty of man is already contained in the Ten Commandments. To yield the conscience to any duty not contained in these laws is to become the servant of man rather than of God.

QUESTIONS

1. Prove that the law of God is always obligatory for man.
2. Did Adam have the law? In what manner?
3. Was the law changed by the fall of man? If not, what was changed?
4. What two important things demonstrate that all men are "under the law"?
5. Is the Christian obligated to keep the law less than is the unbeliever? Prove this.
6. What two positive principles fulfill the law?
7. State the principles contained in the first four commandments.
8. Give an example of a modern-day violation of each of these commandments.
9. Is it right to accept other rules besides the Ten Commandments? Why?

XIX, 3–5

3. *Besides this law, commonly called moral, God was pleased to give to the people of Israel, as a Church under age, ceremonial laws containing several typical ordinances, partly of worship, prefiguring*

Christ, his graces, actions, sufferings, and benefits; and partly holding forth divers instructions of moral duties. All which ceremonial laws are now abrogated under the New Testament.

4. *To them also, as a body politic, he gave sundry judicial laws, which expired together with the state of that people, not obliging any other now, further than the general equity thereof may require.*

5. *The moral law doth forever bind all, as well justified persons as others, to the obedience thereof; and that not only in regard of the matter contained in it, but also in respect of the authority of God the Creator, who gave it. Neither doth Christ, in the gospel, any way dissolve, but much strengthen this obligation.*

These sections of the Confession teach us (1) that God gave the nation Israel ceremonial laws (in addition to and distinct from the moral law) consisting of types and symbols of (a) Christ and his redemptive work, and (b) the Holy Spirit and his work in the application of redemption, (2) that these laws are now abrogated, (3) that he also gave that nation certain civil laws which terminated with the end of the Jewish theocracy, but (4) that the moral law remains in effect (and it was understood under the Old Testament economy that it would be so).

There is an extended discussion of the ceremonial institutions of the Old Testament in the Epistle to the Hebrews, chapters 7–10. We will cite a few quotations to illustrate the teaching of the Confession. For example, in Hebrews 8:4–5, a contrast is drawn between Christ in heaven and the priests who carried out the ceremonial ordinances of the Old Testament. It is stated that they were "the copy and shadow of the heavenly things" (8:5). We are reminded of the tabernacle with "the golden censer and the ark of the covenant overlaid on all sides with gold, in which were the golden pot that had the manna, Aaron's rod that budded, and the tablets of the covenant" (9:4). "The priests always went into the first part of the tabernacle, performing the services. But into the second part the high priest went alone once a year, not without blood, which he offered for himself and for the people's sins committed in ignorance" (9:6–7). But of this the Scripture declares that "the Holy Spirit [was] indicating this, that the way into the Holiest of All was not yet made manifest while the first tabernacle was still standing. It was symbolic *for the pres-*

ent time in which both gifts and sacrifices are offered which cannot make him who performed the service perfect in regard to the conscience— concerned only with foods and drinks, various washings, and fleshly ordinances imposed *until the time of reformation*" (Heb. 9:8–10). These things were "a shadow of the good things to come" (10:1).

In all this two pertinent facts stand out quite boldly: (1) all these things are declared to have testified to the work of Jesus Christ that was yet future, and (2) with the accomplishment of the work of Jesus Christ their usefulness would be at an end. By means of these things the Old Testament believers could see the work of the Savior as in a glass, darkly. But with the coming of Christ himself, they could not but become as unnecessary as they once were essential. Thus the abrogation of the ceremonial law is plainly affirmed. The "handwriting of requirements," says Paul, Christ "has taken . . . out of the way, having nailed it to the cross" (Col. 2:14). He "abolished in His flesh the enmity, that is, the law of commandments contained in ordinances" (Eph. 2:15).

The Jews were loath to learn this. Even Peter was reluctant to accept it (Acts 10:14). But the Holy Spirit himself was pleased to guide the Jerusalem Synod to an unequivocal stand against the continuance of the ceremonial obligations of the Old Testament (Acts 15:5, 10). The political or civil laws of Israel were of a similar temporary character. This is self-evident, for what permanent obligation could there be for the assignment of tribes to particular regions of Canaan, for example (Josh. 18–19), or for the various groups who did service under the reign of David (1 Chron. 25–27)? The Israel of God is now international and therefore no longer subject to these ordinances in any way (Gal. 6:16; Gen. 22:18; Eph. 2:19–22).

This is clear enough to us. But it is sometimes thought that it was not at all clear to those who lived under the ceremonial and civil laws of the Old Testament. No doubt the degree to which the Old Testament believers recognized the transient nature of the ceremonial and civil laws of Israel varied from person to person and from age to age. But there is good reason to affirm that some recognition of this was a possession of true believers even from the beginning.

This we say, first, because of the dramatic difference between the manner in which God revealed the moral law (the Ten Commandments) and the ceremonial and civil laws. God revealed the ceremonial and civil laws through Moses, who wrote them on vellum or parchment. But God himself wrote the Ten Commandments, and he wrote them not on perishable skins but upon tablets of stone—symbolic of the permanence belonging to them.

We say this, secondly, because of the statements of the Old Testament believers which indicated a conscious distinction made by them between the moral law and the ceremonial and civil ordinances. David contrasts the observance of ceremonial and moral laws as follows: "For You do not desire sacrifice, or else I would give it; You do not delight in burnt offering. The sacrifices of God are a broken spirit, a broken and a contrite heart—these, O God, You will not despise" (Ps. 51:16–17). "Sacrifice and offering You did not desire; my ears You have opened. Burnt offering and sin offering You did not require. Then I said, 'Behold, I come; in the scroll of the book it is written of me. I delight to do Your will, O my God, and Your law is within my heart" (Ps. 40:6–8). These statements do not mean that David felt no obligation to observe the ceremonial ordinances. He was not forgiven apart from them, for they were a means by which the grace of Christ was administered to him. But he indicated that he was well aware of the difference between ceremonial and moral legislation. His words anticipated the abolition of the one and the continuance of the other.

So the prophet says, "Thus says the Lord of hosts . . . I did not speak to your fathers, or command them in the day that I brought them out of the land of Egypt, concerning burnt offerings or sacrifices. But this is what I commanded them, saying, 'Obey My voice, and I will be your God, and you shall be My people. And walk in all the ways that I have commanded you' " (Jer. 7:21–23). And Samuel said, "Has the Lord as great delight in burnt offerings and sacrifices, as in obeying the voice of the Lord? Behold, to obey is better than sacrifice" (1 Sam. 15:22). The ceremonial law evidenced its temporary character by its very inability to "make those who approach perfect" (Heb. 10:1). Since it could "never take away sins" actually (10:11), the Holy Spirit himself testified that something better would have to supplant the ceremonial ordinances, namely, the one oblation of Jesus (Heb. 10:12–14; Jer. 31:33–34). Perhaps the most conclusive demonstration of the consciousness of the temporary character of the ceremonial and civil laws in the minds of the Old Testament believers is the fact that predictions of the coming suffering of Christ are given in ceremonial terms (Isa. 53:7, 11; Dan. 9:25–27; Zeph. 1:7–8).

QUESTIONS

1. Besides the moral law God also gave two other types of laws. What were they?
2. What was the purpose of the ceremonial law?
3. Prove that it has been abolished.
4. What was the purpose of the civil laws?
5. Did Old Testament believers themselves recognize a distinction between the Ten Commandments and the ceremonial and civil ordinances? Give two proofs.
6. What defect in the ceremonial law itself indicated the need for something better?

XIX, 6–7

6. *Although true believers be not under the law, as a covenant of works, to be thereby justified, or condemned; yet is it of great use to them, as well as to others; in that, as a rule of life informing them of the will of God, and their duty, it directs and binds them to walk accordingly; discovering also the sinful pollutions of their nature, hearts, and lives; so as, examining themselves thereby, they may come to further conviction of, humiliation for, and hatred against sin, together with a clearer sight of the need they have of Christ, and the perfection of his obedience. It is likewise of use to the regenerate, to restrain their corruptions, in that it forbids sin; and the threatenings of it serve to show what even their sins deserve, and what afflictions, in this life, they may expect for them, although freed from the curse thereof threatened in the law. The promises of it, in like manner, show them God's approbation of obedience, and what blessings they may expect upon the performance thereof; although not as due to them by the law as a covenant of works. So as, a man's doing good, and refraining from evil, because the law encourageth to the one, and deterreth from the other, is no evidence of his being under the law, and not under grace.*

7. *Neither are the forementioned uses of the law contrary to the grace of the gospel, but do sweetly comply with it; the Spirit of Christ subduing and enabling the will of man to do that freely, and cheerfully, which the will of God, revealed in the law, requireth to be done.*

These sections of the Confession teach us (1) that true believers are not "under law" as a covenant of salvation, (2) but that they are "under" it as (a) a rule of practice, (b) a means of knowing their sin and consequent need of Christ, and (c) a revelation of Christ's perfection, (3) that it is also operative upon the unregenerate (a) to restrain them, (b) to warn them, and (c) to reveal God to them, (4) that "a man's doing good, and refraining from evil, because the law encourageth to the one and detereth from the other, is no evidence of his being under the law, and not under grace," and (5) that these uses of law are in no way contrary to gospel grace but, rather, essential to it.

We have mentioned those who say, on the basis of Romans 6:14, that they are "not under law but under grace," by which they mean that they believe themselves to be free from all obligation to keep the Ten Commandments because they are believers. It is mistakenly supposed that grace delivers one from all guilt and punishment of sin without concern for deliverance from the practice of sin. Yet this very text (Rom. 6:14) appears in a passage dealing with deliverance from the practice of sin (Rom. 6:1–23). Paul's great affirmation here is that sin cannot have dominion in the life of a believer (vv. 2, 7, 14, 22). And the reason that sin cannot dominate a believer is precisely the fact that he is "not under law but under grace." If he were still under law, he would still be dominated by sin. Because he is under grace instead of the law, he is no longer dominated by sin.

Many today would say, "Yes, I can violate the Sabbath day, because I am not under law but under grace." But Paul is saying, in effect and principle, "No, I cannot disregard the Sabbath, for I am under grace, not law, and sin shall not have dominion over me." Thus the solution lies in a proper understanding of what it means to be *"under* law" or *"under* grace" to "live under the terms or conditions of" either that covenant that holds out the prospect of eternal life as a result of law keeping by the sinner himself, or that covenant which is called the covenant of grace. But this does not mean that there can be *no* aspect of law in the covenant of grace, nor vice versa.

We are born by generation from Adam under obligation to keep God's law perfectly *as the condition of life*. To be under the law means to have the obligation to keep the commandments perfectly and perpetually or else perish. But because of Adam's fall, and our fall in him, this is a "hopeless" covenant. To be under grace is to be under the terms or conditions of a covenant which grants life to man without his having rendered prior perfect and perpetual obedience to the law. Obedience to the law, then, is not the means of salvation, but grace alone is.

However, note two important aspects of the covenant of grace which involve the law. First, the grace that is given to the sinner has a legal basis. Jesus Christ rendered perfect and perpetual obedience to the law and received the penalty required for the sinner. There is no grace without that fulfilling of the law. And second, the grace that is given leads to greater righteousness than is the case without it. Grace is not only legal but also remedial, providing a renewing work of God in the heart of a sinner, bringing new power and desire for righteousness, the result of which is the keeping of the law to a greater degree by far than is the case with the unconverted (Rom. 6:22; Gal. 5:22–25; Eph. 5:9). Thus it is clear that being under grace, rather than law, is not a case of "being without law toward God, but under law toward Christ" (1 Cor. 9:21).

The law is of great importance to believers. (1) It is (as a summary of God's complete and holy will) the only infallible rule of practice. The apostles frequently quote these commandments as the rule for believers (Rom. 13:9; Eph. 6:2). We are warned against any deprecation of the law (Matt. 5:19) and taught that its demands concern every inward thought (Matt. 5:21–48). It is the "carnal mind" which is "not subject to the law of God" (Rom. 8:7), but for the believer who delights in the law (7:22), it is called "the law of liberty" (James 1:25). (2) The law is also of value in revealing to believers their sin and their need of Christ. Paul said, "I would not have known sin except through the law" (Rom. 7:7). The law instructs (Gal. 3:19–25). It teaches men that they are lost in order that they might seek Christ. "For Christ is the end of the law for righteousness to everyone who believes" (Rom. 10:4). And this is not only true at the time of conversion. It is also true thereafter. The law teaches a believer the duty of perpetual repentance and faith. (3) Finally, the law discloses the glory of Christ. It shows us how holy he is (Matt. 5:17; Rom. 5:18–19). And it shows us the severity of the law and the punishment which it demanded of him.

With respect to the unbeliever nothing rivals the fact that the law executes the sentence of judgment against him. For "we know that whatever the law says, it says to those who are under the law, that every mouth may be stopped, and all the world may become guilty before God" (Rom. 3:19). Yet even in the case of the unbeliever the law accomplishes good. Though it incites enmity and sin (because of his depravity) it also restrains the outward expression of it (Rom. 2:14–15). Even in nations where the gospel has made little headway, there is some knowledge of the moral law, and it has some effect in restraining the progress of sin. But of course it can in no way remedy it.

QUESTIONS

1. What text is frequently misquoted as respects the believer's relation to the law?
2. What error is maintained by those who abuse this text?
3. What is the true meaning of "under" in this text?
4. What does it mean to be "under the law"?
5. What does it mean to be "under grace"?
6. How is law important to the covenant of grace?
7. Of what use is the law to believers?
8. What good does the law do in the case of unbelievers?

19

XX. Of Christian Liberty, and Liberty of Conscience

1. *The liberty which Christ hath purchased for believers under the gospel consists in their freedom from the guilt of sin, the condemning wrath of God, the curse of the moral law; and in their being delivered from this present evil world, bondage to Satan, and dominion of sin; from the evil of afflictions, the sting of death, the victory of the grave, and everlasting damnation; as also in their free access to God, and their yielding obedience unto him not out of slavish fear, but a child-like love and willing mind. All which were common also to believers under the law. But under the New Testament, the liberty of Christians is further enlarged in their freedom from the yoke of the ceremonial law, to which the Jewish Church was subjected; and in greater boldness of access to the throne of grace, and in fuller communications of the free Spirit of God, than believers under the law did ordinarily partake of.*

This section of the Confession teaches us (1) that Christ has purchased liberty for believers, (2) that this liberty consists of freedom from guilt, God's wrath and curse, the love of the world, bondage to Satan, the dominion of sin, the evil of afflictions, the sting of death, the victory of the grave, and eternal punishment; and freedom for access to God, obedience to him, and love for him, and (3) that the difference between liberty enjoyed by New Testament believers and Old Testament believers is one of degree rather than kind.

Chapter IX of the Confession speaks of "that natural liberty" with which God has "endued the will of man" so "that it is neither forced, nor by any absolute necessity of nature determined, to good or evil." And we have shown that man retains this liberty in each of four estates. But man, in his fallen estate, has liberty without ability to do good because of his total depravity. He is free to do as he pleases, but he is not pleased to do good at all.

The liberty that we consider here is that liberty which is purchased for the believer by Christ and bestowed by the Holy Spirit. And it is liberty which, because of a new ability, is liberty indeed. "If the Son makes you free, you shall be free indeed" (John 8:36). This is "the glorious liberty of the children of God" (Rom. 8:21). It consists in more than mere absence of outward constraint (which all men enjoy). It consists also in a restoration of inward ability to will and to do God's good pleasure, and freedom from the disabilities brought upon the sinner by his sin. The unconverted man has liberty, but his liability is such that he might well cry out with Cain, "My punishment is greater than I can bear! . . . I shall be a fugitive and a vagabond on the earth" (Gen. 4:13–14). He has liberty of will, but he is not free from the law, from sin, or from death. But the freedom or liberty of the children of God consists in deliverance from these.

(1) There is, then, freedom from the law. The believer is not under law but under grace. It is just as important to stress the true meaning of these words as to refute the false interpretation. Because Christ kept the law, the believer receives salvation only because of Christ's obedience, and he is freed from the obligation to keep the law of God perfectly as the means of obtaining life.

(2) This liberty also consists in deliverance from the dominion of sin. "The prince of the power of the air . . . who now works in the sons of disobedience" (Eph. 2:2–3) is supplanted in his dominion in the believer's heart by the Holy Spirit. The believer is "set free from sin" in order to become a servant of God (Rom. 6:22). This means that the whole kingdom or domain of sin is no longer his habitation. He is delivered "from this present evil age" (Gal. 1:4), not geographically, but in the sense that

he is alien to it and immune to its fashion of thought and life (1 John 2:15–17; Rom. 12:2). Satan no longer exercises lordship over him (Acts 26:18). Even those things which presently are (i.e., adversity, affliction, etc.) and those things which will be (i.e., death and the grave) the effects or consequences of sin are either immediately or eventually, wholly or partly, denied power over him. Adversity and affliction may be, and often are, wholly for the benefit of the believer and the glory of God. Even when there is chastisement for sin it is ultimately for good (Rom. 8:28; Job; Ps. 119:71). And while the evil of death will not be wholly removed until the resurrection (by which the body is made alive again, as the soul already has been made alive again by regeneration), yet the sting, or penal aspect of death, is removed, and the "victory of the grave" but temporary (1 Cor. 15:54–57).

(3) Thus the believer is liberated even from death itself, which is the end of sin. And even in death the believer does not die "the death," but rather "sleeps" in Jesus (Gen. 2:17; Mark 7:10; Rom. 6:9; 1 Thess. 4:14).

This liberty must not be confused with license. Some have used liberty "as a cloak for vice" (1 Peter 2:16), "as an opportunity for the flesh" (Gal. 5:13). This is not liberty. It is bondage under the disguise of liberty. True liberty is to be made free from sin to become the servant of God. It means restored ability as well as freedom to be the children of God. License is that vain and deceiving thing which Satan has offered as a substitute. It is the suggestion that sinful man be unrestricted in setting his own moral standards and doing his own will. "Do not be deceived," says the apostle, "God is not mocked; for whatever a man sows, that he will also reap. For he who sows to his flesh will of the flesh reap corruption, but he who sows to the Spirit will of the Spirit reap everlasting life" (Gal. 6:7–8). An inner desire and ability to strive to fulfill the law of God— that is true liberty. And the desire and will to do as we please, irrespective of the law, is license, and it is sin.

The difference between the Old and New Testament believer is sometimes described as if the Old Testament believer had no such liberty as belongs to the believer under the gospel. This error is the reverse of that which teaches that the Christian enjoys license (that is, complete freedom from all duty to keep the law). It teaches that the Old Testament believer enjoyed no portion of the liberty of the children of God. This view is refuted by the Scripture teaching that "the blessing of Abraham" has "come upon the Gentiles in Christ Jesus" (Gal. 3:14). Like other errors, this too is an exaggeration of an important truth, namely, that there is an increased degree of liberty belonging to New Testament believers. But this increased degree of liberty is due to the abrogation of the ceremonial law (which was borne by the Old Testament believer and not by the New Testament believer) and not because of any essential difference in deliverance from the moral law, from sin, or death. We have a much greater degree or measure of liberty because that which was administered through types and ordinances is now administered in complete fullness by Christ through the operation of the Holy Spirit.

QUESTIONS

1. What is meant by "natural liberty"?
2. How does the liberty belonging to believers differ from this natural liberty?
3. From what is the believer freed?
4. How is the believer freed from this present evil world?
5. Since believers die, how can it be said that they are freed from death?
6. What is the difference between liberty and license?
7. In what respects was the Old Testament believer free as we are?
8. In what respect was the Old Testament believer not free as we are?

XX, 2–3

2. *God alone is Lord of the conscience, and hath left it free from the doctrines and commandments of men which are in anything contrary to his Word, or beside it if matters of faith or worship. So that to believe such doctrines, or to obey such commandments, out of conscience, is to betray true liberty of conscience; and the requiring of an implicit faith, and an absolute and blind obedience, is to destroy liberty of conscience, and reason also.*

3. *They who, upon pretense of Christian liberty, do practice any sin, or cherish any lust, do thereby destroy the end of Christian liberty, which is, that, being delivered out of the hands of our enemies, we*

> *might serve the Lord without fear, in holiness and righteousness*
> *before him, all the days of our life.*

These sections of the Confession teach us (1) that God alone has legitimate authority over the conscience, (2) that his Word alone is the rule thereof, (3) that the doctrines and commandments of men which are either contrary to or *additional* to God's Word in respect to worship have no authority to bind the conscience, (4) that to permit the conscience to be bound by such is sin, betrayal of true liberty of conscience, and a denial that God alone is one's Lord, and (5) that Christian liberty must be distinguished from antinomianism (which means "freedom to sin").

Here stands one of the glorious benefits of the Reformation for which our fathers gave their all. It was this truth, so clearly taught in Scripture, that was wholly eclipsed in the apostasy of the Roman Church. It was recovered only by the blood of many martyrs. The strong determination of covenanting Presbyterians in Scotland who would surrender to no man the crown rights of Jesus Christ is to be remembered reverently. They recaptured the spirit of the Apostolic Church as they answered those who tried to coerce them to believe or to do what was contrary to the Word of Christ: "We ought to obey God rather than men" (Acts 5:29).

We must not forget that the Reformation was much more than mere separation from the authority of the pope and the errors of Rome. It was not, after all, a struggle against something so much as a glorious witness for Christ. It was a witness made in every sphere of life. For example, there were kings on earth who were not wholly unhappy to see the structure of Roman Catholic power weakened by the rise of Reformed Christianity. Yet sometimes these same kings determined to take charge of the Church themselves. When it dawned on them that Reformed Christians meant to acknowledge none but Christ as "king and head of the Church," they were capable of terrible persecution. Much of the suffering endured by the authors of our Confession came at the hand of such kings. But thanks be to God, they stood by the grand truth of Scripture, and by that mighty principle such tyrants were themselves doomed. God alone is Lord in the Church and in the conscience. We are "bought with a price" and must not be "the slaves of men" (1 Cor. 7:23).

Today we almost take for granted the precious legacy which has accrued from this principle. The separation of Church and State, by which we mean the liberty to believe and to practice one's faith without coercion by men, is an example. We are not saying that this principle is always respected in a nation such as our own. Indeed, we believe that the state control of education increasingly threatens this very principle. A false and anti-Christian philosophy of life, in practical utterance if not in theory, is being forced upon those who teach in the public school system of this nation. And the day may come when those who teach will have to suffer in order to speak and to act as if God were sovereign in all things.

But let us give more detailed consideration to a very common violation of the principle under consideration, a violation found in many Protestant churches and even in those that claim this Confession! In such churches it is customary to make certain specific rules which are imposed upon members of the church as a matter of duty, thus binding the conscience.

These rules are of two kinds: (1) some are contrary to the Word of God. Examples of rules which are contrary to the Word of God are prohibitions requiring total abstinence from the use of certain material things. The Mormon religion forbids the use of coffee. Other sects forbid the use of meat. And truly, time would fail to mention all such forbidden things for the number is legion. However, in not one case is it possible to show that such abstinence is required by God. This is impossible because "there is nothing unclean of itself" (Rom. 14:14). "All things indeed are pure" (14:20). If nothing is unclean, then no such rule forbidding the use of something can be legitimate. If all things indeed are pure, then all things may indeed be used by men without fear of conscience.

It is true, of course, that once a person has allowed his conscience to be bound by such a (false) rule, he cannot partake of the forbidden thing without sinning. We have already shown how and why this is so (chapter XVI). "To him who considers anything to be unclean, to him it is unclean. . . . It is evil for [that] man . . . because [it is] not from faith; for whatever is not from faith is sin" (Rom. 14:14, 20, 23). It is never right to do what we believe to be wrong, even when we believe a thing to be wrong without good reason. But even if a person faithfully obeys his conscience and scrupulously observes a rule forbidding the use of a material thing, he is still guilty of sin. He is guilty of the sin of allowing someone other than God to impose a rule upon his conscience.

To this it is objected that without such rules (forbidding, or at least restricting, the free use of material things) the only possible result will be "all-out intemperance." It is either total abstinence or there is unavoidable certainty of wicked abuse. We have already shown that this is a false expectation. We have shown the difference between true liberty and sinful license (XX, 1). We shall say here only that it is extremely dishonoring to the Holy Spirit of God to maintain such an objection. For this objection is tantamount to saying that a man-made rule will keep a Christian from sin better than will the Holy Spirit who dwells in him. To say that the Holy Spirit cannot guide the Christian in the free use of material things which he has not forbidden is to charge God foolishly.

(2) The second class of rules are those that are, if not contrary, then at least additional to the Word of God. As an example we might mention many of the rules imposed upon members of the Roman Catholic Church. No doubt many of these rules are contrary to the Word of God, but even those that are not are often additions to the Bible. "The chief commandments or laws of the Church," we read in the Roman Catechism, "are these six: (1) to assist at Mass on all Sundays and holy days of obligation, (2) to fast and to abstain on the days appointed, (3) to confess our sins at least once a year, (4) to receive Holy Communion during the Easter time, (5) to contribute to the support of the Church, and (6) to observe the laws of the Church concerning marriage."

We do not think that it could be proved contrary to the Bible to fast on those days which happen to be appointed by the Roman Church. Certainly the Christian ought to confess his sins (to God through Christ alone). And it would be perfectly proper to receive holy communion (if it is rightly administered) on that Lord's Day which Rome presumes to call "Easter." But though it is not wrong to do these things voluntarily, in a proper manner, it is wrong to permit the conscience to be *bound* to do them in the manner and at the time designated by Rome.

Let us cite another example: the Baptist churches insist upon immersion as the form of baptism. It is not contrary to the Word of God to baptize by immersion. But it is an addition to the Word of God to *require* that baptism be by immersion only. And to permit the conscience to be bound by such a rule is wrong even though immersion itself is not.

It has been said that there is "a pope in every man's heart." We are all tempted to think that we could improve our fellow Christians if we had charge of their conscience. We are likewise all liable to imagine that we are doing much better than others in the use of our cherished liberty. We would restrict others and relax strictures against ourselves. But the Scripture requires the reverse: charity towards others, and carefulness in the use of our own liberty. We ought to give our brother the benefit of any doubt. We should esteem others better than ourselves. And even where it appears that our brother has abused his liberty, we should correct in meekness, taking heed to ourselves. Meanwhile, we should guard against the abuse of our own liberty, taking heed that we do not make it an occasion of the flesh, and exercising care that we do not cause a weaker brother to stumble by the exercise of our liberty.

Questions

1. What was the great principle for which our fathers nobly contended?
2. Was this merely a struggle against the authority of the pope? Explain.
3. What principle of our national life is a fruit of this struggle?
4. Is there any threat to this principle in our nation today?
5. In what two ways is this principle denied in Protestant and even Reformed churches today?
6. Cite an example of each.
7. Why is it wrong to submit the conscience to a rule requiring total abstinence from the use of a particular material thing?
8. Why would it be wrong to submit the conscience to a rule requiring immersion?
9. Why has it been said that there is "a pope in every man's heart"?
10. What does liberty require of us as respects others?
11. What does liberty require of us as respects ourselves?

XX, 3 (continued)

It is alleged that such a doctrine of liberty as that set forth above will lead to sin. We have already refuted this in our discussion of license. However, we wish here to emphasize the fact that contrary to common impression, this doctrine (rightly understood) really shows the full scope of God's laws in man's life. It is not because the Reformed faith is interested in eliminating holiness and duty that it rejects all rules contrary or additional to the Word of God. Rather, it does so precisely because it recognizes that it is the Christian's duty—whether he eats, or drinks, or whatsoever he may do—to do all to the glory of God. When man's duty is *reduced* from divine principles to human rules, it is falsified because it is reduced. The Pharisees of old multiplied rules in an effort to cover the whole of life, but they did not even come close to the holiness of Christ, who rejected their rules in favor of the law of God (Mark 7:1–13). Some people cannot imagine that the Ten Commandments cover everything and that they do so without error or defect, but this is the case nonetheless.

Paul says that when the mind is transformed and renewed (by the inward operation of the law applied by the Holy Spirit), the individual believer will be able to prove what the will of God is (Rom. 12:2). He says that he will know (without man-made rules) what is "good and acceptable and perfect." We believe that a careful exegesis of this text will show that the meaning is as follows: (1) By the knowledge of the Ten Commandments, a believer will know that which is good. For example, he will know that playing the piano is good, for the simple reason that it is not forbidden by any one of the Ten Commandments. "We know that the law is good" (1 Tim. 1:8); therefore, that which is in accordance with, or not contrary to, the Ten Commandments is good. The act of playing the piano, considered in itself, is therefore good.

(2) The Christian must also consider the circumstances under which a particular thing is done. A good thing is not always acceptable (under just any and all circumstances). It is good to call upon the name of the Lord. But it must be done in an acceptable time (2 Cor. 6:2). Men who call upon the Lord only when it is too late will not be heard. So again, as an example, playing the piano may, or may not, be acceptable according to such circumstances as time and place. It would be wrong for a child to play the piano when father has forbidden it. It would be wrong to play the piano at any time in a "striptease" emporium.

(3) Finally, it is necessary that an act be done with the right intent or motive. This is what the apostle means by the perfect will of God. Again we will take as an example the act of playing the piano. It is conceivable that a person would do this good thing under proper circumstances and yet violate one or more of the Ten Commandments. Suppose that the purpose was to gain personal fame and fortune rather than to serve God.

Suppose that one played the piano only to make money and not to serve God. Then it would be wrong, not because it is a sin to play the piano, but because it is a sin to make it the chief end of one's life, or even to do it only as a means of making money without seeking to glorify him.

The truth is that when the law of God is rightly observed by a believer, it will prove much more demanding and will be much more stringent than the rules of men. But above all, such a believer will be preserved from the age-old ruin of the Pharisees, who thought that they were keepers of the law when they were really keeping only a few relatively easy rules. The making of rules by men deceives the heart because it reduces the breadth and depth of the Christian's duty to God. For this reason, if for no other, we should stedfastly reject them.

QUESTIONS

1. What false charge is made against the doctrine of Christian liberty?
2. What is the real reason why the Reformed faith rejects such man-made rules?
3. What does Paul mean by the three terms he uses in Romans 12:2?
4. Can a thing be good without being acceptable and perfect?
5. Can a thing be forbidden if God declares it to be good? Why?
6. Take any material thing that is an example of what is "forbidden" by human commandment, and show why it is good, when it may be acceptable, and how it may be perfect.
7. Why is the Reformed position more demanding than the opposing view?

XX, 4

4. *And because the powers which God hath ordained, and the liberty which Christ hath purchased, are not intended by God to destroy, but mutually to uphold and preserve one another, they who, upon pretense of Christian liberty, shall oppose any lawful power, or the lawful exercise of it, whether it be civil or ecclesiastical, resist the ordinance of God. And, for their publishing of such opinions, or maintaining of such practices, as are contrary to the light of nature, or to the known principles of Christianity (whether concerning faith,*

worship, or conversation), or to the power of godliness; or such
erroneous opinions or practices, as either in their own nature, or in the
manner of publishing or maintaining them, are destructive to the
external peace and order which Christ hath established in the
Church, they may lawfully be called to account, and proceeded
against by the censures of the Church, and by the power of the civil
magistrate.

This section of the Confession teaches us (1) that God has ordained authority in Church and State which (when operating in their proper spheres) are to be obeyed as part of our duty to God, and (2) that it belongs to each of these to enforce such authority within its own sphere.

The Christian never has liberty to oppose that which is ordained of God. As the apostle said, "Let every soul be subject to the governing authorities. For there is no authority except from God, and the authorities that exist are appointed by God. Therefore whoever resists the authority resists the ordinance of God, and those who resist will bring judgment on themselves" (Rom. 13:1–2). God has given to the State (or civil rulers) the power of the sword in order to punish crime (Rom. 13:3–6). And he has given to his Church the power of the keys, in order to shut out those who persist in heresy and immorality (Matt. 16:19; 18:15–18). Great harm results when these spheres are confused, or when either Church or State usurps the authority of the other.

For example, in those countries where the pope of Rome is able to determine civil policies, there have been suppression of the Protestant witness, opposition to the distribution of the Bible, and even violent persecution. Civil authority becomes tyrannical when it becomes an instrument of religious coercion. On the other hand, when the State has imposed upon its citizens the religion it wants them to have, or makes the "Church" a mere instrument of the State, the result is equally bad. For example, in Communist countries the State has often sought to control the Church. When this succeeds, error and immorality are not suppressed, but rather, only the "enemies of the State."

When civil or ecclesiastical authority contents itself with the sphere of divine appointment, and exercises that authority in a legitimate manner within that sphere, great blessings result. Much of the strength of our own nation—and of the churches in it—has been due to this principle.

However, we believe that there has arisen a grave threat to this principle in recent developments in both Church and State.

(1) We believe that there is a rising threat to this principle in the fact that liberal churches and church councils have increasingly sought to exercise power or influence more directly within the civil sphere. The older biblical view was that the Church would influence power in the State by bringing individuals under the authority of Christ. But it would not "intermeddle with civil affairs, which concern the commonwealth, unless by way of humble petition, in cases extraordinary; or by way of advice for satisfaction of conscience, if . . . thereunto required by the civil magistrate." If the State acted to the detriment of the spiritual freedom of the Church, it would of course make humble petition. And if, in an extraordinary case, the civil authorities sought advice from the Church, it would be proper for the Church to speak directly of civil matters. But otherwise the Church was "to handle or conclude nothing but that which is ecclesiastical." This does not mean that the Church did not concern itself with civil matters. Nor does it mean that the Church was silent about duties of Christian citizenship. What it means is that the Church taught *principles* revealed in the Word of God respecting civil duties, and that it did not try to formulate *policy,* which is the proper duty of the civil authority.

But it is precisely the reverse in many instances today. Certainly the Church ought to teach that it is the duty of civil magistrates to use the power of the sword "to execute wrath on him who practices evil" (Rom. 13:4). The Church should teach the principles of the Scripture which sanction and require capital punishment, the maintenance of armies and navies, and the duty of self-defense. But in our recent history such organizations as the National Council of Churches have not only failed to teach biblical principles such as these, but also have sought to enunciate policies contrary to these principles, and to influence the civil authorities directly to adopt these wrong policies. Such policies as unilateral disarmament, pacifism, abolishment of capital punishment, and the abandonment of national sovereignty for world government have been advocated. And the evil is, not only that the Church thus intrudes directly into the affairs of State, weakening it, but also that it has neglected its divinely ordained task of suppressing heresy and immorality by spiritual means within the Church and spreading the gospel in the world. By seeking to get at least a measure of control of State power, it has neglected to use the keys of the kingdom of God. In such churches it is now commonly the case that error and heresy are unchecked.

(2) There is also a rising threat to the Christian faith, and to faithful churches, in our nation today. This is an indirect threat in that it does not come from direct interference in the affairs of the Church. It comes rather from the rising trend of state control of education and the like. The family is a divine institution, as are Church and State. And God has given the authority and responsibility for the education of children to parents, rather than to Church or State. This does not mean that Church and State have no authority in this regard. The Church has the authority and duty to see to it that parents bring up their children in the nurture and admonition of the Lord. The State also has the right to require sufficient education as will enable citizens to know and to do their duty and to obey the laws of the land. But the State does not have the right or authority to exclude God from the educational process, as is increasingly the case. Thought control is usually associated with nations that are ruled by dictators, and in which atheism holds sway. Yet public school education in our nation is more and more rigidly non-theistic, because God, the true God Jesus Christ, and his holy Word, the Bible, are excluded from the educational process. And because this intrudes upon an inherent right of Christians, who are members of the body of Christ, and required by him to see to it that their children are always and in everything conditioned by God and his Word, it is a violation of the principle here under consideration.

It is tragic that this violation of the biblical principle has been accomplished under the guise of devotion to this principle. We do not mean that the State should put its imprimatur upon the doctrines of any sect. (This is exactly what *is* being done. The doctrines being imposed today belong to the "sect" called "atheistic humanism.") Rather, the parents should decide which religious viewpoint should be taught their children. Everyone has a religious viewpoint. Thus the correct and biblical answer we believe to be parent-controlled Christian schools for Christians, and not State-controlled non-Christian schools for everyone.

We will discuss the principle of proper separation of State and Church further under chapters XXIII, XXV, and XXX. Here we must note that the original version of this section of the Westminster Confession concludes with the statement that those persons who "are destructive to the

external peace and order which Christ hath established in the Church .
. . may lawfully be called to account, and proceeded against by the censures of the Church, *and by the power of the civil magistrate.*" The italicized
words are deleted by many American revisions of the Confession. No
doubt the reason for this deletion has been a desire to remove all danger
of offering encouragement to the State to interfere in purely ecclesiastical matters. History indicates that the fear of civil abuses in punishment
of this kind is not groundless.

However, we would defend the original formulation. For the Confession carefully limits the civil magistrate to the cases involving that which
is "destructive to the *external* peace and order" of the Church. In other
words, it is not against unlawful *opinions* but only destructive *actions* affecting external peace and order that the civil authority may properly take
action. For example, if a person went around detesting statues of the Virgin Mary, witnessing to men against them, and converting others to his
own view, he could not be justly acted against by the government of the
State. But if he entered the premises of a Roman Catholic Church and
disrupted the worship, or destroyed these statues, he could and ought to
be arrested and punished by the law, not because he held a wrong opinion about such statues, but because he had performed an unlawful act,
namely, destroying someone else's property.

QUESTIONS

1. What other authority is there for the Christian besides the Scripture?
2. What is the proper sphere of each?
3. What happens when the two are confused or violated?
4. Give a modern example of the Church's intrusion into the sphere
   of State.
5. Give a modern example of the State's intrusion into the sphere of
   religion.
6. What are the evils that result?
7. Should the State determine the religious aspect of education? Is there
   such a thing as education without a religious aspect? Explain.
8. Did the original conclusion of this section of the Confession permit or encourage civil rulers to punish people for their convictions?
   Explain.

CHAPTER

20

XXI. Of Religious Worship, and the Sabbath Day

1. *The light of nature showeth that there is a God, who hath lordship and sovereignty over all, is good, and doeth good unto all, and is therefore to be feared, loved, praised, called upon, trusted in, and served with all the heart, and with all the soul, and with all the might. But the acceptable way of worshiping the true God is instituted by himself, and so limited by his own revealed will, that he may not be worshiped according to the imaginations and devices of men, or the suggestions of Satan, under any visible representation, or any other way not prescribed in the holy Scripture.*

2. *Religious worship is to be given to God, the Father, Son, and Holy Ghost; and to him alone; not to angels, saints, or any other creature: and, since the fall, not without a Mediator; nor in the mediation of any other but of Christ alone.*

These sections of the Confession teach us (1) that natural revelation is sufficient to inform men *that* they are obligated to worship the true God, but (2) that it is not sufficient to tell men *how* to worship God, so that (3) "the acceptable way of worshiping the true God is *instituted* by himself, and so *limited* by his own revealed will, that he may not be worshiped according to the imaginations and devices of men" or in "any other way not *prescribed* in the holy Scripture," (4) that God alone is the proper object of true worship, and (5) that he can be worshiped only through the mediation of Christ.

We have already shown (chapter 1) that natural revelation makes the true God known to men so that they cannot but sense that they owe him worship and obedience. But whereas the worship of sinless man in paradise was immediate (that is, without a mediator or savior), sin has made man incapable of such worship. Sin affected man's relationship with God in two ways. God's presence was withdrawn (Gen. 3:22–24), and man's heart was darkened. Accordingly, worship, to be acceptable to God, had to reckon with this alienation. But there was no way in which sinful man could reverse or annul God's withdrawal and his own heart's darkness. Thus, by the nature of the case, true worship could not exist except by divine provision. And this is the same as to say that such worship was— and is—*instituted* by God, *limited* by God, and *prescribed* by God.

(1) By *instituted* worship the Confession means worship which has been authorized, commanded, or established by God. The worship of Cain, for example, differed from that of Abel. God had not respect to Cain or to his offering. But the worship of Abel was approved of God. When Cain refused to change his worship to that which God approved or sanctioned, it was because he did not accept the principle that true worship requires explicit divine approval or sanction. When men worship God in any way not appointed or commanded by God, they worship in vain (Mark 7:7). The sin of Israel, when they "also built the high places" and burned their offerings to Baal, was that they did that *which I did not command* or speak, nor did it come into My mind," said the Lord (Jer. 19:5). Nadab and Abihu were consumed by the fire of the Lord because they "offered profane fire"; it was profane because it was fire "which He had not commanded them" (Lev. 10:1). That which is instituted (commanded or established) by God is true worship. That which is not instituted by God is *for that reason* false worship.

(2) This principle (that true worship is worship that God has instituted) necessarily involves the corollary that it is *limited* by his revealed will. It is limited because God has commanded only certain things in his worship. Sections 3–5 of this chapter show us that God has instituted or prescribed as the usual parts of worship (a) prayer, (b) the reading and preaching of the Word, (c) the singing of psalms, (d) the administration of the sacraments, and—as occasional parts of worship—(e) oaths, vows, and

solemn fastings. Proof of the divine institution of these elements of worship is easily cited from Scripture. God has told us to observe these things in his worship. But he has also revealed his abhorrence of anything and everything that men may presume to invent or to devise without such divine scriptural warrant. Thus we cannot say that true worship is *instituted* (or prescribed) without also saying that it is *limited*.

This view is simple to state, but it has not proved simple to practice. And this is because of the sinfulness of the human heart which ever tends to think along the lines of the wicked Israelites of old who said, "We will walk according to our own plans, and we will every one obey the dictates of his evil heart" (Jer. 18:12). Thus a rival principle has won a wide following, not only among Roman Catholics and Lutherans, but even among those who claim the Reformed faith. This view is that true worship need not consist of only what God has commanded, but that it may also consist of that which he has not commanded, provided it be not expressly forbidden in the Word. We diagram these two views in figure 4.

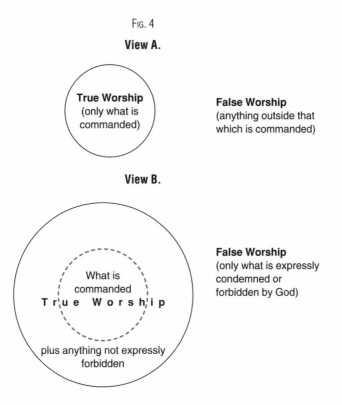

Fig. 4

View A.

True Worship
(only what is
commanded)

False Worship
(anything outside that
which is commanded)

View B.

What is
commanded
True Worship

plus anything not expressly
forbidden

False Worship
(only what is expressly
condemned or
forbidden by God)

View A is explained above. View B, it will be noted, considers the things which God has commanded to be only a part (often it is only a small part) of legitimate worship. Thus, for example, in Roman Catholic worship there is a great mass of ceremonies, symbols, and activities which are allowed, and they can be changed or added to on the basis of this spurious principle. Such worship is offered in vain (Matt. 15:9). It is false worship because it has no sanction behind it other than the will of man. These "things indeed have an appearance of wisdom in self-imposed religion," but they are "of no value against the indulgence of the flesh" (Col. 2:23). To worship in the way that we please, without proof that it is God's will, is to worship our own will rather than God. And what must be vigorously stressed is that there is no other stable safeguard of the purity of true worship if this principle is abandoned, as it has been, and is being, abandoned even by many who profess adherence to this Confession. (For example, what command requires the candlelight service so common today? But if such a "ceremony" as this, invented by Protestants, is not ruled out, how can the ceremonies invented by Rome be condemned?) God will not be worshiped except as he wills. And therefore true worship is both *instituted* (prescribed) and *limited*. There are only two categories: what God has commanded is legitimate, and what God has not commanded is excluded.

Does this mean that there is *nothing* that may be done in a Reformed church except what is commanded in the Bible? Not exactly. There are "some circumstances concerning the worship of God . . . which are to be ordered by the light of nature, and Christian prudence, according to the general rules of the Word" (I, 6). These "circumstances" are such as are "common to human actions and societies." But one must be careful to distinguish between the *circumstances of* worship and the *worship* itself. For example: Scripture does not prescribe the hour of the day at which public worship of the congregation is to be held. Neither has the Lord prescribed the shape, style, or size of the place of worship. In the nature of the case, such circumstances will vary from country to country, season to season, and location to location. There is a general rule, however, which requires that congregations assemble somewhere on the Lord's Day. The general rule controls the particular situation according to the circumstances. But when the congregation has assembled at the agreed place, the worship must then be only that which God has commanded.

True worship is addressed to God, and God exists in three persons—the Father, the Son, and the Holy Ghost. This follows from what has been shown under II, 3, in our discussion of the doctrine of God. But here we note that true worship must also be rendered through the mediation of Christ. As A. A. Hodge points out, the Church of Rome denies this in both theory and practice. Rome teaches (1) that the Virgin Mary and other saints (and even angels) are to be given a degree or kind of religious worship, (2) that they are to be invoked for help in time of need, (3) that they are able to intercede with God or with Christ for us, (4) that God may be asked to save and help us (at least in part) on the ground of the merits of the saints, and (5) that the pictures, images, and relics of saints and martyrs are to be retained in churches and worshiped. (See the decrees of the Council of Trent.) "To avoid the charge of idolatry . . . they distinguish between (a) *Latria,* or the highest religious worship, which is due to God alone, and (b) *Doulia,* or that inferior religious worship which is due in various degrees to saints and angels according to their rank. (Some also use the term *Hyperdoulia* as due to the Virgin Mary alone.) They also distinguish between (a) *direct* worship which is due severally to God, to the Virgin, or to the saints and angels, and (b) that *indirect* worship which terminates upon the picture or image which represents to the worshiper the direct object of his worship" (*The Confession of Faith* [London: Banner of Truth, 1958], p. 273).

In reply to the Roman Catholic teaching, many sound arguments may be given. (1) Jesus said, "It is written, 'You shall worship the Lord your God, and Him only you shall serve'" (Matt. 4:10; Deut. 6:13). The reasons for the worship of God argue against the worship of any other being. God has commanded us to worship him alone. (2) But Scripture also explicitly forbids the worship of men and angels (Acts 14:14–15; Col. 2:18; Acts 10:25–26). (3) The Second Commandment expressly forbids the use of pictures or images to represent Christ or to assist us in our reverencing him (see Larger Catechism, Q/A 109). (4) The saints do not become superhuman merely because they are in heaven. They are not endowed with the divine attributes requisite for receiving worship and making mediation between God and man. (5) And the Scripture states that there is only "one Mediator between God and men, the Man Christ Jesus" (1 Tim. 2:5). The very thought of other mediators is derogatory of the exclusive honor that belongs to him.

But let us again stress this point: if we once admit that true worship is not limited by God's revealed will—if we once allow that man *can* rightly add even one element to divine worship—it becomes exceedingly diffi-cult to refute the devious arguments and distinctions such as those between *latria* and *doulia* and "direct" and "indirect" worship. One reason why Protestantism is experiencing a gradual return of pictures, ceremonies, and the like, is that it has (often without realizing it) lost its hold on the regulative principle of true worship. There is no safeguard for purity of worship except conscious and persistent adherence to this principle: what is commanded is right, and what is not commanded is wrong.

QUESTIONS

1. What must true worship since the fall take into account?
2. What does it mean to say that true worship is "instituted"?
3. What does it mean to say that true worship is "limited"?
4. Why were Nadab and Abihu consumed by fire from God (Lev. 10:1–2)?
5. According to the Reformed view how many types of worship are there?
6. According to non-Reformed churches how many types of worship are there?
7. What is "will-worship"?
8. What is meant by the phrase "some circumstances concerning the worship of God"?
9. Give a general rule which controls an action affected by circumstances.
10. To whom may worship be given according to Rome?
11. What are the kinds of worship according to Rome?
12. State two or three arguments against such worship.
13. Why are Protestants today often weak in their arguments against Rome?

XXI, 3–4

3. *Prayer, with thanksgiving, being one special part of religious worship, is by God required of all men: and, that it may be accepted, it is to be made in the name of the Son, by the help of his Spirit, according*

to his will, with understanding, reverence, humility, fervency, faith,
love, and perseverance; and, if vocal, in a known tongue.

4. *Prayer is to be made for things lawful, and for all sorts of men living,*
or that shall live hereafter; but not for the dead, nor for those of whom
it may be known that they have sinned the sin unto death.

These sections of the Confession teach us (1) that prayer and thanksgiving are prescribed as part of true worship (i.e., they are commanded or
instituted by God), (2) that such is to be offered only through the mediator, Jesus Christ, (3) that the help of the Holy Spirit and the rule of Scripture are required to the proper offering thereof, and (4) that it is to be
offered in a common tongue. To say that prayer must be according to
the rule of Scripture is further explained to mean that it must be (a) for
things lawful (agreeable to the will of God), (b) for men living, (c) for
those who are yet to be born, but (d) not for the dead, or (e) for such as
may be known to have sinned the sin unto death.

That prayer is a prescribed element of true worship is evident throughout Scripture. From patriarchal times true worship was offered with prayer
and thanksgiving to God (Gen. 20:7, 17). "Moses prayed for the people"
(Num. 21:7). The book of inspired hymns and songs contains many references to the constant practice of prayer in Old Testament times (Pss.
4:1; 6:9; 17:1). At the dedication of the temple Solomon "stood before
the altar of the Lord in the presence of all the assembly of Israel" and uttered
a great prayer (1 Kings 8:22–53). In the New Testament this aspect or element of true worship continues. Christ was faithful in private prayer (Matt.
14:23), but he also prayed in the assembly of the Church (John 17). Prayer
was a constant element in the public worship of the Apostolic Church
(Acts 1:14; 2:42). And the apostles commanded prayer to be made in the
churches everywhere (1 Tim. 2:8; 1 Thess. 5:17; Eph. 6:18).

With the coming of Christ to accomplish the work of redemption, the
Old Testament mediatorial offices became exclusively his. He alone is
our great high priest, prophet, and king. For this reason all mediation is
in him. "No one comes to the Father except through Me," he said (John
14:6). "For through Him we . . . have access by one Spirit to the Father"
(Eph. 2:18). It is therefore only "in the name of the Lord Jesus" that we
are to give "thanks to God" (Col. 3:17). The atonement of Christ and
his intercession on our behalf are the basis of all true prayer.

In view of the *regulative principle* of true worship (what is commanded is right, what is not commanded is wrong), it may be thought that true prayer would consist only of a repetition of prayers found in Scripture. This is not the case, as may be proved from the command of the apostle, "Therefore I exhort first of all that supplications, prayers, intercessions, and giving of thanks be made for all men, for kings and all who are in authority, that we may lead a quiet and peaceable life in all godliness and reverence" (1 Tim. 2:1–2). Since it is clear that many kings, and other persons in authority, are not mentioned in the prayers written in the Bible, it is clear that God would not have us to merely recite the prayers of Scripture. But this does not mean that we are left to ourselves to pray according to our own will. (This again would be false worship.)

How then shall we pray out of our own hearts without being guilty of false worship? The answer is that God gives a special assistance by his Holy Spirit so that we can pray as he wills. "For we do not know what we should pray for as we ought, but the Spirit Himself makes intercession for us with groanings which cannot be uttered. Now He who searches the hearts knows what the mind of the Spirit is, because He makes intercession for the saints *according to the will of God*" (Rom. 8:26–27). If the *form* of our prayers had to be exactly the same as those that can be found in Scripture, our particular needs and desires would not be recognized. But if our prayers were not *formed* by the special assistance of the Holy Spirit—in accordance with the Word of God (or will of God)—they would be useless. To say that prayer is "free," then, is not to say that it is not prescribed. It *is* prescribed. But God has prescribed that we pray as the Spirit enables us to pray according to the will of God. And this means that the pattern or basic desires that find expression in true prayer must always be according to the structure of the Lord's Prayer (study the Larger Catechism, Q/A 186–96). All true prayer will conform to this structure. But liturgical (or set-form) prayers are not desirable, as a general rule, because God has commanded us to pray for specific persons and needs, with the immediate assistance of the Holy Ghost, according to the principles of the Word of God.

Prayer must be offered according to the rule of Scripture. "You ask and do not receive," says James, "because you ask amiss" (4:3). But "if we ask anything according to His will, He hears us" (1 John 5:14). Because of this statement in Scripture, there are those who never ask anything without also saying, "if it be Your will." This is not necessary. It confuses that which is known to be God's will with that which is God's secret will or decree. When prayer concerns that which God has not revealed, such as what is to happen at a future time, it is proper to say, "if it be Your will." Even Christ prayed so (Mark 14:35). But when we pray concerning that which is revealed in Scripture to be the will of God, we ought not to say, "if it be Your will."

For example, if we contemplate sinners who never repent, we may not ask God to bless them, saying, "if it be Your will." This is no doubt a crass way to state the matter, but there is a very common instance of this evil! There are those who pray that God will be merciful unto their relatives, and even save them from eternal damnation, even though they do not repent and believe the gospel. They pray, in effect, "Lord, be merciful even though they continue to persist in wickedness, if it be Your will." It is certainly not wrong to pray for God to convert them, if it be his will, for we do not know whether it is his will or not. But it would be wrong to pray that God would save them from eternal damnation even though they do not repent and believe, for we know that this is not the will of God.

Christ provided us with the example of praying for those who are not yet born. He prayed not only for his disciples who were with him, but also for those who would believe on him through their word (John 17:20). In view of the promise of God to believers and to their children (Acts 2:39) there is good reason to pray for our posterity, as Jonathan Edwards, the great New England Puritan, regularly did. But there is no reason to pray for the dead. If they were believers, there is nothing that we can ask for them that they do not already have. And if they were not, there is nothing that can be secured for them because "there is a great gulf fixed" (Luke 16:26). While his infant lived, David prayed for him. But when David knew that the child was dead, he ceased to fast and pray (2 Sam. 12). He said, "While the child was alive, I fasted and wept; for I said, 'Who can tell whether the Lord will be gracious to me, that the child may live?' But now he is dead; why should I fast?" (12:22–23). Before the child died, David could say, "Spare the child if it be Your will, Lord." But when the child died, he knew that it was not the will of God to spare the child, and with death his child was consigned to a place and condition that is irrevocable, and hence, beyond the proper concern of prayer.

There is real difficulty in the concluding statement of section 4, which states that prayer is not to be made "for those of whom it may be known that they have sinned the sin unto death." If this means only that a person persisted in sin and unbelief until he died, then the statement would merely repeat the prohibition of prayer for the dead. But if it means something else, it must then be asked (a) what is the sin designated, and (b) how may it be known when someone has sinned "the sin unto death"? If there is such a sin—as distinct from persistent unbelief—it must be the sin of blasphemy against the Holy Spirit (Matt. 12:31–32). This is willful and malicious refusal of pardon upon terms of the gospel offer (Heb. 10:29; 6:6). It is to sin willfully against the knowledge of the truth (Heb. 10:26) and to suffer the infliction of divine hardening which is final and incurable (2 Thess. 2:11–12). Paul says of such persons that "their folly will be manifest to all" (2 Tim. 3:9).

We believe that there is a sin properly designated "the sin unto death." We believe that it is of such a nature that it *is* manifest to all. When someone who has known the truth (like Judas), professed faith in Christ, and walked in the company of the Lord's people, makes deliberate and open apostasy from Christ—clear for all to see—it is right to pray against, rather than for, such (Ps. 69:22–28). It is important, of course, to pray for all others (1 John 5:16). But "there is sin leading to death," says John, and the Lord does not say that we should pray for such as are guilty of it.

QUESTIONS

1. Cite proof from the Old and the New Testaments that prayer and thanksgiving are prescribed by God as a part of true worship.
2. Why may true prayer be made only "in the name of Christ"?
3. Cite a Scripture text to prove this.
4. If true worship is only that which is prescribed, why are we *not* to use only the prayers written in the Bible?
5. Cite Scripture proof of this.
6. Does this mean that we are left to pray according to our own will?
7. Does Scripture prescribe the basic structure or pattern of prayer? Where?
8. Are all prayers (or petitions) to include the phrase "if it be Your will"? Why?
9. For whom are we to pray? Prove.

10. For whom are we not to pray? Prove.
11. What is "the sin unto death"?
12. Can we know a particular person to be guilty of this sin? Prove.

XXI, 5–6

5. *The reading of the Scriptures with godly fear, the sound preaching, and conscionable hearing of the Word, in obedience unto God, with understanding, faith, and reverence; singing of psalms with grace in the heart; as also the due administration and worthy receiving of the sacraments instituted by Christ, are all parts of the ordinary religious worship of God: besides religious oaths, vows, solemn fastings, and thanksgivings upon special occasions, which are, in their several times and seasons, to be used in a holy and religious manner.*

6. *Neither prayer, nor any other part of religious worship, is now, under the gospel, either tied unto, or made more acceptable by, any place in which it is performed, or towards which it is directed; but God is to be worshiped every where in spirit and in truth; as in private families daily, and in secret each one by himself; so more solemnly in the public assemblies, which are not carelessly or willfully to be neglected or forsaken, when God, by his Word or providence, calleth thereunto.*

These sections teach us (1) that divinely prescribed elements of true worship (in addition to prayer) are (a) *ordinary* (the preaching of the Word, singing of psalms, administration of the sacraments), and (b) *occasional* (oaths, vows, fasting, thanksgiving on special occasions), (2) that true worship is not attached to any special place as if it were more holy than other places, (3) that true worship is spiritual, truth being the essence of it, and (4) that God requires personal, family, and public worship, none of which are to be neglected or forsaken.

We have previously shown that there are two views as to what constitutes worship acceptable unto God. According to the one view, only what God has commanded is legitimate. According to the other, some elements of worship may be added without divine commandment to those elements that are commanded by God, and these together constitute what is considered legitimate. The Confession adheres to the former view and therefore limits true worship to that which can be proved from Scripture to be the will of God. What then are the elements of true worship?

The elements of true worship acknowledged by the Confession (as supplemented by the Larger Catechism, Q. 108) are (1) prayer, (2) reading of Scripture, (3) preaching of the Word, (4) administration of the sacraments, (5) church discipline, (6) the singing of psalms, (7) the receiving of offerings for the maintenance of the ministry, these being elements of the ordinary worship of God. There are also elements of a more occasional sort, namely, (1) religious oaths and vows, (2) thanksgiving upon special occasion, and (3) religious fasting.

Prayer is discussed in the section preceding. But first in the order of importance for true worship are assuredly the reading, preaching, and hearing of the Word of God. In the Apostolic Church the ministry of the Word of God had the pre-eminent place. Paul says, "Christ did not send me to baptize, but to preach the gospel . . . for the message of the cross is foolishness to those who are perishing, but to us who are being saved it is the power of God" (1 Cor. 1:17–18). Important as are the other elements of true worship, it is to be remembered that "faith comes by hearing, and hearing by the word of God" (Rom. 10:17). For this reason the Westminster Larger Catechism mentions "especially the word" and "especially the preaching of the word" as the means whereby Christ communicates to us the benefits of his mediation. True worship of God depends upon this element beyond all others. Despite other defects and impurities, we believe that true worship cannot altogether perish from that place in which there is yet a faithful preaching of the Word.

The sacraments duly administered and properly received are also a part of scriptural worship. This we know because the sacraments were instituted by Christ. He commanded that such as receive the gospel also be baptized (Matt. 28:19). And of the Lord's Supper, he commanded, "Do this in remembrance of Me" (1 Cor. 11:24). The sacraments are not given as a means of converting sinners unto Christ, as is true of the Word of God, but they are—together with the Word—a means of strengthening and confirming faith in the hearts of believers. Because they have been instituted by Christ with the requirement that they be continued in his

Church until he comes, there can be no pure worship where the sacraments are either eliminated or corrupted.

Another element of true worship is the "singing of psalms with grace in the heart." It will be observed that the Confession does not acknowledge the legitimacy of the use of modern hymns in the worship of God, but rather only the psalms of the Old Testament. It is not generally realized today that Presbyterian (and many other Reformed) churches originally used only the inspired psalms, hymns, and songs of the biblical Psalter in divine worship, but such is the case. The Westminster Assembly not only expressed the conviction that the psalms should be sung in divine worship, but implemented it by preparing a metrical version of the Psalter for use in the churches. This is not the place to attempt a consideration of this question. But we must record our conviction that the Confession is correct at this point. It is correct, we believe, because it has never been proved that God has commanded his Church to sing the uninspired compositions of men rather than or along with the inspired songs, hymns, and psalms of the Psalter in divine worship.

It may be questioned that church discipline should be regarded as an element of worship. The Confession does not describe it as a distinct element. Yet indirectly at least it is required. How else can there be a proper safeguard which will ensure that there are a *sound* preaching of the Word and a *proper* administration of the sacraments? And since the censure of the Church is to be administered "in the name of our Lord Jesus Christ, when [the Lord's people] are gathered together" and "with the power of our Lord Jesus Christ," it is, upon such occasions, a distinct element of that solemn worship which God requires of His people (1 Cor. 5:3–5).

In contrast to these divinely ordained elements of true worship, it is not difficult to see the extent to which many modern churches have departed from the principle of worship set forth in the Confession. In many churches today the preaching of the Word of God has lost the central place. The pulpit is often moved to one side. Formalism, elaborate liturgy, and invented ceremonies increase as the faithful preaching of the Word of God is diminished. Even in churches that adhere to the fundamentals of the Christian faith the sermon is often set aside for a motion picture or a religious drama. No doubt, sincere Christians who are used to such things would be shocked at the suggestion that these things are *in principle* the same as the false elements of worship sanctioned by the Church of Rome.

Yet such is the case. It is our conviction that the whole mass of superstition and error in Romish worship can be traced back to departure from the simple rule: what God has not commanded is forbidden.

The beauty of true worship is the beauty of holiness and truth. That which originates from a human source contradicts the glory of this spiritual worship. It is for this reason that the Confession does not allow for human art and imagination in its conception of worship. "Therefore, since we are the offspring of God, we ought not to think that the Divine Nature is like gold or silver or stone, something shaped by art and man's devising" (Acts 17:29). It is true that the tabernacle and temple were filled with symbolic "decorations" (Ex. 31:1–11), but there are two good reasons why this should not be regarded as a sanction for pictorial representations of Christ in murals, stained-glass windows, and the like. First, the whole ceremonial system of visible things has been abrogated. And second, the Old Testament ceremonial system was not created by human wisdom but by divine inspiration (see Ex. 25:40; 28:3; 31:6; 35:30–35; 1 Chron. 28:11–12, 19). Even if someone were to argue that the ceremonial system is still obligatory, there would be warrant only for exactly those symbols that were originally given by divine inspiration. Only that which man receives from God can be returned to God in true worship.

True worship is not attached to any particular place under the New Testament as it was under the Old (John 4:21, 23; Dan. 6:10). God has not commanded his people to assemble at any special place, or at any specific hour, on the Lord's Day. Consequently, there are certain things pertaining to true worship which are left within the province of human determination. Much false argument against the principle of pure worship set forth in the Confession has arisen from this obvious fact. But this argument is entirely due to a failure to distinguish between the *elements* and the *circumstances* of worship. As the Confession itself says (I, 6), "There are some circumstances concerning the worship of God . . . common to human actions and societies, which are to be ordered by the light of nature, and Christian prudence, according to the general rules of the Word, which are always to be observed." Circumstances of worship are such as the time, the place, the length of time to be engaged, the frequency of assembly, and the like. These things God has not regulated by specific command, but has left the Church to determine them. But the elements of worship, those precise things that constitute it, he has regulated by express command. There is no need to confuse these distinct matters.

The Confession also mentions what might be called occasional elements of true worship. Such elements as "religious oaths, vows, solemn fastings, and thanksgivings upon special occasions" are indeed warranted by the Word of God. Why then are they not listed among the ordinary elements of worship? It is because they are proper only upon certain occasions. Consider fasting, for example. In Roman Catholicism (and following the lead of the Roman Church are many Protestant churches today) certain days and seasons are *designated* for fasting. This is contrary to Scripture, which teaches that fasting is not acceptable unto God when it arises out of such mechanical regulation (see Mark 2:18–20; Matt. 6:16–18). For this reason Christ condemned the fasting of the Pharisees. He also stated that his disciples *could not* fast while the bridegroom was with them. When fasting arises out of a spontaneous and inward spiritual desire (i.e., because of mourning for sin, an earnest seeking of divine favor, an urgent personal crisis, or the like), it then becomes a part of true worship. The length of time involved varies (see 1 Sam. 7:6; 31:13; 2 Sam. 12:21; 2 Chron. 20:3; Neh. 1:4; Matt. 4:2; Acts 10:30; 13:2–3; 14:23). Observe once more the admirable consistency of the Confession. Fasting is an element of true worship only if it remains spontaneous and occasional, rather than being made a fixed part of the ordinary worship of God. (For a discussion of oaths and vows see chapter XXII.)

QUESTIONS

1. What are the elements of the ordinary worship of God?
2. What are the elements of worship that are occasional?
3. Which element of worship is especially important?
4. How can we be sure that the sacraments are a part of true worship?
5. What does the Confession allow to be sung in divine worship?
6. Was this practice always as strange as it seems to many today to be?
7. Why did the Westminster Assembly not approve of the use of uninspired compositions of men in divine worship?
8. Why is church discipline essential for true worship?
9. When does church discipline actually become an element of such worship?

10. What modern trends show that many churches have departed from the principle of worship set forth in the Confession?

11. What safeguard is there against the errors and additions of Romish worship?

12. Does the artistic symbolism of the tabernacle and temple justify the modern effort to make worship artistically beautiful? Why?

13. Has God left anything pertaining to worship to human determination? If so, what?

14. What is meant by "occasional" elements of worship?

15. Why does fasting cease to be a part of true worship when it is made a fixed and regular part of worship?

XXI, 7–8

7. *As it is of the law of nature, that, in general, a due proportion of time be set apart for the worship of God; so, in his Word, by a positive, moral, and perpetual commandment, binding all men in all ages, he hath particularly appointed one day in seven for a Sabbath, to be kept holy unto him: which, from the beginning of the world to the resurrection of Christ, was the last day of the week; and, from the resurrection of Christ, was changed into the first day of the week, which, in Scripture, is called the Lord's Day, and is to be continued to the end of the world, as the Christian Sabbath.*

8. *This Sabbath is then kept holy unto the Lord, when men, after a due preparing of their hearts, and ordering of their common affairs beforehand, do not only observe an holy rest, all the day, from their own works, words, and thoughts about their worldly employments and recreations, but also are taken up, the whole time, in the public and private exercises of his worship, and in the duties of necessity and mercy.*

These sections of the Confession teach us (1) that God has (by natural and special revelation) bound all men to observe the Sabbath, (2) that the weekly Sabbath was the seventh day in order of succession from creation to the resurrection of Christ, (3) that it is the first day in order from the resurrection onward, (4) and that God requires that this Sabbath be kept holy by (a) due preparation, (b) resting from worldly employments and recreations (and whatever pertains to these), (c) private and public exercises of divine worship, and (d) works of piety, necessity, and mercy.

Some have vainly tried to eliminate the Fourth Commandment from the sphere of Christian obligation while retaining the other nine commandments. The basis of this attempt is usually the contention that the Sabbath was "Jewish" and that it "went out" with the ceremonial laws of the Old Testament. The truth is that the Sabbath was instituted long before there was any ceremonial legislation (Gen. 2:2–3). It belongs to the order of things which God established for man at the beginning. Even sinless man had the duty of observing the Sabbath. He was made in the divine image. His duty was laid down by divine example. "The sequence for man of six days of labour and one day of rest is patterned after the sequence which God followed in the grand scheme of His creative work" (John Murray). It is inconceivable that anything could make God's example irrelevant for the duty of man.

But even if we were to make no mention of this, it would still remain clear that the Fourth Commandment is moral and not ceremonial. God is a God of order, not of confusion. And he himself inscribed the moral law in tables of stone before he revealed the ceremonial law by his servant Moses. Since God (who cannot err) set this commandment down in stone with the other commandments which are without question moral, it is necessary to regard this as moral too. God did not mistake the character of this commandment, and he set it among other moral laws so that we could not mistake its character either.

The most plausible argument against the binding authority of the Fourth Commandment is that which seeks to show that Christ disregarded it. It is true that Christ disregarded certain false restrictions that the Pharisees regarded as binding. But when the Pharisees charged Jesus and his disciples with infraction of the Fourth Commandment *on that account,* his answer was not that the Fourth Commandment was abrogated, but that the Pharisees were mistaken in their interpretation *and* application of it. He then proceeded to prove from the Old Testament Scriptures that they were wrong indeed (Matt. 12:1–13; cf. Lev. 14:4–9; 1 Sam. 21:6). Christ proved that the priest gave David the showbread in order to preserve his life, even though this was a technical violation of the law. Similarly, Christ proved from Scripture that certain specific types of work *are* legitimate on the Sabbath. These works are works of *piety* (that is, work that must be done in order that God be worshiped, such as the work of a pastor in preaching the gospel on the Lord's Day), works of *necessity* (that is, work that cannot be delayed without harm to life or property, such as rescuing an ox that falls in the ditch, or helping to put out a fire), and works of *mercy* (such as an act of kindness to a person who is sick or in distress). Jesus said, "If you had known what this means, 'I desire mercy and not sacrifice,' you would not have condemned the guiltless. For the Son of Man is Lord even of the Sabbath" (Matt. 12:7–8). The Pharisees put the Sabbath in the place of the Lord, and in doing so perverted the Sabbath. Christ did not eliminate the Sabbath, but placed it where it belonged, that is, subordinate to his own lordship.

The disciples kept the Sabbath in a different way than did the Pharisees because they served Christ. Had there been no sin and misery in the world, there would have been no works of necessity and mercy to be done on the Sabbath. God's Sabbath began when creation was finished. But man's sin and misery required that this Sabbath be "broken" as it were, if man was to be redeemed. This came about when Christ did the "work" of redemption. "For he who has entered His rest has himself also ceased from his own works as God did from His" (Heb. 4:10). The very reason for a "new" Sabbath was that Christ did this work of necessity and mercy on the former Sabbath of God. If this were not so, "then He would not afterward have spoken of another day" (Heb. 4:8). But the work of Jesus Christ did not do away with the Sabbath. Rather, it secured the Sabbath. "There remains therefore a [Sabbath-]rest for the people of God" (Heb. 4:9). But the example of Christ showed us that the Sabbath commandment allows for, or rather requires, works of piety, necessity, and mercy. And it is to be carefully observed that Christ never failed to justify his actions from Scripture (John 7:22–23).

It is sometimes said that the abrogation of the death penalty for Sabbath desecration proves that the Fourth Commandment no longer binds believers. This is to confuse the civil law (which required such sanctions for infraction of the moral law) and the moral law. It is easily shown to be false. The civil laws of Israel required the death penalty for violation of the Fifth Commandment (Ex. 21:17; Deut. 21:18–21), the Seventh Commandment (Deut. 22:22), the Second Commandment (Deut. 13:10), and others (Lev. 24:10–23). But as far as we know, no one argues that Christians are free to violate these moral laws merely because the civil penalties exacted under the Old Testament are not being applied among "the nations." Why then should the Fourth Commandment be treated differently?

But what about those who deny that the Sabbath day has been changed from the last day to the first day of the week? Seventh-Day Adventists, among others, insist that the Fourth Commandment perpetually obligates an observance of the last day of the week as the Sabbath of the Lord. We believe that this view is disproved by two considerations. (1) First, the Fourth Commandment does not say, "Remember the *last* day," but "remember the Sabbath day." There is a difference. The difference is the distinction between proportion and order. When the commandment specifies that six of our days are for one duty, and the remaining portion of the week (one seventh to be exact) for another duty, it avoids precisely what the Seventh-Day Adventist position requires. It avoids commanding us to remember the last day of the week, in order that it might command us to observe the seventh day in the proportion of time. Since the Fourth Commandment directs us to observe a seventh part of our time as a Sabbath, there is nothing in this commandment that does not apply with full force to the first day of the week (as to the order of days), for the first day of the week is still a seventh as far as the proportion of time is concerned.

(2) Second, we simply note that the Apostolic Church observed "the first day of the week" (as to order of days) as a seventh portion, or Sabbath (see Matt. 28:1; Mark 16:2, 9; Luke 24:1; John 20:1, 19; Acts 20:7; 1 Cor. 16:2; Rev. 1:10). It is sometimes argued that, in any case, we cannot be sure that our Sabbath is the same as that observed by the Apostolic Church. It is said that the cycle may have been broken at some time down through the centuries that separate us from the apostles' time. To this we reply that Jesus is the Lord of both his Church and the Sabbath. And he declares that the Sabbath is a perpetual sign of the people of God (Ex. 31:13–17; Ezek. 22:26). Christ promised that there would be an unbroken continuance of his true Church till the end of the world, and this guarantees that the Sabbath has not been and will not be, lost to men.

A proper observance of the Sabbath requires "a holy resting all that day, even from such worldly employments and recreations as are lawful on other days, and spending the whole time in the public and private exercises of God's worship, except so much as is to be taken up in the works of necessity and mercy" (Shorter Catechism, A. 60). For an extended analysis of the proper observance of the Fourth Commandment there is no more profitable study than that provided by the Larger Catechism, Q. 115–20.

We shall content ourselves here with a brief statement of principles. (1) The basic meaning of the word "Sabbath" is cessation. To rest, in terms of the meaning of this commandment, does not mean to sleep. It does not mean to cease performing our work and to continue our favorite recreations. What it means is to *cease* from the whole compass of things which engross us during the other days of the week whether it be our employment or recreations. This does not mean that we are free to do sinful things on other days, but not on the Sabbath; rather, it means that even good things that occupy our attention on other days ought to be set aside on this day. For example, television, reading of newspapers and magazines, and engaging in sports and excursions are all proper to the Christian life. But they are not proper to the Sabbath because "Sabbath" means to cease from these things in order to give one day exclusively to worship and the reading of God's Word.

(2) The meaning of "necessity" is frequently misinterpreted in dealing with this commandment. Works of necessity are *not* such as are required only by our convenience. For example, what should a Christian do if his employer requires him to work on the Lord's Day? Some would say, "I will have to work, or else I will be demoted to a much lower salary." But such a reason does not make the work itself a necessity. If a physician says, "I must operate on this man today or he will die," he speaks of a work of necessity. But if a carpenter says, "I must report on the construction job or I will endanger my position," he is still faced with the fact that the *work itself* is not necessary. One could just as well argue that it is legitimate to steal (I *must* steal because my family needs more money) as to argue that a work is necessary on the Sabbath merely because personal inconvenience or hardship is involved.

QUESTIONS

1. Upon what basis do such churches as the Lutheran remove, or relax, the obligation to observe the Fourth Commandment?

2. How can it be proved that the Fourth Commandment is not ceremonial?
3. Did Christ disregard the Sabbath laws of his day? Explain.
4. How did Christ justify his actions?
5. What three types of "work" did Christ sanction on the Sabbath?
6. What did the Pharisees serve in their Sabbath observance?
7. What did the disciples serve in their Sabbath observance?
8. What do the Seventh-Day Adventists maintain (as to the Sabbath)?
9. What evidence refutes this position?
10. What does the word "Sabbath" mean?
11. From what should we "rest"?
12. What is the difference between necessity and convenience?

21

XXII. Of Lawful Oaths and Vows

1. *A lawful oath is a part of religious worship, wherein, upon just occasion, the person swearing solemnly calleth God to witness what he asserteth, or promiseth; and to judge him according to the truth or falsehood of what he sweareth.*

2. *The name of God only is that by which men ought to swear, and therein it is to be used with all holy fear and reverence. Therefore, to swear vainly, or rashly, by that glorious and dreadful name, or to swear at all by any other thing, is sinful, and to be abhorred. Yet as, in matters of weight and moment, an oath is warranted by the Word of God under the New Testament, as well as under the Old; so a lawful oath, being imposed by lawful authority, in such matters ought to be taken.*

3. *Whosoever taketh an oath ought duly to consider the weightiness of so solemn an act, and therein to avouch nothing but what he is fully persuaded is the truth. Neither may any man bind himself by oath to any thing but what is good and just, and what he believeth so to be, and what he is able and resolved to perform. Yet it is a sin to refuse an oath touching any thing that is good and just, being imposed by lawful authority.*

4. *An oath is to be taken in the plain and common sense of the words, without equivocation or mental reservation. It cannot oblige to sin; but in any thing not sinful, being taken, it binds to performance, although to a man's own hurt. Nor is it to be violated, although made to heretics or infidels.*

These sections of the Confession teach us (1) the nature of a lawful oath, (2) the only name in which it is lawful to swear, (3) the propriety and duty of taking oaths upon proper occasions, (4) the sense in which an oath is to be interpreted, and (5) the extent to and ground upon which it has binding obligation.

It has been questioned by some that we should swear at all. Jesus said, "Again you have heard that it was said to those of old, 'You shall not swear falsely, but shall perform your oaths to the Lord.' But I say to you, do not swear at all: neither by heaven, for it is God's throne; nor by the earth, for it is His footstool; nor by Jerusalem, for it is the city of the great King. Nor shall you swear by your head, because you cannot make one hair white or black. But let your 'Yes' be 'Yes,' and your 'No,' 'No.' For whatever is more than these is from the evil one" (Matt. 5:33–37). It is easy to see how this text could be claimed by those who oppose all oaths. But a careful reading of this text in the light of the context does not support such a view. Christ was not abrogating the law (5:17–18) but clearing it of false interpretations.

One of these false interpretations of the Jews was that only some oaths were binding, depending on what men swore by. Christ said that, to the contrary, such distinctions were vain and iniquitous, and that all oaths are binding. But more than that, he said that men's words ought to be true and binding even without oaths. If men were truthful they would simply speak the truth without feeling the need of constantly adding oaths. Oaths have come into use because men are liars. But it is a grievous error to suppose that a lie is not wicked unless an oath is involved. Yet the Jews went even beyond this, maintaining that perjury was not wrong unless the oath was taken in a particular form (Matt. 23:16–22).

Now observe: Christ did not say that everything stronger than "Yes, Yes" *is* evil; he said only that it *comes from* evil, meaning that it is necessitated by the prevalence of untruthfulness. In the kingdom of God which is to come, there will be no oaths, for all will speak the truth in utmost purity (Rev. 21:8, 27). Meanwhile, in this present evil world falsehood remains so common that special solemn occasions may require oaths, and under proper circumstances they may be made (Luke 1:73; Matt. 26:63; Acts 2:30; Heb. 3:11, 18; 4:3; 6:13–18). Jesus himself took an oath (Matt. 26:63–64). And quite frequently he prefaced his remarks with words of special oath-like character, "Verily, verily, I say unto you."

The oaths which Christ condemned, you will note, avoided the use of God's name. These oaths were regarded as violable by the Jews. And this Christ utterly condemned. One cannot be admitted to the kingdom in which truth reigns who holds that he need not speak truth unless he confirms his word with an oath in a certain form. Yet this in no way contradicts the fact that those who are of the truth may make solemn oaths unto God. "You shall fear the Lord your God; you shall serve Him, and to Him you shall hold fast, and take oaths in His name" (Deut. 10:20).

The proper occasions at which an oath may be taken are those in which serious and lawful interests are involved, and in which an appeal to the witness of God is necessary to secure confidence and end strife, and also whenever the oath is imposed by competent authority upon those subject to it. In the latter case, especially, the taking of an oath is a duty, and its refusal is a sin.

Perjury is the act of willfully making a false oath. It is a serious crime. The Bible calls it swearing deceitfully (Ps. 24:4). The taking of an oath with a secret intention of double meaning, not disclosed to others, or with mental reservations—whereby the *mind* silently voices dissent from part or all of what is being sworn by the *mouth*—is a sin of enormity. Yet this sin is common today even in churches that officially profess adherence to this Confession of Faith! When a Presbyterian minister is ordained and installed, he is required to make certain oaths. He is required, in this oath of office, to affirm that the Bible is the only infallible rule of faith and practice. He is then required to solemnly swear that he receives and adopts the Confession of Faith and the Catechisms as agreeable to and founded on the Word of God, and that he personally accepts the system of doctrine taught in them. To take such an oath of office and at the same time not to believe that the Bible is infallible, or to disagree with the doctrines of the Confession of Faith (such as, for example, the virgin birth of Christ, and bodily resurrection, or the doctrine of election), is to be guilty of perjury. It is little wonder that the spiritual condition of the churches is so low, when it has become accepted practice to swear deceitfully, and that on the part of the shepherds of Israel.

An oath is agreeable to the Word of God only if the one who swears is truly sincere. He must "avouch nothing but what he is fully persuaded is the truth." But it sometimes happens that one will swear to perform a duty which he afterwards comes to realize is contrary to the Word of God. An example would be one who solemnly, and at the time sincerely, swears to educate his children in the false system of Roman Catholicism. The argument is sometimes made that such an oath is binding because it was made sincerely, because, at the time, the one who swore believed it was right to do so (or, at least, not wrong) and was resolved to do as he swore to do. But an oath is binding only if the thing promised is good and just, that is, agreeable to the Word of God. The reason for this is evident: that which is contrary to the Word of God is sin, and it is man's duty not to sin; therefore, swearing to sin cannot justify or obligate sin.

Thus when one discovers that he has promised on solemn oath to sin, his only recourse is to ask forgiveness for having made such a promise in the first place and then to renounce the oath (Matt. 14:1–12). It was wrong to make such an oath in the first place. It would be doubly wrong to keep it after discovering that it was sinful. However, we must take care that we do not confuse what is wrong with what is merely painful. "In any thing not sinful" an oath having been taken "binds to performance, although to a man's own hurt." God honors the man "who swears to his own hurt and does not change" (Ps. 15:4). It is imperative that Christians carefully consider the weightiness of so solemn an act, being certain that they do not swear to do more than they are able and resolved to do. Yet when it is discovered that more hardship and affliction are involved in standing true to one's word than was at first anticipated, one cannot disavow that which is not contrary to the Word of God without being guilty of sin (Ezek. 17:19; Josh. 9:19).

QUESTIONS

1. What interpretation is sometimes given to Matthew 5:33–37?
2. What is the correct interpretation of this passage?
3. Did Jesus say that swearing is evil? If not, what did he say exactly?
4. What was the common error of the Jews with respect to oaths?
5. What proof can you give to show that oaths are legitimate?

6. What is perjury?

7. What doctrines does a Presbyterian minister swear to maintain and to defend? (Give a few examples.)

8. Of what are Presbyterian ministers guilty when they do not believe the doctrines contained in the Confession of Faith?

9. Should one keep an oath if he later discovers that he has promised what is contrary to the Word of God? Why?

10. Should one keep an oath if he later discovers that it will inconvenience him?

XXII, 5–7

5. *A vow is of the like nature with a promissory oath, and ought to be made with the like religious care, and to be performed with the like faithfulness.*

6. *It is not to be made to any creature, but to God alone: and, that it may be accepted, it is to be made voluntarily, out of faith and conscience of duty, in way of thankfulness for mercy received, or for the obtaining of what we want; whereby we more strictly bind ourselves to necessary duties, or to other things, so far and so long as they may fitly conduce thereunto.*

7. *No man may vow to do any thing forbidden in the Word of God, or what would hinder any duty therein commanded, or which is not in his power, and for the performance whereof he hath no promise of ability from God. In which respects, popish monastical vows of perpetual single life, professed poverty, and regular obedience, are so far from being degrees of higher perfection, that they are superstitious and sinful snares, in which no Christian may entangle himself.*

These sections of the Confession teach us (1) that a vow is similar to an oath, (2) that a vow is made to God alone, (3) that it must be made voluntarily, out of faith and conscience of duty, by way of thankfulness for mercy received, or for the obtaining of what we want, (4) that it binds us to duty, (5) that it is to be made only for that which is according to the Word of God, and (6) that Roman Catholic vows of celibacy, poverty, and obedience are contrary to the Word of God.

An oath is a calling upon God to judge (or curse) the one speaking if he has not spoken the truth. A vow is a solemn pledge or promise made to God. In an oath man calls God to witness and to judge what he says or promises to men. In a vow man makes a solemn promise to God. In both cases it is out of reverence for and obligation to God that they are made and kept. And we have scriptural sanction for vows as we do for oaths. "What shall I render to the Lord for all His benefits toward me?" asks the psalmist. "I will take up the cup of salvation, and call upon the name of the Lord. I will pay my vows to the Lord now in the presence of all His people" (Ps. 116:12–14).

As in the case of oaths, great care should be exercised in the making of vows. "Walk prudently when you go to the house of God; and draw near to hear rather than to give the sacrifice of fools, for they do not know that they do evil. Do not be rash with your mouth, and let not your heart utter anything hastily before God. For God is in heaven, and you on earth; therefore let your words be few. . . . A fool's voice is known by his many words. When you make a vow to God, do not delay to pay it, for He has no pleasure in fools. Pay what you have vowed—better not to vow than to vow and not pay" (Eccles. 5:1–5). A man who never vows is better off than a man who does not keep a vow he has made.

But this does *not* mean that a man will be well off if he does not vow at all. Many, perhaps most, of the vows or promises that men make to God are never paid and therefore would be better not made. But every true believer must make and keep at least one vow, namely, that by which he solemnly affirms to God that he receives Jesus Christ as he is freely offered in the gospel and promises henceforth to walk in newness of life with him. In at least this one instance, the Bible says: "Make vows to the Lord your God, and pay them" (Ps. 76:11). It is therefore perfectly consistent with the Scriptures to require that men confess Christ publicly and make vows of faith and obedience (Matt. 10:32).

Membership vows are made in the presence of men, but they are made *to* the Lord. In most Reformed churches these vows are in substance as follows: (1) the vow to believe, to accept permanently, and to obey the Bible as the one infallible rule of faith and practice; (2) the vow or promise to regard oneself as sinful and corrupt, and to renounce oneself in order to receive salvation in Christ alone; (3) the vow or promise to acknowledge Jesus Christ as one's ruler and in reliance upon him to walk in newness of life; and (4) the vow or promise to heed the lawful discipline of Christ administered by his Church in accordance with the Word of God. It is true that a man who makes such vows and then does not keep them is worse off than if he had never made such vows. But it is also true that no man is well off who does not both make and keep these vows.

We must be careful not to vow anything that is unscriptural (Acts 23:12; Judg. 11:30–40). Examples of such vows are to be found today in Roman Catholicism, liberal Protestantism, and even among fundamentalists. The Roman Church requires a vow of celibacy from all priests. But Christ said that "all cannot accept this" (Matt. 19:11). And he taught that such a state must be strictly voluntary when he said, "He who is able to accept it, let him accept it" (v. 12). And in any case the Scripture forbids that any class of men, including church officers, be under such a rule. "Because of sexual immorality, *let each man* have his own wife," says the apostle (1 Cor. 7:2). If one is unable to bear the burden of celibacy, the rule is: "Let them marry" (7:9). And it is rather the rule, than the exception, that "a bishop" will be "the husband of one wife" (1 Tim. 3:2). "Forbidding to marry" is called one of the "doctrines of demons" by the very apostle who apparently practiced celibacy himself voluntarily (1 Tim. 4:1, 3). A vow of poverty obligates a renunciation of all private property. This contradicts the teaching of Peter (Acts 5:4). A vow of obedience is a direct violation of the specific command of God which says, "Do not become slaves of men" (1 Cor. 7:23). "We ought to obey God rather than men" (Acts 5:29). God alone is Lord of the believer. It is a sin to vow or to promise anything to God which is not first required or approved by God. Yet even among Protestants a very serious form of this sin has become commonplace. It is the practice of encouraging people, often by psychological emotional influence, on the spur of the moment, to sign pledge cards.

Most distressing of all, it is often children who are the victims. And we say "victims" *regardless of what the vow may be*—that is, even if the thing vowed is in itself unobjectionable. The reason is that a vow, like an oath, can be properly made only if there are (a) due consideration and awareness of the weightiness of so solemn an act, (b) a full persuasion in a person's own conscience that such a vow is scriptural, and (c) a conviction that one is able and resolved to keep the vow. When a child signs a pledge card, or makes a vow, it is extremely unlikely that these necessary conditions can be met. It is therefore sin, pre-eminently on the part of the adults who both sin and cause to sin, but also sin on the part of the child. "For whatever is not from faith is sin" (Rom. 14:23).

This is not the same as saying that children are not bound by the covenant vows of their parents. To the contrary, we believe that the children of believers are covenant children. They *are* bound by the vows of their parents, in all things commanded of God. A parent cannot place a child under perpetual obligation to anything that is not commanded by God (Matt. 4:10). But parents *can*—and *should*—solemnly charge their children to recognize the covenant obligations placed upon them by their baptism. This is very different from inducing children to vow what they are not yet competent to vow for themselves.

Questions

1. What is the difference between an oath and a vow?
2. In what way are they similar?
3. Prove that vows are not contrary to the will of God.
4. What vow is required of a Christian? What is promised in the same?
5. Give an example of an unscriptural vow common in Roman Catholicism.
6. Give an example of an unscriptural vow common in Protestantism.
7. Why is it wrong to induce children to make vows?
8. Are children ever bound by the vows of their parents?

We shall postpone the discussion of chapter XXIII of the Confession until chapter 29 of this work in order to discuss XXIII, 3 and XXXI, 1–2 (sections pertaining to the power of the civil magistrate with regard to ecclesiastical matters) together.

CHAPTER

22

XXIV. Of Marriage and Divorce

1. *Marriage is to be between one man and one woman; neither is it lawful for any man to have more than one wife, nor for any woman to have more than one husband, at the same time.*

2. *Marriage was ordained for the mutual help of husband and wife; for the increase of mankind with a legitimate issue, and of the Church with an holy seed; and for the preventing of uncleanness.*

3. *It is lawful for all sorts of people to marry who are able with judgment to give their consent: yet it is the duty of Christians to marry only in the Lord. And therefore such as profess the true reformed religion should not marry with infidels, papists, or other idolaters: neither should such as are godly be unequally yoked, by marrying with such as are notoriously wicked in their life, or maintain damnable heresies.*

These sections of the Confession teach us (1) that God has ordained monogamous marriage, (2) that it serves various purposes, (3) that celibacy is not to be regarded as a holier state than marriage, and (4) that Reformed Christians should not marry unbelievers or even those who subscribe to dangerous errors.

That marriage is a divine institution is clearly taught in Scripture (Gen. 2:18–25). Marriage is the divine provision. Inasmuch as God made one

woman only, it is evident that marriage is to be between one man and
one woman only. This was recognized in Adam's prophecy. He spoke
in the singular as he mentioned the wife for whom a man would leave
his father and mother. Christ's comment is implicit in the Genesis account:
"the *two* shall become one flesh" (Matt. 19:5). And it is noteworthy that
departure from this original monogamy first appears in the history of those
who departed from God (Gen. 4:16, 19). It is clear that polygamy was
the result and evidence of man's depravity and a contradiction of the
divine institution (Gen. 6:5).

Frequently mentioned in regard to this matter is the well-known fact
that many Old Testament believers had more than one wife at the same
time. There is even provision (in Deut. 24:1–4) for divorce for sexual
immorality. It is obvious that this does present a difficulty, and some have
sought to argue against the doctrine of the Confession on the basis of it.
But in Matthew 19:3–9 Jesus recognizes and answers this difficulty. In
reply to the Pharisees Jesus insists that the Genesis account is clear: from
the beginning it was one man and one woman, the two made one flesh,
and what God has joined together no man has a right to separate. This
was the divine standard. And every deviation from it was wrong. "Moses,
because of the hardness of your hearts, *permitted you* to divorce your wives,
but from the beginning it was not so. And I say to you, whoever divorces
his wife, except for sexual immorality, and marries another, commits
adultery" (19:8–9). We understand this "hardness" of heart to be descrip-
tive of the state of man as fallen. Thus it is not as if Moses tolerated something in Old Testament times—as if people *then* were more hard of heart,
by nature, than they are *today*. No, the moral and spiritual condition of
the natural man is every bit as bad today as it was then. And it is because
of this that divorce is permitted by God. He permits it today even as he
permitted it in the time of Moses. Yet even so, "from the beginning it
was not so." The unchanged standard to which God calls all men, and
especially his people, is lifelong monogamous marriage.

Marriage fulfills manifold purposes. One of these is the satisfaction of
the sex desire (Gen. 2:20). The Scripture says that in order to avoid a sinful and improper satisfaction of the sex desire every human being is to
have the right to marriage (1 Cor. 7:2). And within marriage there is to
be no failure on the part of either spouse to minister to this need and
desire. "Let the husband render to his wife the affection due her, and

likewise also the wife to her husband. The wife does not have authority over her own body, but the husband does. And likewise the husband does not have authority over his own body, but the wife does" (7:3–4). Even the interests of piety are not to be allowed to interfere with this obligation (7:5). Even if there is mutual consent to temporary abstinence from the sex relation, it must be for only a limited time, so that the sex desire will not become an occasion of Satan's temptation. And in any case, the unilateral denial of the sex relation is as sinful as it is dangerous.

In the witness of Scripture on this aspect of marriage we believe two errors are to be avoided. (1) There is the error which has been called *Puritan* or *Victorian* (with perhaps some justification) and which inclines to view sex as intrinsically evil precisely because it involves such intense desire and pleasure. But sin lies in the *perversion* of these, rather than in them per se. The power of this error has been so strong that it has even led to a very fanciful and strained interpretation of the Song of Solomon, which so frankly recognizes the legitimacy of a proper satisfaction of the sex desire. (2) The other error is that which would restrict the legitimate expression of the sex desire to the procreation of children. This is the view which says the satisfaction of sex desire is proper only when the purpose of it is to beget children. We believe that this position is untenable in the light of 1 Corinthians 7:3–5. The duty here stated would remain even apart from the ability to beget children. For this reason we do not believe that Scripture supports the view that it is *necessarily, unavoidably,* and *invariably* wrong to seek the satisfaction of sex desire apart from a procreative purpose. Therefore, we believe that a church errs when it makes a blanket prohibition of the use of means whereby, in certain instances, the one purpose of marriage may be accomplished while the other is not.

However, for Reformed Christians the danger appears to be in the other direction. To say that Scripture does not teach that the satisfaction of the sex desire must always include the procreative purpose is not the same as to say that the procreative purpose may be neglected. God has ordained marriage not only for the proper satisfaction of sex desire, but also "for the increase of mankind with a legitimate issue, and of the Church with an holy seed." This is the divine commandment (Gen. 1:28). The chief end of man is to glorify God in every sphere of life. When sex desire is not governed by this purpose, it is most certainly abased. When it is governed by the desire to glorify God, it becomes the instrument of God for the increase

of his Church with the promised seed (Mal. 2:15; Acts 2:39). To avoid
bearing children for selfish reasons is the very opposite of a proper fulfillment of the divine purpose of marriage. We must fully recognize this present-day abuse of the modern knowledge of convenient means of avoiding
the begetting of children. And this abuse must be condemned. But abuse
of a thing does not justify absolute condemnation of it.

Section 3 states that "it is lawful for all sorts of people to marry who are
able with judgment to give their consent." It is unlawful for men to be
sinners and to disbelieve the gospel. But there is every reason for Christians to approve of civil laws which require unbelievers to observe the
demands of monogamous marriage as far as it is possible. Forbidding unbelievers to marry would be at least as great an evil as to forbid believers to
marry. Thus we believe that where civil law recognizes a minister of the
Church as an agent of society with civil authority to sanction the marriage
of unbelievers, it may in some cases be his duty to so act, that a greater
evil may be averted. But it would be the duty of a minister, in such a case,
to inquire as to the religious profession of both parties and to proceed only
if both make no profession of the true religion. If one, and only one, does
profess the true religion, however, it would be contrary to the Word of
God to sanction, or in any way facilitate, such a marriage. For the Scripture clearly states that a believer must marry "only in the Lord" (1 Cor.
7:39; see also 2 Cor. 6:14–18; Gen. 6:1–3; Ex. 34:16; Deut. 7:3–4).

It is true, however, that such a mixed marriage, once contracted and
consummated, is binding (1 Cor. 7:12–14). For the believer to initiate
the dissolution of the marriage bond in such a case is wrong. But it is
probable that the cases envisioned by the apostle were due to the conversion of only one spouse, and that subsequent to the marriage. In any
case the believer cannot marry an unbeliever without committing sin.
And church discipline is clearly required in such a case.

It is an added difficulty to discern which of the various denominations
that claim to be Christian actually do adhere to the truth of God to a sufficient degree that one may have confidence that a member of that denomination can be expected to know and to profess the true religion. The
Confession says that "such as profess the true reformed religion should
not marry" adherents of the Roman Catholic faith, nor such as "maintain damnable heresies." It may be argued that a person could conceivably be a true believer and yet be an adherent of a false religion. We

believe that this is a false abstraction. A person's faith is not to be judged apart from his profession and walk, and in this case the profession and walk would be contrary to the judgment that he is a believer. We cannot so separate between personal and corporate responsibility.

Finally, we must admit that the problem of deciding whether or not a person is sufficiently Christian to marry is a difficult one in not a few instances. There are errors that are of various degrees of seriousness. In any case we believe that the believer who knows the true Reformed religion should enter upon marriage only if such *requires* no compromise of God's truth.

QUESTIONS

1. Prove from Scripture that God instituted marriage.
2. Prove that it was monogamous.
3. Does the fact that Old Testament believers practiced polygamy justify it? Why?
4. What is the meaning of the term "permitted" in Matthew 19:8?
5. With what is this permission sometimes confused?
6. What are the purposes of marriage?
7. What two false attitudes toward sex have been, and are, quite common?
8. What danger appears to beset Reformed believers who disavow the two errors mentioned above?
9. Whom may a Reformed minister scripturally join in marriage?
10. Is marriage between a believer and an unbeliever binding and valid?
11. Prove from Scripture that a Christian may marry only another Christian.
12. Would it be right in every instance to marry, though both are Christians? Why?

XXIV, 4–6

4. *Marriage ought not to be within the degrees of consanguinity or affinity forbidden in the Word. Nor can such incestuous marriages ever be made lawful by any law of man, or consent of parties, so as those persons may live together as man and wife. The man may not*

marry any of his wife's kindred nearer in blood than he may of his own, nor the woman of her husband's kindred nearer in blood than of her own.

5. *Adultery or fornication committed after a contract, being detected before marriage, giveth just occasion to the innocent party to dissolve that contract. In the case of adultery after marriage, it is lawful for the innocent party to sue out a divorce, and, after the divorce, to marry another, as if the offending party were dead.*

6. *Although the corruption of man be such as is apt to study arguments, unduly to put asunder those whom God hath joined together in marriage; yet nothing but adultery or such willful desertion as can no way be remedied by the Church or civil magistrate, is cause sufficient of dissolving the bond of marriage; wherein a public and orderly course of proceeding is to be observed; and the persons concerned in it not left to their own wills, and discretion, in their own case.*

These sections of the Confession teach us (1) that there are certain divine restrictions as to whom a Christian may marry because of already existing relationships, (2) that there are two possible grounds for legitimate divorce: (a) adultery or fornication (i.e. sexual immorality), and (b) desertion of a Christian by an unbeliever, and (3) that even though the wickedness of man is such that it ever seeks to overthrow the divine ordinance, yet it is the duty of both Church and State to uphold the divine ordinance.

In Leviticus 18:6–18 and 20:10–21 there is an extended list of the various kinds of relationships considered incestuous. Of course, neither the Old nor New Testament deals with every possible type of incestuous relation specifically. Rather there are a number of representative examples of the various kinds.

An analysis of the Leviticus code will show that sexual intercourse is forbidden within a specific circle of relatives, and the compass of that relationship, according to section 4, includes those who are our kin by marriage as well as those who are our kin by blood. In other words, when we have once contracted marriage, we are thereafter subject to the same limitations with regard to those who have become our relatives through husband or wife as was already the case by blood relation. This section of the Confession is one that has often, and over a considerable period of time, been contested. Many, perhaps even the large majority, of Presbyterian denominations throughout the world have not adopted this section of the original text of the Westminster Confession as a part of their church's version. We certainly do not wish to call into question the faith of all who disagree with us at this point. Many have sincerely believed the system of doctrine taught in the Confession but been unable to accept this particular section. No doubt the lack of unanimity on this point explains the fact that some truly orthodox Presbyterian churches have deleted this section. Be that as it may, the Word of God is the final test of all doctrine, including that of the Confession. And it is for this reason that we do not hide the fact (1) that this doctrine is taught in the original version of the Confession, and (2) that we believe this doctrine to be taught in the Bible. (For those who are interested in further consideration of this matter, we would suggest, in defense of the Confession, consulting John Murray's *Principles of Conduct* [Grand Rapids: Eerdmans, 1957], pp. 49–55, and Appendix B, pp. 250ff. On the other side, see "Marriage," in *The New Bible Dictionary* [Grand Rapids: Eerdmans, 1962], p. 789, and the bibliography included there.)

It is an age-old observation that the first marriages could not have observed the limitations set forth in Leviticus. This cannot be denied. Adam's children must have married one another. How can this be explained? We believe that the explanation is that man's duty is conditioned by divine provision. It was Adam's duty to cleave unto his wife, but not until God had made a woman for him to cleave to. It was the duty of human beings to marry beyond the degrees of consanguinity and affinity, but not before there was a sufficiently wide development of the human race to permit the operation of this duty. When the human race was again reduced to one family (i.e., by the flood), there was again a consequent impossibility of observing this duty. But as soon as Noah's family had increased beyond these degrees of relationship, it was their duty to marry beyond them.

We need not labor to prove that divorce is lawful if the cause be adultery. Since adultery is the one exception explicitly allowed by Christ, while otherwise it is a sin to put away a wife, it can hardly be argued that there is no such exception (Matt. 5:31–32; 19:9). The Roman Church says, "The marriage of two baptized persons who have afterward lived together as husband and wife can never be dissolved except by the death of one of the parties" (Baltimore Catechism, Q. 1194). But Paul says, "Do you not know that he who is joined to a harlot is one body with her? For 'the two,' He says, 'shall become one flesh' " (1 Cor. 6:16). If a man becomes one flesh with a harlot, it is hard to see how it can be denied that the one-flesh relationship with his wife has been disrupted. Unless such a sin is repented of and forgiven, we do not see how it can be denied that the adultery necessitates dissolution of the marriage. And if adultery results in the marriage of the adulterers, divorce from the former spouse is an accomplished fact. In such an instance, return to the previous spouse would simply be another act of adultery (see Deut. 24:1–4).

In 1 Corinthians 7:10–15 Paul discusses the case of those who, being already married, become Christians and then encounter marital difficulty. Under such circumstances the marriage is binding. And in no case is the Christian to evade the discharge of the marital obligation. Even if, in violation of the law of the Lord, separation has taken place (whether because of sin or of necessity), the Christian still is required to regard the marriage bond as in full force. The separated spouses must either be reconciled and reunited, or remain as they are without thought of remarriage, as far as the Christian partner's case is concerned.

But what if the other person (the unbeliever) determines to disrupt the marriage bond? What if it is his (or her) will to desert the marriage, to secure a divorce and to go free (even without immediate prospect of remarriage)? Paul says, "If the unbeliever departs, let him depart; a brother or sister is not under bondage in such cases" (v. 15). Since, in the context, to be "bound" means to be bound to a person in the institution of marriage, to be "not bound" can only mean to be free from the same institution. Thus we see no alternative than to believe that willful desertion of a believer by an unbeliever (which cannot be remedied by Church or civil authority) is just cause for divorce. And a Christian who has secured a divorce on such a ground, or who has been divorced for such a reason, is free to remarry.

Our study of the depravity of man fully supports the Confession when it says that sinners are apt to study ways to circumvent the limitations of God's laws. Even Christians, by reason of the sinful propensities remaining in them, are apt to invent arguments to justify divorce for other than these two reasons only. For example, when fidelity to the marriage requirements entails heartache and suffering, many Christians have tried to justify separation and divorce on such grounds as "extreme abuse," "mental suffering," and "incompatibility." Others have secured divorces from spouses who were imprisoned or hospitalized. But as in the case with other laws of God, so in this, the path of obedience is often the way of self-denial and the bearing of reproach and suffering for the glory of God. And no legitimate divorce can ever be secured on other grounds than these two: (1) adultery, and (2) willful and irremediable desertion of a believer by an unbeliever.

QUESTIONS

1. Where is legislation restricting whom we may marry found in the Bible?
2. Why did this law not apply to the first marriages?
3. According to the Roman Church, what is the one thing that can dissolve marriage?
4. According to Christ, for what may marriage be dissolved?
5. Is there any other lawful ground for divorce? What is it?
6. Would this ground apply for all marriages? Why?
7. On what other grounds do sinful men justify divorce? Is this ever right?

23

XXV. Of the Church

1. *The catholic or universal Church, which is invisible, consists of the whole number of the elect that have been, are, or shall be gathered into one, under Christ the head thereof; and is the spouse, the body, the fulness of him that filleth all in all.*

2. *The visible Church, which is also catholic or universal under the Gospel, (not confined to one nation, as before under the law), consists of all those throughout the world that profess the true religion, together with their children; and is the kingdom of the Lord Jesus Christ, the house and family of God, out of which there is no ordinary possibility of salvation.*

These sections of the Confession teach us (1) the nature of the Church from the divine point of view, and (2) the nature of the Church from the human point of view, but (3) it is not as if there are two different Churches, the visible and the invisible.

In Hebrews 12:23 we read of the "church of the firstborn who are registered in heaven." This is the body of which Christ is the head (Eph. 1:22–23; 5:23, 27) and of which all the elect of all ages are destined to be members. Such are "predestined according to the purpose of Him who works all things according to the counsel of His will" (Eph. 1:11) "just as He chose [them] in Him before the foundation of the world" (1:4).

This is the body of believers for whom Christ prayed (John 17:9). It is invisible to us because it has extension in both time and space. It reaches from one end of the earth to the other, and from the beginning to the end of history. But it is invisible only *to us*. It is not "invisible" *to God*. He who infallibly discerns the hearts of men, knows them that are his. "The solid foundation of God stands, having this seal: 'The Lord knows those who are His'" (2 Tim. 2:19).

However, it is this Church—not another—that becomes visible to men in the world. There is a true visible Church. In other words, the one true Church does manifest itself in the world. And when, and where it does, it is just that Church which is in the absolute sense invisible to us which is nevertheless visible to us at that time and place. The true or real Church of God manifests itself through those who are living in the world at a particular time and place. This manifestation is, therefore, never more than a small portion of the whole (invisible) Church, and it is a portion that is circumscribed by the limitations imposed by the imperfection of things in this world. This Church, in visible manifestation, is also universal in a sense. It consists of all those throughout the whole world who, at the present time, are members of the body of Christ.

But there are two things which obscure the visibility of this true Church: (l) there is the imperfection of each particular member on earth who belongs to Christ, and (2) there is also the hypocrisy of unbelievers who often imitate, in their appearance, true members of the body of Christ. Because there is evil in true believers while they are on earth, and because there is the appearance of faith and righteousness in hypocrites, the visible manifestation of the Church is never perfect. Or to put it another way, the Church of Christ is never perfectly manifested in any denomination or organization so that that denomination or organization possesses the same lines of demarcation as those which belong to the Church of God itself. Every attempt to realize the perfect Church (i.e., in which there are no hypocrites at all) is doomed to failure because the Church is invisible to us in exactly the sense that it would have to be visible to us to realize this goal.

When we speak of a true visible Church, then, we do not mean that it has exactly the same line of demarcation as belongs to the very body of Christ. It is not the will of God that the true visible Church should possess this attribute. Rather, a true Church visible is such, not because its membership is identical with the elect, but because it professes the true religion, maintains the teaching of the true doctrine and sacraments of the Scripture, and maintains the discipline required by the law of the Lord. Where there is fidelity in Word, sacraments, and discipline, there— without doubt—is the true visible Church. And the important thing to stress is that this true visible Church is none other than the body of Christ manifesting itself on earth.

If it be asked: "Could not this be only the semblance of the Church? Could not this be a whole congregation of hypocrites who have gathered together to maintain the true preaching of the Word of God, the sacraments, and discipline, while not one of them is really a member of the body of Christ? Is not this conceivable?" the answer is: "No, it is not conceivable." Hypocrites may join themselves *to* a body of true believers. Hypocrites do so constantly. But Satan's work is destructive and imitative only. He cannot cause an entire body of hypocrites to manifest the marks of God's true Church.

In the New Testament Paul speaks of "the church of God *which is* at Corinth" (1 Cor. 1:2; compare 2 Cor. 1:1; 1 Thess. 1:1; Rom. 16:4, 16; Gal. 1:2, 22; Rev. 1:4, 11, 20). Whether the apostles speak of "the church" at a particular place, or of "the churches" in a certain region, they always speak of particular visible churches as such because therein is manifested none other than the one Church of God which is the body of Christ. Wherever they saw a congregation in which the true religion was professed, and the preaching of the Word, the administration of the sacraments, and discipline maintained, they were in no doubt whatever that they beheld a real manifestation (however obscured by trouble and sin) of the universal Church of Christ.

The Confession states that this "visible Church . . . consists of all those . . . that profess the true religion, together with their children." If this be true, it cannot be denied that unbelievers may be, and *actually* are, *members* of the true visible Church. We believe that this is undoubtedly the case. It may perplex us that God has ordered that his true visible Church should include those who are not, and will never be, members of the body of Christ's redeemed. But our perplexity is not the criterion of truth. God commanded that both Jacob and Esau be circumcised, and thus be visibly identified as members of the Church. And yet it was already revealed that Esau was not to have part in the invisible Church. Does not the Scripture also speak of the place "from which Judas by transgression fell, that he might go to his own place" (Acts 1:25)? This can mean only that he fell from a place in the (visible) Church which was actually his, and not a place in the body of Christ (the Church as invisible to us) which was never his.

Thus we may say that the true Church becomes visible, not by an identification of *persons,* but by an identification of *presence.* The true Church of Christ (his body of elect persons) will manifest itself, not by a disclosure that particular persons are elect, but by a disclosure of certain things that true believers will do (even though there be hypocrites mixed in with them). They will profess the true religion and maintain with fidelity the Word, sacraments, and discipline required of a true visible Church. It is the presence of these activities of elect persons which makes the body of Christ visibly evident.

QUESTIONS

1. What is the invisible Church?
2. What is the visible Church?
3. Are these two different Churches? Why?
4. What is the distinction between visible and invisible as respects the Church?
5. Why is the visibility of the Church obscured?
6. Why cannot the visible Church have the same line of demarcation as the invisible Church?
7. How can the true Church be visibly discerned?
8. What is the difference between identification of persons and identification of presence?
9. Which do we identify in a true visible Church?
10. Does God *require* that some who are not elect be admitted as members of the true visible Church? Prove this from Scripture.

XXV, 3–6

3. *Unto this catholic visible Church Christ hath given the ministry, oracles, and ordinances of God, for the gathering and perfecting of the saints in this life, to the end of the world; and doth, by his own*

presence and Spirit, according to his promise, make them effectual thereunto.

4. *This catholic Church hath been sometimes more, sometimes less visible. And particular churches, which are members thereof, are more or less pure, according as the doctrine of the gospel is taught and embraced, ordinances administered, and public worship performed more or less purely in them.*

5. *The purest churches under heaven are subject both to mixture and error; and some have so degenerated as to become no churches of Christ, but synagogues of Satan. Nevertheless, there shall be always a Church on earth to worship God according to his will.*

6. *There is no other head of the Church but the Lord Jesus Christ. Nor can the Pope of Rome in any sense be the head thereof; but is that Antichrist, that man of sin, and son of perdition, that exalteth himself in the Church against Christ, and all that is called God.*

These sections of the Confession teach us (1) that the degree to which the Church is visible varies, (2) that we are to judge each particular church by its (a) doctrine, (b) worship and (c) discipline, (3) that no church is entirely pure, (4) that some churches become apostate, (5) that there will always be some visible manifestation of the true Church, but (6) that this cannot be the Roman Church because the papacy is anti-Christian.

Those who speak of the Church visible as if it once had absolute purity and unity are suffering a delusion. It is true that at the very beginning "all who believed were together, and had all things in common . . . continuing daily with one accord" (Acts 2:44–46). But it was not long before "there arose a complaint against the Hebrews by the Hellenists, because their widows were neglected" (Acts 6:1). Thus, alongside the grandeur of the true Church, we also see its visible imperfections. The same apostle who urged Christians to "speak the same thing, and that there be no divisions among" them, but that they "be perfectly joined together in the same mind" (1 Cor. 1:10–11), immediately thereafter acknowledged that there were "contentions" among them. And he even acknowledged that such divisions were a necessity. "I hear that there are divisions among you," he said. "There must also be factions among you, that those who are approved may be recognized among you" (1 Cor. 11:18–19). When heresy is at a minimum, the one universal Church manifests itself to a maximum degree. When heresy is at a maximum, the same Church manifests itself with greater difficulty.

As we study the apostolic writings, we clearly witness the difficulty with which the Church sought to manifest unity and purity. Evil men crept in unawares (Jude 4). They brought in damnable heresies (2 Peter 2:1). Some apostolic churches were soon removed from the doctrines of Christ (Gal. 1:6; Rev. 2–3). Some fought against these evils more valiantly than did others. Some became indifferent or neglectful and were thus invaded and overcome. As John wrote from Patmos (Rev. 2–3), there were great differences among the seven churches in Asia. At least some were perilously near to outright apostasy.

The question is: how do we know when a church reaches the "point of no return"? When must the believer come out of her and be separate, declaring her to be apostate? This is a solemn question and one that must be answered with care. The Belgic Confession (Art. xxix) is of some assistance:

> The marks by which the true Church is known are these: If the pure doctrine of the gospel is preached therein; if it maintains the pure administration of the sacraments as instituted by Christ; if church discipline is exercised in punishing of sin; in short, if all things are managed according to the pure Word of God, all things contrary thereto rejected, and Jesus Christ acknowledged as the only Head of the Church. Hereby the true Church may certainly be known, from which no man has a right to separate himself.

The article further states that "the false Church . . . ascribes more power and authority to itself and its ordinances than to the Word of God, and will not submit itself to the yoke of Christ."

Clearly, there are churches that manifest the requisite fidelity to the Bible so plainly that there can be no doubt, while others quite as obviously fail to do so, and of these there is no doubt either. No church is perfectly pure. But some have sufficient purity of Word, sacraments, and discipline that there can be no legitimate question that they are true churches. Again, there are probably no churches in which there is not some trace of these marks remaining, and yet the lack of fidelity to the Bible may be so plain that there can be no reasonable question that such are not true churches. However, no church is without imperfection, and every church is (humanly speaking) liable to apostasy. If a believer were to separate from a church because of any and every imperfection, he would belong to no church at all. But there may come a time when the departure of a church from the truth is such as to either require or justify separation. And we believe that the precise "point of no return" comes when such a church imposes upon its members the unavoidable necessity of participation in sin. When this point is reached, the Scripture is clear: "Come out of her, my people, lest you share in her sins, and lest you receive of her plagues" (Rev. 18:4).

It is sometimes argued that one should never leave a particular denomination as long as it is possible to remain in it. We would rather say that one should never leave a particular denomination as long as it is possible to remain without compromising obedience to Christ. The conditions necessary to an obedience which is not compromised are these: (1) the denomination as a whole must still profess the true religion in its essential integrity, (2) there must be an unrestricted right to contend for the truth against such errors as are present, and (3) there must be an active engagement (on the part of those who remain members) to defend the truth and to seek the purity of the Church.

There are those who have remained in false churches on the grounds that they are in a "conservative" congregation or presbytery, while admitting that the denomination as a whole is apostate. This violates the biblical doctrine of the unity of the churches and the scriptural concept of corporate responsibility (1 Cor. 11:14–27). Others have remained in false churches on the grounds that "they still have the right to preach the fundamentals of the faith." They admit, however, that they are not any longer permitted to preach the whole counsel of God, especially not that part of the counsel of God which condemns the errors that prevail in their church. This contradicts the scriptural duty to preach the whole counsel of God and the special duty to expose error, and is therefore sinful (2 Tim. 2:25–26; 4:2–5). Finally, there are those who remain in a false church because they hope some day to reform it. But they never actually do anything because they realize that such efforts have not been, and will not be, tolerated. This is the least excusable of all.

In conclusion, we believe that in a case of uncertain diagnosis, where there is opportunity to become a member of a church concerning which there is no doubt that it is a true church, a believer should separate with a clear statement of the reasons which have made him doubt that the church he is leaving is a true church. We even believe that it is proper to leave a true church that is much less pure to join a true church that is much more pure, provided the motive is the glory of God, the welfare of one's spiritual concerns (and that of his children), and a testimony against error.

QUESTIONS

1. When was the visible Church perfectly pure?
2. When does the visible Church have maximum unity?
3. What is the cause of disunity?
4. What are the marks of a true visible church (according to the Belgic Confession)?
5. Were churches of apostolic origin immune to apostasy? Prove.
6. When is separation from a particular church required?
7. How long should one remain in a church that is becoming quite corrupt?
8. What are some of the arguments advanced for remaining in false churches?
9. Answer these arguments.
10. Should one remain a member of a church which he doubts is a true church when he has opportunity to belong to a church which he does not doubt to be a true church? Why?
11. When leaving a doubtful or false church, what obligation does one have?

XXV, 6 (continued)

This section of the Confession teaches us (1) that Christ is the only king and head of the Church, (2) that the pope is not the head of the Church in any true sense whatever, and (3) that the papacy is the predicted agency of the devil subversive of the true Church of Christ.

That the Lord Jesus Christ is the only king and head of the Church is stated in so many words in Scripture (Col. 1:18; Eph. 1:20–23). And this truth is fully recognized by most of the Reformers. However, some (along with Roman Catholics) have maintained that the visible Church on earth ought to have a visible head, with authority delegated by Christ. Erastianism, a doctrine held by some Protestants, is named after Thomas Erastus (1524–83), a German theologian. This doctrine maintains the supremacy of the State over the Church in ecclesiastical as well as civil matters. And in various forms and degrees such a theory of church government has had historical manifestation in the state churches of Scandinavia, Germany, and England. For example, King Henry VIII was recognized as "supreme head of the Church of England." And it was enacted "that the king, his heirs, etc., shall be taken, accepted and reputed the only supreme head on earth of the Church of England." This doctrine was even incorporated into the 37th Article of the Church of England: "The Queen's majesty has the chief power in this realm of England, and her other dominions; unto whom the chief government of all estates of this realm, whether they be ecclesiastical or civil, in all causes doth appertain."

When the Westminster Confession of Faith was written, the papal claim to the crown prerogatives of the Lord Jesus Christ was in the forefront of conflict. Inasmuch as the Westminster Assembly had been called into session by the Parliament for the express purpose of establishing the true reformed faith as the form of religion for the Church of England, there did not appear to be any danger that a king or queen would be called the supreme head of the Church. Subsequent events demonstrated, however, that the pope is not the only antichrist (that is, one who seeks to stand in Christ's place). And so we regard the revision of this section of the Confession, as maintained by the Orthodox Presbyterian Church, as having one advantage over the original formulation. It preserves the point made by the Westminster Assembly, that the pope of Rome is not the head of Christ's Church in any sense; but also expressly and equally it denounces all others who would lay such a claim for themselves. The revision reads as follows:

> The Lord Jesus Christ is the only head of the Church, and the claim of any man to be the vicar of Christ and the head of the Church, is unscriptural, without warrant in fact, and is a usurpation dishonoring to the Lord Jesus Christ.

A more difficult question pertains to the identification of the pope with the scriptural "antichrist" and "man of sin." The Westminster Assembly regarded the papacy as the embodiment of these predicted historical developments of Satan's kingdom and work. What are we to say of this identification?

(1) The word "antichrist" occurs in 1 John 2:18, 22; 4:3; and 2 John 7. We read, "As you have heard that the Antichrist is coming, even now many antichrists have come, by which we know that it is the last hour" (1 John 2:18). This shows that antichrist was not something wholly in the future, and that it was manifest in many persons rather than just one person. Again we read, "Who is a liar but he who denies that Jesus is the Christ? He is antichrist who denies the Father and the Son" (2:22). Christ is the anointed prophet, priest, and king. Antichrist denies that Jesus is the anointed one. Every evil spirit manifests itself through some kind of false prophet, or teacher of error (1 John 4:1). And the error here is failure to acknowledge Christ. "This is the spirit of the Antichrist, which you have heard was coming, and is now already in the world" (4:3). This would seem to allow for variety, multiformity, and plurality of agents with one unifying principle—to attack the sole mediatorship of Jesus Christ. All those in whom the spirit of antichrist operates are one in their opposition to this.

(2) The "man of sin" (or lawlessness) is described only in 2 Thessalonians 2. He is there described as arising out of a great "falling away" which precedes the visible return of Christ. Christ will not appear until there first be a falling away "and the man of sin is revealed, the son of perdition, who opposes and exalts himself above all that is called God or that is worshiped, so that he sits as God in the temple of God, showing himself that he is God" (2:3–4). The phrase "the son of perdition" is elsewhere applied in Scripture only to an individual, Judas the betrayer (John 17:12). There would seem to be no doubt, then, that "the man of sin" was to be an individual, a particular person, who would virtually assume the place of God in the temple. And some have maintained that there is a clear distinction between one who opposes Christ (antichrist) and one who assumes the place of God (the man of lawlessness).

The Westminster Confession expresses here (in section 6) what was generally the view of the sixteenth-century Reformers. They saw in the papal system the defection from apostolic Christianity which they viewed as foreseen and foretold in the Scriptures mentioned in the previous paragraphs. Because each pope represented this anti–Christian system, he was therefore personally regarded as an antichrist. And the papacy as an institution emerged as the historic framework from which a final "man of sin" could arise, taking the final step of practical self-deification. Yet we believe the change in this section adopted by the Orthodox Presbyterian Church to be fully warranted. We say this for the following reasons. (1) The view set forth in the original text of this section renders a verdict concerning the interpretation of a few particular texts of Scripture. This, in our opinion, is not a proper function of a Confession. A Confession should summarize and synthesize the whole teaching of the Scripture on a particular head of doctrine, and not attempt to render a verdict about this or that particular text. (2) We are also of the opinion that exegetical work has now been done that casts at least a reasonable doubt on the validity of what the original text of this section teaches. There is, to say the least, much to be said for the view that the phenomenon spoken of in both the 2 Thessalonians passage *and* in 1 and 2 John has reference to events and developments *then* current. (We would here refer the reader to such books as Milton S. Terry, *Biblical Hermeneutics,* 2d ed. [Grand Rapids: Zondervan, 1974]; Gary DeMar, *Last Days Madness* [Brentwood, Tenn.: Wolgemuth and Hyatt, 1991]; and Benjamin B. Warfield, "The Antichrist," in *Selected Shorter Writings of Benjamin B. Warfield,* vol. 1 [Nutley, N.J.: Presbyterian and Reformed, 1970].

QUESTIONS

1. Prove from Scripture that Christ is king and head of the Church.
2. What does Erastianism teach?
3. What advantage has the revised version of this section of the Confession?
4. Which apostle speaks of "antichrist" in his epistles?
5. Which apostle speaks of "the man of sin" in his epistle?
6. What does the Greek term *anti* often mean in Scripture?
7. Why do the concepts of "antichrist" and "the man of sin" require historical development?
8. Was the Westminster Assembly wise in making its interpretation of the man of sin and antichrist passages of the New Testament a part of the Confession?
9. State the author's reasons for thinking it was not wise.

24

XXVI. Of Communion of Saints

1. *All saints that are united to Jesus Christ their head by his Spirit, and by faith, have fellowship with him in his graces, sufferings, death, resurrection, and glory. And being united to one another in love, they have communion in each other's gifts and graces; and are obliged to the performance of such duties, public and private, as do conduce to their mutual good, both in the inward and outward man.*

2. *Saints, by profession, are bound to maintain an holy fellowship and communion in the worship of God, and in performing such other spiritual services as tend to their mutual edification; as also in relieving each other in outward things, according to their several abilities and necessities. Which communion, as God offereth opportunity, is to be extended unto all those who in every place call upon the name of the Lord Jesus.*

3. *This communion which the saints have with Christ doth not make them in any wise partakers of the substance of his Godhead, or to be equal with Christ in any respect: either of which to affirm is impious and blasphemous. Nor doth their communion one with another, as saints, take away or infringe the title or property which each man hath in his goods and possessions.*

These sections of the Confession teach us (1) that believers have vital (life-giving) union with Christ in his work of mediation, (2) that as a consequence they also have communion with each other and in each other's gifts and graces, (3) that this communion entails certain mutual duties and obligations among believers, and (4) that the union and communion with Christ enjoyed by believers does not mean that they become divine, or equal with Christ, nor does the communion of believers with each other destroy the right of private property.

True believers are united to Jesus Christ. And this union is variously described in Scripture. For example, (1) it is shown to be a *representative* union. As Adam represented all men under the covenant of "works," so Christ represented his elect people in the covenant of grace. We have previously discussed this aspect of union with Christ (chapter VII).

But here we wish to stress the fact (2) that this union is also *vital*. Scripture compares our union with Christ to the union of the vine with the branches, the various parts of the body with the head, and the union of husband and wife (John 15:1–8; 1 Cor. 12:13–27; and Eph. 5:23–32). There is in each of these the thought that the life which is found in one is also found in the other. And so what Christ experiences, we experience. What he possesses we possess. What he does, we do. Now to be sure, there *is* a sense in which we cannot say that his sufferings, death, and resurrection are ours. We do not physically experience what he experienced. But real experience is not only physical. It is also spiritual. God did not physically suffer and die. But God, in Christ's divine nature, was united with man, in Christ's human nature, so that the person who suffered and died was the God-man. God and man in one person experienced one life (1 John 1:1–2; John 1:4). If God and man can be one person and have one life, then why may not many men have one living existence as truly as a vine and branches, or the members of a physical body? We do not explain it. We do assert it. Christ and his believing people have one life, and they share together suffering, death, resurrection, and glory.

(3) But this also indicates that the union is *spiritual*. It is the Holy Spirit (a) who is of one substance with Christ as to his deity, (b) who dwells in him without measure as to his humanity, and (c) who also dwells in believers, thus creating, sustaining, and determining in them that life which is the life of Christ. Indeed, Scripture affirms not only that believ-

ers have this life "through His Spirit in the inner man" (Eph. 3:16), but also that in this manner "Christ [Himself] may dwell in [our] hearts through faith" (3:17).

Now it is with good reason that theologians have called this a *mystical* union. For it is in truth something that we can know only because it is revealed by God. We could not know it by self-examination, nor by insight into our own experience. And this is because it far transcends all other union and communion that we know. How can it be said that "our old man was crucified with Him" (Rom. 6:6)? And how can we explain how we have been "raised . . . up together, and made [to] sit together in the heavenly places in Christ Jesus" (Eph. 2:6)? How can the psalmist (Psalm 22) describe his own experiences in the very words that Christ used to describe his suffering on the cross of Calvary? We frankly confess that this is a great mystery (Eph. 5:32). But we believe it is so because the Word of God says it is. In some mysterious way that we cannot describe or even comprehend we have a real participation with Christ in these things that he wrought for our salvation. Yet this does not mean that we are merged into him, or that the work was done by us. He alone is the God-man. And he alone accomplished the work of redemption in which we share.

On the basis of this union which believers have with Christ there is a necessary corollary: it is the union and communion that believers have one with another. The union and communion that believers have with each other is explained by, and is an outgrowth of, their union with Christ. And far from dissolving their individual personalities and differences, it manifests itself through them. Thus when one member of the Church receives a certain gift from Christ, it is conferred for the benefit of the whole Church and not just for that member (1 Cor. 12:18–31). Even those members of the Christian Church who are lacking in ability, knowledge, or usefulness serve a purpose involving all believers. "Those members of the body which we think to be less honorable, on these we bestow greater honor . . . having given greater honor to that part which lacked it, that there should be no schism in the body, but that the members should have the same care one for another" (1 Cor. 12:23–25). Every member of Christ is, therefore, by the nature of the case under obligation to perform certain duties which conduce to the good of all members of the body.

The Confession maintains that the duty of "fellowship and communion in the worship of God" is at least in part an outcome of this union. For example, the Scripture teaches that we are to worship God on the Sabbath. This is the Fourth Commandment. But some have argued that they can worship God by themselves, or at least without any commitment to membership in the visible Church. Others seem to feel no obligation to be loyal and faithful in attendance at the services of worship in a particular congregation at its stated times of worship on the Lord's Day. We do not here maintain that there are no other grounds upon which to urge this duty. But we can see that this section of the Confession condemns such an attitude even apart from other grounds. Membership in the Church of Christ is part and parcel to union with Christ. He who is united to Christ is therefore also united to other believers. And being united to other believers necessarily entails solemn obligations to them.

Thus in the matter of worship, we are not only to consider the Fourth Commandment (which requires the individual to worship God on the Sabbath), but also "let us consider one another in order to stir up love and good works, not forsaking the assembling of ourselves together, as is the manner of some" (Heb. 10:24–25). Faithful assembly with other true believers is a distinct and compelling consideration. When we have residence in a particular place, we especially have the obligation to those believers with whom we are necessarily related by virtue of our union with Christ, although, of course, this union and communion ought to be extended in its expression as far as possible "unto all those who in every place call upon the name of the Lord Jesus." For there is but one Christ and one body of believers who are in union with him. Where the Spirit is, there is the body of Christ. And the fruit of the Spirit is "love, joy, peace, longsuffering," etc. (Gal. 6:22–23). Where such fruit is generated, there will be a manifestation of the communion of the saints.

To say that the saints have union with Christ and communion with one another does not mean, however, that they have *everything* in common. Believers have union with Christ, but they do not partake of deity. They do not become of one substance with God. Because he is God, the Bible says that Christ "alone has immortality, dwelling in unapproachable light, whom no man has seen or can see" (1 Tim. 6:16). Nor does the communion of believers with one another wipe out all differences among them. In history there have been many attempts by Christians to create societies in which all things are common, including the possession of goods and property. Scripture warrant for such is sought in the book of Acts, which says that "all who believed were together, and had all things in common" (Acts 2:44). Concerning this, three comments may be made. First, there is no indication that this practice was commanded by God as normative for believers. Second, there is evidence that even at that time the right of private property was still recognized by the apostles (Acts 5:4). And finally, this attempt at communal property did not work out satisfactorily even in the Apostolic Church (Acts 6:1).

QUESTIONS

1. What is meant by calling our union with Christ vital?
2. What is meant by calling our union with Christ spiritual?
3. What is meant by calling our union with Christ mystical?
4. By what figures is this union illustrated in Scripture?
5. Because believers have union with Christ, what else do they necessarily have?
6. For whose benefit does Christ bestow a particular gift upon a particular member of his Church?
7. Why is it the duty of believers to loyally attend the stated worship services of a particular congregation (where and when possible)?
8. Is it the duty of believers to give money to the support of the work of the Church? Why?
9. Does union with Christ mean that believers have everything in common with Christ?
10. Does union with Christ obligate believers to have all things common?
11. What text is employed by those who maintain that believers must have all things in common? Give at least one argument against this position.

25

XXVII. Of the Sacraments

1. *Sacraments are holy signs and seals of the covenant of grace, immediately instituted by God, to represent Christ and his benefits, and to confirm our interest in him; as also to put a visible difference between those that belong unto the Church and the rest of the world; and solemnly to engage them to the service of God in Christ, according to his Word.*

This section of the Confession teaches us (1) what the sacraments essentially are, (2) by whom and how instituted, and (3) for what end they were established.

The *doctrine* of the Trinity is taught in the Bible, though the *term* itself is not found in the Bible. Similarly, the doctrine of the sacraments is taught in the Bible, but the term is a coinage of Christian theology. Some object to the word. But one could as reasonably object to such terms as "Trinity," "incarnation," or even "theology." What is important is the doctrine. And if the doctrine be taught in the Bible, it is merely an economy of speech to coin a term for it. John Calvin wisely said that we must not be bound to "a confession woven (*contexta*) and sewn (*consuta*) superstitiously with biblical words." It is necessary only to have "words truly in conformity with the biblical truth and offering the least possible of those asperities which can offend pious ears." Provided the meaning of the term be clear and scriptural, nothing more is required.

Sacraments, then, are "holy signs and seals of the covenant of grace." As Scripture says, "the sign of circumcision" was "a seal of the righteousness of the faith" (Rom. 4:11). (1) A sign is something by means of which something else is made known. Moses' rod, which when cast down became a serpent, provided evidence of the fact that God had appeared unto him (Ex. 4:1–5). The destruction of Jerusalem was the sign that Christ's heavenly mediation and reign had begun (Matt. 24:29–30, 34). Abraham's circumcision made known "the righteousness of the faith which he had while still uncircumcised" (Rom. 4:11). To say that a sacrament is a sign is to say that it makes a declaration. It does not make a declaration concerning itself. If it did it would not be a sign of something else. A sacrament is a sign because it makes known or declares the saving grace of Christ. But for this reason the saving grace is to be distinguished from the sacrament which declares it. (When the Roman Church says that baptism regenerates, it confuses the sign with the thing signified.)

(2) A seal is something which authenticates or confirms that to which it is affixed or appended. In Esther 3:12 we read of an official document. "In the name of King Ahasuerus it was written, and sealed with the king's signet ring." A college graduate receives a diploma to which an official seal is affixed. The seal is of benefit to the recipient, not the giver. The seal does not make the recipient an educated person, however; it merely declares officially that the authorities so regard him. The message of Ahasuerus was authentic without the seal; it actually was the king's decree. The seal was added to assure the king's subjects that the message really was from him. It is so with the sacraments. Sacraments do not cause grace. Neither is grace dependent upon the sacraments. The sacrament is of benefit only to those who are the receivers of grace. It is of benefit because it makes known, or declares, the salvation which believers receive and which is therefore distinct from the sacrament. It is a confirming testimony to the believer concerning what he has received.

Sacraments, according to the Reformed definition, are such by virtue of the fact that they are instituted by God. Roman Catholicism says there are seven sacraments. These are baptism, the Lord's Supper, confirmation, penance, extreme unction, orders, and marriage. There is, in our estimate, no convincing and conclusive argument against some or even all of these except that which has already been stated in our discussion of chapter XXI, 1: "The acceptable way of worshiping the true God is instituted by himself, and so limited by his own revealed will, that he may not be worshiped according to the imaginations and devices of men . . . or any other way not prescribed in the holy Scripture." If God may be worshiped in any way whatsoever apart from specific scriptural warrant, then there does not seem to be any good reason why such "sacraments" may not be added. But if God is to be worshiped within the precise limits of divine commandment, then the position of Rome is overthrown and that of the Confession is invulnerable when it says that there are only two sacraments. It can easily be shown that Christ commanded baptism and the Lord's Supper (Matt. 28:19; 1 Cor. 11:23). And there is no evidence that he ever commanded any other sacraments.

The Confession states four ends for which the sacraments were given. We shall briefly mention these. (1) Christ and his benefits are represented. This is another way of saying that the sacrament serves as a sign. A sign is that which represents something. (2) The believer's interest in Christ is confirmed. This is another way of saying that the sacrament serves as a seal. A seal is that which attests or confirms. Observe that the primary importance of the sacraments is to benefit believers. The Word is the great means of declaring Christ to unbelievers. God has chosen the foolishness of preaching, rather than the sacraments, as a means of conversion (1 Cor. 1:17). It is also the most important means of confirming believers in faith and righteousness. But the sacraments are given to make an additional declaration of, and attestation to, the grace which they receive through the gospel. Even when the Confession says (3) that the sacraments put a visible difference between those that belong to the Church and the rest of the world, it is evident that the benefit belongs to believers. Baptism and the Lord's Supper do not visibly mark believers in the eyes of those who do not witness them. It is the Church which makes the distinction, and it is in the Church that the distinction is recognized. (4) The closing statement, that the sacraments solemnly engage believers to the service of Christ, again indicates that the sacraments are a means of grace exclusively to the believer.

QUESTIONS

1. Why do some object to the term "sacrament"?
2. What other terms might also be rejected on this basis?

3. What two requirements must be met to render a coined word acceptable?
4. What is a sign?
5. What is a seal?
6. Give an example of a sign (other than a sacrament).
7. Give an example of a seal (other than a sacrament).
8. If baptism itself cleansed the soul, what could baptism *not* be?
9. State the principle which would weaken or destroy all argument against the seven sacraments of Rome.
10. State the scriptural principle which proves that there are only two sacraments.
11. Quote the words of the Confession which state what a sign is.
12. Quote the words of the Confession which state what a seal is.
13. To whom are the sacraments a means of grace?

XXVII, 2–5

2. *There is in every sacrament a spiritual relation, or sacramental union, between the sign and the thing signified; whence it comes to pass, that the names and effects of the one are attributed to the other.*

3. *The grace which is exhibited in or by the sacraments, rightly used, is not conferred by any power in them; neither doth the efficacy of a sacrament depend upon the piety or intention of him that doth administer it, but upon the work of the Spirit, and the word of institution; which contains, together with a precept authorizing the use thereof, a promise of benefit to worthy receivers.*

4. *There be only two sacraments ordained by Christ our Lord in the gospel, that is to say, Baptism, and the Supper of the Lord; neither of which may be dispensed by any but by a minister of the Word, lawfully ordained.*

5. *The sacraments of the Old Testament, in regard of the spiritual things thereby signified and exhibited, were, for substance, the same with those of the New.*

These sections of the Confession are designed to refute certain errors of the sacerdotal system. We shall state these errors and then give a defense of the Confession. (The following quotations are from the 1941 edition of the Baltimore Catechism #3 of the Roman Catholic Church.) Error 1—"The sacraments give grace through a power which they possess to sanctify the souls of men as the instruments of God." Error 2—"The one administering a sacrament must have the intention of doing what the Church does in giving the sacrament." Error 3—"There are seven sacraments: Baptism, Confirmation, Holy Eucharist, Penance, Extreme Unction, Holy Orders, and Matrimony."

Roman Catholic (and other sacerdotal) writers frequently appeal to such texts as Acts 22:16, "Arise and be baptized, and wash away your sins," and 1 Peter 3:21, where Peter speaks of that "which now saves us—baptism." Without question, in such texts as these the apostles use a form of expression which attributes a spiritual effect to a material sign. But the contention of the Confession is that the relation between the invisible and the visible (the thing signified and the sign) is such that "the names and effects of the one are attributed to the other." A complete quotation of 1 Peter 3:21 amply supports this view: "There is also an antitype which now saves us—baptism (not the removal of the filth of the flesh, but the answer of a good conscience toward God), through the resurrection of Jesus Christ." Why would Peter take the trouble to deny that baptism saves us by cleansing away the filth of the flesh, unless he was aware that his mode of expression had led some to suppose that the outward sign itself could save? The real cleansing accomplished in the work of grace is "the washing of regeneration and renewing of the Holy Spirit" (Titus 3:5). Baptism is spoken of as it is only because it is a sign of "the real thing."

This "sacramental union" may be compared with (although it is not the same as) the union existing between the two natures of Christ. Because divine and human natures are united in his person, it happens that the names and effects "proper to one nature [are] sometimes in Scripture attributed to . . . the other" (VIII, 7). In Acts 20:28 we read of "the church of God which He purchased with His own blood." The divine nature has not flesh and blood. Yet Christ, who had flesh and blood, is God. It is therefore proper to speak of the "divine-human person" according to terminology and description applicable to either nature.

And there is a similar reason to speak of the sign and the grace signified together by means of terminology derived from either one. This is just what Peter does.

The central issue between sacerdotalists and the Confession "is just whether it is God the Lord who saves us, or it is men, acting in the name and clothed with the powers of God, to whom we are to look for salvation. This is the issue which divides sacerdotalism and evangelical religion" (B. B. Warfield, *The Plan of Salvation* [Grand Rapids: Eerdmans, 1942], p. 56). The sacerdotal view is that the saving grace of God is contained *in* the sacraments and conveyed *by* their administration. The Reformed view is that God the Holy Ghost works when, where, and how he will in conferring saving grace, and that the sacraments are dependent upon and subordinate to his sovereign operation. It is because he is pleased to use the sacraments to exhibit and to confer grace that they become efficacious.

At first sight it might seem that a Roman Catholic would, on his view, be more certain of receiving divine grace through the sacraments than would a Reformed Christian, on his view, in complete dependence upon God. This does not prove to be the case, and the reason is that in the Romish view (1) the sacraments must be administered by someone having "the intention of doing what the Church does in giving the sacrament," and (2) the sacraments must be received with "the right disposition" or "proper motive." Thus divine grace is *conditioned on,* and *controlled by,* the uncertain states of men. Even if one could convince himself that he possessed the right disposition and motive, it would never be possible to be sure that one had not received the sacraments from the hand of a Judas without the right intention (John 4:2).

The Reformed faith subordinates the sacramental means of grace to the divine source of grace, thus making the validity and efficacy of the sacraments independent of men. The sacrament is valid and efficacious because it is appointed by Christ, and is made effectual when and where he is pleased to confer saving grace by his Holy Spirit. "For by one Spirit we were all baptized into one body . . . and . . . made to drink into one Spirit" (1 Cor. 12:13).

Rome is compelled by the logic (?) of its position to virtually grant that all church members are—in emergencies—sacerdotal priests. No Roman Catholic other than a priest would be permitted to administer the sacrament of the Lord's Supper (or mass). But since, in their view, saving grace is contained in and conveyed only by the sacraments, "if there is danger that some one will die without Baptism, any one else may and should baptize" (Baltimore Catechism, Q. 824). Only the priests of Rome can really administer the sacraments aright—yet anyone may administer the sacrament of baptism. Such is the inconsistency required for the maintenance of a false system.

The Reformed view is that neither sacrament may be administered by any but a minister of the Word, lawfully ordained. This is not held in the interests of any priestly or superstitious view of the ministry. Strangely enough, that view leads to the opposite conclusion, as we have shown. Rather, the Confession maintains its view because (1) Scripture says that "servants [ministers] of Christ" are to be the "stewards of the mysteries of God" (1 Cor. 4:1). "And no man takes this honor to himself" (Heb. 5:4). There is no evidence in Scripture to show that other than church officers ever administered the sacraments in the Apostolic Church. (2) The fact that sacraments are not containers and conveyers of automatic grace, that they are not instruments of conversion, further supports this view. God has called all believers to witness because no one can be converted without the gospel. If the sacraments were, as the Roman Catholic Church claims, possessed of inherent power to take away original sin and give our souls new life, then it would be expected that every believer would administer them at every opportunity. The position of the Confession safeguards the truth, namely, that the sacraments are but signs and seals of God's grace which he confers wholly without dependence upon them. It is not as if salvation were absolutely impossible apart from the sacraments.

Finally, the Confession teaches that there have been only two essential sacraments throughout the history of the Church, under both the Old and New Testaments. That is, circumcision and baptism are substantially the same. They signify the same thing spiritually. And the same is true of the Passover and the Lord's Supper. The Old Testament ordinances, circumcision and the Passover, have become, under the New Testament, baptism and the Lord's Supper. The new is in the old concealed, and the old is in the new revealed. The bloody signs were superseded by two bloodless signs. But the significance remains the same, as the following table shows:

Circumcision—Baptism	The Passover—The Lord's Supper
1. Administered once only to each.	1. Administered repeatedly to each.
2. Administered to believers and their children.	2. Administered to believers only.
3. Picture of inception of union with God (cleansing, justification, etc.).	3. Picture of maintenance of union with God (nourishment, growth, sanctification, etc.).
4. Recipient wholly passive (he is circumcised-baptized: receives what another performs).	4. Recipient active (he partakes by his own act).

Argument in support of this identification (between the Old and New Testament ordinances) will be provided throughout our discussion of the sacraments. But we here call attention to an aspect of Scripture data that is often overlooked. The apostle Paul sometimes uses the name of an Old Testament sacrament when speaking about those who have literally received only the New Testament sacrament, or vice versa. He says the Israelites were baptized (1 Cor. 10:2), whereas, of course, they were actually circumcised. He also says the Colossians were circumcised (Col. 2:11), though in actual fact they were baptized. He speaks of the Corinthians as having the Passover (1 Cor. 5:7), though we know that it was the Lord's Supper, and not the Passover, that was observed among them. The Passover became the Lord's Supper once and for all on the night in which our Lord was betrayed (Matt. 26:17–30; Luke 22:15–20).

So the question is: how are we to explain this interchange of sacramental terminology in the New Testament? We believe this is the true explanation: (1) "a spiritual relation . . . between the sign and the thing signified; whence it comes to pass, that the names and effects of the one are attributed to the other." This means that there is such a relationship between sacrament and grace that we may speak of the sacrament as if it were the grace, and vice versa. (2) "The sacraments of the Old Testament, in regard of the spiritual things thereby signified . . . were, for *substance,* the *same* with those of the New." The meaning is that circumcision and baptism are linked together because they both sustain the same kind of spiritual relation to the same grace. And since that grace can be spoken of by means of the name of the sacrament related to it, it follows that the name of the one sacrament can be applied to the other sacrament. If the same grace can be called circumcision and also baptism, then there is no reason why the apostle may not speak of baptism as if it were circumcision. This is what he does (see Col. 2:11–12). That he does so argues effectively for the teaching of this section of the Confession.

QUESTIONS

1. What is the first error of sacerdotalism?
2. What Scripture text, for example, would seem at first sight to support this?
3. What Scripture can be shown to refute this interpretation?
4. Why are expressions such as the one in that Scripture passage misinterpreted?
5. With what might the "sacramental union" be compared?
6. What is the central issue between Romish and Reformed religion?
7. Why, at first sight, does the Romish system seem to offer assurance?
8. Why does this not prove to be the case?
9. How does the Reformed system really offer certainty and assurance?
10. Why is Rome compelled to virtually deny its own teaching concerning the exclusive power of the priesthood?
11. Why does the Reformed church allow that only ordained ministers should administer the sacraments?
12. In what ways are baptism and circumcision the same?
13. In what ways are the Lord's Supper and the Passover the same?
14. What phenomenon in the language of the apostle Paul supports the view that the Old and New Testament ordinances are essentially the same?

26

XXVIII. Of Baptism

1. *Baptism is a sacrament of the New Testament, ordained by Jesus Christ, not only for the solemn admission of the party baptized into the visible Church, but also to be unto him a sign and seal of the covenant of grace, of his ingrafting into Christ, of regeneration, of remission of sins, and of his giving up unto God through Jesus Christ, to walk in newness of life. Which sacrament is, by Christ's own appointment, to be continued in his Church until the end of the world.*

2. *The outward element to be used in this sacrament is water, wherewith the party is to be baptized in the name of the Father, and of the Son, and of the Holy Ghost, by a minister of the gospel, lawfully called thereunto.*

These sections of the Confession teach us (1) that baptism is a sacrament (according to the definition made in the preceding chapter), (2) what baptism means, (3) how it is to be administered, and (4) how long this sacrament is to continue in the Church of God.

We have already shown that the sacraments "are holy signs and seals of the covenant of grace" instituted by Christ. This establishes that baptism is a sacrament. It does not save us, but it is a "sign" representing that which does save us (1 Peter 3:21). It is recorded in the Gospel (Matt.

28:19) that Christ instituted, or commanded, baptism. From these two teachings of the Word of God we have proof that baptism is a sacrament.

But what is the meaning of baptism? The Confession indicates that the meaning of baptism is not to be found in one single aspect of the doctrine taught in Scripture but in a complex or manifold concept. Baptism signifies (1) admission into the visible Church, (2) the grace of the covenant, (3) regeneration, (4) the remission of sins, and (5) the duty of new obedience. In other words, the meaning of baptism is rich. It is a sign and seal, not of this or that part of a certain great work of divine grace, and of covenant privilege, but of the whole complex wonder of it. Baptism is, as it were, a great "motion picture" which shows forth that great work of God whereby dead sinners are brought into living union with Christ and with God. And the central concept expressed by baptism is this union itself. The baptismal formula recorded in Matthew 28:19 shows this quite clearly. Believers and their children are to be baptized *into* the name of the Father, and of the Son, and of the Holy Ghost. When Paul says that the children of Israel "were all baptized into Moses" (1 Cor. 10:2), he means that they left Egypt and all the relationships which they had with it, to enter into a new relationship with Moses the man of God. And so it is with those who are baptized into relationship with the Triune God. "Were you baptized in the name of Paul?" (1 Cor. 1:13) asks the apostle, as he argues against the thought that any Christians were especially united to him as over against Peter or Apollos. His argument would have no relevance if union (or intimate and special relationship) were not the central import of baptism.

Yet union with God through Jesus Christ is a relationship which involves a whole complex of integral matters. One cannot have union with God except there be a removal of the guilt and defilement of sin. There can be no relationship of intimate concord with God on the part of one who is yet under the dominion of sin. So it is that Scripture focuses now upon one and now upon another of the several subordinate aspects of this union. Peter speaks of baptism with special reference to "the remission of sins" and the "gift of the Holy Spirit" (Acts 2:38). Paul emphasizes "washing of regeneration and renewing of the Holy Spirit" (Titus 3:5). And again he specifies the duty to walk in newness of life which belongs to those who are baptized (Rom. 4:12). But the predominant theme in Scripture's references to baptism is union with Christ and the

Triune God, which embraces and transcends all other aspects of the meaning of this sacrament (Matt. 28:19; 1 Cor. 12:13; Gal. 3:27; Rom. 6:3).

Baptism (and likewise the Lord's Supper) simply expresses the verbal content of the gospel in a nonverbal form. Baptism expresses and represents that aspect of the gospel and its saving reception which is verbally set forth in the doctrines of grace discussed in the Confession under these heads: (1) effectual calling, (2) regeneration, (3) conversion (repentance and faith), (4) justification, and (5) adoption. This will explain why baptism is rightly administered but once to any individual. It will also explain why the sacrament of baptism, unlike the sacrament of the Lord's Supper, is passively rather than actively received. This is in accord with that work of God of which baptism is a visible representation or "picture." Regeneration is the act of God alone. The sinner is dead. Regeneration is that which makes him alive. We cannot say that the sinner is active in his own regeneration (which is likened to being raised from the dead). He is wholly passive. But as soon as he is regenerated he is alive. And this means that he is in union with Christ. For *in* Christ is life. It is true that the sinner will now be able to repent and to believe. And he will be active in repentance and faith. But he can do this only because the seeds of repentance and faith are already present in him by virtue of regeneration and union with Christ.

Thus baptism represents that in which man is essentially passive, and the apostles characteristically speak of it as such. "We are buried," we do not bury ourselves; "we have been planted," we do not plant ourselves; "our old man is crucified," he does not crucify himself. When baptism is described as if it were a symbol of an activity performed by man (rather than a union created by God), its true meaning is contradicted. This is our ultimate objection to the Baptist view of this ordinance. Baptists say (1) that baptism should be given only to adults, because only adults are capable of performing the activity which baptism signifies, and (2) that baptism signifies that activity by which a man joins himself to Christ. The Baptist theologian A. H. Strong says: "The essence of it is the joining of ourselves to another before the world" (*Systematic Theology,* [Philadelphia: Griffith and Rowland, 1912], p. 943).

The answers to this view are: (1) that baptism should be given to children of believers as well as to believers because God is capable of creating that union in children of which baptism is a sign and seal, and (2) that baptism signifies that union which is created between God and sinners by his own power alone. It is neither the activity of God (which causes this union) nor the activity of man (which results from this union) which is signified by baptism. It is the union itself, which is the result of God's work alone, and which effects the entirety of man's gracious activity. And because such a union is created only once, there can be only one baptism. Repeated baptism would not represent God's grace in the efficacy that belongs to it.

There is no argument among Christians of practically all denominations that the "outward element to be used in this sacrament is water," and that the party to be baptized is to be baptized into the triune name. As the reason is self-evident we need not labor the point. We have also shown why this sacrament is to be administered by ministers of the gospel. We conclude, then, with the assertion that baptism is to be administered until the end of the world, because Jesus Christ said, "Go . . . make disciples . . . baptizing them in the name . . . and lo, I am with you always, even to the end of the age" (Matt. 28:19–20). Since the scope of this Great Commission is worldwide and age-long, and since the promise of the Savior is to sustain his Church in the engagement of this duty to the end of the age, it follows that this sacrament is to be continued until the end has come.

QUESTIONS

1. From what two proofs are we certain that baptism is a sacrament?
2. What is the meaning of baptism?
3. What is the central import of baptism?
4. What are some subordinate aspects of baptism?
5. If baptism has a central meaning, why are these subordinate aspects sometimes mentioned in Scripture apart from the central meaning?
6. What is the relationship between the sacraments and the gospel?
7. Why is it that baptism requires no activity on the part of man?
8. Why do Baptists say that infants should not be baptized?
9. What is the ultimate objection to the Baptist view?
10. Is baptism a representation of God's activity? Explain.
11. Prove that this sacrament is to be administered until the end of the age.

XXVIII, 3–4

3. *Dipping of the person into the water is not necessary; but baptism is rightly administered by pouring or sprinkling water upon the person.*

4. *Not only those that do actually profess faith in and obedience unto Christ, but also the infants of one or both believing parents are to be baptized.*

These sections of the Confession teach us (1) that immersion is not essential to baptism, (2) that no particular mode of baptism is commanded in Scripture, and (3) that professing believers and their children are the proper subjects of baptism.

Some Christian denominations require immersion because they do not believe there is any real baptism without immersion. They insist that the New Testament Greek word (*baptizō*) means "to immerse." The fact is that the word (*baptizō*) does *not* mean immersion. This is not to say that the term cannot be legitimately applied to an action involving immersion. It is only that the term itself does not have that meaning. This is easily shown from Scripture itself.

(1) In 1 Corinthians 10:2 we read of the Israelites, when they left Egypt, that "all were baptized into Moses in the cloud and in the sea." Since Scripture infallibly records the fact that they were *not* immersed (the Egyptians were), but that they passed through the sea upon dry ground, it is obvious that in this instance the term (*baptizō*) does not mean immersion (Ex. 14:22).

(2) Again, in Hebrews 9:10, we read that under the Old Testament ceremonial law there were "various washings" (*diaphorois baptismois*). But the book of Hebrews reminds us that these consisted of the sprinkling of the blood of bulls and goats (9:13), the sprinkling of the book and all the people (9:19), and the sprinkling of the tabernacle and the vessels of the ministry (9:21). In other words, we are told that various Old Testament ceremonial acts of cleansing were not performed by immersion, but nonetheless they were "baptisms." How then could the term (*baptizō*) mean immersion?

(3) In Acts 1:5 we read the promise of Christ to his disciples: "You shall be baptized with the Holy Spirit not many days from now." Then

in Acts 2 we find the fulfillment of that promise. The Holy Spirit came upon them, "and there appeared to them divided tongues, as of fire, and one sat upon each of them" (2:3). When people thought them drunk, Peter said, "These are not drunk, as you suppose. . . . But this is what was spoken by the prophet Joel: 'And it shall come to pass in the last days, says God, that I will pour out of My Spirit on all flesh . . . I will pour out My Spirit in those days . . .' " (2:15–18). To be baptized with the Spirit was to have the Spirit *poured out upon* the disciples, not for them to be *immersed into* the Spirit. So again it is clear that baptism does not mean immersion. This does not prove that baptism was never administered by the mode of immersion (although it cannot be *proved* that it was in a single instance in Scripture). It does prove that the term (*baptizō*) does not mean immersion. It does not mean immersion any more than it means sprinkling or pouring. What it means is (as we have shown) union with Christ and the Triune God by means of cleansing from sin, whether by immersion, sprinkling, or pouring.

Baptists also insist that adults are the only proper recipients of baptism. This they maintain on two grounds: (1) that children are not capable of such experience and activity as baptism requires, and (2) that the Bible does not give evidence for the baptism of children (that is, infants). We have already shown that baptism is a sign and seal of union with Christ and with God, and that this union is an absolute creation of God which he bestows upon whomever he will. Children are no more incapable of effecting their own union with Christ than adults are. *All* (adults and infants alike) are totally depraved and unable to do *anything* whatsoever to effect union with God. But God is omnipotent, and he can and does effect this union in his own power. And Jesus Christ said that this saving work is found in children, and even in tiny infants (Luke 18:15). "For of such is the kingdom of heaven," he said (Matt. 19:14). If children—and even tiny infants—are members of the kingdom of God (Luke 18:16), then it can scarcely be argued that they cannot experience that which baptism signifies and seals. What is membership in the kingdom of God if it is not union with Christ? It is interesting to observe that Baptists themselves do not consistently abide by their own argument. At least most Baptists allow that believers' infants who die in infancy may be saved. And this is the same as allowing that they may have that of which baptism is a sign and seal.

As to the second argument, we agree, of course, that the New Testament does not contain a specific command to baptize infants. Neither does the New Testament contain a specific command that women are to receive the Lord's Supper. But this is not the same as saying that the Bible contains no such command. The New Testament does not always repeat specific commands which are already recorded in the Old Testament Scriptures. In other words, the apostles do not act as though the commandments of God are of no effect unless they repeat them in their writings. The apostles nowhere expressly repeat the words of the Second Commandment. But there is no doubt that they continued to regard the Second Commandment to be binding (Acts 17:29; Rom. 1:23). So we may not say that God has not commanded the baptism of children. God, at the beginning of patriarchal history, commanded that the sign and seal of the covenant of grace be given to the children of believers (Gen. 17:1–14). Furthermore, it was explicitly stated that this was an everlasting requirement. It is not true, then, that God has given no commandment with respect to the baptism of children.

The Baptist argument is that with the coming of Christ circumcision was abrogated, so that this command is no longer in force. But the apostle makes it clear that circumcision continues, with this change, that it is now called baptism—"In Him you were also circumcised with the circumcision made without hands . . . in baptism" (Col. 2:11–12). The Baptist contention is that children may not be baptized without a New Testament commandment. But the need is rather for the Baptists to produce the "New Testament command" that excludes what God previously commanded. The disciples felt that little children should not be brought to the Lord. But he said, "Do not forbid them" (Matt. 19:14). Our argument is this: (1) God commanded believers to give the sign and seal of the covenant to their children; (2) baptism is now the sign and seal of that covenant concerning which God gave this command (Gal. 3:16–17); (3) God changed the form of the sign and seal but not the everlasting covenant; he did not revoke his command to give the sign and seal to the children of believers; and (4) the New Testament evidence confirms this position.

While the New Testament does not contain a verbal repetition of God's original command to give the sign and seal of the covenant to the children of believers, it does contain information and evidence agreeable to no other view but that which assumes the continued force of that commandment. We shall cite a few instances. (1) In Acts 2:38–39 Peter urged the Jews to receive baptism in the name of Jesus Christ, and he gave as a reason that "the promise is to you and to your children." This form of expression is wholly consistent with the Old Testament concept of "covenant children" included in the promise to believers and consequently circumcised. And the fact that Peter urges baptism on precisely this ground is a strong presumption in favor of the continuance of that concept in the New Testament era.

(2) In Acts 17:11 we are informed that the Jews of the Berean synagogue, unlike most Jewish congregations scattered through the Roman Empire, "received the word with all readiness." They even "searched the Scriptures daily" to see whether or not the things that Paul taught were in agreement with them. They tested Paul's doctrine by God's Word as they found it in the Old Testament. But how could they have accepted Paul's doctrine of baptism if it was not in agreement with the command to give the sign to covenant children?

(3) In 1 Corinthians 7:14 Paul gives comfort, hope, and instruction to Christians who find themselves under the burden of being married to unbelievers. Evidently, there were such in Corinth who, because of this "yoke," felt themselves to be at a great disadvantage as compared with others because of a presumed difference in the status of their children. The Baptist view is that all children are outside of God's grace and covenant, and therefore not to be baptized. They recognize no distinction between the children of believers and the children of unbelievers. But the apostle said, "The unbelieving husband is sanctified by the wife, and the unbelieving wife is sanctified by the husband; otherwise your children would be unclean, but now they are holy" (1 Cor. 7:14). In other words, the apostle *did* recognize a distinction between the children of believers and the children of unbelievers. And he was able to assure believers in mixed marriages that in their case also he that worked in them was greater than he who works in the world. Therefore, their children, like those of two believing parents, were holy. It is interesting to observe the complete silence of Baptists regarding this text. And if it be objected that the term "holy" does not mean that these children are merely entitled to the sign and seal of the covenant, but that it means much more than that, we reply, so be it, but in any case it means something, and something wholly inconsistent with the Baptist view.

QUESTIONS

1. Why do Baptists insist upon immersion?
2. How do Reformed Christians sometimes lend needless support to this view?
3. How may we prove that the word *baptizō* does not mean immersion?
4. Does this prove that this term is never used to describe an instance in which immersion may be involved?
5. What are the two main Baptist arguments against infant baptism?
6. What proof can be presented to refute each of these arguments?
7. Give an example of evidence in the New Testament which conflicts with the Baptist view, and which supports the Reformed view.

XXVIII, 5–7

5. *Although it be a great sin to contemn or neglect this ordinance, yet grace and salvation are not so inseparably annexed unto it, as that no person can be regenerated or saved without it, or that all that are baptized are undoubtedly regenerated.*

6. *The efficacy of baptism is not tied to that moment of time wherein it is administered; yet notwithstanding, by the right use of this ordinance, the grace promised is not only offered, but really exhibited and conferred by the Holy Ghost, to such (whether of age or infants) as that grace belongeth unto, according to the counsel of God's own will, in his appointed time.*

7. *The sacrament of baptism is but once to be administered unto any person.*

These sections of the Confession teach us (1) that it is sinful to neglect the ordinance of baptism, (2) that salvation is not absolutely inseparable from it, (3) that salvation is not guaranteed by it, (4) that the efficacy of baptism is not tied to the moment of administration of it, and (5) that it is a means of grace when rightly administered (but once, and according to the Word of God).

If baptism is "a sacrament of the New Testament, ordained by Jesus Christ," which is "to be continued in his Church until the end of the world," then it follows that it is a great error to deprecate or to neglect it. If neglect of circumcision elicited the wrath and displeasure of God against Moses (Ex. 4:24–26), and if the spurning of the baptism of John by the Pharisees and lawyers is likewise condemned (Luke 7:30), then how much more ought we to consider the gravity of a like disposition toward that which our Lord commanded! And it is important to remember that God's wrath against Moses was not because Moses had neglected the ordinance for himself, but because he had neglected the circumcision of his children. Baptism is a moral duty. And a person who could be baptized (or who could present his children for baptism) but will not, is in a very different position from a person who would be baptized but cannot. There may be instances in which it is physically impossible for a believer to receive this sacrament (Luke 23:39–43). Because such an individual neither deprecates nor neglects the ordinance, we cannot say that he errs merely because divine providence prevents his baptism. But if a person is not baptized for the reason that he either condemns or neglects the ordinance, he is guilty of sin.

In effect we are saying only that all error is sinful. We must remember that every one, including Presbyterians as well as Baptists, are sinful and thus not free from error in varying degrees. It should be noted in this connection that sin is less heinous in the sight of God when it is not done in conscious disobedience or neglect. He who knows the truth and *then* disobeys is guilty to a greater degree than he who obeys a misinformed conscience. It is when "we sin willfully after we have received the knowledge of the truth, [that] there no longer remains a sacrifice for sins" (Heb. 10:26).

To say that baptism is required by the law of God (for believers and their children) does not mean, then, that baptism is absolutely necessary for salvation itself. What man must do as a moral duty must not be confused with what God may do. Scripture shows that it is possible to have everything signified and sealed by baptism without having baptism itself. Everyone knows that the thief on the cross was saved. And he was saved in that era when John the Baptist and Jesus himself required that men be baptized for the remission of sins. But he was prevented from being baptized by providential circumstances over which he had no control. God did not change these circumstances preventing baptism but saved him without baptism. This proves that it is possible for there to be circumstances in which men may have the saving effects of God's grace without the divinely appointed sign and seal, and this by the will of God.

On the other hand, Scripture also shows that men may have baptism *under proper administration* without actually experiencing the saving grace of which it is a sign and seal. Simon (Acts 8:13) was baptized lawfully by the apostle. Yet he remained "poisoned by bitterness and bound by iniquity" (v. 23). He could not have had rightly administered baptism together with a sin-bound heart if it were not true that baptism is separable from the grace of which it is a sign and seal, and if it were not also true that baptism may be rightly administered to those who do not really possess the grace of which it is a sign and seal.

The case of Esau also demonstrates this point. He was circumcised by divine command. Yet it was certain (even before he was born) that he would never have union with Christ (Rom. 9:11-13). In this instance it cannot be argued that Esau was improperly circumcised. Neither can it be argued that Esau was circumcised because it was presumed that he was, or would be, in union with Christ. It can be argued only that God commanded believers to give the sign and seal of the covenant to their children even though it could not be presumed that they were, or would be, in union with Christ. The Bible does not teach that the proper *administration* of the sacrament of baptism requires that those who receive it actually possess union with Christ. There is, in other words, a real discrepancy between the sphere of the proper administration of baptism and the sphere of the working of saving grace. God has given orders which do not provide for the baptism of *all* true believers (Luke 23:33, 43) and which do provide for the baptism of some who are *not* destined to eternal life.

We must not limit the efficacy of baptism to the moment of administration. For example, we are not to think that when a child is baptized the effect of his baptism terminates then and there. Again we cite the case of Jacob and Esau. (1) Both were given the sacrament by divine command. (2) Esau never received the grace of which he had the sign and seal. And (3) Jacob did not experience the efficacy of the sacrament until his conversion many years later (Gen. 25–32, esp. 32:24–28).

Opponents of infant baptism frequently point out that in a great many cases there seems to be no evidence of the work of God's grace in those who have been baptized as infants. They truly state the fact that baptism has no saving effect upon such infants at the time they are baptized. But we must not allow this truth to mislead us; to say that baptism has no effect at the time is not the same as to say that it has no effect at all. Baptism *never* causes union with Christ. It never has that effect. That is not the purpose of baptism. The purpose of baptism is not to effect union with Christ but rather to confirm and testify such. And this is precisely why baptism is of increased efficacy inasmuch as it is not tied to the moment of administration only. In this way baptism testifies that God gives union with Christ to whom he will, as he will, and when he will. The effect of baptism is not that it causes union with Christ, but that it testifies of this union. Baptism, like circumcision, may have no saving effect upon some people. But infant baptism, like infant circumcision, does have a profound effect upon those who are converted long after their baptism. The order then may be either (1) baptism, then effectual calling into union with Christ, and then the efficacy of baptism, or (2) effectual calling, then baptism, and then the efficacy of baptism. It cannot be in any other order. For one cannot experience the efficacy of baptism prior to baptism, nor can one experience the efficacy of baptism prior to effectual calling.

Questions

1. Why is it a sin to contemn or to neglect baptism?
2. What Scripture can be cited to prove this?
3. Does the Baptist who sincerely believes that it is wrong to baptize his children sin in not having them baptized? Why?
4. In what sense is baptism not necessary?
5. What is willful sin?
6. What biblical evidence proves that one can be saved without being baptized?
7. What biblical evidence proves that one can be baptized without being saved?
8. What biblical case proves that baptism is not given to infants on the ground that we are to regard them as elect?
9. Why then was he baptized?
10. What biblical case proves that the efficacy of baptism is not tied to the moment of its administration?
11. What two things (in either order) must a person first have before baptism can have efficacy for him?

27

XXIX. Of the Lord's Supper

1. *Our Lord Jesus, in the night wherein he was betrayed, instituted the sacrament of his body and blood, called the Lord's Supper, to be observed in his Church unto the end of the world, for the perpetual remembrance of the sacrifice of himself in his death, the sealing all benefits thereof unto true believers, their spiritual nourishment and growth in him, their further engagement in and to all duties which they owe unto him, and to be a bond and pledge of their communion with him, and with each other, as members of his mystical body.*

This section of the Confession teaches us (1) that the Lord's Supper is a sacrament instituted by Christ, (2) that it was instituted on the night in which he was betrayed, (3) that it is to be observed in his Church until the end of the world, (4) that it is given for (a) the perpetual remembrance of his sacrifice, (b) the sealing of all benefits thereof to true believers, (c) their spiritual nourishment and growth in him, (d) their further engagement in and to all duties which they owe him, and (e) a bond and pledge of their communion with him, and with each other, as members of his body.

The institution of the Lord's Supper is recorded in three Gospels and one of the epistles of Paul. "For I received from the Lord that which I also delivered to you" (1 Cor. 11:23–26; Matt. 26:26–29; Mark 14:22–25; Luke 22:17–20). In this fourfold account we are repeatedly told that Jesus commanded, "Do this." And the time of this institution is as clearly revealed as the duty itself. It was on the night in which he was betrayed. It was at the time of the Passover. And while the frequency with which it was to be observed was not specified in a particular way, it was his command that it be frequent. His exact term is "often." Calvin strongly urged the weekly observance of this sacrament. Such frequency would certainly not be a violation of Christ's institution. But the Scripture requires only a frequent administration of the sacrament and does not give a rigid rule *requiring* weekly observance. Finally, we note that in Christ's words of institution, as is true of baptism, there is warrant to continue this sacrament until the end of the world. For, says the apostle, "As often as you eat this bread, and drink this cup, you proclaim the Lord's death *till He comes*" (1 Cor. 11:26). If this sacrament is observed until he comes, it will be observed until the end of the world, because that is when he will come.

The Lord's Supper "is a visible sermon, wherein Christ crucified is set before us" (Thomas Watson, *The Ten Commandments* [London: Banner of Truth, 1965], p. 165). The sacrament of the Lord's Supper represents and exhibits salvation through the one perfect sacrifice of Christ. So the central emphasis of the ordinance is the "remembrance" of "the Lord's death." The *elements* recall the body and blood rendered unto God in his sacrifice of himself. The *words* instill within us the remembrance of him whose body and blood it was, and of the wondrous fact that he gave himself for us. "This is My body which is broken for *you*" (1 Cor. 11:24). And even the *actions* call to mind the suffering and pain endured by the Savior in rendering unto God this great oblation. "This is My body which is *broken* for you."

When Christ distributed the elements of this sacrament to his disciples, he did not, by that sacramental act, actually give them salvation. In the case of all but one they already had salvation. In the case of one there was never to be salvation. What then did the sacrament do for them? It signified and sealed the benefits of his sacrifice. It represented them. It vividly "pictured" them. It showed the disciples what they possessed. And it testified to them that they did possess it. It assured them of this great salvation that was theirs in Christ.

Yet this is not all. The Lord's Supper, unlike baptism, does not represent only something that is fully accomplished. It does not signify merely a finished state of existence (union with Christ which never again changes essentially). It does not represent the Christian's saving interest in that work of God as if it were already fully received. The Lord's Supper is to be frequently observed, because it represents a work of God that continues throughout the life of the believer. Again and again the believer is to eat, drink, and remember, because the Lord's Supper is a sign and seal of the work of God's grace whereby a believer continually derives spiritual nourishment and strength, forgiveness, cleansing, and sanctification, from the benefits of Christ's one sacrifice and his present mediation of those benefits to believers.

The believer does not, of course, derive those benefits from the sacrament itself but from Christ and his sacrifice. What the believer receives in and by the sacrament itself is not the same as what he receives in Christ and his sacrifice. The precise thing received in and by the sacrament is a testimony of and confirmation (attestation as to the validity) of saving grace which is received from Christ through the Holy Spirit. The saving grace (which nourishes, sustains, and sanctifies the believer) is operative in the believer by virtue of vital union with Christ. But this saving grace is strengthened by the witness and attestation conveyed by the sacrament.

Since this sacrament is a sign and seal of union and communion with Christ, it is also a means whereby the believer is reminded of the fact that he is to be—and is strengthened in his will to be—faithful and obedient to Christ. Being reminded that he is "bought at a price," he will know that he must "therefore glorify God in . . . body and in . . . spirit, which are God's" (1 Cor. 6:20).

In this same epistle Paul says, "You cannot drink the cup of the Lord and the cup of demons; you cannot partake of the Lord's table, and of the table of demons" (10:21). It is not merely that a believer ought not to drink of the two cups; rather, he cannot. Of course the apostle realized that there is a sense in which such a thing can be done: a person can partake of the elements of the sacrament of the Lord's Supper and also partake of the ceremonial elements of a false religion. But in such an instance there is no efficacy in the Lord's sacrament, so far as that person is concerned. It has efficacy only as a sign and seal of real union with Christ. And he who has real union with Christ cannot—at the same time—have union with Satan.

The Lord's Supper is *not* a means of grace to those who have no grace (1 Cor. 11:27–29). The preaching of the Word of God, by contrast, is a means of grace to those who have no grace. No one is required to discern the Lord's body before he hears the gospel. But this requirement proves that the Lord's Supper is not a converting ordinance. It is not a means of effecting union with Christ. It is rather a means of strength and assurance to those who have union with Christ.

The Lord's Supper is also "a bond and pledge" of the union and communion shared by true believers with Christ (the head) and with each other (the members of his body). The bread was distributed. But it was one loaf that was distributed. "For we, though many, are one bread and one body; for we all partake of that one bread" (1 Cor. 10:17). And again we read that "He took the cup, and gave thanks and said, 'Take this and divide it among yourselves'" (Luke 22:17). The many are one. They have as much, nay, even more in common than have Adam and his posterity. Thus through this sacrament, we receive testimony and assurance of the fact that we have become members of a new race in Christ. We are strengthened in our realization and assurance of this blessed fellowship and communion with Christ and his people which is ours by virtue of our union with him.

QUESTIONS

1. Where is the institution of the Lord's Supper recorded?
2. When was the Lord's Supper instituted?
3. How often does Christ require its observance?
4. How long is this sacrament to be continued? Prove.
5. What is the central emphasis of this sacrament?
6. In what three ways is this shown?
7. Does the sacrament of the Lord's Supper convey saving grace? If not, what does it convey?
8. What truth is testified to by the frequent observance of this sacrament?
9. What requirement is made of those who receive this sacrament that is not made of those who hear the gospel?
10. What aspect of this sacrament portrays the union of many believers with Christ and their communion with each other?

XXIX, 2

2. *In this sacrament Christ is not offered up to his Father, nor any real sacrifice made at all for remission of sins of the quick or dead; but only a commemoration of that one offering up of himself, by himself, upon the cross, once for all, and a spiritual oblation of all possible praise unto God for the same; so that the Popish sacrifice of the mass, as they call it, is most abominably injurious to Christ's one only sacrifice, the alone propitiation for all the sins of the elect.*

This section of the Confession teaches us (1) that the sacrament of the Lord's Supper is not a sacrifice but only a commemoration of that one all-sufficient sacrifice of Christ, and (2) that the Romish doctrine of the mass is nothing less than an attack against the glory and efficacy of the one true sacrifice of Christ.

In the Baltimore Catechism we read these words: "The Mass is the sacrifice of the New Law in which Christ, through the ministry of the priest, offers Himself to God in an unbloody manner under the appearances of bread and wine" (Q. 925). "In the New Law there is no other sacrifice acceptable to God save the sacrifice of the Mass" (Q. 929). "The Mass is the same sacrifice as the sacrifice of the cross, because in the Mass the victim is the same, and the principal priest is the same, Jesus Christ" (Q. 931). By this, the official teaching of Rome, it is to be believed that one is saved, not because Christ *died* for him, but because Christ *dies* for him. As often as the sinner sins, so often must Christ also die. According to Romish dogma this is what Christ does. He does not appear to do so. But this is only because he presents himself under the appearance of bread and wine. He looks like bread and wine. But he is really physically present in human flesh and blood in order to suffer and to die again. And, says Rome, there is no salvation except by this continually repeated sacrifice.

It would be difficult to invent a doctrine more detrimental to the true glory of the work of Jesus Christ. For the Scripture says that "by one offering He has perfected forever those who are being sanctified" (Heb. 10:14). When he died he said, "It is finished" (John 19:30). And, unlike the Old Testament priests, Christ "does not need daily, as those high priests, to offer up sacrifices" (Heb. 7:27). If daily forgiveness of sin required daily sacrifice of Christ, "He then would have had to suffer often since the foundation of the world" (Heb. 9:26). The fact that forgiveness was given before Christ's sacrifice was made, establishes the fact that forgiveness can be given after that sacrifice has been finished. So "now, once at the end of the ages, He has appeared to put away sin by the sacrifice of Himself. . . . So Christ was offered once to bear the sins of many" (Heb. 9:26, 28). Well might we say of the supposed physical presence of Christ at the mass what the angel once said to the disciples: "He is not here, but is risen!" (Luke 24:6). "Heaven must receive [Him] until the times of restoration of all things" (Acts 3:21).

Because of the infinite worth, the absolute perfection, of Christ's one sacrifice of himself, Scripture teaches us to remember it, and to rest our hope of salvation and eternal life upon it. Thus the past tense is used: "knowing that you *were* not redeemed with corruptible things . . . but with the precious blood of Christ. . . . He indeed was foreordained before the foundation of the world, but was manifest in these last times for you" (1 Peter 1:18–20). "Christ also *has* loved us, and given Himself for us, an offering and a sacrifice to God" (Eph. 5:2). "For Christ also suffered once for sins, the just for the unjust" (1 Peter 3:18). If Christ's one sacrifice were not sufficient, Scripture could hardly speak in this manner. It speaks this way because Christ's one offering was sufficient to atone for all the sins of his elect people, whether they be past sins, present sins, or future sins. The Romish mass, in denying this, undermines the integrity of Christ's work and leads sinners to trust in the priest, the mass, and the Church rather than in the only sacrifice that can deliver them from their sins. To the extent that Rome persuades men to believe her doctrine, she also persuades men to abandon legitimate hope.

If one death of the God-man is not sufficient for all human need, how could many such deaths suffice? Of course, Rome teaches that the death which Christ dies in the mass is not another but somehow the same death as that which he died on the cross. But if this be so, how can we regard it as a real death? If the death that Christ died on the cross is no more "real" than that which he is supposed to die in the mass, then it is not of much value. And again, one does not *really* die one death many times. But even if we try to follow the incredible logic of Romish dogma, we still must say that the death of Christ is of no value, because (on their own testimony) he is not through dying. A sacrifice has no value until the dying is finished. But if Christ has not finished dying after two thousand years, how can we be sure that he will ever finish dying? Then what becomes of our hope of the resurrection; indeed, how can there be a resurrection from a death that is perpetual? In a word: the Romish doctrine is as absurd as it is unbiblical and detrimental.

QUESTIONS

1. According to Rome what sacrifice is alone acceptable to God?
2. According to Rome what sacrifice is identical with the sacrifice of the cross?
3. According to Rome why is the mass designated a real sacrifice?
4. According to Rome how often must Christ die? According to Scripture how often must Christ die? Give proof text.
5. Why cannot Christ be physically present in the mass?
6. What characteristic mode of expression shows the sacrifice of Christ to be already finished?
7. From what does the Romish doctrine lead men's trust?
8. To what does the Romish doctrine lead men's trust?
9. To what extent are Roman Catholics "hopeless"?

XXIX, 3–4

3. *The Lord Jesus hath, in this ordinance, appointed his ministers to declare his word of institution to the people, to pray, and bless the elements of bread and wine, and thereby to set them apart from a common to a holy use; and to take and break the bread, to take the cup, and (they communicating also themselves) to give both to the communicants; but to none who are not then present in the congregation.*

4. *Private masses, or receiving this sacrament by a priest, or any other, alone; as likewise the denial of the cup to the people; worshiping the elements, the lifting them up, or carrying them about for adoration, and the reserving them for any pretended religious use; are all contrary to the nature of this sacrament, and to the institution of Christ.*

In this section of the Confession we learn (1) that Christ has appointed his ministers to administer the sacraments with the word of institution, prayer, and blessing, (2) that the elements to be used are bread and wine, (3) that both elements are to be received by ministers and members of the Church alike, and (4) that it is to be given to none who are not present in the congregation at the time of the administration of the sacrament.

We have already shown (XXVII, 4) that the sacraments are to be administered by ministers of the Word, lawfully ordained. We shall therefore concentrate upon the other truths set forth in this section of the Confession.

According to the Confession of Faith, the elements to be used in the Lord's Supper are bread and wine. It is our conviction that when the Lord instituted the sacrament he used unleavened bread and fermented wine. Scripture clearly indicates that the Supper was instituted during the observance of the Passover (Mark 14:12–16), and according to the law of Moses no leavened bread was permitted on the premises at this occasion (Ex. 12:15–20). "Modern custom in Palestine, among a people who are traditionally conservative as far as religious feasts are concerned, also suggests that the wine used was fermented" (*The New Bible Dictionary* [Grand Rapids: Eerdmans, 1962], p. 1331). Alfred Edersheim says that "the contention that it was unfermented wine is not worth serious discussion" (*Life and Times of Jesus the Messiah* [Grand Rapids: Eerdmans, 1943], vol. 2, p. 485). It must have been fermented wine in order for drunkenness to occur in connection with the sacrament at Corinth (1 Cor. 11:21). And with this evidence agrees the known practice of the ancient Church, in which unleavened bread and fermented wine were used.

However, we would not argue that the sacrament cannot—under any circumstances—be valid without unleavened bread and fermented wine. We can readily envision circumstances under which it might be necessary to use either leavened bread, or grape juice, or even both. Though technically irregular, we would not maintain that the sacrament may not be observed under such conditions. Even those who ordinarily use leavened bread and grape juice out of mere convenience we will not condemn. But if the decision to use grape juice instead of wine is based on the influence of the Temperance Movement, we must regard this as seriously unbiblical. It is a false doctrine, a legacy from the ancient Gnostics, to locate sin or evil in material things. The cause of the sin of drunkenness was located by Christ in man's depraved heart (Mark 7:14–23), not in wine. Those who have fallen prey to this error have been forced to conclude either (1) that Christ must have used unfermented grape juice at the last supper, or (2) that he must have been ignorant of the evil character of wine. Modernists have often chosen the latter alternative because in their view Christ was capable of sin and error. Evangelicals have all too often adopted the first alternative because of the mistaken notion that certain material things are evil in themselves. This inevitably leads to a disregard for certain portions of Scripture which clearly teach that wine (that is, fermented wine) is neither intrinsically evil nor forbidden to the people of God (John 2:1–11; Ps. 104:15; 1 Tim. 5:23). It is not biblical to locate evil in the handiwork of God rather than in the heart of man. Nor can the sacrament of the Lord's Supper be rightly administered on the basis of deference to such error.

It is clear from Scripture that it is *essential* to the proper observance of the Lord's Supper that both elements be received by all believers (ministers and members of the church alike). Jesus said of the cup, "Take this and divide it among yourselves" (Luke 22:17). "And they *all* drank from it" (Mark 14:23). "As often as you eat this bread *and drink* this cup, you proclaim the Lord's death till He comes" (1 Cor. 11:26). How then can we show the Lord's death if we only eat and do not drink? There is no justification for the denial of the cup to the laity, nor is there warrant to assert that those who have received only one element have received the whole sacrament. The example of Christ is decisive, and his words are normative in this matter.

A most difficult problem concerns the question, "Who is properly to be admitted to the Lord's table?" We shall discuss this question further under section 8 of the present chapter, but we will mention one aspect of the problem here. It is *not* proper to admit to the Lord's table those who do not receive it in the midst of the congregation of believers. In other words, private administration of the sacrament is contrary to the ordinance of Christ. This error used to be associated only or at least primarily with Rome. But today many Protestant ministers have "private communion" sets, and it is even said that some ministers now invite listeners in a television audience to partake of the sacrament in the privacy of their own home. We give the following reasons for rejecting all such practices.

First, the example of Christ is not consistent with such practices. He instituted the sacrament in a gathering of believers. They were commanded to divide the cup and to partake together of a common loaf. Manifestly, this example cannot be followed where there is no assembly of believers. Second, every New Testament reference to the observance of this sacrament shows us that it was an ordinance of the visible Church, administered when and where there was a gathering together of the members (Acts 2:42; 1 Cor. 11:18–20). Third, the Lord's Supper is an expression or representation of communion between believers. But this it cannot be unless there are at least "two or three . . . gathered together in my name" (Matt. 18:20).

Finally, the sacraments are not to be severed from the preaching of the Word and the administration of church discipline. Christ is our prophet and king as well as our priest. As our prophet he teaches us the will of God by his Word and Spirit. As a king he rules us by his Spirit and Word. As our priest he offered himself a sacrifice to satisfy divine justice and to reconcile us to God. But private administration of the sacrament obscures or even denies that these are necessarily interrelated and interdependent. This does not mean that the sacrament must be administered in a church building. Certainly, in the Apostolic Church the administration of the sacraments was tied to no such location (Acts 2:46; 5:42; Rom. 16:5). The sacrament of the Lord's Supper may be administered in private homes, provided there are an assembly of believers there, and provided there are faithful preaching of the Word and the administration of church discipline in that place also.

QUESTIONS

1. What are the proper elements to be used in the Lord's Supper?
2. Does the Scripture permit the use of substitutes for these?
3. Why is it that so many Protestant churches today do not use wine?
4. What are the two convictions to which this principle has led?
5. Why should Reformed Christians retain the use of wine?
6. Prove from Scripture that all members of the Church (not just ministers) ought to receive both elements.
7. Why is it improper to administer this sacrament *privately?*
8. Why is it not necessary to administer the sacrament in a church building?

9. Could this sacrament be administered properly in the home of a sick person?

XXIX, 5–7

5. *The outward elements in this sacrament, duly set apart to the uses ordained by Christ, have such relation to him crucified, as that truly, yet sacramentally only, they are sometimes called by the name of the things they represent, to wit, the body and blood of Christ; albeit, in substance and nature, they still remain truly and only bread and wine, as they were before.*

6. *That doctrine which maintains a change of the substance of bread and wine into the substance of Christ's body and blood (commonly called Transubstantiation) by consecration of a priest, or by any other way, is repugnant not to Scripture alone, but even to common sense and reason; overthroweth the nature of the sacrament; and hath been and is the cause of manifold superstitions, yea, of gross idolatries.*

7. *Worthy receivers, outwardly partaking of the visible elements in this sacrament, do then also inwardly by faith, really and indeed, yet not carnally and corporally, but spiritually, receive and feed upon Christ crucified, and all benefits of his death: the body and blood of Christ being then not corporally or carnally in, with, or under the bread and wine; yet as really but spiritually, present to the faith of believers in that ordinance, as the elements themselves are to their outward senses.*

These sections of the Confession teach (1) the nature of the sacramental representation of Christ crucified in the elements of the Lord's Supper, (2) that the doctrine of transubstantiation is a gross error and a cause of much superstition and even idolatry, and (3) that the manner in which true believers partake of the benefits of Christ is to be distinguished from the Lutheran error of consubstantiation.

"There is in every sacrament a spiritual relation, or sacramental union, between the sign and the thing signified; whence it comes to pass, that the names and effects of the one are attributed to the other" (XXVII, 2).

This "spiritual relation, or sacramental union" exists because of divine appointment. God has appointed bread to represent Christ's body and wine to represent his blood. When the bread and wine are "duly set apart" by the words of institution (that is, by the minister reading the words which Christ spoke at the last supper) and prayer, they then have "such relation to him crucified, as that truly, yet sacramentally only, they are sometimes called by the name of the things they represent." Yet as to their material substance and nature they remain just what they were before, bread and wine, and this only. When Christ said "this is my body" and "this is my blood," he spoke *truly* though not *literally*.

This sacramental union, as we have indicated, is analogous to that of the two natures of Christ. When Christ became man he did not cease to be God. His human nature was not mixed or confused with his divine nature. Neither did his human nature change into deity. This would have been "transubstantiation." Yet "by reason of the unity of the person, that which is proper to one nature is sometimes in Scripture attributed to the person denominated by the other nature" (VIII, 7). It is similar with the sacramental union: Scripture can speak as if Christ were the thing which represents him, and yet the reason is not that there has been transubstantiation but only that there is a sacramental union.

The doctrine of transubstantiation teaches "that the whole substance of the bread is changed into the literal body, and the whole substance of the wine is changed into the literal blood, of Christ; so that only the appearance or sensible properties of the bread and wine remain, and the only substances present are the true body and blood, soul and divinity, of our Lord" (A. A. Hodge, *The Confession of Faith* [London: Banner of Truth, 1958], p. 359). According to this doctrine a cannibal does not eat flesh more literally than a Roman Catholic eats the flesh and drinks the blood of Christ. And because the flesh and blood of Christ are literally, physically "there," every recipient, believer and unbeliever alike, who receives the elements of the mass eats and drinks the very material substance of Christ. If a bit of the body (under the appearance of bread) were accidentally spilled on the floor and a mouse ate it, it would be necessary to say that the mouse had eaten the very body of Christ!

As the Confession truly states, this doctrine is not only nonbiblical, but also it is nonsense. To speak of holding a piece of flesh or a glass of blood, which do not look like, feel like, taste like, or smell like, flesh and blood,

is nonsense. The Roman Catholic Church says that a miracle takes place
in the mass, namely, the miracle of changing bread into flesh, and wine
into blood. But this is an exceedingly poor "miracle." If true miracles
were reduced to this sad condition, the testimony of Scripture would
have to be "rewritten." John tells us of an actual instance of *transubstantiation* (John 2:1–11). Jesus turned water into wine. But this change of
substance was apparent to all, believers and unbelievers alike. They knew
that the wine was no longer water, precisely because it looked, felt, tasted,
and smelled like wine—the best wine at that. The miracle was given as
a sign of Christ's glory and of his messianic work. But it was a sign of
these invisible things because it was visible. How else could it have been
a sign or a miracle? It was a sign and miracle because it was self-authenticating. A miracle which is not self-authenticating is not a miracle at all.
It is a "lying sign and wonder."

The doctrine of transubstantiation is untrue, and it can be believed
only by those who do not receive the love of the truth. And it is a falsehood of so great a consequence that it must be said of those who receive
and practice this doctrine that they are guilty of idolatry. Idolatry is the
worship of that which is not God as if it were God. To worship any created thing as though it were God is to worship a false god. It is not wrong
to worship Christ, because he is God as well as man. But it is wrong to
worship the "host" as if it were Christ, because it is not. It only represents him. The mass is the heart of Romanism. And idolatry is the heart
of the mass. The Confession only speaks the truth, therefore, when it
denotes Romanism as idolatry (XXIV, 3).

The Lutheran doctrine of *consubstantiation* is different from the Roman
Catholic doctrine of transubstantiation in that it does not teach that the
substance of the bread and wine is miraculously changed *into* the substance of flesh and blood. For this reason it cannot be called as gross an
error and superstition. But it is nonetheless a serious error. Lutheran doctrine teaches that the physical or material substance of Christ's flesh and
blood is literally present *in, with, and under* the bread and wine. This would
be similar to the way in which a sponge can be filled with water. To the
substance of the sponge is added the substance of the water. One still sees
just a sponge. But the substance of the water is everywhere present. However, it must be realized that such a view of the sacrament virtually denies
the true human nature of Christ. How can Christ have a true human

nature which is literally capable of being at any number of places at the same time? Lutherans say that his human nature is "ubiquitous." They maintain that Christ is able to be omnipresent in human nature. Human nature, on this view, ceases to have the properties of human nature.

Romanism teaches a doctrine which says that bread and wine are changed into flesh and blood which do not look, feel, taste, or smell like flesh and blood. Lutherans, on the other hand, say that Christ's human nature is not of a certain size and shape, located at a certain place, as true human nature always is. Yet Jesus said, "It is to your advantage that I go away; for if I do not go away, the Helper will not come to you; but if I depart, I will send him to you. . . . I came forth from the Father and have come into the world. Again, I leave the world and go to the Father" (John 16:7, 28). These words teach the *physical absence* of the literal human nature of Christ from this planet. When Christ ascended into heaven a certain number of pounds of real human flesh (albeit with new qualities) were lifted from the earth, as eyewitnesses testify in Scripture. It is not too much to say that the Lutheran view of Christ's *physical presence* in the sacrament is a virtual denial of his true human nature.

The Reformed view teaches that which is in accord with Scripture, and it is a view that does not require a direct contradiction of the testimony of the senses. Scripture teaches what the senses confirm, namely, that Christ is *not in any way physically present* in the sacrament of the Lord's Supper. He is truly present but spiritually only. Through the personal and immediate presence of God the Holy Spirit, true believers, and they only, receive and feed upon Christ and have union and communion with him, not only as to his divine nature but also as to his human nature. This union and communion with Christ is not essentially different from that enjoyed by those believers on the night in which our Lord was betrayed. True, Christ *was* physically present with them *at* the supper. But he was not physically present *in* the sacramental elements. In the sacramental elements his believing disciples received a spiritually communicated benefit. And thus, so far as the sacramental elements are concerned, there is no difference whatever in the way in which we eat and drink Christ in this sacrament and the way in which they did so.

QUESTIONS

1. Between what two things does sacramental union exist?
2. With what may this be compared?

3. Because of this sacramental union we may speak of Christ *as if* he were what? Because of this sacramental union we may speak of what *as if* it were Christ?
4. What does the term "transubstantiation" mean?
5. What actual instance of transubstantiation is recorded in Scripture?
6. How does transubstantiation cause idolatry?
7. What does the term "consubstantiation" mean?
8. What does the term "ubiquitous" mean?
9. Cite a text which teaches the *physical absence* of Jesus Christ from the world.
10. What harm comes from the Lutheran doctrine of consubstantiation?
11. How is Christ really present in the Lord's Supper?
12. What difference is there between the way in which Christ was received in this sacrament on the night in which he was betrayed and in the present observance of this sacrament?

XXIX, 8

8. *Although ignorant and wicked men receive the outward elements in this sacrament, yet they receive not the thing signified thereby; but by their unworthy coming thereunto are guilty of the body and blood of the Lord, to their own damnation. Wherefore all ignorant and ungodly persons, as they are unfit to enjoy communion with him, so are they unworthy of the Lord's table, and cannot, without great sin against Christ, while they remain such, partake of these holy mysteries, or be admitted thereunto.*

This section of the Confession teaches us (1) that the unconverted who partake of this sacrament receive the sign but not the thing signified, (2) that they do incur guilt by this action, and (3) that it is therefore necessary for the Church to refuse admittance to all except those who give a credible profession of faith in Christ.

Someone has said that Judas ate bread with the Lord, but did not eat the Lord with the bread. This must be true because Jesus said, "Whoever eats My flesh and drinks My blood has eternal life, and I will raise him up at the last day. . . . He who eats My flesh and drinks My blood abides in Me, and I in him. . . . He who eats this bread will live forever" (John 6:54, 56, 58). Since there are unquestionably those who receive the elements of the sacrament of whom this is not true, it is evident that "ignorant and wicked men" may "receive the outward elements" and yet "receive not the thing signified thereby." But the Bible also leaves no doubt that no one can receive even the outward signs and seals alone without important consequences. "For he who eats and drinks in an unworthy manner eats and drinks judgment to himself, not discerning the Lord's body" (1 Cor. 11:29). A man's inward condition of heart determines what he receives in the sacrament. But what he is cannot determine what the sacrament *is*. The sacrament is a divinely instituted sign and seal of the covenant. It represents Christ because of divine institution. And it does so even if it be by judgment against rather than reception by the sinner.

From these rather obvious facts some have drawn an unwarranted and dangerous conclusion. They say that, since the Scripture does not envision a situation in which only true believers would receive the sacrament, there is no reason to exercise any restriction with respect to those who would receive it on their own responsibility. This is the basis of the common practice of "open communion." Open communion means that the Lord's table is to be approached at will by all who, in their own judgment, are able to do so. We believe that this is a manifestly unscriptural view. And we give the following reasons:

(1) Christ preached the gospel to all without distinction. We might well say that there was "open" gospel proclamation. But he did not administer the sacraments to all. Many who heard him preach refused the terms upon which baptism was given (Luke 7:30). And when he administered this sacrament (i.e., the Lord's Supper), he did not administer it in a public place but in private to his disciples only. No one was admitted except those who possessed an adequate knowledge of the truth, and who professed to be his disciples *and* appeared to be such. Until that very night the other disciples did not know that Judas was not the believer he pretended and appeared to be. *"Lord, is it I?"* asked each one.

(2) Moreover, in the Apostolic Church none were admitted to this sacrament who were not first instructed, then baptized, giving evidence of faithfulness to the things of the Lord (Acts 2:41–42). And whenever a

false pretender was later discovered, the command of the apostles was: "Put away from yourselves the evil person" (1 Cor. 5:13). And even this is not all. There were even instances in which *believers* were to be prevented from participation in the fellowship of the saints. "Withdraw from every *brother* who walks disorderly," said the apostle (2 Thess. 3:6). Even Christians must be set apart from the ordinances of the Church when they violate their profession, until they change their ways.

No doubt the sacrament of the Lord's Supper was administered in the Apostolic Church according to the practice which we will call "closed communion." In this view the sacrament is to be administered only to those who are baptized and professing members of the church (or denomination) which is administering the sacrament. When there was relative purity in the visible Church, such a practice was both practical and proper. Under such circumstances it would have been the only alternative to open communion, which is improper. If conditions were such today that all churches were true visible churches, it would be incumbent upon each church to receive from every other church all members certified as in good standing, and to admit them to the Lord's table. But closed communion is not scriptural today for the simple reason that some denominations (and congregations) have ceased to be true churches, on the one hand, and because no single denomination alone is "the true Church," on the other. Open communion is wrong because it would admit members of false churches without evidence that they are Christians, and closed communion is wrong because it would exclude members of true churches without evidence that they are not Christians.

The proper administration of the sacrament is therefore "restricted communion." This simply means that a particular true church does not indiscriminately admit members of other churches to the Lord's Supper. If a person comes from another church body and desires to partake of the Lord's Supper, it is necessary to determine (1) whether or not such a person has sufficient understanding of the truth to be a believer, and (2) whether or not such a person professes faith in Christ and gives evidence of walking in obedience to his commandments. If the person in question comes from another congregation of the same denomination (and that denomination is faithful), he may be admitted on the basis of such evidence. But if such a person comes from another denomination, the integrity of the denomination must be accounted for. Unless that denomination is known to be of like purity in doctrine and discipline, the consequent uncertainty can be resolved only if the applicant is personally questioned as to his faith and life.

Thus in *every case* there must be admission to the Lord's table only on the basis of a credible profession of faith, or rather a profession of faith that is considered credible by the church administering the sacrament. As the Confession says, "All ignorant and ungodly persons . . . cannot, without great sin against Christ, while they remain such, partake of these holy mysteries, or *be admitted* thereunto." To abdicate this responsibility is to invite sinners to harm themselves. And for such harm the Church is guilty perhaps even more than the ignorant and ungodly who are thus needlessly encouraged to eat and to drink damnation to themselves. Proper restriction will not prevent any believer from coming to the Lord's table, and it will warn the secret unbeliever in such a way that he and he alone will bear the guilt if he eats and drinks unworthily (that is, without really being a believer as he professes and appears).

QUESTIONS

1. Prove from Scripture that a man may receive the sacrament and not receive Christ.
2. Prove from Scripture that a man cannot receive the sacrament without receiving either benefit or harm.
3. What is meant by "open communion"?
4. Why is this unscriptural?
5. What is meant by "closed communion"?
6. Why is this improper?
7. What is meant by "restricted communion"?
8. What fault from each of the erroneous views is avoided by restricted communion?
9. How does restricted communion benefit ignorant and ungodly persons?
10. How does it benefit the Church?

28

XXX. Of Church Censures

1. *The Lord Jesus, as king and head of his Church, hath therein appointed a government in the hand of church-officers, distinct from the civil magistrate.*

2. *To these officers the keys of the kingdom of heaven are committed, by virtue whereof they have power respectively to retain and remit sins, to shut that kingdom against the impenitent, both by the word and censures; and to open it unto penitent sinners, by the ministry of the gospel, and by absolution from censures, as occasion shall require.*

These sections of the Confession teach us (1) that Christ is king and head of his Church, (2) that he has appointed (under his headship) a government, (3) that this government is in the hand of church officers, (4) that this government is distinct from that of the State, (5) that true administrative power belongs to these church officers, and (6) that this power (called the power of the keys) consists in opening and closing the kingdom of God to men by means of the Word and discipline (or censures).

We have shown (XXV, 6) that Christ is the only king and head of his Church. Here we shall show that Christ, as king and head of the Church, has "appointed a government" therein, and that this government is of apostolic authority and presbyterian in form. The fact that Christ has instituted a government in his Church is clearly stated in Scripture. "And God has appointed these in the church: first apostles, second prophets, third teachers, after that miracles, then gifts of healings, helps, administrations, varieties of tongues. Are all apostles? Are all prophets? Are all teachers?" (1 Cor. 12:28–29). When Christ ascended into heaven, "He Himself gave some to be apostles, some prophets, some evangelists, and some pastors and teachers" (Eph. 4:11; see also Matt. 18:17; John 20:23). This is the government predicted by the prophet Isaiah (Isa. 9:6). And it is apostolic and presbyterian.

It is *apostolic* because the authority of Jesus Christ in the Church is constitutionally embodied in the apostles and in their inscripturated Word. The Church is "built on the foundation of the apostles and prophets" (Eph. 2:20). Of those set by God in the Church, the apostles are first. During the apostolic age this authority, which was final in the Church, was *personally embodied* in the apostles. Thus Paul could say, "If anyone thinks himself to be a prophet or spiritual, let him acknowledge that the things which I write to you are the commandments of the Lord" (1 Cor. 14:37). No one, not even another apostle, could question the official declarations of an apostle (2 Peter 3:17). Even the Old Testament testimony of the prophets has authority only in conjunction with the witness of the apostles (Heb. 1:1–2; Luke 24:27; and especially 1 Peter 1:10–12).

Then, with the passing away of the apostles, this authority remained in the deposit of apostolic truth inspired by the Holy Ghost and recorded in the New Testament. The authority of the apostles was not delegated to any successors of the apostles (as Roman Catholicism teaches), but rather, it was transferred from their *persons* to the written *Word* of God in the New Testament. Because the New Testament is apostolic, and because the New Testament alone (not tradition, or other "revelations") is apostolic, it is *the constitution* (final revelation of Christ's authority here on earth) of the Christian Church, together with the Old Testament of which it is the completion. This constitution (the Bible) is the permanent and only supreme authority in the Church because Jesus Christ was pleased to institute his authority through the apostles.

However, the *administration* of this authority is by the hands of church officers, who are called elders (*presbyteroi*) or bishops (*episkopoi*) in the Scriptures. Even in the days of the apostles this was true (Acts 16:4). As Paul said, "Let the elders who rule well be counted worthy of double honor, especially those who labor in the word and doctrine" (1 Tim. 5:17). These are "the elders of the church . . . which the Holy Spirit has made . . . overseers [or bishops]" (Acts 20:17, 28). Inasmuch as the only persons mentioned in the Scripture as having lawful ruling authority in the Church are elders or bishops, and since elders are bishops (and vice versa), it is clear that the scriptural form of government is presbyterian (that is, government by the administration of ruling elders).

It may be objected that in the apostolic era the apostles also exercised rule. That is true. But it is also true that the apostles regarded themselves as elders when it came to the administration of government. "The elders who are among you I exhort, I who am a fellow elder," says Peter. "Shepherd the flock of God which is among you, serving as overseers [bishops]" (1 Peter 5:1–2). When it came to writing the Scripture (the apostolic constitution), Peter said, "I exhort." But when it came to *administering* that constitution in oversight of the Church, Peter regarded himself as one of the elders. The structure of divinely instituted government in the Church then is as follows: (1) Christ is the only head of the Church, (2) under Christ the apostles embodied, and then transcribed in Scripture by divine inspiration, the regulative constitution of the Church, and (3) under Christ the elders or bishops administer the authority of Christ according to this constitution.

Historically speaking, there have been three basic types of government in the visible Church. (1) The *hierarchical* form of church government is that type of church government which has a visible gradation of church officers with authority centralized in the hands of those who hold the highest rank. This type of church government is exemplified by the Church of Rome in the most fully developed form, but is also found in such churches as the Methodist, Eastern Orthodox, and Church of England. (It is also found in the Erastian type of church government, which grants supreme ecclesiastical authority to the civil ruler.) (2) The *congregational* form of church government is that which holds the autonomy of government in each particular congregation of Christ. Often, but not always, there is but one elder in a congregation. Yet in this type of church government it is maintained that no one outside a particular local congregation has any administrative authority over it. (3) The *presbyterian* form of church government is that which recognizes the government of the whole church by the body of elders or bishops. This form of church government is scriptural, and it avoids the false elements in both of the other forms of government. These can best be seen if the essential principles of church government, as revealed in the Scripture, are tabulated in relation to the three types of church government:

The Principles of Scripture	Hier.	Cong.	Presb.
1. Christ alone is head of the Church (Eph. 5:23; Col. 1:18).	No	Yes	Yes
2. Elders are chosen by the people over whom they are to rule (Acts 1:15–26; 6:1–6).	No	Yes	Yes
3. All ruling officers (elders-bishops) are equal in authority (Acts 20:17, 28; Titus 1:5, 7).	No	Yes	Yes
4. Each particular church must have a plurality of elders (bishops) (Acts 14:23).	No	No	Yes
5. Church officers (elders-bishops) are ordained by the presbytery (i.e., a large body of elders drawn from churches in communion with one another) (1 Tim. 4:14).	No	?	Yes
6. The right of appeal is made from the smaller to the wider assembly of elders (Acts 15:1–31).	No	No	Yes

Since the presbyterian form of church government is the *only* form of church government agreeable with these six biblical principles, truth requires us to testify that it alone is sanctioned by Christ, and that the other systems are without warrant from the Word of God. This does not mean that churches without presbyterian government are necessarily to be declared false churches (nor that all churches that preserve presbyterian government are true churches). But as far as government is concerned, no church is pure unless it is presbyterian.

We have previously shown that the Church is independent of the State in government (XXV, 6). We shall therefore turn to a consideration of the "power of the keys." These are the controversial words: "And I also say to you that you are Peter, and on this rock I will build My church, and the gates of Hades shall not prevail against it. And I will give you the keys of the kingdom of heaven, and whatever you bind on earth will be bound in heaven; and whatever you loose on earth will be loosed in heaven" (Matt. 16:18–19). We hardly need to remind the reader that these words have been variously interpreted. And we cannot here deal with every shade of difference among these interpretations. Suffice it to say that two extremes are to be studiously avoided: first, the view which holds that Peter received absolute authority, and second, the view which holds that Peter received little or no authority at all.

The Roman Catholic view is, of course, that Christ here conferred supreme authority over his Church on earth to Peter and his successors. But there is no mention by Jesus of successors of Peter. The assumption is purely gratuitous. Moreover, the authority given by Christ was undoubtedly resident *with* Peter, but resident *in* the keys. The power or authority was unquestionably in Peter's hand, but it was the power of the keys. Therefore, we are led to the conclusion that Christ gave Peter the administration of the keys. Jesus said, "Behold . . . I have the keys" (Rev. 1:18). And in Matthew 18:17–18 and John 20:21–23, Jesus clearly stated that others could administer the same keys with the same results as Peter would have. The essence of the Romish error then is a gratuitous transference of the power from the *keys* to the *person* of Peter alone, and then to his successors. The truth is that the power to open and to shut the kingdom of heaven is inherent in Christ alone, and administered by all officers (elders, bishops) of the Church.

But many Protestants err in the other direction. They do not believe that men on earth can be administrators of such power as to open and to close the kingdom of heaven to other men. Yet Christ said, "Assuredly, I say to you, whatever *you* bind on earth will be bound in heaven, and whatever *you* loose on earth will be loosed in heaven" (Matt. 18:18). To avoid the error of transferring power from the keys to Peter himself, many Protestants would transfer all administration of that power back to Christ in heaven. But Christ has made the earthly administration of his keys powerful notwithstanding. And the keys are the Word of God and church discipline.

(1) The preaching of the Word of God *is* "the power of God to salvation for everyone who believes" (Rom. 1:16). This is so, not because men have decided it, but because God has ordained it. "For the message of the cross . . . to us who are being saved . . . *is* the power of God" (1 Cor. 1:18). When the Word of God is authoritatively preached with purity, it administers the power of God by opening the kingdom to sinners. It does so because it is one of the keys given by Christ to his Church for this purpose.

(2) The administration of church discipline is the other key. The apostle commanded: "Reject a divisive man after the first and second admonition" (Titus 3:10). When a sinner "refuses even to hear" the command of Jesus, "let him be to you like a heathen and a tax collector" (Matt.

18:17). And when this discipline is administered according to the Word of Christ, it is no mere form nor a powerless pretense. It is an actual administration of the power of Christ by which the kingdom of heaven is actually closed to the sinner unless and until he repent. This does not mean that the key of faithful preaching only opens and that the key of faithful discipline only closes the kingdom. When the gospel is faithfully preached, it also shuts the kingdom to the neglectful and indifferent; and when church discipline is faithfully administered, it also opens the kingdom to the penitent sinner (2 Cor. 2:6–8). But the main point is that it is as serious a mistake to imagine that these keys have no power, as it is to imagine that a mere human person can open and close the kingdom of heaven at his own will.

It will be noted that the sacraments are *not* keys of the kingdom. They neither open nor shut the kingdom to men. They are signs and seals of that to or from which the keys admit or exclude men. We would also call attention to the fact that Christ has joined the two keys of the kingdom together. When men fail to properly exercise or administer these keys, Christ gives them to others (Rev. 1:18; 2:5; 3:7–8). And this happens when either of these two keys is not faithfully used. When a church, for example, fails to exercise church discipline, it must not be imagined that it will long retain the power to open and close the kingdom of God to men by preaching. And be a church ever so diligent in maintaining rigid discipline, it will not long possess such power without the faithful preaching of the gospel. To lose *either* faithful preaching *or* church discipline is to lose the right and the power to open and to shut the kingdom of heaven.

QUESTIONS

1. What is meant by saying that Christ has "appointed a government" in his Church?
2. What is meant by calling this government apostolic in authority?
3. How was this authority made constitutional?
4. By whom is this constitutional authority administered?
5. What are the three types of church government displayed in history?
6. What are the six principles of church government revealed in Scripture?

7. How many of these are found in each of the historic types of church government?
8. What error does Roman Catholicism make in its interpretation of the power of the keys?
9. What error is made by many Protestants in regard to this power?
10. What are the keys?
11. Prove from Scripture that the keys actually open and close the kingdom of heaven by earthly administration.
12. What happens when men try to separate the two keys?

XXX, 3–4

3. *Church censures are necessary for the reclaiming and gaining of offending brethren; for deterring of others from the like offenses; for purging out of that leaven which might infect the whole lump; for vindicating the honor of Christ, and the holy profession of the gospel; and for preventing the wrath of God, which might justly fall upon the Church, if they should suffer his covenant, and the seals thereof, to be profaned by notorious and obstinate offenders.*

4. *For the better attaining of these ends, the officers of the Church are to proceed by admonition, suspension from the sacrament of the Lord's Supper for a season, and by excommunication from the Church, according to the nature of the crime, and demerit of the person.*

These sections of the Confession teach us (1) why church discipline is necessary, and (2) how church discipline is to be carried out.

We live in a day in which church discipline is practically nonexistent in much of the visible Church. Even churches that endeavor to preserve faithful preaching of the Word of God are often lax in this matter. And this laxity is even defended on the grounds that church discipline is harmful to erring sinners and an unwarranted "judging" of a brother's soul before God.

Before we answer these plausible-sounding arguments against church discipline, we will state the biblical requirements for it. And the supreme argument for church discipline is that Jesus commanded it. In Matthew

18:12–20 we have his commandment and plan for church discipline. And there can be no higher reason for any ordinance of the Church of Christ than this: Christ commanded it. Indeed, without this reason other reasons would be insufficient. Christ is king and head of his Church. And there can be no other law than that which he commands. In the light of his clear commandment, the validity of arguments against church discipline is obliterated, however attractive or plausible they may sound. And what are these arguments against church discipline? We believe that they can be reduced to the following types.

(1) Perhaps the most common argument against church discipline is the contention that *people will be offended*. It is said that church discipline will offend and alienate, not only the erring brother who is the subject of discipline, but also others in the congregation (and perhaps even more those who are contemplating membership in the congregation). It is usually proposed that, instead of church discipline, the Church content itself to pray for the Holy Spirit to trouble the conscience of the erring brother and thus to restore him to the right path and the fellowship of Christ. This method is supposed to display love (toward the erring brother) and humility (toward self) in contrast to a spirit of harsh judgment and pride.

This view can be made to sound very pious. But it is no exaggeration to say that it is the very soul of hypocrisy. How can obedience to the command of Christ be harsh, unloving, or prideful? To lay such a charge against faithful church discipline is to lay that charge against Christ who instituted it. The truth is that it is a sin to pray for an erring brother in the way here suggested. To ask the Holy Spirit to reclaim an erring brother when at the same time we refuse (out of pretended piety) to use the divine ordinance (church discipline) given to effect that end is sin. And the ironic fact is that church discipline is really the very opposite of what it is commonly said to be: it is the very means of "reclaiming and gaining of offending brethren" who are said to be alienated by it. Scripture proves this. The evil practicer of fornication in the Corinthian church was "put away" by faithful discipline (1 Cor. 5:13). And this "punishment, which was inflicted by the majority" (2 Cor. 2:6), was the very means of bringing him to repentance (v. 7) and eventual restoration (v. 8), humanly invented arguments to the contrary notwithstanding. Church discipline thus proved to be what Jesus said it was: an act of love and concern like unto that of a good shepherd who seeks out a wandering sheep (Matt. 18:12–18).

Church discipline is loving concern in action, the blessed result of which will often be: "you have gained your brother" (Matt. 18:15).

Lack of church discipline ought to be seen for what it really is—not a loving concern as is hypocritically claimed, but an indifference to the honor of Christ and the welfare of his flock. Not only is the erring brother himself harmed by the lack of church discipline. Others also are evilly affected. "Do you not know that a little leaven leavens the whole lump? Therefore purge out the old leaven, that you may be a new lump" (1 Cor. 5:6–7). When error and sin are left alone they will spread. Men are sinners. Nothing is more natural for them than to sin. A sinful example that is openly tolerated will therefore become an open invitation for others to go and do likewise. Thus the Scripture commands: "Those who are sinning rebuke in the presence of all, that the rest also may fear" (1 Tim. 5:20).

(2) Another common obstacle to church discipline is the seemingly pious attitude that refuses to judge another person. Does not the Scripture itself say, "Judge not, that you be not judged" (Matt. 7:1)? It is not uncommon that even church officers refuse to administer church discipline on the grounds that they too are sinners and are therefore not qualified to judge someone else.

This argument also can be made to sound very attractive and plausible. But it too is utterly false. It should be plain that this is so when we recall that it was our Lord who commanded us to exercise church discipline. The fallacy is quite apparent. Exercising church discipline is no more an attempt to judge another man's soul before God than is the act of admitting people to the visible Church. The least that can be said about this kind of argument is that those who are not willing to exercise the keys of the kingdom in *excluding* people from the kingdom should also renounce the right to exercise these keys to *admit* people to the kingdom. But Scripture makes it clear that church discipline is to be exercised in some cases even when the offender is not regarded as an unbeliever, but only as an erring brother. "Withdraw from every brother who walks disorderly," says the apostle (2 Thess. 3:6). Even if a brother's sin is such that we need not call into question his whole Christian profession, we must still exercise discipline as long as he walks in a disorderly manner.

Ordinarily, no doubt, church discipline is of such a character. The purpose of church discipline is rather the reclamation of a brother than the judgment of the soul. And even when excommunication is required, it is rather a declaration of what a person has undeniably evidenced himself to be than an attempt to know the heart. When sinners are admitted to the Church, it is because they give *evidence* of an external sort that men must judge without presuming to judge the heart. And it is the same with the extreme censure of church discipline by which men are excluded from the visible Church. Evidence of an external sort is judged. When a person gives no evidence that he is a true believer, the Church declares that fact by excommunication. But in every case the judgment of the soul is left to God alone.

But above all arguments, we again stress the fact that church discipline is necessary because it is the ordinance of Christ. Above the welfare of any individual (who deserves God's wrath and curse to begin with) and above all considerations of the feelings and attitudes of any number of individuals, are the honor of Christ and the cause of his truth. It is better to maintain the honor of Christ than to keep a thousand sinners on the rolls of the visible Church to his dishonor. It is better to maintain the truth of Christ than to cater to men. It is more important to God that Christ be honored and obeyed than that sinners be pampered. We must choose between the two: we must either maintain the honor of Christ at all costs, or else sacrifice the honor of Christ in order to satisfy the wishes of men. And if the latter, the Church will be "good for nothing but to be thrown out and trampled underfoot by men" (Matt. 5:13).

When church discipline is avoided, a very great price is paid. The supposed evil that is feared and avoided is nothing in comparison with the evil that is sure to follow. Christ does not care for the reputation of any church—no matter how "great it has been"—when it is spiritually dead. Church discipline may result in a smaller church, but—if it is faithful discipline—it will still be a true church. "You have a name that you are alive," said Christ of one church, "but you are dead" (Rev. 3:1). But he praised "a few names even in Sardis who have not defiled their garments; and they shall walk with Me in white, for they are worthy" (v. 4). Those who cherished purity were not of reputation among men, but they were highly esteemed by their Lord because they had maintained *his* honor rather than their own.

(3) Church discipline is also argued against by those who say something like this: "I just can't see throwing people out of the church for

every little sin." This ends all thought for some people. But this is nothing more than knocking down a straw man. For scriptural church discipline is (a) not a mere matter of casting people out of the church, nor (b) is it for "little" sin. The *purpose* of church discipline is the removal of sin from the sinner, not the removal of the sinner from the church. That is why excommunication is warranted only as a last resort, and then only for sin in the extreme. Prior to excommunication, as Christ instructed (Matt. 18:16–18), repeated earnest and tender efforts are to be made to encourage an erring brother to turn from his sin.

That this process is *not* a mere matter of casting people out of the church is evident from the following principles taught in Matthew 18:16–18. (a) Every church member has the right and duty to seek recovery of an erring brother. Obviously, an individual church member who goes to a brother privately does not seek his brother's excommunication, but only his reformation. (b) If possible, public knowledge of the sin in question should be avoided. Even if the first private approach should fail, the matter should still not be made public. Two or three others (presumably elders of the church) and no more should be informed of the difficulty. (c) There is to be instruction from the Word of God in order that the erring brother may realize what the law of God requires, in the hope that he will then be persuaded to abandon his sin. (d) Above all, it is clear that final excommunication is only a last resort. It follows every reasonable effort to reclaim the erring brother.

Therefore it may be said that excommunication requires two specific conditions: (a) there must be undeniable violation of one of the Ten Commandments. Sin is want of conformity unto or transgression of the law of God. Mere nonconformity to custom or tradition is not punishable by discipline. And (b) the sin must be persisted in without repentance. It is sometimes thought that excommunication is justified only when some notorious sin such as murder or adultery is committed. The truth is that excommunication is not related to the *notoriety* of the sin but to the *persistence* of the sinner in any sin. Let the sin be slanderous gossip or neglect of divine worship, which are neither uncommon nor "notorious," and if the sinner hardens his heart and persists in such a sin without evidence of repentance, excommunication is warranted. When an erring church member has been faced with his error, when he has been shown from the Word of God what his error is and what his duty is, if he then still "refuses even to hear" the church (or in other words, pays no heed, but persists in his error with hardness and obstinancy), the duty of the church is clear: "let him be . . . a heathen and a tax collector." This is right and good because Jesus said to do it.

QUESTIONS

1. What is the supreme reason for maintaining church discipline?
2. What is the first type of argument urged against church discipline?
3. Why is it a sin to pray for the reclaiming of an erring brother when church discipline is not also exercised?
4. What is the real effect of church discipline upon the erring? Prove.
5. Who is harmed when church discipline is neglected? Prove.
6. What is the second type of argument against church discipline?
7. What is the fallacy of this argument?
8. What other activity presumes no less authority over sinners than does discipline?
9. Why is it important to maintain church discipline?
10. What becomes of a church that forsakes church discipline?
11. What is the purpose of church discipline if it is not to cast people out of the church?
12. What must precede excommunication?
13. Who has the right and duty to initiate the process of church discipline?
14. What two conditions must exist before excommunication is required?

CHAPTER

29

XXIII. Of the Civil Magistrate

1. God, the supreme Lord and King of all the world, hath ordained civil magistrates to be under him over the people, for his own glory, and the public good; and, to this end, hath armed them with the power of the sword, for the defense and encouragement of them that are good, and for the punishment of evildoers.

2. It is lawful for Christians to accept and execute the office of a magistrate, when called thereunto, in the managing whereof, as they ought especially to maintain piety, justice, and peace, according to the wholesome laws of each commonwealth; so, for that end, they may lawfully, now under the New Testament, wage war upon just and necessary occasions.

4. It is the duty of people to pray for magistrates, to honor their persons, to pay them tribute and other dues, to obey their lawful commands, and to be subject to their authority for conscience' sake. Infidelity, or difference in religion, doth not make void the magistrate's just and legal authority, nor free the people from their due obedience to him: from which ecclesiastical persons are not exempted; much less hath the Pope any power or jurisdiction over them in their dominions or lives, if he shall judge them to be heretics, or upon any other pretense whatsoever.

At this point we again depart from the order of the Confession of Faith in order to consider together certain sections of the Confession which present difficulty when seen in relation to one another (XXIII, 3 and XXXI, 1–2). The difficulty pertains to the power of the civil magistrate with regard to ecclesiastical matters. We shall proceed at this point to discuss, first, the sections of chapter XXIII which occasion no difficulty, second, the sections of chapters XXIII and XXXI which present the problem, and then, the remaining portions of chapter XXXI, 3–5.

These sections of the Confession teach us (1) that God has ordained civil government on earth, (2) that the purpose of it is his glory and our good, (3) that he has given to civil officers the power of the sword, (4) that Christians may lawfully hold civil office and exercise the power of the sword upon just and necessary occasions, (5) that Christians are required by God to honor this ordinance and to pray for and be subject to those who lawfully use the office of civil government, (6) that this duty is not exempted because of difference in religion, and (7) that the pope of Rome does not have any right to civil power.

The classic Scripture passage dealing with the ordinance of civil government is Romans 13:1–7. In this passage most of the teaching of these sections of the Confession is sustained. "Let every soul be subject to the governing authorities," says the apostle. Certainly the Christian is therefore required to be subject to those who are in authority by the will of God. "For there is no authority except from God, and the authorities that exist are appointed by God. Therefore whoever resists the authority resists the ordinance of God." A. A. Hodge well says, "Some have supposed that the right or legitimate authority of human government has its foundation ultimately in 'the consent of the governed,' 'the will of the majority,' or in some imaginary 'social compact' entered into by the forefathers of the race at the origin of social life" (*Commentary on the Confession of Faith* [London: Banner of Truth, 1958], p. 239). But the Scripture teaches us that civil government comes from God, and that it has authority by the will of God, with or without the consent of the governed. This clearly implies that the Christian (at least ordinarily) is to regard the *de facto* government of any particular country in which he may reside as *de jure*.

No particular form of civil government is designated in Scripture. And the Christian is not at liberty to render or to withhold obedience depending upon whether or not he happens to like the type of government that exists. "The authorities that exist are appointed by God," said Paul. And he was referring to the totalitarian government of the Roman Empire! If Paul, and even Jesus, could teach that people should render to Caesar, it is difficult to think of any type of civil government that should not be obeyed by a Christian today in civil matters. In the light of the context of the apostolic age (when the civil government was totalitarian), we do not believe that Christians have the right to advocate, or to participate in, the violent overthrow of civil authority whether it be monarchy or democracy (see Rom. 13:2; 1 Peter 2:13–14; Titus 3:1). If every *de facto* government is ordained of God, and resistance is resistance to the ordinance of God, then no other conclusion is possible.

Yet to assert that civil authority is of divine origin is not to say that it has unlimited rights. All divinely constituted authority in human affairs is limited by divine statute. The civil magistrate is ordained of God as "minister" or servant of God "for good." His task is to "bear the sword" of physical power as "a terror" to evil works. His task is that of "an avenger to execute wrath on him who practices evil" (Rom. 13:4). As long as a civil government is content to restrain and to punish crime and violence, protecting the good and punishing the evil, the Christian must support, pray for, and honor that government. But when that government punishes the righteous, and rewards the evil, becoming militaristic and bent upon aggression, it is the duty of Christians to resist that power because it subverts the ordinance of God.

It is, without doubt, difficult in many cases to determine precisely when and to what extent a Christian must resist a particular civil government. We do not seek to make it appear simple. But certain principles are very clear, and, if rightly applied, will enable one to make the proper decision in a given instance. (1) We ought *always* to obey the "lawful commands" of our government. We are in any and every instance "to be ready for every good work" (Titus 3:1). (2) We must *always obey* God rather than man when there is a conflict between the two (Acts 5:29). (3) We may resist *actively* as well as passively if that is necessary for obedience to God. When a civil authority becomes a terror to good works rather than evil, we believe that Christians have the right of active self-defense (of life and property) by sanction of law (Ps. 82:4; Prov. 24:11–12). Thus "the proximate end for which God has ordained magistrates is the promotion of the public good, and the ultimate end is the promotion of his own glory" (Hodge, *Confession of Faith,* p. 295).

But let us consider more particularly certain modern errors which have gained wide currency, and which confuse the thinking of many Christians. (1) The first that we shall consider is the modernist attempt to overthrow the practice of capital punishment. In our own nation, in recent decades, there has been a powerful effort to bring about the abolishing of capital punishment. And many liberal Protestant groups have sanctioned this change on the grounds that capital punishment does not benefit society, reform the criminal, or reflect the humane teachings of the New Testament. In other words, for various reasons, it is widely advocated today that the civil government cease to use the power of the sword to punish evil.

Such a view of civil authority is, to say the least, highly unbiblical. We do not think that it can be proved that capital punishment does not benefit society. We believe that it does, if for no other reason than that the Scripture says that the faithful exercise of justice is a terror to evil works and an encouragement to good. Opponents of capital punishment deny this, but they deny it in vain. It may be true that capital punishment fails to reform the criminal. But we completely doubt that the absence of terror against evil reforms the criminal either. Furthermore, we doubt not that it encourages evil. But above all, we deny that civil power and authority is supposed to reflect the modernist notions of the "humane" teachings of the New Testament. Justice is not any more "humane" in the New than in the Old Testament. And the ordinance of civil government is not meant by God to impose what it may think the New Testament teaches; it is to punish crime and to protect those who do good. However, we doubt that the scheme of the liberals who advocate abolishing capital punishment is "humane." We believe that much modern crime is due to the fact that there is too much unbiblical concern for the wicked and too little biblical concern for the upright.

(2) Another modern attack on the ordinance of civil government is to be seen in those who advocate the pacifist line. Modernist church councils have advocated such things as these: (a) complete disarmament of our nation, (b) unilateral disarmament, (c) negotiations rather than armed defense in the face of aggression, and (d) the recognition of those who are aggressors without just punishment of any kind. The Confession main-

tains that civil magistrates (even if they be Christian persons) "may law-fully, now under the New Testament, wage war upon just and necessary occasions." Those people who advocate policies which virtually call upon our national government to renounce the power of the sword, and to renounce all attempts to be a terror to evildoers, and to renounce the execution of revenge upon them, advocate nothing less than the over-throw of the ordinance of God (Rom. 13:1–5). And precisely because they "resist the authority" they "resist the ordinance of God" (v. 2). This *sin* should be denounced for what it is. It is a sin against our government and a sin against God.

The last part of section 4 of this chapter deals with two historic evils associated with the Roman Catholic Church. (1) The first of these evils is that which maintains a privileged status for church officers in civil mat-ters. There are still some countries dominated by the Roman Church in which priests cannot be tried in civil courts for their crimes. There is per-haps some humor in the traditional stories about the embarrassment of the Irish policeman when he finds that he has stopped a priest for speed-ing. But the Scriptures teach that Christians, whether they be church offi-cers or not, must not consider themselves exempt from civil jurisdiction. We believe that the Confession is in line with Scripture when it states that "ecclesiastical persons are not exempted" from this authority. And that "infidelity, or difference in religion" between the Christian citizen and the civil ruler "doth not make void the magistrate's just and legal authority."

(2) The other evil is that which maintains that the pope of Rome pos-sesses civil authority. This has been and still is the claim made by the Roman pontiff. He insists that he exercises both the spiritual and tem-poral swords of power and authority. "According to the strictly logical ultramontane view, the whole nation being in all its members a portion of the Church universal, the civil organization is comprehended within the Church for certain ends subordinate to the great end for which the Church exists, and is therefore ultimately responsible to it for the exer-cise of the authority delegated. Hence, whenever the Pope has been in a condition to vindicate his authority, he has put kingdoms under inter-dict, released subjects from their vow of (civil) allegiance, and deposed sovereigns because of the assumed heresy or insubordination of the civil rulers of the land" (Hodge, *Confession of Faith*, p. 298). Scripture pre-

dicted what history has shown, namely, that such a usurpation results in the persecution of true believers (Rev. 13; 18:24).

QUESTIONS

1. What is the basis of the authority of civil government? Prove.
2. What type of government is of divine authority?
3. May a Christian advocate the violent overthrow of civil government?
4. Can a Christian rightly resist a civil government? If so, when?
5. When ought Christians to obey their government?
6. When ought Christians to disobey their government?
7. State two modern errors espoused by liberal "Christians" which are contrary to the divine ordinance of civil government.
8. Why are these contrary to the divine ordinance of civil government?
9. What are the two errors refuted in section 4?

30

XXIII. Of the Civil Magistrate (continued) and XXXI. Of Synods and Councils

XXIII, 3

3. *The civil magistrate may not assume to himself the administration of the Word and sacraments, or the power of the keys of the kingdom of heaven: yet he hath authority, and it is his duty, to take order, that unity and peace be preserved in the Church, that the truth of God be kept pure and entire, that all blasphemies and heresies be suppressed, all corruptions and abuses in worship and discipline prevented or reformed, and all the ordinances of God duly settled, administered, and observed. For the better effecting whereof, he hath power to call synods, to be present at them, and to provide that whatsoever is transacted in them be according to the mind of God.*

XXXI, 1–2

1. *For the better government, and further edification of the Church, there ought to be such assemblies as are commonly called Synods or Councils.*

2. *As magistrates may lawfully call a synod of ministers, and other fit persons, to consult and advise about matters of religion; so if magistrates be open enemies to the Church, the ministers of Christ, of themselves, by virtue of their office, or they, with other fit persons upon delegation from their churches, may meet together in such assemblies.*

These sections of the Confession of Faith teach us (1) that the civil magistrate may not assume to himself the administration of the Word, sacraments, or discipline, (2) that he does have authority to see that unity and peace be preserved in the Church, and that error and abuses in worship and discipline be prevented or reformed, (3) that he has power to call synods, and to be present at them to see that what is transacted is according to the mind of God, (4) that there ought to be synods or councils for the government of the Church, and (5) that while a civil magistrate may lawfully call a synod, the ministers of the Church have the power to call such synods themselves if the civil magistrate happens to be an open enemy of the Church.

We come, in this part of the Confession of Faith, to what can only be called an acute difficulty. On the one hand, we read that "the civil magistrate may not assume to himself the administration of the Word and sacraments, or the power of the keys of the kingdom of heaven," and on the other hand, we read that "he hath authority . . . to take order, that unity and peace be preserved in the Church, that the truth of God be kept pure and entire, that all blasphemies and heresies be suppressed, all corruptions and abuses in worship and discipline prevented or reformed, and all the ordinances of God duly settled, administered, and observed," and that in order to do this "he hath power to call synods, to be present at them, and to provide that whatsoever is transacted in them be according to the mind of God." In chapter XXX, 1, we read that Jesus Christ, "as king and head of his Church, hath therein appointed a government in the hand of church-officers, distinct from the civil magistrate." But here we read that independent action is envisioned only "if magistrates be open enemies to the Church," in which event "the ministers of Christ, of themselves, by virtue of their office, or they, with other fit persons upon delegation from their churches, may meet together in such assemblies." What is this if it is not a direct contradiction?

This difficulty is not found in the Westminster Confession of Faith alone. For example, in the Belgic Confession, as revised by the Synod of Dordt, these words are found in Article XXXVI ("Of Magistrates"): "And their office is, not only to have regard unto, and watch for the welfare of the civil state; but also that they protect the sacred ministry; and thus may remove and prevent all idolatry and false worship."

We find that practically every Presbyterian and Reformed church has addressed itself in one way or another to the difficulty presented by this contradiction. Some churches, for example, the Reformed Presbyterian Church of North America, have not changed the original text of the Confession, but have made a special declaration on the subject. The Reformed Presbyterian Declaration and Testimony says: "No ecclesiastical authority is lodged in the hands of private Christians or civil Magistrates; Church judicatories are subordinate only to Christ Jesus. They appoint, by an exclusive right, their own times and places of meeting and adjournment . . . " (xxiii, 4).

It is difficult to see how this statement can be reconciled with the Confession. We can understand the reluctance that might be felt in changing the text of so venerable a document as the Westminster Confession of Faith. But when it can be shown that the Confession of Faith is incorrect, we believe that it ought to be changed. For, as the Confession itself is careful to teach us, "The supreme judge by which all . . . decrees of councils, opinions of ancient writers, doctrines of men . . . are to be examined, and in whose sentence we are to rest, can be no other but the Holy Spirit speaking in the Scripture" (I, 10). For our part we believe the only proper solution to the difficulty involved in this portion of the Confession is that which most Presbyterian and Reformed bodies have adopted, namely, a revision of these portions of the Confession of Faith. In such revision as that of the Orthodox Presbyterian Church and the Presbyterian Church in America, for example, all ambiguity and error are removed, and the following principles are clearly stated: (1) that the government of the Church is distinct and separate from that of the State, (2) that civil magistrates may not interfere in the affairs of any church so long as it is not subversive of the civil order, even in controversies of doctrine or discipline, and (3) that church officers alone have the authority to appoint synods or councils, with which the civil government may not interfere. Here is the revised text as adopted by these churches.

XXIII, 3 (revised)

3. *Civil magistrates may not assume to themselves the administration of the Word and sacraments; or the power of the keys of the kingdom of heaven; or, in the least, interfere in matters of faith. Yet, as nursing fathers, it is the duty of civil magistrates to protect the Church of our common Lord, without giving the preference to any denomination of Christians above the rest, in such a manner that all ecclesiastical persons whatever shall enjoy the full, free, and unquestioned liberty of discharging every part of their sacred functions, without violence or danger. And, as Jesus Christ hath appointed a regular government and discipline in his Church, no law of any commonwealth should interfere with, or hinder, the due exercise thereof, among the voluntary members of any denomination of Christians, according to their own profession and belief. It is the duty of civil magistrates to protect the person and good name of all their people, in such an effectual manner as that no person be suffered, either upon pretense of religion or of infidelity, to offer any indignity, violence, abuse, or injury to any other person whatsoever: and to take order, that all religious and ecclesiastical assemblies be held without molestation or disturbance.*

XXXI, 1–2 (revised)

1–2. *For the better government, and further edification of the Church, there ought to be such assemblies as are commonly called synods or councils: and it belongeth to the overseers and other rulers of the particular churches, by virtue of their office, and the power which Christ hath given them for edification and not for destruction, to appoint such assemblies; and to convene together in them, as often as they shall judge it expedient for the good of the church.*

We believe that this is a more excellent way. The Westminster Confession of Faith ought to be revered, but not merely because it is old. It ought to be revered because it is true to the Bible. We do not believe this Confession will require further correction in anything but minor detail. But it does not lower our regard for the wonderful integrity of this document to know that it was in error in one or two particulars. The same careful examination of this Creed in the light of Scripture that convinced the church that this portion was faulty at the same time confirmed the truth of the rest. When this Confession was adopted originally by various Presbyterian bodies, it was sincerely believed. Where it has been found to err from Scripture it has been amended. And true Presbyterians have always believed that the Confession could and ought to be amended when it can be shown to be in error. But this is a far cry from the modern-day attitude toward the Confession which is evident in many quarters, where ministers give lip service to this Creed—even in its correct and scripturally accurate revision—while not believing the biblical doctrines which it teaches. If modernists were honest they would either (1) not subscribe to such a Creed, or (2) they would revise it to express what they really do believe. In either case they would have no association with those who approach this Confession with the integrity evidenced by those who—in four centuries—have found only a few errors to correct in an otherwise true statement of faith.

The famous Council of Nicea (A.D. 325) was the first to be summoned by a civil ruler. Constantine sought in this way to reconcile the contending parties in the Arian controversy. The Emperor himself presided. But not only did he fail to fully appreciate the issue at stake, he also set a precedent for the intrusion of civil authorities into the sphere of church government. It is no doubt understandable that our Reforming Fathers should have tended in the direction they did. On the one hand, there was the claim of Roman Catholicism to supremacy in both ecclesiastical and civil matters. And on the other hand, there was the fact that benevolent civil authorities had on various occasions protected and nourished the struggling Reformed churches. But it is not to be forgotten that subsequent to the Westminster Assembly, the Scottish Covenanters were called upon to suffer unto death from *civil* oppression. To these rugged Presbyterians, who more than others of that time resolutely adhered to the testimony of the Confession, we owe much, for it was to assert the absolute spiritual independence of the Church of Jesus Christ from civil authority that they gave their all. Those who loved the testimony of the Confession best, suffered most for the principle which was—after all—compromised in the original formulation of these sections.

QUESTIONS

1. What are the two irreconcilable principles stated in these sections of the Confession?
2. Is this difficulty manifest in the Westminster Confession of Faith only?
3. What two methods of resolving this difficulty have been used?
4. Which of these is to be preferred? Why?
5. What principles are clearly stated in such a revision as that of the Orthodox Presbyterian Church and the Presbyterian Church in America?
6. Does revision of a venerable Creed such as this detract from its worth?
7. Why is it very important that a creed be revised at any point where it errs?
8. If time has proved the Confession incorrect at this point, what else has it proved?
9. Give an example of the interference of civil rulers in ecclesiastical affairs.
10. To whom do Presbyterians owe a great debt for asserting the spiritual independence of the Christian Church from civil government?

XXXI, 3–4

3. *It belongeth to synods and councils ministerially to determine controversies of faith, and cases of conscience; to set down rules and directions for the better ordering of the public worship of God, and government of his Church; to receive complaints in cases of maladministration, and authoritatively to determine the same: which decrees and determinations, if consonant to the Word of God, are to be received with reverence and submission, not only for their agreement with the Word, but also for the power whereby they are made, as being an ordinance of God, appointed thereunto in his Word.*

4. *All synods or councils since the apostles' times, whether general or particular, may err, and many have erred; therefore they are not to be made the rule of faith or practice, but to be used as an help in both.*

These sections of the Confession teach us (1) the sphere of authority belonging to synods and councils, (2) the degree or measure of authority belonging to them, and (3) the limitation of their power within the realm of fallible administration.

The government of the Church is wholly spiritual and ministerial. That is, (1) it has to do with matters of doctrine, worship, and spiritual discipline, and (2) its power is only administrative and declarative. It must do and say according to the will of God as it is revealed in Scripture. When there is a controversy as between two opposing views, both claiming to be according to the truth of God, then it is proper for a synod or council to convene to determine which view (if either) is according to the Word of God. This is what happened at the Synod of Jerusalem (Acts 15). At that synod it was determined that one view was correct and the other incorrect by test of the Word of God.

Again, when there are questions as to whether a certain practice is right or wrong, in which there is disagreement in the conviction of men's consciences, it is proper for a synod to consider the matter and to endeavor to ascertain the proper answer to the question from the Word of God. Provided it adheres to the Scripture, such a synod would also have the right to set down rules and directions for the better ordering of the public worship of God and the government of the Church. In the Synod of Jerusalem "decrees . . . were determined" concerning certain matters affecting the practice of Christians, and these were "delivered" for them "to keep" (Acts 16:4).

It is important to stress the fact that the power in evidence here is strictly limited. It is limited to the *declaration of* that which God has said in his Word and the proper *order by which* the commands of God are to be observed. For example, it would be proper for a synod to make rules concerning the *order* of worship to be observed in a church where difficulty has arisen over such a question. But it would not be permissible to make new laws additional to the Bible as to the proper elements of divine worship. No synod may lawfully legislate the *content* of true worship. It can only decree with respect to the *order* of worship.

If the decrees and determinations of church assemblies are "consonant to the Word of God," they are to be "received with reverence and submission." This is true not only because these decrees are scriptural (although that is of primary importance), but also because these decrees

are made by a church government instituted by Christ. There is authority not only in Scripture, which is declared, but also in the synod which
declares. For example, if a synod decrees that the Lord's Supper be
observed at least four times every year, this ought to be done not only
because Christ has commanded the frequent observance of the sacrament
in the Bible, but also because an assembly of Christ's Church has decreed
a particular order, lawfully, in his Church. To disregard a particular order
which is agreeable to the Word of God, is sinful not only because of the
general command which the order implements, but also because of the
specific command by which it is implemented. To disregard a specific
decree which implements a general command of Christ is sinful because
Christ has authorized church courts to make such decrees.

However, as the Confession reminds us, "all synods and councils since
the apostles' times, whether general or particular, may err, and many have
erred," so that "they are not to be made the rule of faith or practice, but
[only] to be used as an help in both." When a church assembly issues a
decree or order, or makes a determination of a controversy, which is itself
in conflict with the Word of God, it *must be disobeyed*. For example, when
the General Assembly of the Presbyterian Church in the U.S.A. in the
1930s ordered all members of the Church to support certain agencies and
boards of the Church even though modernists were employed by them,
it was perfectly scriptural and right for believers to refuse to obey. Yet
such disobedience would be exceedingly reprehensible in a case where
the General Assembly required that which was according to the Word
of God. This is just to say that the authority belonging to church councils is limited. It is limited to the *declaration* and *implementation of* the doctrines and commandments of Christ contained in Scripture. And it is to
say that synods and councils can never put forward any decree or determination which is inherently, and by virtue of the authority of the synod
or council itself, infallible.

The limitations of the authority and power of synods and councils,
recognized by the Reformers, are not so widely recognized nor scrupulously observed today. In the modern ecumenical movement, for example, there has often been a tendency to subordinate the authority of the
Bible to that of councils. The truth, in such circumstances, is not sought
in Scripture alone but in a consensus of various traditions and opinions.
As one writer has expressed it, "He who feels he already 'has' the truth

does not enter fully into dialogue" (Floyd H. Ross, "The Christian Mission in Larger Dimension," in *The Theology of the Christian Mission,* ed. Gerald H. Anderson [New York: McGraw-Hill, 1961], 227).

It is no exaggeration to say that Luther's bold stand at the Diet of Worms was the exact antithesis of this view which has been revived in the modern ecumenical movement, to the effect that the whole Church speaking synodically or by council is the voice of truth. It must also be said, however, that even in orthodox Reformed churches there has sometimes been a tendency to gradually elevate the deliverances of synods or assemblies to a place of practical supremacy as the rule of faith and practice. There are orthodox Reformed churches in which the members believe certain things and adhere to certain practices, not because the declarations of Synod or the General Assembly have been presented to them in such a way as to persuade them that such is the teaching of Scripture, but merely because a church rule has been made. We believe this to be dangerous and harmful, even if a particular rule is in accordance with Scripture. There may be a temporary appearance of strict obedience and piety. But it will soon decay and prove powerless to restrain sin. The more difficult way is the right way. When synods and councils put forth the effort to *prove* their declarations by Scripture, and administer them by persuasion as well as by discipline, the supreme authority of the Bible will be both safeguarded and expressed. And in such a process the Church will not turn a deaf ear to those who dissent on the basis of conviction supported from Scripture.

QUESTIONS

1. What is meant by saying that the government of the Church is spiritual?
2. What is meant by saying that the government of the Church is ministerial?
3. What matters are properly determined by synods and councils?
4. Give an example of something a synod or council may not decree.
5. When do the decrees of synods or councils have authority?
6. Why do the decrees of synods or councils have authority in such cases?
7. When a church council makes a decree or determination contrary to the Word of God, what must the individual Christian do? Why?
8. What tendency is manifest in much of the modern ecumenical movement?

9. Do orthodox Presbyterian/Reformed bodies sometimes tend to disregard the limitations of the authority of synods or councils? If so, how?
10. What is necessary to guard against this?

XXXI, 5

5. *Synods and councils are to handle or conclude nothing but that which is ecclesiastical; and are not to intermeddle with civil affairs, which concern the commonwealth, unless by way of humble petition, in cases extraordinary; or by way of advice for satisfaction of conscience, if they be thereunto required by the civil magistrate.*

This section of the Confession teaches us (1) that synods and councils are to concern themselves with the affairs of the Church, (2) that they are not to intermeddle in the affairs of the State, (3) that they may, however, speak out on civil issues in extraordinary cases involving matters vital to the Church, and (4) that they may also give advice to the civil magistrate when it is requested.

During the week of November 18–21, 1958, the World Order Study Conference met in Cleveland, Ohio. This conference had been called by the President of the National Council of Churches of Christ in the U.S.A., and it was convened by the Division of Life and Work of the Department of International Affairs. From this conference came the "Message to the Churches" in which the following purely political or civil matters were considered, and certain positions advocated. The message called for (1) diplomatic recognition of Communist China by the United States, (2) admission of Communist China to the United Nations Organization, (3) avoidance of the posture of general hostility toward communist nations, (4) internationalism to supersede national patriotism, (5) the seeking of the goal of universal disarmament, (6) the use of military force only when sanctioned by, and under the control of, the United Nations, (7) the creation of a permanent United Nations police force, (8) the abolition of the system of military conscription, and (9) the approval of unrestricted trade between the United States and communist nations.

Perhaps this is an extreme case. But it illustrates exactly what our Confession opposes. It is a clear example of what the Scripture does not sanction as the proper business of the Church. It is our conviction that such bodies as the World Council of Churches and National Council of Churches have frequently advocated civil causes, political programs, and social schemes that are nothing short of perverse. No Christian concerned to maintain the honor of Christ should be a part of such organizations. But we stress here the fact that even if a particular position taken by such a body was correct, we would still have to reject such organizations because it is contrary to the Word of God for synods and councils to intermeddle in civil affairs in this way. Even if they were right on particular issues, they would be wrong in assuming the right to meddle in civil affairs.

We believe that the following arguments are sufficient proof of the teaching of the Confession. (1) Christ said, "My kingdom is not of this world" (John 18:36). Christ not only made no effort to wield political power or to influence political events directly by making pronouncements on civil matters, but also when his followers tried to make him a political power he frustrated their attempt. Instead, he preached the gospel of the kingdom of God. He taught that men must be changed, and that as they were changed they would leaven the social and political order (Matt. 13:33). (2) There is no evidence that the apostles or the Apostolic Church intermeddled in civil affairs. Even the Jerusalem Synod concluded nothing that was not ecclesiastical. (3) There is no Scripture teaching that warrants such interference in the affairs of the State on the part of the Church.

The Reformed concept of "sphere sovereignty" is the scriptural teaching, and it indeed recognizes that God is supreme in every realm or sphere of life. It teaches that the individual Christian is to glorify God in all that he does. And the law of God is quite as relevant in the political realm as in any other. Moreover, it is the task of the Church to teach the whole counsel of God, even as it pertains to political affairs. But there is a world of difference between the *teaching of principles* of the Word of God to members of the Church and the attempt to directly *interfere* in the affairs of the State. It is the task of the Church to provide instruction that will guide church members in political matters—civil magistrates included. But it is the task of Christians as citizens to effect that which is in accord with the gospel. The Church is a mighty force in the affairs of State. But it is so indirectly. It is the Christian individual in the exercise of his civil rights—rather than the Church as such—that must influence politics with Christian principles.

There are, however, two instances in which the Church may directly concern itself with civil matters. (1) When the State presents a direct threat to the spiritual concerns of the Church, the latter has the right to speak on that matter as an organized body. This happened in recent years when certain laws were passed which attempted to silence what the Bible says about homosexual sin. In both San Francisco and the State of New Jersey the Orthodox Presbyterian Church had no choice but to speak out—*to the State*—for satisfaction of conscience. It said to the State—and properly we maintain—that it must continue to denounce what the Bible denounces.

(2) There may also be times when the civil authorities request from the Church a statement of opinion on matters involving morals. The writer of this study once appeared before a select committee of the Parliament in New Zealand for precisely this reason. The church that the writer served at that time held that it would be a right and even a duty for the Church to comply. But, in such instances, care must be exercised to avoid confusion between a faithful declaration of principles from the Word of God and any attempt to dictate administrative policy, which is the proper task of the civil magistrates and not of the Church.

QUESTIONS

1. What are the proper matters with which church synods should concern themselves?
2. What modern Council flagrantly violates this principle?
3. Why is such activity wrong even if the particular thing advocated be right?
4. Give three arguments against such intermeddling.
5. Does this principle of the Confession mean that the gospel is not regulative of political matters for the Christian?
6. How does the Church rightly influence political affairs?
7. When may the Church concern itself directly, as an organized body, with political matters?

31

XXXII. Of the State of Men after Death, and of the Resurrection of the Dead

1. *The bodies of men after death return to dust, and see corruption; but their souls, (which neither die nor sleep), having an immortal subsistence, immediately return to God who gave them. The souls of the righteous, being then made perfect in holiness, are received into the highest heavens, where they behold the face of God in light and glory, waiting for the full redemption of their bodies; and the souls of the wicked are cast into hell, where they remain in torments and utter darkness, reserved to the judgment of the great day. Besides these two places for souls separated from their bodies, the Scripture acknowledgeth none.*

This section of the Confession teaches us (1) that at death the physical bodies of all men alike return to dust and see corruption, (2) that the souls of all men then enter upon the intermediate state, (3) that the intermediate state differs as respects the righteous and wicked, and (4) that purgatory is a fiction.

It is a fact supported by common experience, as it is the infallible teaching of Scripture, that "the bodies of men after death return to dust, and see corruption." As God said to fallen man, "For dust you are, and to dust you shall return" (Gen. 3:19). Neither Scripture nor our own observation indicates any difference between the righteous and wicked so far as the physical body in death is concerned. "For David, after he had served his own generation by the will of God, fell asleep, was buried with his fathers, and saw corruption" (Acts 13:36), even though he was a man after God's own heart. As far as the body is concerned, the believer, like the unbeliever, is subject to this consequence of Adam's sin, for the present. Death is the effect of sin. The wages of sin is death, and so death passed upon all men because all sinned.

The question is, why is there no difference between believers and unbelievers so far as physical death is concerned? The answer is that it has pleased God to delay the physical benefits of Christ's redemptive work until the end of time. "The last enemy that will be destroyed is death" (1 Cor. 15:26). At the resurrection on that final day of history the physical aspect of man will be reconstituted, and the righteous will have a body changed into the glorious likeness of the resurrected body of Christ (Phil. 3:21). The wicked will be raised also, but in dishonor and vileness, to receive just punishment of sin in body as well as soul (2 Cor. 5:10).

While we cannot, and need not, explain the ways of God, we would suggest at least a few reasons for this delay in the redemption of the body. (1) Since the physical benefits of redemption are delayed, no one is encouraged to be a Christian merely for the sake of liberation from sickness, suffering, and death. Christ's miracles gave a foretaste of the final victory over disease and death, and there were many who followed after him because of the miracles. But they did not desire deliverance from sin but only from the effects of sin. (2) Death, like sickness, adversity, and weakness of body, is a means of sanctification. It causes us to remember our frame, that we are dust. It helps to wean us from the pride of life and the love of this present world. It encourages us to cast ourselves more and more upon God and to cry out to him for that final deliverance. (3) Death is also a means of attaining something better, which otherwise would not be attained. The resurrected body of Lazarus was not like that glorious body which will be his, and ours, on the resurrection day, if we believe in Jesus. "Foolish one, what you sow is not made alive unless it dies. And what you sow, you do not sow that body that shall be" (1 Cor. 15:36–37). The death of the physical body (Paul calls it "this body of death," Rom. 7:24) is prerequisite to the resurrection of that same body with new and glorious qualities. There is *continuity of substance* but *transformation of qualities*. In much the same way, the "old man" (which is our sinful self, our egocentric fallen nature) must die, being crucified with Christ, in order for the "new man" (which is our regenerate self, self-less and Christ-centered) to be created. (See the discussion of V, 2–6.) (4) Finally, if there were no death for the righteous, there could be no world history. Either the righteous would go out of the world (as Jesus did in his resurrection body), or else they would have to live a wholly separate existence in a segregated society. There could be no order in which believers and unbelievers could dwell together. And the righteous could not beget children. There would be no covenant seed (Matt. 22:30).

While the temporal destiny of the physical bodies of believers and unbelievers is the same until Christ returns, their souls (or spirits) at death enter upon entirely different estates. The spirits of believers immediately become sinlessly perfect and enter upon the joy of immediate presence with God (Heb. 12:23). As the apostle said, to be "absent from the body" is to be "present with the Lord" (2 Cor. 5:8). "To depart" is to "be with Christ," he writes, and this is (in comparison with our present estate) "far better" (Phil. 1:23).

But we must understand that this intermediate state is simply a more perfect development, a more advanced phase, of that new life which has its beginning *in the soul* of the believer at regeneration. When we are made alive by God's Holy Spirit, we have already passed from death unto life, as far as the soul is concerned (John 5:24). We have already begun to sit in heavenly places in Christ Jesus (Eph. 2:5–6). And from the moment of regeneration the soul cannot be touched by death. Death, in the full scope of it, as a punishment for sin, incurs the payment of the wages of sin, and this is its sting. This sting is removed at the moment of regeneration, so that at physical death, there is nothing that can touch the soul or spirit, not even any insurmountable fear, and least of all, the sting of the law. Death merely marks an advance in the progress of the believer's spirit in that eternal life which began with regeneration. And the advance is one of both inward holiness and immediate communion with God. When Paul said, "O wretched man that I am! Who will deliver me from this body of death?" (Rom. 7:24), he associated death with his physical body, and life with his regenerated soul. At death the soul or spirit is wholly free from that body, which is still under the power of sin and death. At the resurrection the body will be at last delivered also, and reunited with the spirit, and then the whole man will be spiritual. This does not mean that the body will not be physical; it means only that both body and soul will be perfectly holy and under the rule of the Holy Spirit of God.

But the wicked are dead already in this life, in both body and soul. The soul is dead from the very beginning of its natural existence because it is derived from Adam. All men are by nature "dead in trespasses and sins" (Eph. 2:1). But the unbeliever remains dead. And his physical death merely marks an advancement into death as a more complete experience. Unbelievers are already without God and without hope in the world, and yet—in the world—still enjoy some of God's common blessings. But at the time of physical death, they will lose even that which they now have. Then there will be no more blessings of any sort to alleviate the torment and darkness of their condition. Neither will there any longer be a free and gracious invitation of God to salvation through Jesus Christ. All hope will then be abandoned. Their soul (or spirit) will descend into hell.

Yet the condition and place of these wicked unbelievers after physical death, and prior to their resurrection, is not a totally new development. It is rather a more complete manifestation, a yet fuller development, of that spiritual condition which began with their natural birth in a lost and sinful condition. The wrath of God *remains* on them. But then it will come to greater expression. But even this intermediate state, in which the lost soul or spirit alone reaches mature development in sin and experiences the unalleviated consequences of sin, is not the final and complete manifestation of the damnation of the wicked. That must await the resurrection of the body. Then, and only then, can the reconstituted man experience the physical and spiritual torment that God has reserved for them that are not his. Thus, paradoxically enough, physical death has the effect of delaying not only the full perfection and joy of the righteous, but also the full misery and suffering of the wicked.

"Besides these two places [i.e., heaven and hell] for souls separated from their bodies, the Scripture acknowledgeth none." Roman Catholic theology teaches that most men at death go to neither heaven nor hell, but to a place called purgatory. Purgatory, according to Romish teaching, is the place where those "who die in the state of grace but are guilty of venial sin, or have not fully satisfied for the temporal punishment due to their sins" go to receive that punishment and make that satisfaction. Not only is this contrary to the teaching of Scripture in that Scripture teaches the immediate departure of souls (spirits) to either heaven or hell, but it is also contrary to the teaching of Scripture because it undermines the sufficiency of the work of Jesus Christ for the full satisfaction for all the sins of his people. "By one offering He has perfected forever those who are being sanctified" (Heb. 10:14).

QUESTIONS

1. Is there any difference in the physical death of believers and unbelievers (that is, in the purely physical aspects)?
2. Of what is death the effect? Prove.
3. Why then are not the righteous freed from physical death now rather than later?
4. When do the souls of men begin to experience essentially different conditions?
5. When do the souls of men begin to experience entirely different estates?
6. Of what is the intermediate state a more mature development?
7. How is the believer's soul advanced in its condition by physical death?
8. How is the unbeliever's soul advanced in its condition by physical death?
9. What is the purpose of purgatory according to Rome?
10. What teaching of Scripture does this contradict?

XXXII, 2–3

2. *At the last day, such as are found alive shall not die, but be changed: and all the dead shall be raised up with the self-same bodies and none other, although with different qualities, which shall be united again to their souls for ever.*

3. *The bodies of the unjust shall, by the power of Christ, be raised to dishonor; the bodies of the just, by his Spirit, unto honor, and be made conformable to his own glorious body.*

These sections of the Confession teach us (1) that there will be a general resurrection at the last day, (2) that those who live until that day will be changed without the usual (time-consuming) process of physical decay, (3) that it will be a resurrection of the same body (identical in essence or substance, but different in qualities) that died, (4) that this body will again be united to the soul, so to remain forever, and (5) that this resurrection will be different for the righteous and the wicked.

The Westminster Larger Catechism (Q. 84) says, "It is appointed unto all men once to die; for that all have sinned." But the Confession says that "at the last day, such as are found alive shall not die, but be changed." On the surface, at least, this would seem to be a contradiction. One or the other cannot be an absolute statement. But far from objecting to this feature of the Westminster Confession and Catechism, we see in it the willingness to be controlled by Scripture.

There is no greater difficulty in reconciling these two statements in the Westminster standards than there is in reconciling various similar statements of Scripture. Scripture also clearly states the universality of death. "Death spreads to all men," says Paul, "because all sinned" (Rom. 5:12). "It is appointed for men to die once" (Heb. 9:27). This is a statement of what we see as the universal fact of our existence. There is no class or race of men that escapes this appointment. Generation after generation has faced the same terminus. But obviously, there will be one generation that will not "pass away" from this earthly scene as others before them, for the simple reason that Christ will return while they are yet alive. "For this we say to you by the word of the Lord, that we who are alive and remain until the coming of the Lord will by no means precede those who are asleep" (1 Thess. 4:15). Some will be alive when Jesus returns. How then could they partake of death as did those who preceded them? In their case the body and soul will not be separated, neither will the body rest for a period to suffer decay. This difference is self-evident.

But it is unwarranted to imagine, as many have, that those who are alive and remain will have an advantage over others. Paul refutes this very notion in 1 Thessalonians 4:15. He says that those who are alive and remain will "by no means precede" or "come before" those who have been asleep. We believe that this means that they will not have any advantage over them. And we believe this is so for the following reasons. (1) Christ's second coming will be at least as fearful a thing to face as physical death could possibly be: "when the Lord Jesus is revealed from heaven with His mighty angels, in flaming fire taking vengeance on those who do not know God, and on those who do not obey the gospel of our Lord Jesus Christ" (2 Thess. 1:7–8). (2) The change that will then occur in the believer who is alive and remaining will be no less awesome a crisis than is death itself or the resurrection of the dead. That which is accomplished by death, the intermediate state, and the resurrection at the last day (in the case of most believers), will also be accomplished in a drastic and sudden fashion in the case of those who are alive and remain till Christ comes. Neither will have any advantage since both will undergo a like change. (3) Further, while we strenuously resist the notion that believers have no consciousness during the intermediate state (as some false sects teach), we are not certain that they will have the same consciousness of time that we have here on earth. It may be that, at death, the believer begins to have a consciousness that is no longer circumscribed by our present temporal boundaries. (4) In any case, since death has no sting and no victory (1 Cor. 15:55), and since we are assured that it is far better to be absent from the body and present with the Lord (2 Cor. 5:8), there can be no disadvantage to those who sleep in Jesus. Therefore, since the change experienced by believers who are alive and remaining at the last day is to the same effect as the change experienced by other believers in death, the intermediate state, and the resurrection at the last day, there is a proper sense in which both statements (that all will die once; that some will not die) are perfectly true.

But what will be the nature of the resurrection? This is a great mystery, and we cannot do more than stress certain great teachings of Scripture that keep us from error in our thinking on this matter. (1) It will be a *physical* resurrection. That is, actual earthly material will be involved. There will be some kind of continuity between the identity of the body that is laid in the grave to suffer corruption and the identity of the body that is raised up at the last day. "And after my skin is destroyed, this I know, that in my flesh I shall see God" (Job 19:26). There will be as real an identity in our case as there was in the case of Jesus himself. It was the same body, although the body was not the same (in qualities). Just as there is continuity between the fetus in the womb and the full-grown human being, so there will be continuity between the body that dies and that which lives again. A century ago no one knew of the existence of DNA.

Today it is possible to read the DNA code of Pharaohs who have been dead for millennia. This is not to try to explain the continuity factor, but just to remind the reader that there are surprising things that have long been unknown. Why then should we have any doubt as to God's ability to recover—and reconstitute—the very same physical body as that which was burned to ashes in a fire?

(2) The resurrection body (at least in the case of the righteous) will be radically *different* from what it was before. It will no longer be subject to corruption (1 Cor. 15:42). It will be glorious (v. 43). It will have great power (v. 43). And it will be completely and perfectly subject to the rule of God's Spirit (v. 44). It will be much more radically changed than we can even imagine. But it will not be a "new body" in every sense of the word, but will be the "old body" made into a "new body." It will have no less continuity with the old than does the soul of the believer have with the soul which he had before regeneration. As one may take scrap metal and melt it down to produce a new object, so of the body: the body "sown in corruption" will be "raised in incorruption." The new will be made out of the old. "There is a natural body, and there is a spiritual body" (1 Cor. 15:44). If "flesh and blood cannot inherit the kingdom of God" (v. 50), what is needed is not annihilation of the old body but rather a radical change of it. And that is what shall be: "We shall all be changed— in a moment, in the twinkling of an eye, at the last trumpet . . . the dead will be raised incorruptible, and we shall be changed" (vv. 51–52).

The Scripture does not tell us nearly so much with respect to the resurrection of those who are lost. We do know (1) that it will be at *the same time* as the resurrection of believers. "For the hour is coming in which all who are in the graves will hear His voice and come forth—those who have done good, to the resurrection of life, and those who have done evil, to the resurrection of condemnation" (John 5:28–29). (2) In their case it will also be a resurrection of *the same body* that was buried. For among "those who sleep in the dust of the earth [who] shall awake . . . some [will awake] to shame and everlasting contempt" (Dan. 12:2). But (3) while *there may be radical changes* in the bodies of the unsaved, they will not be such as take place in the bodies of the saved. Whatever changes there may be, they will only be such as will be appropriate to shame, contempt, dishonor, and everlasting suffering of pain and loss. "This is the second death. And anyone not found written in the Book of Life was cast into the lake of fire" (Rev. 20:14–15).

QUESTIONS

1. What are the two apparently contradictory statements in the Westminster standards concerning death?
2. Give a Scripture reference to support each of these statements.
3. What three proofs can you give to show that those who are alive and remain at Christ's return will have no advantage over those who die in Christ before this?
4. What does the Confession mean when it says the resurrection will be of "the self-same bodies"?
5. What does the Confession mean when it speaks of "different qualities"?
6. When will the lost be raised?
7. In what sense will their bodies be the same?
8. What is the second death?

32

XXXIII. Of the Last Judgment

1. *God hath appointed a day wherein he will judge the world in righteousness by Jesus Christ, to whom all power and judgment is given of the Father. In which day, not only the apostate angels shall be judged, but likewise all persons that have lived upon earth shall appear before the tribunal of Christ, to give an account of their thoughts, words, and deeds and to receive according to what they have done in the body, whether good or evil.*

2. *The end of God's appointing this day is for the manifestation of the glory of his mercy in the eternal salvation of the elect, and of his justice in the damnation of the reprobate, who are wicked and disobedient. For then shall the righteous go into everlasting life, and receive that fullness of joy and refreshing which shall come from the presence of the Lord; but the wicked, who know not God, and obey not the gospel of Jesus Christ, shall be cast into eternal torments, and be punished with everlasting destruction from the presence of the Lord, and from the glory of his power.*

3. *As Christ would have us to be certainly persuaded that there shall be a day of judgment, both to deter all men from sin, and for the greater consolation of the godly in their adversity; so will he have that day unknown to men, that they may shake off all carnal security, and be*

always watchful, because they know not at what hour the Lord will come; and may be ever prepared to say, Come, Lord Jesus, come quickly. Amen.

These sections of the Confession teach us (1) that God has appointed a day of general judgment, (2) that Christ will be the judge, (3) that all angels and men will appear before him, (4) that they will be judged for every thought, word, and deed, (5) that God's purpose in appointing this day is the manifestation of his glorious justice and grace, (6) that the righteous and wicked will then enter upon their eternal reward, and (7) that the great day cannot be predicted or known before it comes.

As the Larger Catechism says, "We are to believe, that at the last day there shall be a general resurrection of the dead, both of the just and unjust" and that "immediately after the resurrection shall follow the general and final judgment of angels and men" (Q/A 87–88). The teaching of the Westminster standards is that there will be a general resurrection of all men, and then, without delay, a general judgment. "For the hour is coming in which all who are in the graves will . . . come forth" (John 5:28–29). John describes the scene: "And I saw the dead, small and great, standing before God, and books were opened. And another book was opened, which is the Book of Life. And the dead were judged according to their works, by the things which were written in the books. The sea gave up the dead who were in it, and Death and Hades delivered up the dead who were in them. And they were judged, each one according to his works" (Rev. 20:12–13). Observe: two kinds of books were opened, and there were present those who were judged on the basis of each kind, and every man was included. We are thus shut up to the fact that "He has appointed a day on which He will judge the world in righteousness by the Man whom He has ordained" (Acts 17:31).

This teaching of Scripture is so plain that it might seem unnecessary to dwell upon it. But there is today widespread acceptance of a form of doctrine at variance with the teaching of Scripture concerning both the general resurrection and the general judgment. It is the doctrine called premillennialism. In order to understand this doctrine, and also to present the other two classic views, we will introduce at this point a brief discussion of the millennial positions.

Millennial Views

The word "millennium" comes from the Latin words meaning "thousand years." It has come to have a special meaning in the realm of doctrine. There are some who associate with the return of Christ the idea of an extended period (hence, millennium) of unparalleled prosperity and blessedness on earth during which Christianity will virtually reign supreme. (1) Some hold that Christ will return *before* this period begins. They are called premillennialists. (2) Others believe that a period of unparalleled prosperity and blessedness (i.e., the millennium) will come first, and that the return of Christ will come *after* this. They are called postmillennialists. (3) And there are those who do not believe that the Bible warrants expectation of any extended period of triumph of Christianity prior to the end of the age. It has become traditional to call these amillennialists, because they believe there will be no millennium. (These persons do believe that there is a proper interpretation to be given to Revelation 20:1–10, and so it is not correct to associate the term "amillennialist" with disbelief of Scripture.) We shall now endeavor to give a brief description of certain characteristic examples of these three basic views.

Premillennialism

Classical Premillennialism. This view was held in early church history by Irenaeus and others. The main outline is as follows: (1) world history is expected to extend six thousand years, a thousand years for each of the days of creation (cf. 2 Peter 3:8); (2) toward the end of this period (the sixth day, which began with Christ's first coming) suffering and persecution of believers will increase until climax in the rise of Antichrist (cf. 2 Thess. 2:3–10; 1 John 2:18); (3) at the height of Antichrist's power Christ will appear in heavenly glory to triumph over all his enemies, resurrecting the saints and establishing his kingdom, which will last a thousand years (the seventh day, Sabbath, or Millennium). (During this period Jerusalem will be rebuilt, the earth will prosper, and there will be universal peace); (4) at the end of this period the wicked will be raised for the final judgment; (5) finally, the new creation will appear (cf. 2 Peter 3; Rev. 21–22).

This basic scheme has had advocates throughout church history, although this must be called a distinctly "minority" view. In the nineteenth century this view became much more popular, and was held (with some variation) by such able scholars as Bengel, Godet, Van Oosterzee, Moorehead, and others. Then toward the end of the century and throughout the twentieth century to an even greater degree, there came a new and radically different type of premillennial doctrine. To this we now turn.

Modern Dispensational Premillennialism. This view can only be called a recent innovation. It is rather a product of the dispensational system, of which it is a part, than of the ancient teaching of the Christian Church. The dispensational premillennial scheme is as follows: (1) There are seven dispensations: Innocency (creation to the fall), Conscience (the fall to the flood), Human Government (the flood to the tower of Babel), Promise (from the patriarchs to Moses), Law (Moses to Christ), Grace (Christ to the Millennium), and Kingdom (the millennial period). (2) The nation (or kingdom) of Israel occupies a special place in the divine economy. It was the provisional form of the kingdom of God. Because of apostasy it was overthrown, but the prophets predicted its reestablishment. The Messiah came and offered to establish this kingdom. The Jews refused. Christ was therefore forced to delay the establishment of the kingdom. He temporarily withdrew (going into a far country, Matt. 21:33) but will return to do what he was then kept from doing. (3) The Church is regarded as a mere parenthesis in the history of the kingdom. It has no connection with the kingdom and was unknown to the prophets. It is a sort of unexpected "break" which resulted in the "windfall" of the gospel of grace for the nations. Most dispensationalists do not look for very profound results in the preaching of the gospel. The real hope is only in Christ's return. The work of surpassing greatness will then follow in the millennial period. (4) Christ's return is imminent. He may come at any time. There are no predicted events which must first be fulfilled. (5) Christ's second coming will consist of two separate events (comings) with seven intervening years between. The first will be his coming for his saints (see Matt. 24:40–41; 1 Thess. 4:17). The second will follow the seven-year period in which the gospel of the kingdom will again be preached (by believing Jews), widespread conversion effected (though not universal), Israel reconstituted (some, however, put this event later), and in the latter part of this period Antichrist revealed and God's wrath poured out upon the human race (2 Thess. 2; Rev. 16; Matt. 24:14–22). After this period Christ will come with his saints. The living nations will then be judged, the saints that died during the great tribulation raised up, Antichrist destroyed, and Satan bound (Rev. 20:1–2). (6) The millennial kingdom will then be established. It will be an earthly, visible kingdom in which only the Jews will be natural citizens; the Gentiles will be merely adopted citizens. Christ will sit on a throne in Jerusalem. The temple will be rebuilt, and sacrifices made once more (Ezek. 40–48). Universal peace and prosperity will prevail (Isa. 11:8). During this period the world will be converted, some say by the gospel, but most say by might and by power. (7) At the end of the millennium Satan will be loosed for a little season. Gog and Magog will rise against the holy city (Rev. 20:7–8). But God will intervene with fire from heaven. Satan will be cast into the pit, and the dead that have not yet been raised (i.e., the wicked) will be raised to appear before the judgment seat of God. (8) Then will follow the eternal kingdom of heaven.

Postmillennialism

Postmillennialism has presented a stable view throughout the history of the Church. However, in recent times modernism has adapted a semblance of the view to its own naturalistic reconstruction of Christianity. Unfortunately, many who know of postmillennialism assume that postmillennialism is invariably associated with modernist views. It is actually not even accurate to speak of modernists as postmillennialists at all, because the former do not believe that Christ will return in a visible way at any time. Therefore, in our discussion we will not even consider the modernist position. We are here presenting only the views of those who can be called Christians.

Most postmillenarians believe (1) that the Holy Spirit will gradually bring about a period of virtual triumph of true Christianity before Christ returns. (2) Some believe that a great apostasy will precede the "golden age," others (perhaps most) believe that it will follow it. (Some believe that the papacy at its height was the great apostasy, and that the Reformation began the course of events that will bring about the golden age.) (3) Christ will return after the world is evangelized, the Jews converted (en masse), and the Church established in great purity and unity. (4) The resurrection will be general (all men at the same time). (5) The general judgment will follow. (6) Then the eternal kingdom will begin.

Postmillennialists believe that the kingdom of God is a present reality, that it is spiritual in character, and that the Church is the divine institution which effects this coming of Christ in his kingdom power (John 18:36; Luke 17:20; Matt. 16:19; Col. 1:13; Dan. 2:44). They point to various passages to prove that Christ's kingdom is in existence, and that it is a fulfillment of Old Testament prophecies (Acts 15:14–18; Heb. 12:22–23). (Cf. Acts 2:34–36; Ps. 110:1; Eph. 1:20; Col. 3:1; Heb. 1:3, 13; 8:1.)

Amillennialism

Amillennialists do not believe that the Scripture predicts a golden age in world history prior to Christ's return, nor do they believe that it predicts such an age in history after Christ's return before the final judgment. They believe (1) that there will be a progressive maturation of the forces of good and evil (Matt. 13:24–30, 37–43, 47–50). (2) Some believe there will be tribulation and much (or great) apostasy throughout this era, while others believe that the apostasy will come as an event concentrated in time immediately prior to Christ's return. Still others believe there will be (a) the great (concentrated in time) apostasy, (b) conversion of the Jews (en masse), and (c) a state of affairs in which it can be said that all nations of the earth have been blessed in the seed of Abraham (Christ). (3) Christ will return and resurrect all men at one time. (4) The general judgment will follow. (5) The new heavens and the new earth will appear in their full beauty and glory to abide forever.

It is important to note that postmillennialism and amillennialism agree in the conviction that Revelation 20:2–3 describes a present reality, and that Jesus will not return until the period here described comes to an end. In other words, strictly speaking, both of these positions are postmillennial in the sense that they see Christ's return as taking place *after* the millennial period of which John wrote. So the difference is essentially a matter of the degree of optimism with which they view the unfolding of present-and-yet-future church history. The writer of this study does not mind being called an optimistic amillennialist. Neither does he mind being called a non–utopian postmillennialist.

The various millennial views (without attention to particular variations) are illustrated in figure 5. One thing should be obvious: it is no easy task to chart the future! But two questions may profitably concern

Fig. 5

A. Classical Premillennialism

| O. T. Kingdom | Christ's 1st Coming | Pentecost | Evil matures / Good matures | Apostasy—Antichrist | 2nd Coming of Christ | Saints' resurrection | Millennium (1,000-year reign of Christ on earth) | Resurrection of lost | Judgment of wicked | The Eternal Kingdom |

B. Modern Dispensational Premillennialism

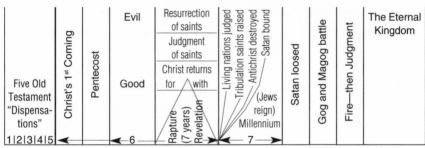

| Five Old Testament "Dispensations" 1\|2\|3\|4\|5 | Christ's 1st Coming | Pentecost | Evil / Good | Resurrection of saints / Judgment of saints / Christ returns for ∧ with / Rapture (7 years) / Revelation | Living nations judged / Tribulation saints raised / Antichrist destroyed / Satan bound / (Jews reign) Millennium | Satan loosed | Gog and Magog battle | Fire—then Judgment | The Eternal Kingdom |

←—6—→ 7 →

Rise of Antichrist
Great Tribulation

C. Postmillennialism

| O. T. Kingdom | Christ's 1st Coming | Pentecost | (Great Jewish Apostasy) | ←----------- Tribulation -----------→ Evil (gradually decreases) / Good (gradually increases) | (Christian Apostasy) | 2nd Coming of Christ | General Resurrection | General Judgment | The Eternal Kingdom |

D. Amillennialism

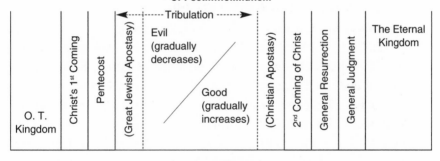

| O. T. Kingdom | Christ's 1st Coming | Pentecost | (John 16:33) Tribulation / Evil / Good / (Matt. 13:24–30, 37–43, etc.) | (Apostasy) | 2nd Coming of Christ | General Resurrection | General Judgment | The Eternal Kingdom (1Cor. 15:24–28) |

us: (1) how shall we look upon those who hold these differing views, and (2) how shall we determine which (if any) should be given preference?

In answer to the first question, we believe that all who believe in (1) the visible bodily return of Jesus Christ, (2) the general resurrection of all men, and (3) the general judgment of all men, should be regarded as holding the Christian faith. And we believe that those who hold these three principles steadfastly are able to subscribe to this portion of the Confession of Faith.

As to the second question we offer the following suggestions, believing that if we hold firmly to these truths we will avoid serious error. First, Scripture warns us that *no one knows the times or the seasons* (Acts 1:7; Matt. 24:36–44; 1 Thess. 5:1). No man knows, or can know, the chronology of the future (this is the meaning of the Greek word *chronos*) nor the precise events (or timing of events, *kairos*) which will mark the unfolding of God's plan. Therefore, any scheme (such as that of the dispensationalists) which claims such knowledge cannot be accepted by those who believe and know the truth.

Second, Scripture clearly teaches that Christ's kingdom is (a) *already existent* (Matt. 4:17; 5:3; 16:19; Mark 9:1), (b) *spiritual and invisible,* not worldly and material (Luke 17:20; John 3:3–8; 18:36; 1 Thess. 2:12; Col. 1:13), (c) *not millennial only* (Dan. 2:44; 2 Peter 1:11), (d) *not the possession of national Israel,* from which it was taken and given to all nations (Luke 12:32; Rev. 11:15), (e) *to end, as to the present mediatorial administration,* only when "He delivers the kingdom to God the Father, when He puts an end to all rule and authority and power. For He must reign till He has put all enemies under His feet. . . . Now when all things are made subject to Him, then the Son Himself will also be subject to Him who put all things under Him" (1 Cor. 15:24–28). Then will the kingdom appear in its final form (2 Tim. 4:1; Matt. 26:29), but even then it will be a continuance of the kingdom that now is.

Third, the Bible states that Christ's return will be (a) without warning (that is, without signs) (Matt. 24:36–39, 42–44). It is compared with the days of Noah when life went on "as usual" until, without warning signs, the flood suddenly came. Noah's preaching was the only warning, but this was not different from the preaching of today, which is the only warning of Christ's coming. Christ also used as an illustration of this truth the thief that comes without warning signs, and the lightning that shines

XXXIII ℭ THE LAST JUDGMENT

without warning from east to west. (b) When he does come, he will summon all men to rise from their graves (John 6:28–29; Acts 24:15). (c) In that day the heavens and the earth as we now know them will "pass away" because "the elements will melt with fervent heat" (2 Peter 3:10–11).

Fourth, the Bible says that this is the final period of human history (Heb. 1:2; John 6:39; 11:24; 12:48; Acts 2:17; 2 Tim. 3:1; 2 Peter 3:3; 1 John 2:18). As the apostle Paul said, we are those "upon whom the ends of the ages have come" (1 Cor. 10:11). This can mean only that we live in the final age marking the history of salvation.

Fifth, the great apostasy cannot be something in the distant future from the perspective of the apostle, because he said that "the mystery of lawlessness" which causes this apostasy was already at work in his day (2 Thess. 2:7–9; and see 1 John 2:18, 22, and 4:3).

Sixth, no view can be correct which envisions a period of "good-without-evil" or the separation of the righteous from the wicked prior to the end of this age, because Jesus said, "At the end of this age . . . the Son of Man will send out His angels, and they will gather out of His kingdom all things that offend and those who practice lawlessness (Matt. 13:40–41, 49).

Finally, no view can be correct which envisions Christ's present reign as terminating before "He has put all enemies under His feet." "For He must reign till He has put all enemies under His feet" (1 Cor. 15:25) and "the last enemy that will be destroyed is death" (v. 26). It follows that entire victory will coincide with the defeat of death by the general resurrection. There can be no complete triumph of the kingdom of Christ until world history comes to an end.

We do not maintain that only postmillennialists or optimistic amillennialists are entitled to the name Christian. But we do believe that a premillennial view is difficult to harmonize with the clear teaching of Scripture and the Confession.

QUESTIONS

1. What basic truths must be held by those who rightly claim this Confession?
2. Cite Scripture proof for each of these truths.
3. What does "millennium" mean?
4. What are the three millennial views? (Give title and brief definition of each.)

5. What errors do you find (if any) in the chart depicting classical premillennialism?
6. What errors do you find in the chart depicting dispensational premillennialism?
7. What errors do you find in the chart depicting postmillennialism?
8. What errors do you find in the chart depicting amillennialism?
9. What, under whatever view, must be held by those entitled to be called adherents of the historic Christian faith?
10. Seven principles of Scripture can help guide us in discerning millennial errors. State as many of these as you can.

The Westminster Confession of Faith has been called both good and evil names. Certainly it enjoyed a wider loyalty in times past than it does today. And not a few who claim the Presbyterian *name* consider this standard to be an outworn relic of the past. With this conclusion we cannot agree. Even though we have only touched upon the vast field of truth unfolded in the Confession, we have tried to show two things: (1) the firm scriptural foundation of the teaching of this Confession, and (2) the relevance of this Confession for today.

Truth does not change. And advance in acquiring more of the truth of God does not come by disregard for, or contradiction of, that which the Lord has taught his Church in the past. If there is to be a new day of advance, in which the Church will again recover genuine zeal and faithfulness, we believe it must be brought about by raising up the banner of truth that is expressed in this Confession. It will not be to a lesser gospel than this Confession expresses that we can look for glorious conquest and victory. The need of the hour is not for new creeds—or still worse, no creeds—but rather, to recover the faith of our fathers as it is so wonderfully set forth in this statement of faith—the greatest of all Christian creeds.

It is for this grand purpose that this humble effort has been made. And we send it forth with the earnest prayer that it may be used to bring many to see the glorious heritage of our Presbyterian faith.

Answers to the Questions

Chapter 1: Of the Holy Scriptures (I)

I, 1

1. Two. Natural revelation (this is also called general revelation, given to all men) and word revelation (this is also called special revelation, given only in the Bible).
2. Ps. 19:1–3; Rom. 1:20.
3. Yes. Everywhere in everything. (There is nothing that does not testify of him.)
4. They assume a deficiency in natural revelation. (They say that natural revelation proves that a god possibly exists; in reality natural revelation shows that the true God certainly exists.)
5. His *being* and his *will*. (The being of man, like that of God, is not a matter of choice. But the purpose of man, like that of God, is voluntary.)
6. His voluntary (or willing) likeness to God.
7. His being in God's image (this is involuntary).
8. The purpose of man.
9. No. Because it contained no directive for the test of man's voluntary obedience.
10. The wrath of God (Rom. 1:18).
11. Yes. To lose the image of God would be to cease to be man.
12. Men suppress the truth by a sinful effort of their minds and hearts.
13. Because natural revelation does not disclose God's remedy for man's guilt and depravity (i.e., atonement and conversion of the heart).
14. They believe that the charismatic gifts that occurred in the age of the apostles are still occurring today.
15. To show that the prophets and apostles were God's spokesmen.

16. No. The Bible makes it clear that this process came to completion in the finished work of Christ and the apostolic testimony.

I, 2–5

1. The proof is evidence. This evidence is partly (and primarily) within the Bible itself, and partly (and subordinately) external to the Bible.
2. (a) The Old Testament (by the testimony of its inspired writers) claims to be the Word of God.

   (b) The New Testament (by the testimony of its inspired writers) acknowledges the Old Testament to be the Word of God.

   (c) Christ promised divine inspiration to his apostles.

   (d) The apostles claimed the divine inspiration promised them by Christ.

   (e) The apostles recognized each other's writings to be inspired.
3. Authority cannot rest upon that which is subordinate to itself. (To put it another way, authority can rest only upon that which is greater than itself. The authority of God's Word can depend only upon God himself.)
4. That the authority of the Bible depends upon the authority of the Church. (Or, in other words, the authority of what God says depends upon the authority of what men say.)
5. By resting the proof of the authority of the Bible upon human reason, archaeology, or the like.
6. Primarily, and conclusively, in the Bible itself.
7. Because men are incapable of receiving the evidence aright. (This is because of their total depravity.)
8. No. It means that the Holy Spirit enables men to see the Bible for what it actually is—the inspired Word of God.

I, 6

1. John 14:6; Heb. 1:1–2; John 15:15; 2 Tim. 3:15–17; Rev. 22:18–19.
2. Acts 20:20, 27; Jude 3; 2 Tim. 3:16–17.
3. (a) The Bible would be exceedingly bulky if it contained rules for every particular instance of human need.

   (b) There would be no thought process in man (as God's image) corresponding to that of his Creator.
4. By universal principles that apply to all men in all times and places.

5.

	Circumstances	Principles
(a) Worship—	The exact hour of worship	The day of worship
	The exact order of worship	The elements of true worship
	The place of fellowship	The terms of fellowship
(b) Government—	The number of elders in a particular church	That there be two or more elders in each
	The exact system of delegation to presbytery and assembly	That there be presbyteries and general assemblies

6. The Fourth Commandment controls all circumstances relating to divine worship, and circumstances cannot be allowed to change the day of worship or duties of worship required by this commandment.

I, 7

1. That the Scripture is clear in meaning. It is not obscure. What it says it says with perfect accuracy. The difficulty in understanding Scripture is due to a condition in us, not to any defect in Scripture.
2. That the meaning of the Scripture is not clear in itself, but can be understood only by the interpretation of the Roman Catholic Church.
3. The Reformed view is that the creeds (what the Church says that the Bible says) are less than a perfectly clear expression of the truth, and therefore subordinate to the Scripture. The Romish view is that the truth is made clear and final only by the testimony of the Church.
4. No. There are things taught in Scripture that are hard to understand, but this is not due to any obscurity in the teaching of these things (doctrines), but rather to the character of the doctrines themselves. (For example, divine predestination and human responsibility are *clearly* taught in Scripture, but they are hard to understand.)
5. Study them diligently and persistently. Those who complain that Scripture is hard to understand usually, if not always, are unable to say that they have made a real effort to understand and to study them.
6. (a) All Christians are required to search the Scriptures.
   (b) The Scriptures are addressed to ordinary Christians, not just the learned.
   (c) The Scriptures are, by their own testimony, clear.

(d) The Scriptures require obedience because they are clear in what they teach.

7. The Bible should be studied in a translation that one can understand. It should be studied systematically. It should be studied with the help of other believers (so, of the historic creeds, etc.).

I, 8

1. There is only one Bible in the ultimate sense: the absolutely perfect, infallible, or inerrant Word of God.

2. It is that original text (the exact letters, words, sentences, etc.) written down by men under divine inspiration.

3. We do not now possess the original manuscripts upon which this text was written.

4. The modernist says that it is of no use to believe in such a text when we don't have it in our possession. (He fails to distinguish between the original manuscript, which has been lost, and the original text, which has not been destroyed.)

5. Yes. If the text of a copy were the same as the text of an original, it would be exactly as infallible as the original. (A photographic copy does not differ as far as the text is concerned.)

6. No. They were copied by hand by men who made mistakes.

7. (a) Each copyist made "his own" mistakes. Thus the copies made by others tend to differ with his at that point. In other words, copies agree in witnessing against each other's errors.
   (b) The Greek-speaking Church, through great familiarity, guarded the correct text against corruption.

8. We believe that the first factor is weightier, but we also believe that the second factor is a real one and is often neglected in accounting for the preservation of the true text of the Bible.

9. Because we now have mechanical means of reproducing the text and of preserving it without further corruption.

10. We actually possess the very words that God deposited in the text of the Bible by divine inspiration. (We do not say that every difficulty has been removed. We do say that almost all of the very words God inspired are known to us beyond all doubt. There is *not* some doubt about all words. There is, rather, no doubt about almost all words.)

I, 9

1. That it is self-interpreting.
2. Not in any practical sense.
3. True preaching of the Word of God is the interpretation of Scripture by Scripture. The minister proves the meaning of one text by constant reference to the rest of Scripture.
4. No, some portions of Scripture are more difficult to understand than others. No, the Scriptures are still self-interpreting. We must explain the more difficult portions of Scripture by comparison with that which is already clearly understood.
5. It denies, in effect, that Scripture has been clear to others before us.
6. Because they express the teaching of Scripture accurately.

I, 10

1. In Roman Catholicism the decisions of the Church are final. There is no right of appeal against them. In a Reformed church only the Bible has final authority, and anyone has the right of appeal to the Word of God from the decisions of the Church.
2. No. Only God can speak infallibly. The Church speaks with authority and value when it declares the Word of God.
3. No. Peter had no more authority than the other apostles and elders. The apostles and elders made the decision. The decision was based upon the Old Testament Scriptures and the revelation given to, and by means of, the apostles.
4. (a) 1 Cor. 11:23–26; (b) 2 Cor. 6:14–18; 2 Thess. 3:14.

Chapter 2: Of God, and of the Holy Trinity (II)

II, 1–2

1. Everywhere.
2. That God has no body like men. (He is not composed of material that is created.)
3. Scripture speaks of God by means of human expressions. Man's being is analogous to God's being; therefore, God can speak of himself by way of analogy.
4. That which cannot be communicated to (and shared by) the creature.

5. Those qualities or properties we ascribe to God (or man, as the case may be).

6. God is eternal, infinite, and unchangeable. He is omnipotent, omniscient, and omnipresent.

7. That which can be communicated to (and shared by) the creature.

8. Being, wisdom, power, holiness, justice, goodness, and truth.

9. No. God knows everything with an exhaustively complete and absolutely perfect knowledge. (It cannot be increased by further study, for example.)

10. Nothing. He is absolutely self-sufficient.

11. That God is absolutely independent, and that in comparison with him, all things are as nothing, man included.

II, 3

1. The doctrine of the Trinity is revealed by the events which took place after the Old Testament was written and before the New Testament was written. However, since the New Testament records these events, and the Old Testament prepared the way for these events, the doctrine of the Trinity is revealed to us in the Bible as a whole.

2. The Old Testament is a partial revelation of the true God, who is triune. This can be proved from scriptural data that are inexplicable by any interpretation other than a trinitarian interpretation.

3. Gen. 1:26 (Gen. 32:24–30; Ex. 23:20–25).

4. Ex. 23:20–21.

5. Isa. 9:6 (or 7:14).

6. Because each of the three persons manifested himself to the apostles as personally distinct, and yet as essentially one God.

7. That the three persons have one being; that the one being exists in three persons.

8.

	GOD THE FATHER	GOD THE SON	GOD THE SPIRIT
(a) *Names*	John 20:17	John 20:28	Acts 5:3–4
(b) *Attributes*	Matt. 6:8	John 2:24–25	1 Cor. 2:10–11
(c) *Works*	Prov. 16:4	John 1:1–3	1 Cor. 12:4–11
(d) *Worship*	Rev. 22:9	Heb. 1:6	Rev. 2:7

Chapter 3: Of God's Eternal Decree (III)

III, 1–2

1. A person acts according to purpose.
2. An eternal and unchangeable plan.
3. Eph. 1:11.
4. Matt. 10:29.
5. 1 Kings 22:1–40.
6. Acts 2:23 (and Acts 4:27–28).
7. Matt. 18:7 (also Acts 2:23; 4:27–28).
8. Phil. 2:13.
9. He is not forced to act against his will.
10. They are evil. All their actions are determined by their evil nature. They desire to do only evil because they are evil.
11. God has given them a new nature which is inclined to that which is good.
12. No, God cannot foresee that a thing actually will be until he has determined that it shall be. Nothing can have existence except God determine that it shall exist. (To say that God foresees what he has not determined is to say that he is not the only self-existent being.)

III, 3–5

1. Because of human perversity. (Sinful men do not like what Scripture teaches.)
2. Man deserves nothing but damnation.
3. The example of Jacob and Esau.
4. Everything. Nothing.
5. Since God chose Jacob and rejected Esau, though they were not different, and before they had done anything good or evil, it is proved that the whole basis for God's discrimination between them was in him, not in them.
6. Rom. 9:21.
7. God does not decide whom he will choose and whom he will reject on the basis of anything in them.
8. (a) That salvation is all of grace, and not of works at all.
   (b) That repentance and faith are given to sinners by God.
   (c) That men are dead in trespasses and sins.
   (d) That election is conditioned upon God's good pleasure.

9. Because it pleased him to do so.
10. In order to manifest his glory in the display of grace to some and justice to others.

III, 6

1. God promised that all on board ship would be saved from shipwreck and destruction. The inspired apostle said that all must remain aboard ship in order to be saved from destruction. All were saved from destruction. The means of their being saved from destruction was obedient compliance with the apostle's warning. God decreed that all would be saved from destruction and therefore also decreed what was necessary to realize this end (namely, obedience to Paul's warning).
2. It denies that God predetermines all things. (It denies that God predestines what I must do now, though it admits that God predestines what will happen to me later.)
3. The work of God (what God does) never contradicts the plan of God.
4. Because (a) Scripture does not say that Christ's death was intended for the salvation of all men, and (b) because the Scripture says that God will not actually save all men.
5. In the context these words are incorrect: "a ransom *for all*," "*free access to God for*," and "*though made for the sin of the world.*"
6. (a) Under the correct view (1858) the death of Christ secures eternal redemption.
   (b) Under the incorrect view (1925) Christ's death secures only "access to God for pardon and restoration." In other words, it makes such *possible*.
7. The teaching of the 1925 Confessional Statement in effect abolishes God because it teaches that the work of the Holy Spirit is not in harmony with that of Christ. (Christ works to save all; the Holy Spirit works to save some.)

III, 7–8

1. God has determined to pass them by (i.e., not to give them the gift of saving grace).
2. Because it pleased him to do so.
3. Because they have sinned and thus deserve damnation.

4. It has been abused by those who assert that the fault as well as the determination to punish the reprobate is in God. (Man's condition as well
as his disposition is attributed to God.)

5. Because many are unwilling to accept God as he has revealed himself
to be, that is, as absolutely sovereign.

6. Yes.

7. No. He has absolute right to do as he will with creatures he has made,
especially in view of their sin.

8. John 3:36. God's sovereign discrimination concerns those who are
already under his wrath and curse. His discrimination concerns who
shall not be left in that condition.

9. Yes. Because it is taught in the Scripture. With special care and prudence, that is, accurately, fully, and with concern to refute erroneous
impressions.

Chapter 4: Of Creation (IV)

IV, 1

1. The Triune God.

2. (a) That the universe is self-existent.

(b) That it was not created out of nothing.

(c) That the present form of things is the result of an evolutionary
principle.

(d) That there is no ultimate reason for things beyond things themselves.

3. No. Because it is not the truth.

4. The truth is that which really is (or was, or will be).

5. In nature and in Scripture.

6. (a) That fossils were produced very slowly.

(b) That the Bible does not allow the necessary time after its story of
creation to account for these fossils.

(c) That the Bible necessarily teaches that the days of creation were
ordinary (twenty-four-hour) days.

(d) That God did not create (in six twenty-four-hour days) with the
appearance of age.

7. (a) The fossils *may* have been produced suddenly (as by the flood).

(b) The Bible does not say how long a time elapsed between creation and
later events.

(c) Orthodox Bible scholars have shown that the Hebrew word for "day" does not always mean a twenty-four-hour period.

(d) God may have created the whole world suddenly, and with the appearance of age. God certainly did so create Adam.

8. We believe that it refers to days similar to ours (not vast stretches of time).

9. The Hebrew term for "day" sometimes denotes an indefinite period of time.

10. We believe that the first chapter of Genesis was written so as to give the impression that creation took place in a supernatural rather than in a time-consuming natural process.

IV, 2

1. The Bible and evolutionists superficially agree in teaching (a) that man is the highest (known) creature, (b) that the higher forms of life came after the lower, and (c) that the whole human race has come from one pair.

2. Because these propositions are held for totally different reasons.

3. No. Since all of God's works are the expression of perfect wisdom, we would expect similarity in the different things God has created.

4. That the human species is derived or evolved from some prior lower species the Christian cannot admit.

5. No. Because the Scripture clearly states that man's spirit came directly from God, and that the fusing of this spirit with matter made man a living soul.

6. That it was on an animal level (cavemen are depicted as animal-like).

7. That it was exalted. It was higher than any subsequent life known to sinful men in this present world.

8. It was not technical or composite. It was not accumulated or highly developed.

9. Because they could not well believe that nature could simultaneously produce identical "accidents."

10. Because of the Scripture teaching that God created just one man and one woman.

11. Man *is* the image of God. (Perhaps also: the soul is the image of God, if the soul means man's physico-spiritual nature. Man became a living soul.)

12. Because of the influence of the ancient error teaching that spirit is good and matter is evil.

13. Diversity. (Man has one personality, but various faculties—mind, heart, and will.)
14. Yes, the Scriptures teach that man is a rational, emotional, volitional personality (Isa. 1:18; Acts 24:25; Col. 3:9–10; Rom. 12:10; Matt. 26:39; John 1:13).

Chapter 5: Of Providence (V)

V, 1
1. Chance. Fate.
2. Arminians also believe that things happen by chance, that is, for no necessary reason.
3. Prov. 19:21; 21:1.
4. There is no "chance" that God will do evil. He cannot do so because it is contrary to his nature.
5. Because the actions of men are determined by their character.
6. Fate is mechanical (things must happen a certain way, but not for a reason), while divine sovereignty is purposive.
7. (a) That God created all things.
   (b) That God has perfect foreknowledge.
   (c) That God is all-powerful (omnipotent).
   (d) That God is free to do as he will.
8. Dan. 4:35; Ps. 135:6; Eph. 1:11.

V, 2–7
1. (a) If God controls everything, then I am not responsible for what I do.
   (b) If God controls everything, then things will work out the same no matter what I do.
   (c) If God controls everything, then he must be the author of sin.
   (d) If God controls everything, then there is no explanation for the evil in good men and the good in evil men.
2. (a) God is able to control everything, including our free acts, without destroying our genuine liberty.
   (b) God controls everything; therefore all things must work out as he has planned, and this includes the things I do.
   (c) God is able to control those who author sin without himself being the author of sin.

(d) It is because God controls everything that we can account for the evil in good men (which God permits for good reasons), and the good in evil men (which God causes for good reason).

3. Because God permits a temporary resurgence of indwelling sin as a chastisement and warning.

4. Because God sometimes enables the conscience of the unbeliever to overrule him.

5. No. The Christian *was* the old man, he *is* the new man. However, sinful effects from the old nature remain with the new man.

6. Yes. It is the (new) *man* that sins, even though the source of that sin is not the *new* man.

7. No. The figure attempts to indicate only the basic character of men. (All actions of a regenerate man, for example, are affected by the remaining imperfection.)

8. Romans 7:20 traces the source of sin to the remnants of Paul's former nature. Romans 7:24 blames the execution of the sinful act upon Paul himself.

9. It emphasizes that God's providential control works all things together for the redemptive good of those who love God.

Chapter 6: Of the Fall of Man, of Sin, and of the Punishment Thereof (VI)

VI, 1–2

1. Because of the wide acceptance of neo-orthodoxy, a theology which denies the historical basis of the Christian faith.

2. The new orthodoxy.

3. The older modernism or rationalism.

4. Because it attacked the old modernism and used a terminology that sounded orthodox.

5. It separates doctrine from historical fact. It denies that what the Bible says actually happened in this world did actually happen in this world.

6. It means that it symbolizes something. (It is not literally true but only a sign of that which is true.)

7. Because it desires (a) to have the appearance of historic Christianity, and (b) to have the appearance of scientific credibility.

8. (a) They had to accept the Bible and lose standing in the modern world, or else (b) maintain a scientifically credible view of the Bible, and lose its historical trustworthiness.

9. They managed to adopt the second alternative and yet make it sound as though they had also adopted the first alternative.

10. It denies that the fall of man was due to the act of a real individual. It seeks to place the fall "behind" history as Adam did.

11. (c)

12. The extent of the damage is complete in fallen human nature, but not the degree of the damage. (The degree is becoming worse and worse in the reprobate, and will finally be absolute.)

13. No. All that he does issues out of that which has been corrupted by sin.

VI, 3–4

1. (a) Adam sinned and fell, becoming totally depraved.

   (b) In Adam we sinned, fell, and became totally depraved.

   (c) We are therefore born in sin.

   (d) Death therefore reigns over us.

2. It is difficult to understand how we can be guilty and depraved by the act of another person.

3. The Scripture says that God does only what is right, and that God has condemned us for the sin of Adam.

4. The Bible teaches that we are not merely individuals, but also members of an organism or corporate body—the human race.

5. That it comes directly from God (at the time of conception, or later).

6. That it comes indirectly from God in the same reproductive chain as does the body. (Parents beget both body and soul of their child.)

7. The traducian view seems preferable because (a) Adam is said to have begotten in his own image and likeness (Gen. 5:3), (b) the souls of offspring are said to have been in their fathers (Heb. 7:10), and (c) there seem to be inherited traits of the mind as well as of the body, not the least of which is sinful inclination.

8. The representative principle.

9. Because only in his first sin did Adam act officially (as a representative).

10. They are all effects of the first sin.

VI, 5–6

1. No. The believer is only a new man.

2. 2 Cor. 5:17 ("If anyone is in Christ, he is a new creation; old things have passed away; behold, all things have become new").

3. Perfectionism teaches that a believer may be perfectly free from all sinning (or at least from all conscious sinning) in this life.

4. Antinomianism teaches that the believer need not strive to be perfect because the sins he commits are the responsibility of "his old nature."

5. 1 John 1:8, 10; James 3:2 ("We all stumble in many things").

6. Rom. 7:14; 1 John 3:4; 1 John 1:8, 10 ("If we say that we have no sin, we deceive ourselves").

7. Indwelling sin has dominion in the unregenerate man; in the regenerate man it does not.

8. Antinomianism.

9. Because there is greater reason for the believer to overcome sin.

10. Antinomian practice (sinning because we are not concerned with overcoming sin) is willful sin.

Chapter 7: Of God's Covenant with Man (VII)

VII, 1

1. That he is a mere creature.

2. Even Reformed Christians have sometimes spoken in such a way as to suggest that man has certain inalienable claims upon God.

3. They have sometimes described covenants between God and man as a mutual agreement rather than as a sovereign imposition made by God alone.

4. Nothing.

5. God is bound only by his own promises in his covenants with men.

6. God institutes his covenants unilaterally.

VII, 2–3

1. Because the elements of such a covenant are clearly revealed in Scripture.

2. (a) Such a covenant is not formally stated in Scripture (nor the precise phrase itself used).
   (b) The designation "covenant of works" suggests that man's works could merit something from God and thereby obligate him.

3. (a) A thing need not be formally stated, nor need a term be used in Scripture, to have validity. (The doctrine of the Trinity is an example of this fact.)

(b) When the doctrine of the covenant of works is carefully stated, there will be no danger of this unwarranted inference.

4. It focuses upon the fact that the works of man were the means of, and condition for, the fulfillment of the gracious provisions of the first covenant.

5. God did not ask man's permission before instituting this covenant. It was determined by God's will, and not by mutual agreement.

6. The Arminian conception of the condition of the covenant of grace is that certain works of man are the means of, and condition for, the fulfillment of it.

7. The Reformed conception of the condition of the covenant of grace is that the work of God (wrought for us and in us) is that which secures fulfillment.

VII, 4–6

1. The basic error of dispensationalism is the tendency to teach an essentially different way of salvation in different periods of history.

2. Periods of Bible history in which a particular way of dealing with men was in evidence.

3. Not if by dispensations we mean periods in which the one way of salvation was administered with the limitations imposed by the development of the progress of redemption.

4. The Reformed Christian means a period in which the one way of salvation was administered in a certain way.

5. A change in the administration of grace (the means by which grace is administered).

6. (a) There is but one Church extending through all ages.
   (b) The Old Testament ordinances (circumcision and the Passover) administered the same grace as do the New Testament ordinances (baptism and the Lord's Supper).

Chapter 8: Of Christ the Mediator (VIII)

VIII, 1

1. Christ is the last person in history to act as a covenant head or representative, as Adam was the first.

2. The offices of prophet, priest, and king.

3. Because of man's depravity and inability. (Men were no longer personally able to render unto God that which each of these offices exemplified.)
4. (a) Abraham.

    (b) Moses.

    (c) There has been no prophet since the coming of Christ and completion of the Bible.
5. (a) Melchizedek.

    (b) There is no record of his beginning or termination of days.

    (c) Aaron.
6. (a) Saul.

    (b) Gen. 17:6—to Abram.

    (c) It was the will (decree, or secret purpose) of God that Israel have kings, but contrary to the will (revealed in commandments) of God that Israel desire and secure them as they did.
7. (a) As a prophet he teaches us God's (revealed good pleasure or) will.

    (b) As a priest he atoned for our sins and intercedes for us.

    (c) As a king he rules us and all things for us and his own glory.
8. Christ's prophetic and priestly offices. (They do not accept his Word as infallible, nor do they believe in his substitutionary atonement.)
9. Christ's kingly office. (They believe that Christ does not yet rule over all.)
10. By acting as if one could honor God without doing so by the mediation of Christ.

VIII, 2

1. Christ promised that there would be conflict and said that his truth causes it.
2. The Word of God.
3. Error and deception whereby error is made to seem truth.
4. The conflict was not centered on any one aspect of the truth, but was general, touching the Christian faith as a whole.
5. The doctrine of the Trinity.
6. The Council of Nicea in 325 and the Council of Constantinople in 381.
7. The Council of Chalcedon in 451.
8. Two, the divine and the human.
9. One.
10. Because the Second Commandment forbids it. Those who argue that it is proper to do so because Christ has a human nature virtually repeat

the Nestorian error, which teaches that there are two Christs: a divine Christ which cannot be depicted, and a human Christ which can be depicted.

11. Such texts as Acts 20:28 show that the apostles held firmly to the unity of Christ's person. (They believed the human Christ to be divine, the divine Christ to be human.)

VIII, 3

1. Because he had a real human nature.
2. No. Because there were operations of the Spirit enabling them to perform their office apart from operations pertaining to their personal salvation.
3. He was sinless and thus did not need or receive the Holy Spirit for personal salvation from sin. He did receive the Holy Spirit in order that he might be equipped to do his official work.
4. Prayed, suffered, was tempted, died.
5. Suffering an infinite penalty, rising again from the dead, defeating all his and our enemies, sending the Holy Spirit.
6. The diverse requirements must be met by one representative person.

VIII, 4

1. Heb. 2:12–17.
2. God can predestine that which is performed voluntarily even by sinful men; how much more that which is performed by Christ who was without sin (whose will was never in conflict with the will of God).
3. His birth, poverty, subjection to the law (ceremonial as well as moral), misery, curse, and death.
4. His resurrection, ascension, mediatorial reign, coming again at the last day, and judging the world.
5. Yes, in every detail.
6. His coming to judge the world.

VIII, 5

1. That Christ's death was designed, appointed, or intended to secure the salvation of a definite (or limited) number of men.
2. Definite or particular atonement.
3. That some, and not all, will actually be saved.

4. The design of it (what God purposed to provide in it and accomplish by it).

5. The opposing view limits the atonement as to what it is designed to effect and what it does effect.

6. In order to extend the atonement to a greater number it was forced to reduce or weaken the actual effect of the atonement.

7. Salvation (i.e., pardon, restoration, righteousness, forgiveness).

8. John 6:37, 39; Rom. 8:29–30.

9. Heb. 2:9; 1 Tim. 4:10.

10. Christ's sacrifice secures certain limited temporal benefits for all men, and certain unlimited and eternal benefits for some men.

11. (a) Regard for context.

    (b) Distinction between general and absolute statements.

    (c) Distinction between common and special grace.

VIII, 6–8

1. No. Ps. 51:16; Heb. 9:9.

2. Christ, by his Holy Spirit.

3. John 10:16.

4. All men who hear the Word. Matt. 11:28; 20:16.

5. All who accept the offer of salvation will be saved. John 6:37.

6. Because they are depraved and unwilling to accept it.

7. Because God enables them to accept it. (He gives them a new heart inclined to desire salvation on God's terms.)

Chapter 9: Of Free Will (IX)

IX, 1–5

1. That it denies free will.

2. Liberty (i.e., being permitted to do as we please).

3. Ability to do good or evil irrespective of our natures.

4. Liberty and ability.

5. We have complete liberty and total inability.

6. Character (the moral condition of one's being).

7. In every estate man is at liberty to do good or evil.

8. In the estate wherein he was created (i.e., before the fall), and in the estate of glorification.

9. In man's present fallen estate, and in the final estate to which the wicked will be brought.

10. Gen. 6:5; Jer. 13:23; John 6:44.

11. God has not yet finished his work in the regenerate man in this life.

Chapter 10: Of Effectual Calling (X)

X, 1–2

1. (a) *Calling*—God's free offer of grace in the gospel to all.

   (b) *Regeneration*—creation of a new heart in the elect enabling them to receive the gospel.

   (c) *Conversion*—the exercise of the newly regenerated heart in responding to the gospel by repentance and faith.

   (d) *Justification*—the act of God declaring such to be righteous before him.

   (e) *Adoption*—the act of God conferring the status of sons upon them.

   (f) *Sanctification*—the work of God the Spirit enabling them to persevere more and more in faith and good works unto holiness.

   (g) *Glorification*—the act of God by which the believer is at last constituted perfect in body and soul.

2. The first two. (Conversion is the response which proves that the call is effectual.)

3. All men.

4. All those ordained of God to hear the gospel.

5. Because God had ordained that his elect people there should hear the gospel.

6. The elect and those who are not elect, i.e., the reprobate.

7. Because of their spiritual condition.

8. (a) Prevenient.

   (b) Monergistic.

   (c) Mysterious.

   (d) Sovereign.

   (e) Effectual.

9. Birth, creation, resurrection.

10. None.

11. Man's moral and spiritual nature.

12. Accept or receive it.

13. It makes the activities of the natural man decisive in salvation by making regeneration an effect of human activity rather than the cause of all saving activity performed by man. (It says conversion precedes regeneration, whereas it is really the other way around.)

X, 3

1. Elect infants dying in infancy, and other elect persons incapable of being outwardly called.
2. More.
3. Because it does not make regeneration dependent upon man's ability.
4. Luke 18:15–16.
5. It does not presume to declare that all infants dying in infancy are elect.
6. That all infants dying in infancy are elect.
7. The guilt of all, and the just liability of all to eternal damnation.
8. No. None deserve to be.

X, 4

1. (a) Those who do not hear the gospel.
   (b) Those who do hear the gospel but do not accept it.
   (c) Those who hear the gospel and accept it.
2. Yes. 2 Peter 3:9; Ezek. 18:32.
3. A person may have been enlightened and may have tasted the good word of God and the powers of the age to come (Heb. 6:4–5).
4. They are not willing.
5. No. Man's depravity and inability are the results of his own sin.
6. They only.
7. God only.
8. No.
9. Because those blessings are an effect of the gospel.
10. That they may "save" men as truly as Christianity "saves."
11. Acts 4:12; 1 John 5:12.

Chapter 11: Of Saving Faith (XIV) and Of Repentance unto Life (XV)

XIV, 1–3; XV, 1–5

1. The Confession first discusses what God does, then what man does by way of response.
2. After effectual calling (calling and regeneration) and before justification.

3. Regeneration is the source of conversion (repentance-faith); conversion is the effect of regeneration and calling.
4. No. Because they are two aspects of one great change (or transformation) of the heart, mind, or soul.
5. Because it involves all the faculties of the soul (reason, emotion, will) and is both a turning from sin and a turning to Christ.
6. Reason, affection, will.
7. Repentance and faith.
8. (a) Revival-meeting conversion—insufficient knowledge.
   (b) Conversion to dead orthodoxy—no feeling.
   (c) Spectator religion—no change of the will.
9. Because the ability and inclination manifest in repentance and faith are created or begun in regeneration.
10. Constant conditions.

XIV, 1–3; XV, 1–5 (continued)

1. Inward sorrow for sin, and turning from sin unto God.
2. Satisfaction—or some painful work imposed by the priest and performed by the penitent to satisfy divine justice for sins committed.
3. Recognition of, conviction of, and assent to the fact that there is no possible way in which the sinner can satisfy divine justice (except by eternal damnation).
4. That the natural man is not totally depraved and unable to do good.
5. It regards repentance as a meritorious work.
6. That repentance is precisely the opposite of an act of obedience well-pleasing to God. It is, rather, conscious realization of the inability to please God.
7. Human ability and merit.

XV, 6

1. No. It actually reduces the scope of this duty very much.
2. (a) In its recognition that all sin must be confessed to God.
   (b) In its concern with *sin* (corruption, depravity) even more than *sins*.
   (c) In its requirement that sinfulness and sins be continually mourned.
3. Yes. To remove God's wrath and our sinfulness and guilt.
4. Because of his own corruption and guilt.
5. Because of his true humanity. (He was tempted in all points as we are, and in our nature, yet without sin.)

6. Because he did not sin, though human, and because of his infinite power as God.
7. Those sins which are committed against men. (They are still against God.)
8. Those sins which are committed only against God and ourselves.

Chapter 12: Of Justification (XI)

XI, 1–2
1. All the benefits of redemption belonging to the elect.
2. How a sinful man can be just with God.
3. The extent and magnitude of our guilt and depravity.
4. God.
5. To be, or become, personally and inherently good, holy, or sinless.
6. No. They will be made holy by sanctification (completed at death).
7. It is instantaneous.
8. To declare one to be righteous. Deut. 25:1; Luke 7:29.
9. Because it concerns the judgment which is declared.
10. Yes. Because they cannot provide a just and legal basis for such a declaration.
11. No. Because God can and does provide a just and legal basis for such a declaration.
12. Double imputation.
13. To reckon, think, or regard.
14. (a) That our sin and guilt are reckoned or regarded as belonging to Christ.
    (b) That Christ's righteousness is reckoned or regarded as belonging to us.
15. Because we have no righteousness of our own that is acceptable to God.
16. Yes. Because trust in Christ and his righteousness is all that God requires of those whom he justifies (not apart from repentance, of course).
17. No. Because those who have true faith also have grace productive of good works.

XI, 3–6
1. (a) God permitted a substitute to take our place.
   (b) God gave his only begotten Son to take our place.
   (c) God chose many to be represented by Christ.
   (d) God bestows the benefits of Christ upon them.

2. The erroneous view which teaches that the elect have never been unjust before God.

3. The distinction between the eternal plan of God and the execution of that plan in time.

4. The erroneous view which teaches that the elect have all been just in God's sight from the time that Christ died.

5. The distinction between Christ's work done for us and the application of the benefits of that work to us.

6. When we believe. Gal. 2:16; Rom. 4:24.

7. Confusion of justification and sanctification.

8. Because a person made holy would not have the inclination to sin again.

9. The distinction between justification and sanctification.

10. No. Because (a) a justified person envisions justification together with the other benefits and effects of grace, and (b) a justified person regards the warnings and teachings of Scripture concerning God's dealings with his people (chastisement, etc.).

11. It falsely teaches that Old Testament believers were justified by works (or that this was expected of them).

Chapter 13: Of Adoption (XII)

XII, 1

1. God's decree, and all the benefits of Christ's redemptive work.

2. Eph. 1:5.

3. An act of God whereby believers are constituted members of the family of God.

4. No. The relationship between God and unbelievers is rather one of enmity and alienation. (The relationship of Satan and unbelievers is properly denoted as a father-and-son relationship.)

5. No. The relationship between unbelievers is no longer one of trust, love, and mutual affection.

6. The relationship of intimate love, loyalty, and esteem.

7. Christ's sonship is eternal, by generation from the Father, such as constitutes him equal with the Father in power and glory. Our sonship is begun in time, by adoption, such as does not decrease the infinite distinction between us and God.

8. This difference increases the wonder of adoption, because we are joint heirs with Christ in spite of the infinite difference between ourselves and Christ.

9. No. Because prayer is the activity and expression of sons of God.

Chapter 14: Of Sanctification (XIII)

XIII, 1–3

1. Sanctification is the continuation of (i.e., the nurture and development of) the new creation effected by regeneration.

2. Because of regeneration the believer is no longer under sin's dominion.

3. The power of sin has been broken and the dominion of the law has been established.

4. (a) That (only) some believers attain freedom from sin's dominion in this life.

   (b) That one may be justified without also having sin's dominion broken.

   (c) That complete victory over sin (or conscious sinning) is attainable in this life.

5. (a) Every believer is free from the dominion of sin (Rom. 6:14, 22).

   (b) All who are justified are free from the dominion of sin (Rom. 5:1; 6:1–2).

   (c) No one attains to complete victory over sin in this life (1 John 1:8, 10).

6. The Holy Spirit.

7. No. Because the Holy Spirit works in us in order that we might have the will and desire to work out our salvation with fear and trembling.

8. The relation is that of cause and effect: the Holy Spirit's work is the ultimate cause, and our work is really the effect of the Holy Spirit's work as it is the means by which he sanctifies us.

9. The diligent use of the Word of God (reading and hearing), the sacraments, prayer, and church discipline.

Chapter 15: Of Good Works (XVI)

XVI, 1–2

1. Anything done out of common "charity" or "kindness."

2. (a) The work must be defined as a good work by the Word of God, and

   (b) it must be done with sincerity of conscience and right purpose.

3. Because the unbeliever's conscience is not under the control of the Word of God, and because he frequently violates his own conscience.

4. Yes. Because the act is not performed out of conscious and sincere obedience to the Word of God.

5. Because the conviction of conscience is not under control of the Word of God, and the sincerity is not that of seeking to please God.

6. Because of imperfect conformity of the conscience to the Word of God.

7. One who sincerely believes a thing to be wrong which God has not actually declared to be wrong.

8. We should not induce a weaker brother to do anything against his own conscience.

9. We should seek to convince him of his error, thus educating his conscience by the Word of God.

10. Because God alone is Lord of the conscience. (Voluntary abstinence from the use of a material thing to avoid tempting a weaker brother to use it against his conscience is proper. But to make the erroneous conviction of that weaker brother a rule binding the consciences of others is wrong.)

11. Not in this life.

12. Sanctification is by means of the truth. (We are strong to the degree we conscientiously adhere to the truth as it is taught in the Word of God. We are weak when we are conscientious about that which is not taught in God's Word but which is taught only by our own false scruples.)

13. All true believers have a true desire to obey the Lord and to be subject only to his authority.

XVI, 3–6

1. That all is of God. That we can do nothing of ourselves.

2. Yes. But it is a God-given ability and power. It does not originate within the believer or come from his own nature.

3. By means of a mysterious operation whereby the truth is effectually applied to the activities of the soul.

4. Inability.

5. The reason for man's inability is that he sinned in Adam and fell with him in the first transgression.

6. Continually.
7. The feeling of reverence for and obligation to heed the commandments of God.
8. They may be (a) unconverted or (b) mistaken as to their notions of
   how the Spirit leads believers.
9. Through the actual performance of the duties which God commands.
10. Good works that go beyond what God requires.
11. That none has even come close to doing all that God requires (Ps.
    130:3).
12. Because we have union with Christ.
13. Those who have the greater gifts and attainments. Because they have
    received from God the ability to do all that they have done, and because
    they will also receive a greater reward. "For whoever has, to him more
    will be given, and he will have abundance" (Matt. 13:12).

XVI, 7

1. Acts or deeds performed by unbelievers which are, as far as the acts or
   deeds considered in themselves are concerned, the same as those performed by believers. (They are outwardly, externally wholly the same;
   and inwardly, or internally, wholly different.)
2. Yes. Because they are caused by God for good ends.
3. Because God brings certain influences to bear upon them which induce
   them to do these things. (These instrumentalities and their operation
   are commonly called "common grace.")
4. Because all that proceeds from the unbeliever in these works is evil.
5. Yes. Because the activities and purpose of God in effecting these works
   are wholly good.
6. Because the degree of his sinfulness would have been still greater without such responses to these influences.

Chapter 16: Of the Perseverance of the Saints (XVII)

XVII, 1–3

1. No. John 5:24; Jer. 32:40.
2. There are those who appear to be true believers who do fall away.
3. Such cases really prove that men may appear to be believers when they
   are not.
4. Because their salvation is wholly of God.

5. By making the saving effect of divine grace dependent upon the will of man.
6. Divine grace which is brought into effect by man's will can also, at any time, be put out of operation by man's will.
7. He knows that he possesses a salvation that he cannot lose.
8. No. This doctrine teaches that we will continue to strive if we have really believed.
9. No. Ps. 38:9–17.
10. Yes. Such believers as David and Peter did fall (into grievous sin).
11. The appeal of the world, the temptation of Satan, the corruption remaining in the believer's heart, neglect of the means of grace.
12. Divine displeasure, loss of comfort and assurance, dishonor to God and his truth, encouragement to the enemies of God, and temptation to others.
13. The record of the lapse of true believers is meant to teach us (a) the seriousness of such, (b) the danger of such, (c) the consequences of such, and (d) the way in which true believers will rise from such to continue striving against sin until death.

Chapter 17: Of Assurance of Grace and Salvation (XVIII)

XVIII, 1–2
1. Yes. Jer. 17:9; Gal. 6:3.
2. Because he thought that he was better than other men.
3. The Scripture does affirm that there is true assurance.
4. Yes. Heb. 6:11; 2 Peter 1:10.
5. The qualities and bases are different.
6. (a) Unfeigned humility (having a low opinion of oneself).
   (b) Diligence in the things of God.
   (c) Self-examination and a desire to be searched and corrected by God.
   (d) Unfeigned desire for increase of grace.
7. (a) Spiritual pride.
   (b) Sloth, neglect, indifference to duty.
   (c) Self-satisfaction.
   (d) Lack of aspiration for greater attainments in grace.
8. (a) The infallible certainty of God's Word.
   (b) The evidence of the possession of true grace in believers.
   (c) The joint testimony of the spirit of a believer and the Holy Spirit.

9. (a) The uncertain testimony of men.

    (b) The mere appearance of grace.

    (c) The testimony of one's own heart apart from that of the Holy Spirit.

10. Both are indispensable.

11. Some erroneously believe that the Holy Spirit reveals immediately *to* our spirits that we are saved. (We believe that this witness is by means of the Word.)

12. The Holy Spirit testifies that we are the children of God by enabling us to know (a) that his Word is sure, and (b) that his Word applies to us because we see undeniable evidence of true grace in ourselves.

13. It denies the sufficiency of the Word which he has inspired.

XVIII, 3–4

1. (a) The Bible nowhere states that one cannot be saved without assurance.

    (b) The Bible shows that true believers have sometimes lacked it.

    (c) The Bible contains exhortations to true believers to seek it.

2. Jesus Christ as he is freely offered in the gospel.

3. His faith and other graces.

4. All believers. Heb. 6:11.

5. Every believer who will give diligence to attain it.

6. Because it is in part the *product of* diligence and care.

7. Because believers may temporarily become neglectful, etc.

8. Ps. 88:14.

9. He continues to put his confidence and hope in God (and in Christ) alone.

10. Because true faith cannot fail.

11. Because the grace out of which it comes, and of which it is an effect, cannot cease to exist in a true believer.

Chapter 18: Of the Law of God (XIX)

XIX, 1–2

1. Pss. 19:7; 119:160; Prov. 6:23. The law is perfect because it is a revelation of God and of that duty imposed upon man as man. The law could cease to be obligatory only if God ceased to be God or if man ceased to be man.

2. Adam had the law written in his heart. He knew the law as a positive holy desire or inclination.

3. No. Man's relation to the law was changed by the fall.

4. (a) All men are able to condemn others for doing wrong.

    (b) All men possess the inward witness of conscience.

5. The Christian, above all, is obligated to keep the commandments (not as a means of obtaining righteousness before God, but as a means of expressing gratitude for having received the righteousness of Christ). Matt. 5:17–19; 1 John 2:4.

6. Love God above all. Love your neighbor as yourself.

7. (a) Only the true God is to be acknowledged, reverenced, and worshiped.

    (b) He is to be worshiped only as he commands in his Word. .

    (c) He is to be worshiped with sincerity.

    (d) He is to be worshiped one whole day in seven (works of piety, necessity, and mercy are acceptable).

8. (a) Union worship services with those who do not acknowledge Jesus Christ to be the one living and true God.

    (b) The use of ceremonies (such as a candle lighting service) unauthorized by God.

    (c) Worshiping God in proper form, but without earnest concentration.

    (d) The observance of "holy days," and the observance of Father's Day, etc. (i.e., making other than the Sabbath to be a "holy day," and making the Sabbath other than the Lord's Day).

9. No. Because God alone is the Lord of the conscience, and he has given only ten commandments. He has declared these sufficient (Pss. 19:7; 119:96).

XIX, 3–5

1. Ceremonial and civil.

2. To represent (by way of anticipation) the mediatorial work of Christ and the work of the Holy Spirit in applying the benefits of Christ to believers.

3. Col. 2:14; Eph. 2:13; Acts 15:5, 10.

4. To regulate the nation Israel during that era in which it was the instrument of messianic preparation. (After Christ came, the Church was no longer to be confined to one nation.)

5. Yes. (a) The manner in which the moral law was given, and (b) the statements of Old Testament believers (Ps. 40:6–8).

6. It did not make perfect those who observed it. It had to be repeated over and over (the symbolic sacrifices, etc.) because it was only symbolic.

XIX, 6–7

1. Rom. 6:14.
2. That they are free from all obligation to keep the Ten Commandments because they are "not under law."
3. It refers to being under terms or conditions of the covenant of works or covenant of grace, as the case may be.
4. It means to be under obligation to render perfect and perpetual obedience to God according to the Ten Commandments as a means of attaining life.
5. It means to be granted eternal life as a free gift on condition that one trust Christ to fulfill both the positive and negative demands of the law for him.
6. The free grace given to the unworthy sinner has a legal basis. Christ met the full demands of the law through his obedience in order that we might have life without first meeting the demands of the law (which would have made it impossible for us).
7. The law is of use to believers:
   (a) as a rule of practice,
   (b) as a constant reminder of their sin and unworthiness, ever increasing their repentance of sin and their faith toward Christ,
   (c) as a revelation of the excellency and glory of Christ and his work.
8. The law does good with respect to unbelievers in that it
   (a) justly condemns them,
   (b) warns them,
   (c) restrains them.

Chapter 19: Of Christian Liberty, and Liberty of Conscience (XX)

XX, 1

1. That man (whatever his moral and spiritual condition) is free to do as he will.
2. The regenerate man is free to do as he will, and also *able* to will and do God's will.
3. (a) The believer is free from the obligation to keep the law of God perfectly as the means of obtaining life.

(b) The believer is free from the dominion of sin.

(c) The believer is free from the evil consequences of sin.

4. God gives the believer a heart that is alienated from the world.

5. The believer is free from death (a) in that he does not receive the penal consequences of sin in death, and (b) because he will be raised from the grave as was Christ.

6. Liberty means freedom from sin. License means freedom to sin.

7. The Old Testament believer, like the New Testament believer, was free from (a) the obligation to keep the law of God perfectly as a means of obtaining eternal life, (b) the dominion of sin, and (c) the evil consequences of sin.

8. The Old Testament believer was not free, as we are, from the ceremonial law. He did not possess the same measure of grace as is ours with the completion of Christ's redemptive work and the outpouring of the Holy Spirit.

XX, 2–3

1. That God alone is Lord of the conscience.

2. No. Many kings sought to impose their own will upon the churches.

3. The separation of Church and State.

4. Yes. The increasing measure of federal control of education, including the insistence that the Christian interpretation of life be excluded from that education, is such a threat.

5. (a) By making rules contrary to the Bible.

   (b) By making rules additional to those contained in the Bible.

6. (a) Rules which forbid church members to use certain things (e.g., coffee).

   (b) The rule requiring baptism by immersion.

7. Because God has declared all things to be pure (that is, the use of any material thing is legitimate). See Rom. 14:14, 20.

8. Because it is not the *requirement* of God. Immersion is not a sin, but requiring immersion is a sin.

9. Because there is a tendency in each of us to desire to rule over the consciences of others.

10. We should exercise charity. We should place the best possible interpretation upon our brother's actions.

11. We should exercise great caution in the use of our own liberty, being careful to avoid all intemperance and all offense to a weaker brother.

XX, 3 (continued)

1. That it will lead to sin.
2. Because it is opposed to reducing man's duty from the perfect requirements God has laid down in the Ten Commandments.
3. (a) That which is forbidden by the Ten Commandments is evil; that which is not forbidden by the Ten Commandments is good.

   (b) A good thing is acceptable when it is done under circumstances that are not contrary to the Ten Commandments.

   (c) A good and acceptable thing is "perfect" when it is done with a motive or intent that is not contrary to the Ten Commandments.
4. Yes (depending upon the circumstances and intent with which an act is performed).
5. No. Because God would not declare it to be good if there were not circumstances in which those with a right motive could use that thing. (God declares as evil, and absolutely forbids, only that which is never good.)
6. Coffee is good because God has declared all things to be pure (Rom. 14:14, 20). It may be acceptable when it is used with moderation. It will be perfect if it is received with thanksgiving (1 Tim. 4:3).
7. Because man-made rules cover only a few things, whereas God's rules (laws) apply to all things, all circumstances, and every intention of the heart.

XX, 4

1. The authority of the Church and of the State (not to mention parental authority).
2. The State has the power and authority to maintain law and order. It is concerned with the outward behavior of citizens and nations. The Church has the power and authority to maintain truth and exclude error, promote godliness, and discipline sinners. It is concerned with what men believe and with their obedience to God's commandments.
3. There is persecution of true believers.
4. The Roman Catholic control of civil policies which oppresses Protestants in such countries as Spain and Colombia.
5. The Communist use of orthodox churches as instruments of the State.
6. Both Church and State are perverted and/or weakened by intrusion into or by the other.

7. No. No. All education must have a religious position, even if it is that of considering the true God as unimportant as far as education is concerned.

8. No. It speaks only of acts *destructive* of *external* peace and order.

Chapter 20: Of Religious Worship, and the Sabbath Day (XXI)

XXI, 1–2

1. God's enmity and man's alienation from God.

2. Instituted worship is worship that God has commanded.

3. It means that true worship consists only of what God has commanded or instituted.

4. Because they presumed to offer that which God had not commanded them to offer.

5. Two. Legitimate (commanded) and forbidden (not commanded).

6. Three. Two types of legitimate worship (what God has commanded and what God has not expressly forbidden), and one type of illegitimate worship (what God has specifically forbidden).

7. Worship which is offered only because it is man's will to offer it and not because it is God's will (command).

8. Things which cannot always be the same because of the natural situation, such as time and place of worship on the Lord's Day.

9. We must worship God on the Lord's Day as he has commanded us. We must do all things decently and in order.

10. God and certain creatures.

11. Highest and inferior; direct and indirect.

12. (a) God commanded us to worship only himself (in three persons).
    (b) Scripture forbids the worship of any creature.
    (c) The Second Commandment forbids the use of pictures and images.
    (d) The saints are incapable of mediation.
    (e) Christ is the only mediator.

13. Because they themselves often (and perhaps unwittingly) disregard the regulative principle of true worship.

XXI, 3–4

1. Gen. 20:7, 17; Num. 21:7; Pss. 4:1; 6:9; 17:1; Acts 1:14; 2:42; 1 Tim. 2:8; 1 Thess. 5:17; and Eph. 6:18.

2. Because he is the only mediator, and no prayer is acceptable except in his mediation.

3. John 14:6; Eph. 2:18; Col. 3:17.

4. Because God has not prescribed the use of the prayers written in Scripture.

5. Rom. 8:26–27. (These verses show that God has prescribed prayers that are formulated under the impulse and direction of the Holy Spirit.)

6. No. It means that we are led to pray according to the will of God.

7. Yes. In the Lord's Prayer.

8. No. Because some petitions concern the will of God revealed to us in Scripture. It is proper to say "if it be Your will" only when the petition concerns the unknown or secret purpose of God.

9. All men except those who are dead, and those of whom it may be known that they have sinned the sin unto death (1 Tim. 2:1–2).

10. The dead, and those who are known to have sinned the sin unto death (2 Sam. 12:22–23; Luke 16:26; 1 John 5:16).

11. Willful and deliberate blasphemy against the Holy Spirit. Deliberate and undeniable apostasy from Christ and the truth.

12. Evidently. John seems to indicate that it can be known (1 John 5:16).

XXI, 5–6

1. Prayer, reading of the Scripture, preaching, administration of the sacraments, church discipline, the singing of psalms, and the receiving of offerings.

2. Religious oaths and vows, thanksgiving, and fasting.

3. The preaching of the Word.

4. The Scripture tells us that Christ commanded them to be observed until he comes again.

5. The Psalms only (that is, the psalms, hymns, and songs of the Old Testament Psalter).

6. No. At one time it was the practice of virtually all Presbyterian and Reformed churches.

7. Because it had no proof that God commanded anything else to be sung in divine worship. (No one has yet proved that God has commanded anything but the psalms to be sung in divine worship.)

8. It safeguards the purity that is necessary to it.

9. When, as a part of worship, censure is applied. Also, when the Lord's table is opened only to those who make a credible profession of faith.

10. Formalism, elaborate liturgy, invented ceremonies, motion pictures, etc.

11. There is no other safeguard but the principle set forth in the Confession: what God has not commanded is forbidden.

12. No. Because (1) the ceremonial symbols have been abrogated with the ceremonial system, and (2) the ceremonial symbols were given by divine inspiration and so cannot give sanction to symbols that are merely of human origin.

13. Yes. Circumstances only (i.e., time, place, duration of service, etc.).

14. Elements of worship that are proper only on certain occasions imposed by the providence of God.

15. Because true fasting is motivated from within the heart and by divinely imposed circumstances.

XXI, 7–8

1. That the Fourth Commandment is Jewish or merely ceremonial.

2. (a) It was man's duty long before the ceremonial law or the Jewish nation was instituted. It was a duty imposed upon man at creation.
   (b) God inscribed this commandment with the other moral laws on tables of stone.
   (c) Christ observed this commandment.
   (d) The Apostolic Church observed this commandment.

3. No. He disregarded only the false views of the Pharisees concerning this day.

4. By proving from Scripture that they were correct.

5. Works of piety, necessity, and mercy.

6. The Pharisees served a legal system.

7. The disciples served the Lord.

8. That the Fourth Commandment requires the perpetual observance of the seventh day in the order of days as the Sabbath.

9. (a) The Fourth Commandment does not say, "remember the seventh," but "remember the Sabbath," and requires only that a seventh portion of our time be observed as the Sabbath.
   (b) The example of the Apostolic Church.

10. To cease from, or to rest.

11. The employments and recreations that are lawful on other days.

12. In the one the work itself is a necessity, in the other it is not.

Chapter 21: Of Lawful Oaths and Vows (XXII)

XXII, 1–4

1. That all oaths are forbidden by the Word of God.
2. Christ was really teaching that the Jews were wrong when they taught that only when men swore certain oaths were they obligated to keep their word.
3. No. He said that all oaths are (in one way or another) the result of the prevalence of untruthfulness. They come from evil.
4. That only some oaths were binding.
5. Christ himself took oaths.
6. Deliberate deceit in the making of an oath.
7. The system of doctrine contained in this Confession.
8. Perjury.
9. No. Because it is never right to do wrong even though we have promised to do wrong.
10. Yes. Ps. 15:4.

XXII, 5–7

1. An oath concerns what we say or promise to men. A vow concerns what we promise to God.
2. Both are made out of reverence for and obligation to God.
3. Ps. 116:12–14.
4. The vow of faith in obedience to Christ. In this vow the following are stated or implied:
   (a) Acknowledgment of the authority of God's infallible Word.
   (b) Confession of sin, guilt, and unworthiness, with trust in Christ.
   (c) Promise of obedience to Christ.
   (d) Promise of due submission to scriptural church discipline.
5. The vow of chastity, poverty, and obedience to an ecclesiastical superior.
6. A vow of total abstinence from the use of some material thing.
7. Because they are unable to make such vows in a proper way; that is, with (a) due consideration and awareness of the weightiness of so solemn an act, (b) persuasion that such a vow is according to the will of God, and (c) conviction that one is able and resolved to keep the vow.
8. Yes. Parents may bind their children by covenant vows that are in accordance with the Word of God. For example, children are under the covenant obligations of baptism.

Chapter 22: Of Marriage and Divorce (XXIV)

XXIV, 1–3
1. Gen. 2:18–25; Matt. 19:3–9.
2. Matt. 19:5.
3. No. Because Christ condemns it, and also points out that even though it was allowed by Moses, there was severe disapproval.
4. Tolerated as an unavoidable evil.
5. Approval.
6. (a) Satisfaction of sex desire.
   (b) Avoidance of uncleanness.
   (c) The begetting of a godly seed.
7. (a) That sex is intrinsically wrong.
   (b) That the satisfaction of sex desire is proper only when the purpose of it is to beget children.
8. The sinful neglect of the duty to bear children.
9. Two believers or two unbelievers (under proper circumstances).
10. A marriage between a believer and an unbeliever is valid once it has been contracted or consummated.
11. 1 Cor. 7:39; 2 Cor. 6:14–18.
12. No. Because there may be serious errors in a Christian's profession and life which would require the Reformed Christian to compromise if marriage were contracted. (For example, if a Reformed Christian woman married a Baptist, she might be forced to deny baptism to her children, and this would be sin.)

XXIV, 4–6
1. Lev. 18:6–18; 20:10–21.
2. Because the conditions envisioned by this legislation were not yet in existence.
3. Death.
4. Adultery.
5. Yes. Willful desertion of a believer by an unbeliever which cannot be remedied.
6. No. Because it is conceivable that a believer might desert a believer, and the Scripture does not say that a brother or sister is not bound in such cases.

7. Mental cruelty, incompatibility, extreme abuse, etc. The Christian can never lawfully secure a divorce on such grounds.

Chapter 23: Of the Church (XXV)

XXV, 1–2

1. The whole body of God's elect people.
2. Those who profess the true religion together with their children.
3. No. They are different aspects of the same Church.
4. The Church is "invisible" to us in the sense that we cannot (but God can) see who is elect. The church is "visible" to us in the sense that we can discern those who profess the true religion, and who maintain the faithful preaching of the Word, administration of the sacraments, and discipline.
5. Because of sin in believers and hypocrisy in unbelievers.
6. God has not ordained that it shall.
7. By (a) faithful preaching of the Word, (b) right administration of the sacraments, and (c) faithful exercise of church discipline.
8. We cannot infallibly determine who is elect. But we can be sure that where the three items in answer (7) are manifest, there is a true visible Church.
9. We identify the presence rather than the persons of true believers.
10. Yes. God has commanded all children of believers to be included as members of the visible Church, even though some (Esau) are not elect.

XXV, 3–6

1. Never.
2. When truth flourishes and error is minimal.
3. Error and sin.
4. (a) True preaching, (b) proper administration of the sacraments, and (c) faithful exercise of church discipline.
5. No. Some have apostatized (see Rev. 1–3).
6. When remaining in that church makes obedience to Christ impossible.
7. As long as one can do so without compromise, and with reasonable hope of bringing about a reformation. The following conditions are essential to this end:
(a) The denomination as a whole must still have the marks of a true church.

(b) There must still be freedom to contend for the truth.

(c) There must be an active contending for the truth.

8. (a) It is still possible to preach the fundamentals of the faith (that is, part of the faith).

(b) My particular church or presbytery is still "sound."

(c) There is hope that some day things might improve.

9. (a) The Bible requires the preaching of the whole counsel of God.

(b) If the whole church is not sound, then the local church is not sound unless it forsakes the denomination.

(c) There is no hope of improvement apart from separation where error has command.

10. No. Because it is our duty to belong to a true visible church. It is not our duty to belong to a church whether or not it is a true visible church.

11. One should bear witness against the error, and seek to arouse others to the knowledge of the truth.

XXV, 6 (continued)

1. Col. 1:18; Eph. 1:20–23.

2. The supremacy of the State over the Church in ecclesiastical matters.

3. It is more inclusive (i.e., it condemns not only the usurpation by the Roman pontiff, but also any others who claim headship of the Church).

4. John (in his first and second epistles).

5. Paul (in 2 Thessalonians).

6. "In the place of" or "in stead of."

7. Because there are antichrists as well as the Antichrist, and "the mystery of lawlessness . . . already at work" (2 Thess. 2:7) as well as "the man of sin."

8. No.

9. (a) Their view renders a verdict concerning the interpretation of only a few particular texts. (b) Exegetical work suggests that 2 Thessalonians and 1 and 2 John may actually refer to events then current.

Chapter 24: Of Communion of Saints (XXVI)

XXVI, 1–3

1. The life which is found in Christ is shared by the believer.

2. This life is nourished and sustained by the Holy Spirit.

3. It is known by divine revelation. We cannot fathom or explain this.

4. Union between the vine and its branches, the head and the members of the body, and husband and wife.
5. Communion (and union) with one another.
6. The whole body of believers.
7. Because they have obligations not only to Christ but also to the members of his body.
8. Yes. Because the work of the Church, growth of the body, care of the poor are the concerns of every member (1 Cor. 12:25).
9. Believers do not share in Christ's deity.
10. A Christian should use all that he has for the glory of God and the advancement of his kingdom, but this does not imply that he is to renounce what God has given him.
11. Acts 2:44.
    (a) God has not commanded the practice of "community of goods."
    (b) The apostles acknowledged the right of private property.
    (c) The apparent attempt in the Apostolic Church did not work out satisfactorily.

Chapter 25: Of the Sacraments (XXVII)

XXVII, 1
1. Because the term itself is not found in the Bible.
2. Trinity, incarnation, theology.
3. If the meaning of the term is clear and is in accordance with the teaching of Scripture, it is acceptable.
4. Something by means of which something else is made known.
5. Something by means of which something else is confirmed or declared authentic.
6. Moses' rod, the destruction of Jerusalem, the rainbow.
7. The king's seal on a document of State, the seal on a diploma.
8. A sign and seal.
9. The principle which maintains that true worship consists not only of what God has commanded, but also of what God has not forbidden (and which is instituted by men).
10. True worship consists of that only which God has commanded.
11. "To *represent* Christ and his benefits." (A sign is that which represents.)
12. "To *confirm* our interest in him." (A seal is that which confirms.)
13. Believers only.

XXVII, 2–5

1. That the sacraments contain grace and operate grace automatically.
2. 1 Peter 3:21; Acts 22:16.
3. 1 Peter 3:21 (when carefully analyzed); Titus 3:5.
4. Sacramental union (between the sign and the thing signified).
5. The union of Christ's two natures.
6. Whether God saves men himself, or whether men acting in his name and clothed with his power do this.
7. Because grace is supposed to be automatically conferred by the sacraments.
8. Because this operation is supposed to be dependent upon (a) the intention of the one who administers the sacrament, and (b) the disposition or motive of the one who receives the sacrament. (Either can void the operation of grace.)
9. It acknowledges the sovereign and immediate grace of God. That is, the will of Christ is alone determinative, and the sacraments are subordinate to his grace.
10. Because otherwise many would have no "chance" to receive grace.
11. Because (a) Scripture warrants no other view, and (b) because salvation is not dependent upon the sacraments.
12. (a) Each is administered but once.
    (b) Each is administered to infants of believers as well as believers.
    (c) Each signifies union with Christ, cleansing from sin, and justification.
    (d) Each is received passively.
13. (a) Each is administered often (repeatedly).
    (b) Each is administered only to adults (believers, not their children).
    (c) Each signifies union with Christ, nourishment, growth in him.
    (d) Each is actively received.
14. He calls Old Testament ordinances by New Testament names and vice versa.

Chapter 26: Of Baptism (XXVIII)

XXVIII, 1–2

1. (a) Scripture calls baptism a *figure of* that which saves us.
    (b) Scripture records the divine command to administer baptism.
2. Union with God through Jesus Christ, and all that pertains to this.

3. Union with Christ (and God through him).

4. Regeneration, remission of sins, newness of life, justification, the duty of new obedience.

5. Because there can be no union with Christ apart from any of these.

6. Baptism and the Lord's Supper represent in nonverbal form the same saving grace that is verbally set forth in Scripture and in the faithful preaching of the gospel.

7. Because union with Christ and the other persons of the Trinity is not the result of human activity.

8. Because they believe that only adults are capable of performing that activity which they believe to be symbolized by baptism.

9. The ultimate objection to the Baptist view is that baptism is not a symbol of what believers do, but of what God has made them to be.

10. No. It is a representation of that living union effected by his activity.

11. Matt. 28:19–20.

XXVIII, 3–4

1. Because they believe that the word "baptize" (*baptizō*) means "to immerse."

2. By speaking of baptism as if it were not true baptism but only "christening."

3. By Scripture passages where the term is used in a context in which we know that immersion did not take place (e.g., 1 Cor. 10:2; Heb. 9:10).

4. No.

5. (a) That children are not capable of experiencing or doing that of which baptism is a sign.

   (b) That the Bible does not show that infants should be baptized.

6. (a) Baptism is not a sign of what a believer does, but of what God makes him to be. Scripture says that children (even tiny infants) are members of the kingdom; therefore, they have that of which baptism is a sign.

   (b) The Bible does show that infants should be baptized.

7. (a) Peter's appeal to the Jews (Acts 2:38–39).

   (b) The Bereans tested Paul's teaching by the Old Testament (Acts 17:11).

   (c) The apostle Paul declares the children of believers (even in mixed marriages) to be holy.

XXVIII, 5–7

1. Because it is an ordinance of Christ.
2. Ex. 4:24–26; Luke 7:30.
3. Yes. Because sin is transgression of the law (divine commandment) and not merely transgression of conscience.
4. A person may be saved without it.
5. Knowing what God commands and then deliberately failing to do what he commands.
6. Luke 23:39–43.
7. Esau; Simon (Acts 8:13, 23).
8. Esau.
9. Because God commanded that the sign be given to the children of believers.
10. Jacob.
11. Effectual calling and baptism.

Chapter 27: Of the Lord's Supper (XXIX)

XXIX, 1

1. In three Gospels (Matthew, Mark, and Luke) and in 1 Corinthians.
2. On the night in which Christ was betrayed; at the time of the Passover.
3. Often.
4. Until he comes. 1 Cor. 11:26.
5. Remembrance of the one sufficient sacrifice of Christ.
6. The elements, the words of institution, and the sacramental actions.
7. No. It conveys assurance of that grace.
8. That the work of grace in a believer is continual.
9. They must discern the Lord's body.
10. The distribution of the one (loaf and cup) to the many (believers).

XXIX, 2

1. The sacrifice of the mass.
2. The sacrifice of the mass.
3. Because the victim is the same and the principal priest is the same.
4. Often. Once. Heb. 9:26, 28.
5. Because he is physically absent from the world and will be until he returns at the end of time.
6. The use of the past tense when the apostles refer to his sacrifice.

7. Christ's finished work.
8. The Church, the priest, and the sacrament.
9. To the extent that they trust in Rome's doctrines rather than in Christ.

XXIX, 3–4

1. Unleavened bread and fermented wine.
2. The Bible is silent on this matter; perhaps other types of bread and wine may be used under necessity.
3. Because they subscribe to the erroneous view that wine is evil per se.
4. Either (a) that Christ used unfermented grape juice, or (b) that Christ erred in ignorance.
5. Because this was what Christ used, and because it is the duty of the Church to testify against the erroneous view that wine is evil per se.
6. Luke 22:17; Mark 14:23.
7. Because (a) Christ instituted the sacrament in a gathering of saints, (b) the Apostolic Church administered the sacrament in a gathering of such believers, (c) the Lord's Supper is an expression of the communion of the saints, and (d) the sacraments are not to be separated from the preaching of the Word and administration of church discipline.
8. Because a church building is not "the church"—believers are.
9. Yes, provided other believers are assembled there, and provided the Word was preached and discipline maintained.

XXIX, 5–7

1. The sign and the thing signified.
2. The union of Christ's two natures.
3. The bread and wine. The bread and wine.
4. The change of one substance into another.
5. The changing of water into wine.
6. The bread and wine are adored as the very body and blood of Christ who is deity.
7. The addition of one substance to or with another.
8. That Christ's human nature is (or may be) everywhere.
9. John 16:7, 28.
10. It has the effect of denying the true human nature of Christ.
11. Spiritually.
12. There is no difference.

XXIX, 8

1. Judas may have received the last supper, which, if so, would be proof. But the warning of Paul (1 Cor. 11:29) leaves no doubt.
2. 1 Cor. 11:27–29.
3. Anyone is permitted to come to the Lord's table who, in his own estimate, is able to do so.
4. (a) Christ did not administer the sacrament to any but those who had professed the true religion, and who appeared to walk with him.
   (b) In the Apostolic Church, instruction, baptism, and credible profession were required of those who received this sacrament.
   (c) There are commands in Scripture to put away unbelievers and disorderly believers.
5. No one is permitted to come to the Lord's table except the members of the church (or denomination) administering the sacrament.
6. Because no single denomination is the only true Church.
7. Communion which is administered to all those who are able to present credible evidence of Christian faith and life, and those only.
8. (a) No unbeliever is knowingly allowed to approach the table.
   (b) No believer is knowingly prevented from coming.
9. It offers no encouragement to their eating and drinking damnation to themselves.
10. It removes from the Church all blame for such judgment as may fall upon secret unbelievers or hypocrites.

Chapter 28: Of Church Censures (XXX)

XXX, 1–2

1. That there is a particular type of government commanded by Christ, or revealed in Scripture as his will for the Church.
2. The apostles were the instruments by which Christ's authority was manifested to the Church.
3. The written revelations of Christ made by and through the apostles were infallible, and possessed inherent and final authority.
4. Elders (or bishops).
5. Hierarchical, congregational, presbyterian.
6. (a) Christ is the only head of the Church.
   (b) Elders are chosen by the people they rule.

(c) All elders (or bishops) are equal in authority.

(d) Each particular church is to have two or more elders.

(e) Elders are to be ordained by presbytery (elders from churches in communion with one another).

(f) The right of appeal from a lesser assembly to a higher is to exist.

7. (a) Hierarchical—none.

(b) Congregational—the first three.

(c) Presbyterian—all.

8. It locates supreme authority *in* Peter rather than *with* him and other elders (that is, in the keys administered by them).

9. They deny that there is real administrative power in the keys.

10. The faithful preaching of the Word, and the faithful exercise of discipline.

11. Matt. 18:18; Matt. 16:18–19; John 20:21–23; Rom. 1:16; 1 Cor. 1:21; Titus 3:10.

12. They lose the power to open and close the kingdom.

XXX, 3–4

1. Christ commanded it.

2. It is argued that people will be offended.

3. Because we may never pray for God's blessing when we neglect the means which he has appointed to secure that blessing.

4. It often results in reclamation. It did so in Corinth.

5. The erring sinner and the other members of the church. Before church discipline was applied, the erring sinner in Corinth was not reclaimed but waxed worse in his sin. First Corinthians 5:6–7 also shows that such had an evil effect on others.

6. That we ought not to judge others is also urged against church discipline.

7. It confuses the judgment of the soul (which is the prerogative of God alone) with the judgment of one's profession (which is the duty of the Church).

8. Preaching the gospel and admitting professed believers into church membership.

9. Because Christ commanded it, and because it cannot be neglected except to his dishonor and the detriment of truth.

10. It becomes corrupt and spiritually dead.

11. The reclamation of the sinner.

12. Repeated, earnest, and loving efforts to persuade the erring brother to repent.

13. Any member of the church.
14. (a) The sin must be real (i.e., actual violation of one of the Ten Commandments).

(b) The sin must be persisted in (i.e., continued with unwillingness to repent).

Chapter 29: Of the Civil Magistrate (XXIII)

XXIII, 1–2, 4

1. Divine institution. Romans 13:1–7.
2. Any *de facto* government.
3. No.
4. Yes. When it is necessary to obey God rather than man.
5. Whenever and in whatever respect its requirements are not in conflict with Scripture.
6. Whenever and in whatever respect its requirements are in conflict with Scripture.
7. (a) The advocacy of the abolishment of capital punishment.

(b) The advocacy of the policy of pacifism.
8. Because the divine ordinance requires the use of the sword to punish crime, etc.
9. (a) The error which teaches that ecclesiastical persons are not subject to civil authority.

(b) The error which teaches that the pope of Rome has proper civil authority.

Chapter 30: Of the Civil Magistrate (continued) and Of Synods and Councils (XXXI)

XXIII, 3; XXXI, 1–2

1. (a) That "the civil magistrate may not assume to himself . . . the power of the keys" (that is, the power of government) and that Christ has "appointed a government in the hand of church-officers, distinct from the civil magistrate."

(b) That "he [the civil magistrate] hath authority . . . to take order, that unity and peace be preserved . . . that the truth of God be kept pure and entire, that all blasphemies and heresies be suppressed. . . ."

2. No. It is also a difficulty in such creedal documents as the Belgic Confession.

3. (a) A declaration disavowing the teaching of these phrases.

   (b) A revision of these sections of the Confession.

4. The latter. It seems to recognize more honestly the error made in the original formulation. It also relieves all uncertainty in subscription to the Confession.

5. (a) That the governments of Church and State are separate and distinct.

   (b) That civil magistrates may not interfere in the affairs of the Church in anything that is not subversive to civil order.

   (c) That church officers alone have authority to summon synods.

6. No. The same careful test of time and the comparison with Scripture which have revealed this section to be in error have vindicated the rest of the Confession.

7. It is the duty of the Church to testify to only the truth in its Confession.

8. The truth of the remainder.

9. The struggle in Scotland.

10. The covenanting Presbyterians.

XXXI, 3–4

1. It has to do with matters of doctrine, worship, and discipline. And it cannot enforce its decrees and declarations with bodily punishment as civil authority can.

2. It has the power only to carry into effect the teachings of Scripture. It cannot make new laws.

3. (a) They may authoritatively declare what the Bible teaches.

   (b) They may authoritatively decree how God's commands are to be implemented.

4. A synod could not decree the observance of a new sacrament with divine authority.

5. When they are in accord with Scripture.

6. (a) Because they are in accord with Scripture.

   (b) Because they are made by God-given authority.

7. Disobey. Because the authority of synods is limited to that which is according to the Word of God.

8. The tendency to make the authority of the council superior to that of the Bible.

9. Yes. By regarding the deliverances of synods as authoritative in and of themselves, without proper regard for the requirement that synods prove them to be scriptural and persuade the members of the Church that they are scriptural.

10. Effort to prove and to persuade that all decisions are scripturally grounded.

XXXI, 5

1. Ecclesiastical matters. (They are to strive to bring men to believe and obey the Scripture, and to administer discipline to members of the Church accordingly.)
2. The National Council of the Churches of Christ.
3. Because this Council interferes in civil matters.
4. (a) The example of Christ and his teaching.
   (b) The example of the Apostolic Church.
   (c) The complete absence of any Scripture teaching which would warrant such interference by the Church in the affairs of State.
5. No. The gospel is regulative of all that the believer does.
6. By teaching the members of the Church the principles of the Word of God that have bearing on political questions.
7. (a) When the State interferes with or threatens the Church.
   (b) When the State requests advice or opinion from the Church.

Chapter 31: Of the State of Men after Death, and of the Resurrection of the Dead (XXXII)

XXXII, 1

1. No, all men return to dust and see corruption.
2. Sin. Rom. 5:12; 6:23.
3. (a) In order that there be no carnal inducement to repent and believe.
   (b) In order to promote sanctification.
   (c) In order to provide for something better for the believer.
   (d) In order that believers and unbelievers might dwell together in the world while God's purpose is worked out.
4. When they are regenerated.
5. At death.
6. That which begins at regeneration (in the case of the elect), or birth (or conception, in the case of the reprobate).

7. His soul is made perfect in holiness.

8. His soul is then completely (in degree) evil.

9. To enable those who die in a state of grace but with the guilt of venial sin to make satisfaction by enduring suffering.

10. That Christ has suffered the whole penalty for all the sins of his people.

XXXII, 2–3

1. (a) That all men will once die.

   (b) That some men will not die.

2. (a) Rom. 5:12; Heb. 9:27.

   (b) 1 Thess. 4:15.

3. (a) The fearfulness of that day.

   (b) The change in the body and soul that will then be accomplished.

   (c) The fact that death has no sting or victory, and that it is far better to be absent from the body and present with the Lord.

4. The body that is raised will be that body which is buried. It will be a physical resurrection (against the view that only the soul will survive death).

5. The body that we now have will be raised and also changed so that every imperfection, weakness, and deformity will be gone.

6. At the last day, when Christ comes again.

7. In much the same sense as the soul of a believer is the same as the soul which was once dead in sin.

8. The terrible experience of suffering in both body and soul which unbelievers will have to endure forever.

Chapter 32: Of the Last Judgment (XXXIII)

XXXIII, 1–3

1. (a) The general resurrection when Christ returns (i.e., all men will be raised physically from the grave at the same time).

   (b) The general judgment of all men at the same occasion.

2. (a) John 5:28.

   (b) Rev. 20:12–13; Acts 17:31.

3. "One thousand years."

4. (a) Premillennialism, the belief that Christ will return before the millennium; (b) Postmillennialism, the belief that Christ will return after the millennium; (c) Amillennialism, the belief that the Bible does not

warrant expectation of any extended period of triumph before the end of the age.

5. The separation of the time of the resurrection of the saved from the time of the resurrection of the lost. The judgment is not general.

6. There are multiple future comings of Christ. There is no general resurrection. There is no general judgment. There is a presumed knowledge of the chronology of future events.

7. None.

8. None.

9. (a) The visible bodily return of Christ.

   (b) The general resurrection.

   (c) The general judgment.

10. (a) No one knows the chronology or precise order of events of the future.

    (b) Christ's kingdom exists, is spiritual, is not millennial only, is not Jewish, and will continue until the end of time.

    (c) Christ's return will be without warning signs, will signal a general resurrection, and will terminate the world as we now know it.

    (d) The present period is the last in history.

    (e) The great apostasy is not wholly future.

    (f) Good will not completely triumph until the end of the world.

    (g) Christ will have complete victory when the resurrection comes.

Index of Scripture

G. I. Williamson graduated from Drake University in 1949, and received the B.D. degree from Pittsburgh-Xenia Theological Seminary in 1952. An ordained minister, he has served congregations in the Old United Presbyterian Church of North America, the Associate Reformed Presbyterian Church, and the Reformed Presbyterian Church of North America. But most of his ministerial service has been with the Reformed Churches of New Zealand and the Orthodox Presbyterian Church, which he continues to serve.

Williamson has written several other books that have been well received by Reformed Christians, including *The Westminster Shorter Catechism: For Study Classes* and *The Heidelberg Catechism: A Study Guide*. He is also editor of *The Westminster Larger Catechism: A Commentary,* by Johannes G. Vos.